Book of Quests

Seven Scenarios Against the Sorcerer

For Mythras

MYTHRAS is a trademark of The Design Mechanism. All rights reserved. This edition of Book of Quests is copyright © 2013. This book may not be reproduced in whole or in part by any means without permission from The Design Mechanism, except as quoted for purposes of illustration, discussion and game play. Reproduction of the material in this book for the purposes of personal or corporate profit, by photographic, electronic, or other methods of retrieval is strictly prohibited.

For details please contact The Design Mechanism
(designmechanism@gmail.com).

Published under license in the UK by Aeon Games Publishing
www.aeongamespublishing.co.uk

ISBN 978-1-91147-103-5

Printed in Great Britain

CREDITS

Developed and Written By
Darren Driver, Tom Griffith, Russell Hoyle, Bruce Mason, Keane Peterson,
Marko Vojnovic, Jonathan Webb, John White, and Lawrence Whitaker

Editing
Lisa Tyler, Pete Nash

Proof Reading
Alexandra James

Design and Layout
Fred Hicks and Lawrence Whitaker

Artists
Dan MacKinnon, Pascal Quidault
Cover by Pascal Quidault

Cartography
Colin Driver, Carl Pates, Richard Lawrence

Special Thanks
John Hutchinson

Playtesters
Jordyn Beavan, James Carrington, Milan Dolašević, Chris Donnelly, Tim Eldred, Chris Gilmore, Paul Harrison, Kevin Hicks, Jude Hornburg, Leila Hoyle, Sophie Hoyle, Marcus Knapp, Brad Milburn, Daniel. J Mooney, Alex Morris, Eric Oates, Ian Pachner, Dušan Pavlović, Marko Poznanović, Shaun Rimmer, Gideon Roberts, Bruce Royle, Nick Southwick, Brian Spencer, Braden Spooner, Stephen Watson, Ioan Wigmore, Erik Willis, Russ Zabel, Janko Zafirovski, Ivan Žuvela,

---

About the Cover

At Dark Child's Tower, hidden deep in the Gartharis Mountains, Jedakiah and his Ophidian allies surveyed the army they had engineered. Creatures bred to kill in the crystal vats of Yagelan's Bluff; hybrids of chaos trained to destroy in the wildlands, preying on the innocent of The Realm.

The Chaos Mother had, through dreams and visions, guided Jedakiah to this day. With an army of Chaos he would lay waste to the weak and foolish mortals of the lowlands, delivering to them the Chaos Mother's power and wrath. His army pleased him; it begged to be unleashed to begin its onslaught and, oh, how Jedakiah wished he could release these willing warriors...

But there was one, last task. The culmination of decades of study, manipulation, corruption and murder. The transformation of the Pure Beauty, Bria, into the Daughter of Chaos. A rite that would transform the sorcerer into the Son of Chaos and channel anew the abeyant powers of the Chaos Mother. With one ritual a new race of Gods, terrible and merciless, would be created. The Chaos Mother's rule would be restored and enhanced.

Then would his armies march.

March and kill, not pausing until The Realm in its entirety surrendered...

CONTENTS

Map of The Realm	4
Introduction	5
The Realm *By Lawrence Whitaker*	7
Caravan *By Keane Peterson*	19
Beneath the Black Water *By Tom Griffith*	39
Shadows Behind the Throne *By Marko Vojnovic*	55
The Chaos Mother's Chalice *By Jonathan Webb*	87
Curse of the Contessa *By Bruce Mason*	116
Raid on Yagelan's Bluff *By Russell Hoyle and Darren Driver*	160
Reckoning at Distaff Peak *By John White*	192
Index	222

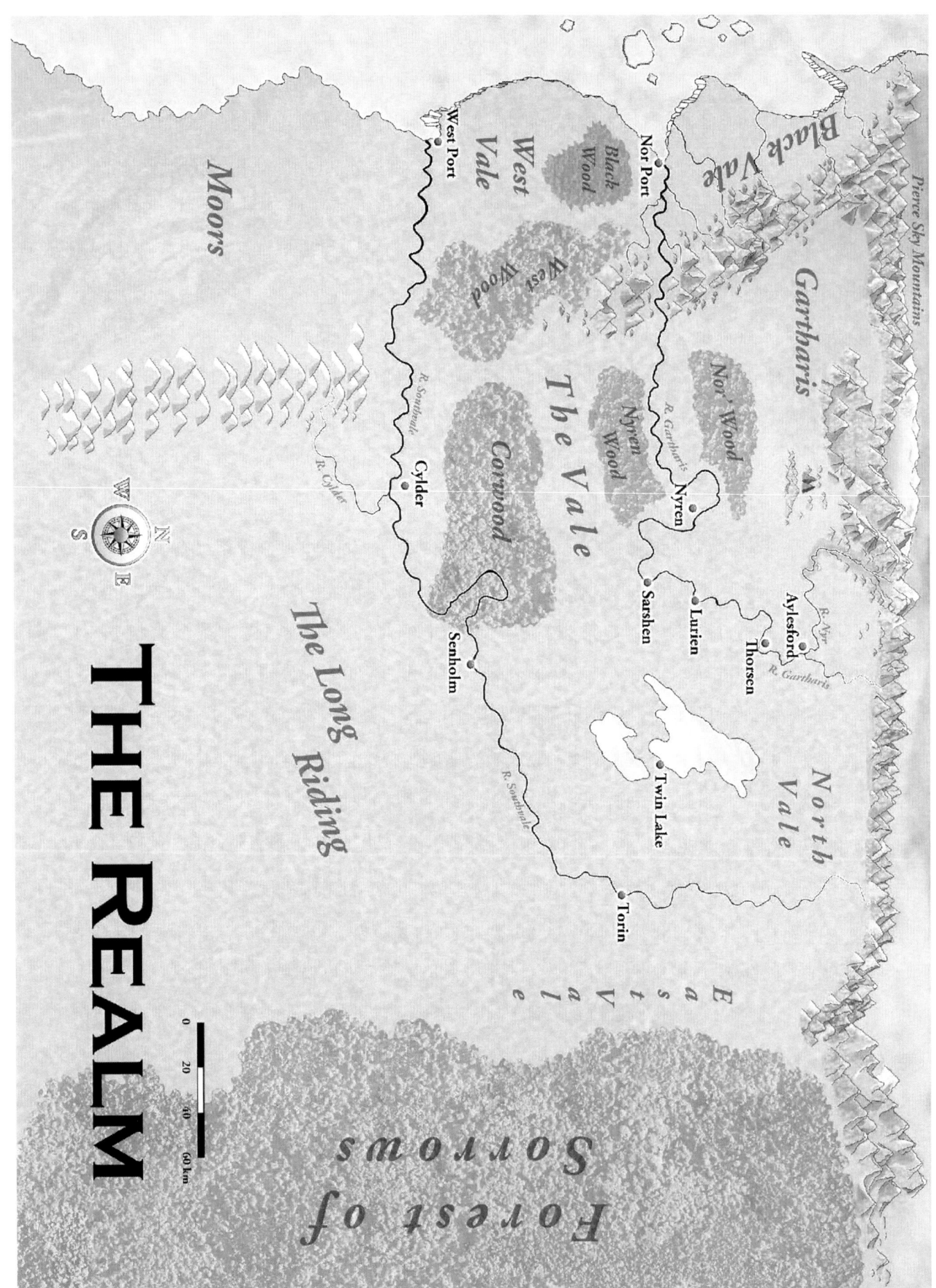

Introduction: Book of Quests

This is the first volume of an occasional series. It features seven connected scenarios forming a loose campaign. Each scenario is set against the backdrop of a fantasy region known, for simplicity, as *The Realm*; however the intention is that Games Masters can take some, or all, of the adventures from Book of Quests and slot them into their own campaigns without needing to use The Realm at all. Those Games Masters who do not have a developed setting for their games should find The Realm provides enough detail to act as a coherent backdrop that can be developed and built on for future games.

Each scenario is complete, with non-player characters, diagrams, maps and handouts. They can played in just about any order although the sequence presented forms a natural arc with the characters becoming more deeply immersed in the nefarious schemes of the sorcerer Jedakiah, leading to a show-down at Distaff Peak, the final scenario in this volume.

Using Book of Quests as a Campaign

If you are intending to run Book of Quests as a complete campaign we recommend that you read through all the scenarios to see how they connect and then plan the preferred order of presentation. Several non-player characters recur, so noting where, and how, they appear may be of importance.

You may also want the players to create fresh characters for The Realm campaign. Standard MYTHRAS rules apply and the following points are worth noting for character creation.

- All the basic cultures are supported, although Barbarian, Civilised and Nomadic are most suitable.
- The Realm is not magic-rich. Folk Magic is taught only through the different cults and regaining Magic Points can occur only at sacred and holy sights.
- Of the different magic systems found in MYTHRAS, Animism and Theism are the most apt. Sorcery is an ancient, long-forgotten and feared art, known only to corrupted individuals such as Jedakiah. There is

Scenarios

The scenarios occupying the rest of the book are structured along similar lines. All necessary maps and diagrams are included in the main body of the text, and Non-Player Character statistics are provided at the end of the chapter.

We've presented these statistic blocks in two ways. Major Non-Player Characters have a full range of characteristics. Those that are likely to just be combatants or casual encounters are not presented with characteristics - although all other pertinent details, such as Attributes, Skills and Combat Styles, are there in full.

no inherent Mysticism tradition in The Realm although it can be introduced if Games Masters so wish.

- Membership of the Founding Four cults is recommended for some characters, especially if they want to wield magic. Cult details are provided in the chapter outlining The Realm.
- Character may also be members of the Order of Truth: see page 17 for more details.
- Non-human species exist but are rare. Dwarves and Elves are possibilities although Games Masters will need to develop a rationale for their existence and decide on likely locations for their homes. Minotaurs are a further possibility: their herds are found in the south of The Realm.

Using Book of Quests in Existing Campaigns

If you are intending to use these scenarios in your own setting, a little work will need to be done to ensure compatibility.

- Geography, place names and non-player characters will need to be adjusted to fit. We have tried to keep specifics as loose as possible to make it easier for Games Masters to do this.
- Magic may need some adjustment depending on its use in your campaign. You may, for instance, want to increase the access some of the non-player characters have to Folk Magic – or reduce, as appropriate.
- The cults of The Realm will need to be adjusted to fit those of your campaign world. The Founding Four are generic gods of trade, fertility, war and knowledge and most fantasy campaigns have corresponding religions making translation easy. The Chaos Mother cult can be quite easily turned into any 'evil' cult or force within the campaign world.

The Realm

The Realm is in the west of a larger continent. Its western border faces the Ocean; its eastern border is the huge, expansive, Forest of Shadows; its northern border is the Gartharis Mountains and the southern border is the immense savannah known as The Long Riding.

Two major rivers, Gartharis River and River Southvale, divide The Realm roughly into three regions.

- The northern region is Gartharis itself; a cold, damp, forbidding place of mountains, sparse forests, deep gorges and tiny, isolated settlements.
- The central region is The Vale and this is the civilized band that runs between the rivers from forest to coast. The land is rolling and fertile with great pastures, productive woodlands and forests and several towns of reasonable size. It is ruled by an ageing king who is supported by regional dukes who control the various towns and cities within The Vale's borders.
- The southern region is split into the Moors and The Long Riding. These huge, empty areas are home to the barbarian moorland peoples and the nomads of The Long Riding. Both trade with The Vale and sometimes with each other, but they are fractious, divided and frequently fight.

Climate

The Realm is a temperate west maritime climate. Gulf-Stream like currents keep the coast and hinterland relatively warm but still susceptible to cold, hard winters and long, hot summers. The mountains mean that precipitation is high: rain is a frequent feature year-round, but the mountains also shelter The Realm from strong winds – save for those coastal areas west of the mountains.

Terrain

Gartharis and North Vale are bleak uplands with occasional wooded regions of pine and spruce. The land slopes upwards to the Gartharis Mountains creating many valleys and foothills. The two lakes of North Vale are glacial residue: deep and teeming with freshwater marine life.

- The Vale is gently undulating with pleasant pastures, low hills, many vales and dells and small copses and woodlands.
- The Moors are typical moorland: rough ground pocked with stones, boulders, and low-lying, hardy shrubs such as gorse, bracken and heather.
- The Long Riding and East Vale are uncultivated grassland steppe. Largely flat, it suffers the most from

Meeros

The Realm occupies a continent roughly analogous with Northern Europe. On a separate continent, and further south - and roughly analgous with the Mediterranean lands - is Meeros.

If Games Masters have used Meeros, found in the MYTHRAS rules, for previous games, then there is no reason why characters from Anathaym's home city and region cannot find their way to The Realm. They might be traders perhaps, or have picked-up on rumours of Jedakiah through dealings with the sorcerer Kratos.

The Cult of Myceras may even send members to The Realm to act as emissaries, seeking help in the battle against the Badoshi Warlords. Indeed, the Badoshi may even have their roots in the Gartharis Barbarians or the nomads of the Long Riding.

The links between The Realm and Meeros are not explicit, but are loosely intended.

what winds make their way through The Realm and suffers from frequent rains and storms. As a result, the barbarians and nomads revere the gods of rain and storm.

- The Forest of Sorrow is a mixture of coniferous and deciduous trees. Very dense in places, light struggles to penetrate the canopy. There are, however, many small settlements – loggers and charcoal burners for instance – scattered throughout the forest, although they are a superstitious bunch and keep largely to themselves. On the fringes of the forest the Vale Lords have hunting and game trails as well as in the various woodlands of the Vale itself.

Governance

No one person rules The Realm. Jedakiah seeks to change all that.

- The Vale is ostensibly ruled by its ageing king, Myur the Third; local government is administered by the Court Nobles – Lords who have been granted specific territories in return for support, allegiance and advice. The approach taken by these Lords differs from one domain to another. Some are benevolent, others far less so. As Lords are responsible for collecting taxes and paying dues to King Myur, the people of The Realm live in a feudal state with differing levels of freedom, and dependent solely on the will or whim of the local ruler. The cities are part of these Lords' fiefdoms, but old traditions maintain that a city must also appoint a governing council made-up of minor nobles, high priests of the temples and elder guildsmen of the trade guilds. This removes some of the burden from the individual ruler, but as the local ruler makes the council appointments, his (or her) influence still pervades.
- Gartharis is ruled by fierce barbarians who propitiate the old gods of Chaos and War. Black Vale is similar. Gartharis is a lawless land, subject to constant feuds, petty struggles, and the predations of local warlords. Some of these warlords are in thrall to the sorcerer Jedakiah, who keeps them in check through the supply of arms and goods bought from the south, gifts of magic, demonstrations of chaotic power, and promises of high positions when The Realm is returned to the authority of the Chaos Mother.
- The moors are ruled by a tribe of nomads who seasonally move into the Long Riding with their herds and compete with the resident barbarians and nomads. Again, there is no central government; simply a twice yearly council of the tribes where certain things are agreed, settled, or brought to bear. Both the nomad and barbarian tribes attend the council, but before it begins there is generally much political trading and bargaining between allied groups that ensure particular agendas are set for the grand council. Otherwise the barbarians and nomads are governed by their own beliefs and traditions which vary greatly from one tribe to another and frequently conflict.
- The Forest of Shadows is largely unknown. Communities there are small, frequently animistic, and as driven by traditions and superstitions as the Long Riding tribes. They keep themselves to themselves and only rarely venture into The Realm at large.

Non-Human Races

The Realm is largely human. There are no dwarves, elves or halflings (although Games Masters wanting to accommodate such species may do so making appropriate judgments regarding their homelands and spheres of influence).

Ophidians

A race of chaos-serving Ophidians live deep beneath the Gartharian Mountains maintaining blasphemous subterranean laboratories and worshipping the Chaos Mother (which they embody as a vast, multi-headed serpent).

Minotaurs

The Long Riding has a tribe of minotaurs that maintain their own cattle herds but largely shun the remainder of the barbarian and nomad tribes.

Boar-Kin

Boars and Boar-Kin are found in the Forest of Sorrows.

Chaos Hybrids

Jedakiah, with the aid of the Ophidians, has been breeding chaos hybrids based on human, bear, wolf, goat and sheep amalgams. These are kept in underground caves and released to cause havoc according to scenario needs.

Cultures

All four cultural backgrounds from MYTHRAS are present in The Realm. The predominant cultures found in each region are as follows:

Gartharis and Black Vale:

Barbarian. The tribes herd sheep, cattle and goats, raise cereals and other crops, and raid each other sporadically for things they lack (and, sometimes, for pleasure). They also raid into North Vale, and far more frequently than their raids against each other.

North Vale:

Civilised. Several small cities, each controlled by a Duke or similar noble, paying fealty to King Myur.

The Vale:

Civilised. The political structure is very similar to North Vale although the Dukes are all loyal kinsmen of Myur and his line. The various cities of North Vale and the Vale are relatively small – 10,000 residents being the uppermost.

The Moors and Long Riding:

Barbarian and Nomad respectively.

Forest of Sorrow

Primitives and low-end Civilised

Economy

The Realm is analagous to early Middle Ages Europe - anywhere from around 700AD to 900AD. Iron and steel are the dominant metals.

The Vale uses the silver coin known as the *Founder*. Copper pieces are known as *Pennies* or *Scraps*. The gold coin is the *Royal*. The default MYTHRAS currency rules otherwise apply. Each city of The Vale mints its own coins, carrying the name and crest of the local Lord.

The Long Riding and Moors tribes shun coinage and prefer to trade in goods and useful commodities.

Magic

Magic is scarce in The Realm, and what little is known remains from that time when the gods were active in the world and chose to gift their followers with some of their knowledge and power.

- The Northern Barbarians know Folk Magic, Animism, and a little sorcery gifted to them by Jedakiah.
- The Long Riding/Moors tribes know Folk Magic and Theism gifted to them by Renamos and Feyr.
- The Sorrowing Forest folk have a few animist shamans.
- In North Vale is the secretive Order of Truth, a brotherhood seeking to prevent any further slides into disorder and chaos. The Order of Truth can call upon extensive reserves of knowledge and

Notes on Magic

The Realm is intended to emulate the classic Sword and Sorcery stories of authors such as Fritz Leiber, Robert E Howard, Clark Ashton Smith and Michael Moorcock. To this end, it is not magic-rich. The gods, whilst worshipped, are distant from humans and the main forms of magic available are the province of those who have devoted their life to its study.

However, Games Masters may wish to allow characters access to magic in a wider sense, especially Miracles for Theist characters. The cults presented on page 10 therefore list available Miracles should Games Masters permit their use.

lore to aid its members and those who work for them indirectly.

- Sorcery is *generally* unknown in The Realm – or at least outlawed. This makes Jedakiah all the more dangerous.

Magic Point Economy

Replenishing Magic Points is wholly reliant on a temple, shrine or holy place recognised by the cult. Magic Point recovery is at the rate of 1 per Day and requires prayers, offerings and sacrifices to the cult deity. The Founding Four require prayers only. The Long Riding gods require a sacrifice of some herd animal or poultry.

Religions

Understanding the religions of The Realm requires understanding of the Chaos Mother and the Founding Four.

The Chaos Mother once dominated the whole of The Realm until she was defeated by the great hero Sayalis some five hundred years ago, when the Vale was settled and the northern tribes driven back towards the mountains. Sayalis is considered a demigod in most Vale settlements. The Chaos Mother is only revered by the northern tribes who remain loyal to her memory.

The Vale worships the Founding Four: two pairs of gods and goddesses who called upon the folk from the east to come to the region and defeat the Chaos Mother. Each god has two aspects, represented by the two runes each holds:

Xalgith (Male)
Trade and Knowledge
Runes: Communication and Mastery

Aliya (Female)
Healing and Fertility
Runes: Fertility and Plant

Sormund (Male)
War and Death
Runes: Motion and Death

Menissa (Female)
Light and the Sun
Runes: Fire and Motion

Every large settlement of The Vale has a main temple dedicated to The Four and usually a series of smaller temples dedicated to one of the pantheon. The vast bulk of the populace venerates The Four as an entire pantheon although particularly devout individuals can, and do, initiate into a specific cult. Xalgith is considered the Father of the Four, and Aliya is his consort. Sormund and Menissa are considered to be the son and daughter of Xalgith and Aliya although there are conflicting myths surrounding their origins.

Each god has a Holy Day each year, and the first day of the new year (the first day of spring) is All Gods' Day – a festival day celebrated everywhere in The Vale.

Although revered, The Four are distant from mortals. Some very special heroes in the past, such as Sayalis the Bright, received help in the form of Miracles and, in the past few hundred years, a handful of exceptionally devout worshippers have also been similarly favoured.

Miracles from The Four are therefore rare, but if Games Masters wish to include more magic in their campaigns, then the gods can offer miracles to their devotees and these are available through any major temple for those of the appropriate rank. The miracles differ according to whether one worships all four gods without preference, or a single god through specific cult initiation.

Only the Chaos Mother should be handled differently: she does not offer Miracles at this time, as is explained on page 14.

The Founding Four

Those who worship the Founding Four as a pantheon attend the holy day ceremonies for each deity and make appropriate offerings as needed, but hold allegiance to no single god. Pious member of the cult have the Miracles for the pantheon available as listed below.

The cult structure follows the basic format found in the Mythras core rules, from page 196 onwards. Initiating into either the general cult of the pantheon, or into that of a specific deity, follows the standard Mythras procedure. Devotees of a cult must perform the expected duties as per rank (Mythras, pages 196 – 199) with the associated rank benefits.

Miracles

Aegis, Awaken, Behold, Consecrate, Dismiss Magic, Excommunicate, Exorcism, Lay to Rest, Sacred Band, Soul Sight, Spirit Block

Those who choose a single god of the pantheon for veneration observe the same holy days but also choose a personal day of veneration where they spend time in private prayer only to their chosen deity. Dedicated members of these individual cults have the above miracles available to them, but also the Miracles listed for each god, below.

Each sub-cult follows the same structure as the overall pantheon.

XALGITH

Xalgith is the god of knowledge, understanding, communication and trade. Considered the First of All Gods most believe that he came into being when the Mastery Rune was created from the primordial surge that brought the universe into being. First, Xalgith was but an idea and a notion; but that turned into comprehension, and, from comprehension, understanding. He took the Communication Rune and used it to barter with the elemental forces of the universe to create the earth and the sun, setting each in motion with the sun trading warmth and light. From this trade, Aliya was born and she became Xalgith's consort and the mother of All Life.

Xalgith is represented in several forms. As a sage-like individual with flowing hair and beard, as well as a travelling merchant equipped for long journeys. Scholars and traders venerate Xalgith as the source of reason and negotiation; others venerate him simply as the First of the Four.

MIRACLES

As for the Founding Four plus: *Extension, Harmonise, Heal Mind, Mindlink, Spirit Block.*

ALIYA

Aliya was born from the egg of the world after Xalgith created the earth and sun. With her birth life flowed into the barren world, first as plants and then as animals and the sapient species. Her first tears created the seas and rivers and her breath is the wind that drives the clouds.

She has many aspects: the wise and fertile Earth Mother; the airy and capricious wind; the Garden Daughter of the fields and forests. Different cultures venerate her in different ways. Her healing powers are recognized ubiquitously and this is magic she was gifted by Xalgith in return for becoming his consort and Second of the Four.

MIRACLES

As for the Founding Four plus: *Bless Crops, Cure Malady, Fecundity, Growth, Heal Body.*

SORMUND

Sormund was born when the sun was stolen by the Devil. Xalgith created a god from the Motion Rune to give chase and return the Sun to its rightful place above the earth. He gave Sormund the power of Death to kill the Devil, but although Sormund succeeded in stealing back the sun, the Devil tricked him, turning the power of death against the living things that were Aliya's children.

Sormund became the defender of the earth, a general for its armies and also the protector of the dead. When one dies, one is taken into Sormund's hall where souls are protected from the ravages of the Devil and Hell. Sormund's enemies are condemned to eternal death, denied the Halls of Heaven and cast into the Devil's pits.

MIRACLES

As for the Founding Four plus: *Backlash, Shield, Sureshot, True Sword, True Spear.*

MENISSA

Menissa was born when Sormund stole back the sun from the Devil. As the rays of the sun fell upon the earth once more, Aliya sang Menissa into being to ward against the Devil's tricks and to give comfort to sorrowing, bitter Sormund. She is the first light of dawn and the last rays of the evening, her hair bathing the world and flowing over it in waves of beauty, chasing the night back to its lair. She is considered to be Aliya's daughter and Sormund's sister, sharing as she does, the Motion Rune with him.

MIRACLES

As for the Founding Four plus: *Clear Skies, Growth, Heal Wound, Ripen, Sunspear.*

THE RENEGADE GODS

The Renegade Gods are so named because they rebelled against the Four and were driven from Heaven, only to be summoned back when the fight was taken to the Chaos Mother in The Realm, and the two deities found ample worship amongst the Long Riding barbarians and nomads. Since then their powers have grown although their worship is shunned in the civilised Vale, which still considers them barbaric, rebellious deities.

The Long Riding and Moors barbarians worship the Renegade Gods: Storm God Renamos and his sister/wife, the Weeping Goddess Feyr. Neither deity has a

The Mad Rule of King Chandanar

Once the power of the Chaos Mother came to an end, the Eastern Empire blossomed, spanning the known lands of The Realm. Led by Sayalis the Bright, they venerated the gods and nature spirits. It was a golden age for man.

The empire became strong and rich, fuelled by a powerful army and a cogent set of beliefs. One of the great wonders of the Empire was the construction of the Earth Mother temple on sacred ground in a valley between great mountains. Once complete, worship to her augmented soil fertility in the surrounding farm lands and made them bountiful. The prayers of the faithful and the toil of the farmers fed the citizens of the empire.

With the madness and then death of Sayalis, the Empire became quiescent. With it the powers of the Earth Mother also began to fade. Was it that her priests had forgotten true worship to her? Were the new farming practices causing her harm? Did the citizens not show true veneration? Nobody knew, but everyone could feel her power fading. Whatever the reason it gave rise to the worship of some nameless power of Chaos

formal structure although every clan maintains priests and priestesses who lead ceremonies based on particular traditions and rituals. These differ from clan to clan and form the basis of disputes. All seem to work though; Renamos and Feyr care more for the devotion than for how it is made, although both require blood sacrifices as part of general rituals and those used to recoup Magic Points.

Renamos the Rising Storm

Renamos is the belligerent father of the winds and storms. He is the Darkening Sky and the Icy Hand. Unforgiving and crazed he is a god of battle and elemental energies.

Folk Magic
Bladesharp, Fanaticism, Might, Pierce, Preserve.

Miracles
Berserk, Call Winds, Cloud Call, Consecrate, Elemental Summoning (Sylph), Rain of Ice, Sacred Band, Thunderclap.

Feyr the Weeping Goddess

Feyr weeps constantly for the torments of her brother, Renamos, who shuns her love and prefers destruction to growth. She is the goddess of bounty and promise, but is also a goddess of fierce fury and jealous corruption.

Folk Magic
Avert, Darkness, Disruption, Extinguish.

Miracles
Corruption, Elemental Summoning (Sylph), Growth, Perserverance, Rain of Blood, Ripen, Sever Spirit, True Spear.

The Chaos Mother

The scenarios of Book of Quests all concern Jedakiah and his veneration of the Chaos Mother, attempting to restore her power, destroyed five hundred years ago when the Founding Four (and Renamos and Feyr of the barbarians), broke her hold over The Realm and made her a prisoner of her intricate Spirit Maze in between Heaven and Hell. The Gartharis tribes are the only ones who have worshipped her in this long period although as a prisoner goddess the Chaos Mother has never been able to offer miracles to her devotees.

History

The Chaos Mother is a fragment of the Chaos Rune, created when the Great Expansion of All Time created the Founding Four and the renegade gods of the barbarians. Whilst these gods were fixed in their natures, Chaos was without a single form and adapted constantly and randomly, destroying – though often without plan or deliberation – the work of the other deities. One of its many forms was the being that came to be known as the Chaos Mother, a fickle, inquisitive goddess that switched its appearance between Aliya, Menissa and Feyr, tricking the male gods and creating all manner of havoc.

Shunned from the Lands of Heaven she took the form of World Spider and spun the Spirit Maze as her web in parody of Heaven. Its pathways burrowed far into the mountains of Gartharis and so she came to The Realm which was, in those times, filled with frightened primitives, reliant on many spirits and totems that offered only limited power. The Chaos Mother steadily replaced them as the dominant deity and gifted those early priests with secret knowledge of creation and change. With these miracles the primitive priest-shamans created the Chaos Hybrids from prisoners, slaves and sacrifices. To further guide them the Chaos Mother created a rift in her Spirit Maze that allowed a colony of strange serpentine people to come to The Realm and form a new stronghold under the Gartharis mountains. They offered the Chaos Mother a certain degree of worship, but also brought with them a new magic – sorcery – which they cunningly spread throughout the world using select agents and intermediaries. Otherwise they are The Realm's greatest secret: shadowy, ophidian manipulators who dwell in darkness and tamper with reality in subtle, obscene ways.

As the primitives of The Realm gained in knowledge and power, the gods saw that the Chaos Mother had seized control of The Realm and decided to take action against her. Armies commanded by the priest-kings of the east marched into The Realm to establish the rule of The Four. The Renegade God and Goddess, Ramanos and Feyr, came too – howling, vengeful gods who took war to the Long Riding and supplanted the Chaos Mother's rule there.

In the north, Sayalis the Bright, born to battle Chaos, and a mortal son of Sormund and a human priestess, led the armies against the Gartharis worshippers of the Chaos Mother. The fighting was terrible with the hybrid armies of the barbarians falling upon the regiments of The Four in dreadful battles. Many of the things sacred to the Chaos Mother were destroyed by Sayalis. Eventually he travelled into the Spirit Maze and carved through its myriad pathways. In the labyrinth's centre, surrounded by twisted, mutated foes, he challenged the Chaos Mother directly in a series of deadly contests. He won each, aided by treasures gifted by the Four gods and secrets known by the Renegade gods. The Chaos Mother was defeated, and although she could not be killed, Sayalis re-made the Spirit Maze into a prison that cut the Chaos Mother's cords from the fabric of The Realm. As her maze became her tomb, the Chaos Mother decreed that, just as a mortal, born of a god, had imprisoned her, so two mortals would become gods and free her. These gods would be the The Chaos Daughter and The Chaos Father: mortals who would become one with the Chaos Rune and so rework the Spirit Maze to find and release the Chaos Mother.

Sayalis returned to The Realm, became its first king, and, in his greatest tragedy, kept the Chaos Mother's valediction to himself. The secret eventually drove him into madness and then death, but before he died he established the Order of Truth, drawing its members from amongst the wise and knowledgable of The Realm. He gave them hints and records of the Chaos Mother's power and charged them with preventing the Chaos Mother from returning.

He died after a reign of a hundred and fifty years. The Realm was at peace; the Founding Four the dominant gods of the world. Chaos returned briefly under the insane reign of King Chandanar, but this was broken by the Order of Truth and sanity restored to the world, including the strengthening of the goddess Aliya. King Myur, the current ruler, is a direct descendent of Sayalis and the Order of Truth prevails, though its importance has diminished with time because the Chaos Mother's power is broken.

Until, ten years ago, a corrupt and vengeful sorcerer, a recipient of ophidian secrets (though he never knew their origin), called Jedakiah, stumbled upon the legends of The Chaos Mother and, through blasphemous research and eldritch magic, reached through the Spirit Maze and heard her calling. The Chaos Mother revealed her prophecy and spoke of how to fulfil it. Jedakiah has made it his life's work to create The Chaos Daughter, become The Chaos Father, and resurrect the Chaos Mother.

If he succeeds, a new and infinitely more dreadful reign of terror will engulf The Realm's peace and stability. Gods and goddesses will die and the Father, Mother and Daughter of Chaos will rule Heaven, Earth, and all places inbetween.

out of desperation - a diabolic cornucopia cult where fertile lands and bountiful harvests were exchanged for blood offered into a chalice. Initially this cult was small but it festered and grew over time, blooming in parallel with the empire's decadence.

Finally, Chaos rose again, two hundred years ago. King Chandanar (a descendent of Sayalis and ancestor of King Myur), secretly guided by the Ophidians, turned to Chaos. In his insanity he perpetrated one act that triggered doom. Manipulated by the Ophidians he and his agents smuggled the chaos chalice (hidden carefully by the Ophidians, so Sayalis could not destroy it) into the great Earth Mother temple. It had a cataclysmic effect – the Earth Mother withered. The priests and their followers within the temple were either tainted with chaos or slain trying to flee from it; the fertile fields surrounding the temple burst into life with corrupted crops which mutated those that ate them.

KEEPING THE FAITH AND THE HOUSEHOLD OF LUCIUS

Through the years of Chandanar's cruel dominance, those who remained true to the Founding Four prayed and kept vigil in the hope that their supplications would bring about a return to sanity.

One family in particular is remembered; that of Lucius and his household. Duke Lucius had married one of the Earth Mother temple acolytes a few years before it had been corrupted. A beautiful and pious woman, she suffered from visions and nightmares. A particular theme was the birth of a new goddess, pure and fecund, in replace of what the Mother had become. Her visions were often addled but one aspect was clear - that the new goddess manifests above the image of the Earth Mother Temple before it had become corrupted. Troubled by this dream, knowing that this would now be impossible, her melancholy pervaded the whole household. Acting in love of his young wife and in faith that her visions would prove correct, Lucius commissioned a mosaic of a vista of the Earth Mother within his villa. For later generations this mosaic became the focus of worship to the 'Goddess yet to be born'. The Lucius household kept up the

THE CULT OF THE CHAOS MOTHER

Unlike the cults of the Founding Four and the Renegade Gods, that of the Chaos Mother has little power in the world. It cannot offer miracles and it has no formal infrastructure, save for those who have been corrupted into its service as agents of Jedakiah and the Ophidians of the Gartharis Mountains. Until the Chaos Father and Chaos Daughter are created, the cult has no power – although much malign significance – and is reliant on the sorcery of Jedakiah and the Serpent Sorcerers of the Ophidian laboratories.

Nevertheless it is a very real threat. Jedakiah has learned how to create the Chaos Hybrids, controlling them through corrupt shamans and Ophidian grimoires. His power is amassing and, if he succeeds in his schemes, then the power of Chaos will come again and be a thousand times stronger than when Sayalis broke it. For now, the Cult of the Chaos Mother is nothing more than a brotherhood bent on one particular goal. But should Jedakiah succeed, it will become a cult of awesome power with both Dark Miracles and Dark Sorcery at its disposal.

For the purposes of Book of Quests then, the Cult of the Chaos Mother is not detailed beyond its history. Jedakiah is its High Priest, and it consists of lay members only (the Ophidians, the Gartharis barbarians, the Batrachians and many warped and insane individuals corrupted by Jedakiah).

TRAVEL IN THE REALM

Most roads in The Realm are little more than rutted tracks, worn down by countless sets of cart wheels - and even then, roads this good are found only in The Vale. Elsewhere, it is a question of following old drovers' paths, hunting trails, animal trails, and so on. Travel can be slow and, outside the boundaries of villages and towns, bandits, particularly in the north, are common occurrences. Bodyguards are frequently hired by merchant caravans but sometimes these bodyguards are merely scouts for bandit groups who lure wealthy pickings into ambush sites. Merchants who must travel to do business are always on their guard.

The temperate climate leads to heavy rains year-round, and so, save for dry spells in the summer, roads and paths are mud-shod, waterlogged and often flooded. Travel then, is slow, fraught with danger, and keeps most people within their settlements, travelling only when needs must.

River travel is frequent. The Southvale River is navigable for much of its length and deep enough to take ships capable of sailing into open waters. The northern reaches of the Gartharis River are plied by barges and its lower reaches are, like Southvale River, navigable to larger vessels.

NOTABLE PLACES

Most of the scenarios in Book of Quests take place in The Vale and north of there. Notable places of this region are:

AYLESFORD

A small, but prosperous, town of the north, it is famed for its market. It has suffered from barbarian raids in the past and these have grown in strength in recent years.

CYLDER

Cylder, The Vale's capital and home to King Myur, was once a border fort. Being on the confluence of two rivers of which Southvale is still deep enough for ocean vessels, Cylder became more of a trade town than a military outpost. Still, wealth came only after silver was found in the hills north of the city. At that time the third king of Vale took his court east from the West Vale and made Cylder the capital.

Cylder is built out of black granite from the nearby quarries and roofed with red tiles. While the city is built on the hills surrounding the confluence of River Cylder into River Southvale the land around it is swampy. A few kilometres north of the city dry land starts in earnest and farmland abounds.

The wet surroundings provide Cylder with plenty of fog, mists and oppressively high humidity levels. River Southvale is also prone to flooding which is why Lower Cylder and Cylder Harbour are built on stilts.

The city consists of four quarters: Upper and Lower Cylder, the Harbour with its shipyards and the Trades Quarter encompassing the marketplace on the Plaza of Kings.

Lurien

A small market town on the Gartharis River; the starting point for the first of the scenarios in Book of Quests, *Caravan*.

Nor Port

Most northerly of the two coastal ports in The Vale. Nor Port's harbour is famous (or infamous) and is a staging post for many ocean-going vessels leaving this continent and arriving from others.

Nyren

Second largest of the cities, after Cylder, Nyren takes its name from Nyren Wood and is a large logging and woodworking community. Ruled by Duke Astomvar, a cousin of the king, it is noted for the quality of its craftsmen and the quality of the game, hunted in the nearby forest. A lively and vibrant place, it is younger than Cylder and considered cleaner and more peaceful. Legend has it that Sayalis the Bright wanted to make Nyren the capital but was persuaded otherwise. The people still consider themselves affiliated with Sayalis and statues of him are found all over the city.

Senholm

Province of Lord Drystan, this large town is close to an area known as the Frogfens and is close to Corwood. The town is unremarkable but the Frogfens have a poor reputation - desolate swamps and marshes plagued by insects and home to the Batrachians - toadmen with vile practices.

West Port

Situated at the mouth of the Southvale River between the forbidding Moors and the downs of West Vale, Westport jealously guards its status as an independent city state, granted five centuries ago during after the Chaos wars. It is a bustling port, a destination for exotic goods from across the seas and the starting point for many a caravan into the interior. The city itself was once ruled by the 171 Peacock Princes and is home to styles of buildings, names and social customs foreign to the rest of the Vale.

The Sorcerer

Jedakiah is an archetypal mad sorcerer. He is arrogant, commands powerful magic and is thoroughly insane. He can be tailored to fit into most fantasy situations and he is intended to be the evil mastermind whose presence and influence is slowly revealed as each scenario is completed. Games Masters should tailor Jedakiah's background to fit their own campaign, so Book of Quests does not present a huge amount of back-story for him, although a suggestion for his origins is given below to act as inspiration for Games Masters who might be at loss to explain where he comes from.

History

Jedakiah was always a selfish individual. The youngest son of a noble family he resented the attention given to his brothers. Bookish and awkward he sought refuge in the arcane tomes of his father's library and was there exposed to the first dark secrets of chaos. Expelled by his family for dabbling in sorcery Jedakiah wandered the cities of his native country and eventually found himself accepted as an apprentice to a sorcerer of some repute. This tutor abhorred chaos and so Jedakiah had to hide his fascination for it. His tutor introduced the young Jedakiah to the nature of the runes and how all things in the universe have an innate connection with the

faith for years, hoping beyond hope that she would appear.

Through the dark days that followed, their worship was secretive, always beyond the prying eyes of Chandanar's agents. In many respects the villa became temple to this 'goddess to come', but the secretive nature of the worship, the nature of the goddess and the lack of priestly mentors meant that their prayers were initially not answered.

Throughout this time the household of Lucius still kept up their faith that the goddess to come would be born and one day their prayers were answered. The new goddess made her presence known in the guise of a copper coloured snake basking upon the mosaic. Divinations and dreams about the snake were clear; a messenger come to tell the faithful that Aliya, in her aspect of The Vengeful Sister, was ready to march on her corrupted Earth Mother aspect. It was time to cleanse the Earth temple of corruption and reclaim it for herself. Her followers took up their relics and other holy items and chanted prayers to their new goddess along the road to war.

The Temple's Destruction

An army marched on the corrupted temple with the new followers of Aliya. Nearing the temple, the priests called upon her, and she responded by waking one of the great mountains above the temple. It erupted violently sending a huge pyroclastic wave into the valley, killing hordes of chaotic mutants, covering the corrupted temple in ash and burying the Chaos Mother's Chalice deep beneath the earth.

A Goddess for the People

Now unable to reclaim the temple for their new goddess, the priests returned to The Realm with all her holy items. The ranks of her followers swelled and the worship of Aliya become almost universal. Her priests cast divinations and determined that her presence had spread across the land, venerated by the common folk at simple shrines or worshipped in the grand temples to the Founding Four. Her holy items were distributed amongst these sites and in such she become a goddess of the land.

runic forces. Jedakiah grasped this relationship easily and his studies showed him that the chaos rune's ability to corrupt all other runes meant it was surely the most powerful of them all. Jedakiah steadily accumulated as much knowledge of the Chaos Rune as he could and, as he did so, became more selfish, spiteful and resentful.

His tutor recognised the signs and refused to school Jedakiah any further. In a fit of rage Jedakiah murdered his teacher and hid the body (later using it in vile experiments). Jedakiah then set about studying every single one of his master's grimoires and tomes, scouring them for spells linked with Chaos. He discovered the exiled Chaos Mother and pledged to worship her. He also created his own grimoire – The Entropic Revelations – using both his own research and the Chaos Mother's help.

Jedakiah's work, and the murder of his respected tutor, came to the attention of the authorities, and Jedakiah was forced to flee. He travelled many, many miles to escape his foes, eventually coming to the lands where the

scenarios in this book are set. Magic is weak here, and Jedakiah's command of sorcery makes him very powerful indeed. The people are nowhere near as sophisticated as those of his home nation and Jedakiah has decided to corrupt, manipulate and abuse these people, making himself their feared ruler and then raising an army with which to crush those who drove him from his home.

Jedakiah's description and statistics are provided on pages 219 to 220.

Jedakiah and The Realm

Jedakiah has lived in The Realm for a decade remaining in relative isolation and coming and going in secret. In this time he has established a small but fervent cult worshipping the Chaos Mother, a primal god that is a fragment of the Chaos Rune that once held sway long ago in The Realm but had become all but forgotten until Jedakiah reinstated her worship. The cult is such that it can now function without Jedakiah's direct guidance although the sorcerer maintains a keen interest in its activities and revels in the destruction it is wreaking. Jedakiah has many agents and servants - willing and unwilling. His desires are largely conducted through them while he remains safe and sound in his remote tower, consorting with the mysterious Ophidians.

No self-respecting sorcerer is without a lair, and Jedakiah makes his home in The Realm's desolate, mountainous north, occupying Dark Child's Tower, on Distaff Peak. The tower once stood guard against the Chaos Mother back in the legendary days when she had considerable influence. Only those who know the north of The Realm intimately are likely to find Jedakiah's tower and Jedakiah has managed to pervert the few remaining barbarian clans to Chaos Mother worship. His true evil has spread far south and this is where the scenarios of this book are concentrated.

Jedakiah's ultimate plan is to create The Chaos Daughter – a demonic demigod who will lead the Chaos creatures Jedakiah has been breeding to lay waste to The Realm and invade the lands beyond the sea – the same lands Jedakiah was hounded from before coming to The Realm. He also intends to become the Chaos Father and so transform into a demigod of terrifying supernatural power himself. To perform the summoning ritual he requires three things:

- The Chaos Mother's Chalice
- The Chaos Father's Blood
- The life of one who has Pure Beauty

The scenarios in Book of Quests concern all three.

Jedakiah works through agents he has corrupted to his schemes. These include a barbarian chief, a few high-ranking city-state nobles, and the Chaos creatures he has bred in his northern dungeons. These agents then recruit their own hirelings – mercenaries, thieves, reavers and so forth – to accomplish the goals Jedakiah has set for them. Eventually though, all roads point back to the sorcerer and, if he is slain, his schemes come to an end (or, *do they?*)...

ADVENTURERS OF THE REALM

If using The Realm as the backdrop for the scenarios, creating a Realm native is recommended. Characters hailing from The Realm can be of any culture with the region of their origin determining the cultural backgrounds most suitable. Long Riding, for instance, has no civilised settlements and so the Barbarian or Nomadic cultures offer the best fit.

Otherwise standard MYTHRAS character creation applies. The one area where Games Masters may wish characters to deviate slightly is in the determination of their Passions.

REALM PASSIONS

In addition to the standard Passions, Realm characters may also create a Hate Sorcery or Hate Jedakiah Passion, beginning at the same percentage as their other Hatred (or in place of it).

Sorcery looms large in the history and myths of The Realm. Before Sayalis cleansed the land of the Chaos Mother sorcerers frequented the place, bringing misery and slavery in their wake. Most cultures in The Realm have an innate hatred of sorcery (and magic generally) as a result and it would therefore be natural for characters to share such feelings.

Although sorcery has been largely destroyed, Jedakiah's interest in The Realm has caused a resurgence of hatred. The sorcerer's agents have reached deep into and across The Realm, often in subtle ways, and brought fresh misery to some of The Realm's inhabitants. There are several ways in which characters may have developed a Hate Sorcery or Hate Jedakiah Passion:

- Someone they know, love or care for has been killed by those who work for or serve Jedakiah.
- Barbarians of Gartharis have raided settlements of The Vale and taken loved ones into slavery.
- Attempts have been made to convert the character into one of Jedakiah's agents: the character has resisted.
- The character has been brought up to believe in sorcery's evils and, through membership of one of The Realm's cults, decided to actively work against it.

Use the Background Events as part of standard character creation to help shape how the Passion has come into being. As the characters play through the scenarios of Book of Quests they will be exposed more and more to Jedakiah's corruption and find their Passion developing - something that may aid them, and inform their choices, as the campaign reaches its climax.

THE ORDER OF TRUTH

Established to guard against sorcery and to protect The Realm from subversive enemies, the Order of Truth is a secretive brotherhood that works independently of the monarch. It possesses wealth and resources that have taken centuries to accrue and is a powerful secret society that can act as a benefactor and patron for the characters. Its leaders are nobles who, having proved their loyalty to The Realm, have sworn oaths to maintain the Order's independence but to always serve The Realm's best interests. Jedakiah knows of it and would dearly love to gain control of it, subverting it to Chaos and his own ends. So far he has failed in his few attempts.

Characters may belong to the Order of Truth either before play begins, or become members during play. Only those of the Noble social classes can join before play and, even then, they have limited access to its secrets and most likely do not even know how many people control it or who they all are. Such characters will therefore be Associates or, at best, Apprentices (see page 197 of the Mythras rules). The Order itself should be treated as a College (page 194 of Mythras) and will have been made to swear an oath of loyalty and secrecy to the Order. It offers no Gifts, but does offer training and access to its resources - mostly knowledge and history, although it can provide equipment and training too.

The Order of Truth's base is the palatial home of its Arch Counsellor, Duke Kornis of Nyren, but it has several other havens in Cylder and Nor Port, all administrated by local nobles. The Order's high ranking members greet each other with a special handshake (thumb clasped into the palm) and wear a discreet silver band on the little finger of the left hand. Those who progress to the rank of Master are given this ring of membership: all other ranks are merely taught the handshake.

Where nobles address commoners there is always the chance that a he or she might be a member of the Order and so nobles always ask after the health of the subject's cousin. Those who are members answer 'In rude health, as always'. This confirms membership if a ring is not present or the handshake would be an inappropriate gesture.

The Order's members are always assured hospitality by its noble members - one of the founding precepts of the society - and can expect, at the very least, a bed for the night, food and drink. A good example of one of the noble leaders of the Order is Lord Drystan, encountered first in the scenario *Beneath the Black Water*.

Scenario 1: Caravan

Overview

Caravan routes form a vibrant lifeline of trade, interconnecting the small towns, hamlets, and farmsteads that spread across the Vale. The caravans bring processed trade goods from the towns to the smaller communities. And, in return, they transport raw materials and foodstuffs back from the rural communities – a cyclical pattern of prosperity.

There is great reward, and great risk, to be had plying the trade routes. Shrewd caravan masters seek out skilled warriors to protect their interests. They offer high wages, but they demand loyalty and responsibility from their employees for the welfare of the caravan.

This scenario presents characters with the opportunity to join a merchant caravan as it prepares to depart a small town. The adventure begins with the characters being interviewed by the caravan master. From there, the journey proceeds – mundanely, at first. But, as days pass, it becomes clear that there is trouble brewing in the wilderness they travel through. It will take sharp steel, and a sharp eye, to overcome the dangers the characters will face.

The foul sorcerer Jedakiah has powerful allies among the barbarian tribes of Gartharis. He has forged an alliance with the barbarian chieftain, Delell, and is working towards unifying all of the tribes under his control. Delell provides Jedakiah with loyal warriors in exchange for gifts from the cult of the Chaos Mother and promises of greater power.

The corrupt shaman, Manuun, initially served as an emissary between Delell and Jedakiah. He travelled to Jedakiah's watchtower on many occasions, and returned to share Jedakiah's wishes with the tribe. Over time, Jedakiah began to see great potential in Manuun as a trustworthy servant. Manuun now serves Jedakiah as one of his chief lieutenants.

Manuun has been indoctrinated into the cult of Chaos Mother, and has gained the trappings, and the scars, from this allegiance. He is a dangerous and ruthless opponent, driven by a lust for power.

Jedakiah has provided Manuun with a gift - a chaos hybrid, bred in the laboratories of the Ophidians. The beast is a tool of destruction that must be controlled carefully. The barbarians transport it shackled and muzzled, and release it to feed and destroy. The shaman is the only one that can safely control the chaos hybrid and Manuun is eperforming an experiment to determine how far it can be controlled when it has tasted blood.

This scenario follows the actions of Manuun's warband that brings them into conflict with the characters. Over the past two weeks, the warband has been rampaging across the Northern border of the Vale. They have waylaid travellers, either forcing them into slavery or brutally sacrificing them. During the characters' journey, the barbarians set the chaos hybrid loose upon a hamlet. It is up to the characters to deal with Manuun and his men before they can cause any more death or destruction.

A Games Master can easily drop this scenario into any rural region of his game world. The only requirements are a populated starting point and some scattered rural communities. The barbarian raiders can be substituted with any appropriate threat in the campaign (orcs, goblins, etc.).

This scenario is not intended to be run during any specific season, though it would be unlikely for merchant caravans to be very active during winter months.

Non-Player Characters

- Jhonen, the merchant venturer operating the caravan between Lurien and Aylesford.
- Utuk, Jhonen's mute, barbarian assistant.
- Manuun, a shaman in Jedakiah's employ and responsible for the murder of Aylesford.

Key Points/Timeline

1. Jhonen hires the characters for his caravan in the town of Lurien.
2. The first day's travel allows the characters to get to know Jhonen, Utuk and other caravan members.
3. Arrival at the village of Thorsen, where Jhonen's past catches up with him.
4. Travel from Thorsen to Aylesford, with various hazards along the way.
5. Arrival at Aylesford - and discovery of the town's dreadful fate.
6. The Chaos Hybrid goes a-hunting.
7. Manuun and his barbarian escort arrive to catch the monster and may become entangled with the characters and the caravan.

Areas to Be Covered

This adventure begins in the town of Lurien, which lies at the border of Vale and North Vale on the banks of the River Gartharis. The caravan travels north, following the winding, upstream path of the River Gartharis, through lush farmland and woods. Its planned journey takes it through the village of Thorsen and the hamlet of Aylesford, before plunging into the heavy woods of North Vale.

A few additional encounter locations are also included in the scenario. The caravan faces an ambush, on the North Road, as it comes within Aylesford's proximity. Also, the characters may stumble upon the barbarian encampment, five kilometres to the north east of Aylesford.

Introduction: The Interview

The market square of Lurien is bustling at this time of year. In the early morning air, hawkers can be heard loudly extolling their goods for sale; caravans arrive and depart in billowing clouds of dust; and criers announce news, opportunities, and executions to the gathering crowds. For those characters gifted with Literacy, signs are posted throughout the square advertising the same information that the criers bellow.

Employment opportunities are abundant – whether that is the manual labour of unloading or loading wagons, the clearing of animal waste, or accompanying the caravans as they depart the town. Word travels fast that Jhonen, the caravan master, is seeking skilled outriders to protect his caravan as it travels northwards. The characters overhear from a few mumbling townsfolk that Jhonen pays very well, but only trusts in the most loyal and competent applicants. Indeed, minutes later, a town crier announces Jhonen's employment opportunities, and reveal that he offers 6 founders, per day, for the journey he is about to embark upon. If that's not enough motivation for the characters to seek out Jhonen, then mention the number of young men walking quickly in the direction of Jhonen's wagons. Competition for employment might pique their interest.

Jhonen can be found interviewing candidates as his wagons are loaded by porters, in a swirl of activity. He questions all of the applicants intently, and many glum young men turn away when it's clear that they will not qualify for the work.

Preparing for Play

This scenario is a good opportunity for Games Masters to bring together a new party of players with disparate characters. It is also a good opportunity to have already assembled the caravan guard in advance, with each player taking a ready-made guard position without the need for the Interview section of the scenario. This speeds-up play and provides a convenient reason for the characters to become adventurers, colleagues and, perhaps friends.

If Games Masters choose this latter option, it can be approached in a number of ways:

1. The Games Master creates a set of guard characters for the players, allowing the players to choose which guard they prefer playing. The pre-designed characters can be from very different backgrounds and if so, the players should be encouraged to devise reasons for why their characters have chosen to join the caravan. Some may be professional guards and mercenaries; others might be traders. Some may have secretive reasons for escaping The Realm for a time.
2. Alternatively, all the characters may be of a similar type - professional guards - who have worked with Jhonen before, or been recommended to him. This restricts the amount of say the players have in their characters' backgrounds and reasons for working for Jhonen, but is a simple option for rapid play.
3. Or, the Games Master allows the players to create their characters normally, but introduces, during character creation, the common background that all of them are working for Jhonen so that they have a ready starting point for play. Again, the players should decide how and why they have come to be part of the caravan, but they retain full control over what kind of character they are playing. Constructing a raison d'etre for being in Jhonen's employ is a great exercise in developing a character's background and for forming links and relationships between disparate characters.

Utuk, Jhonen's assistant, stands silently near Jhonen, eyes applicants, and nods or shakes his head to answer simple questions. He is quite an imposing figure to behold – a Long Riding nomad with graphic scars across his face, and a blackened stump for a tongue. Adventurers from the Long Riding recognise the scars as symbols of criminal prosecution and banishment from his native lands, and it could colour their perception of Utuk.

When it is the characters' turn to be interviewed, Jhonen asks them a simple question: "Tell me of your deeds and exploits". An Influence or Oratory test is required and, if successful, Jhonen hires them on the spot and offers to pay them daily at the advertised rate. A failed test results in Jhonen questioning their competence – he still employs them but at 75% of the advertised rate. (A successful, opposed Commerce check increases the salary amount, but not over the advertised rate). This is also a good opportunity for the characters to use their Passions - either augmenting their Influence or Oratory, or using a Passion in place of either to sell themselves. Characters with high Deceit, and a tendency to lie or exaggerate, may use this skill instead of Influence/Oratory, but a failed roll will have grave consequences, depending on the depth of the lies or embellishment.

A Day's Travel

Jhonen gives the characters the rest of the day to prepare for travel. He intends leaving Lurien at dawn the next day and does not want to waste daylight. If any characters attempt to gain more preparation time, Jhonen starts questioning their integrity: time is money.

The caravan consists of four horse-drawn wagons, each pulled by a pair of horses. The wagons are covered and loaded with a variety of trade goods: dyed textiles, ground herbs and medicinals, tanned leather, and forged metalwork (ploughs, tools, short swords). The wagons are driven by a pair of men – Jhonen and Utuk drive the lead wagon, and the remainder follow in single file. Characters are loaned a horse for the journey if they don't have one of their own.

The caravan departs that morning if all goes according to plan. The procession heads out of Lurien's eastern gate, following the road through the abundant farmland that surrounds the town. The eastern road is busy during the daylight hours; the caravan passes many travellers making their way to and from Lurien. After two kilometres, the caravan veers onto the northern road. It becomes clear, over the next hour, that there is far less foot and horse traffic travelling this road.

The caravan proceeds at a steady pace, slowing at times to navigate sudden twists in the road. When there is clear visibility of the path ahead – perhaps at the rise of a small hill – the caravan picks up the pace. At intervals, side trails lead off from the western side of the road, leading down to the raging Gartharis River. They become commonplace after a few hours of travel.

The characters are instructed to act as outriders on the roadway. At times, they need to cluster close to the wagons, guiding the caravan through treacherous ground or obstructions, and providing protection from bandits, if necessary. Pairs of guards are asked to ride ahead – on "point" – to spot potential threats and survey the land.

The characters should plan their task, deciding who rides ahead of the caravan and who will bring-up the rear. This is a good opportunity for the characters to make rolls for the following:

- Perception - to ensure that there are no visible hazards or bandits lying in wait.
- Ride - to successfully get ahead of the caravan to scout and then return, negotiating potholes, road debris or the odd deer that bolts from nearby bushes.
- Locale - to spot any potential herbs, hedgerow vegetables, game and so on to supplement the supper pot or be sold later.

Jhonen attempts to strike up conversations with the characters at different points in the journey. He naturally inquires about their backgrounds – from where they hail and where their lives have taken them thus far. He asks them to go into more detail about their exploits and accomplishments. He also asks what plans they have for the future.

If a character gains Jhonen's trust – or professes to follow the same religious faith – Jhonen 'opens up' and discusses more personal topics. He asks them of their family and friends. He, uncomfortably, asks how they are able to maintain their relationships with the distance that their travel and activities involve. Jhonen does not come out directly and ask for advice for his own unrequited love, but he vaguely describes his troubles if an character enquires for details.

Jhonen is very obvious about his cult membership. He fills pauses in dialogue with short phrases, such as: "Surely Xalgith guides our actions", or "Oh, this is fortuitous; praise be to Xalgith!" Jhonen distances himself from any character that questions his faith, or openly rejects the wisdom of Xalgith. He is far less likely to trust that person in the future, and speaks with the other characters rather than deal with the blasphemer directly.

The Village of Thorsen

The caravan's first stop on the north road is the village of Thorsen, famed for its pig herders. This small community, of two hundred inhabitants, is bound by a crude wooden palisade. A cluster of buildings stand at the core of the village. They include an inn, a smithy, a butcher, and a number of trinket shops. Dozens of hovels radiate out from the village centre, each with an attached pen crowded with swine. A foul stink hangs over this village – it can be nauseating to travellers, but locals have become inured to it. Have the characters make Endurance rolls when entering Thorsen: if they succeed, the stench does not overwhelm them. If they fail, all skill rolls for the next 1d4 hours are at one grade more difficult as they become used to the smell.

When the caravan is admitted through the gates of the village, a great commotion is raised and a large group of villagers congregate around the wagons. The caravan pushes through the growing crowd until they reach the north end of the village core. The wagons halt, and Jhonen's men work to unpack trade goods and deal with the stabling of the horses.

Jhonen informs the characters that he and his men will be occupied for much of the afternoon in trade negotiations with local shop owners and village folk. He will not need their services during this time, and he suggests that they brush off the road dust and relax at the inn with a beverage. He'll send one of his men if he has any need for them. Otherwise, he'll meet them at the inn later and settle their accommodation.

There are not many attractions in the Village of Thorsen for tourists. There are a few small shops that sell various sundries, but nothing that couldn't be acquired cheaper in Lurien. The local inn is one of the few highlights in the characters' stay in Thorsen. The following are some suggestions for activities that can be used for engaging the characters while Jhonen conducts his business.

Lump Hefting

Old Merrow, a colourful local of the village, possesses a pig called Lump, the biggest porker for miles around. Lump is almost the size of a small pony, can barely move, and spends its days munching turnips. Every so often, the men of Thorsen engage in the sport of Lump Hefting. The men, usually drunk, wager on who can push Lump over and roll the poor creature across Old Merrow's pig-pen. The gambling is good-natured and relies on Brawn and achieving a degree of momentum. A Lump Hefting session has begun when the characters arrive at The Hog's Trotters with the locals making their wagers. The current Lump Hefting champion is Nevis the Blacksmith: a massive figure of a man, his muscles are like boulders and his fingers the size of small crowbars. He wagers 3 Founders that he can topple Lump and roll him across the pen there and back three times without breaking a sweat. A group of six or so locals are betting he breaks into a sweat after the first trip. If the characters want to join the gambling, they can. If they want to challenge Nevis in the Hefting, then they are welcomed enthusiastically and asked to better Nevis's claim.

Eventually the group staggers out of the inn and down to Old Merrow's shack and pig pen. Lump is there, immobile, face squashed into a trough of turnips that it steadily munches. The pig doesn't even bother to look up as the group surrounds it. Nevis prepares to make his Hefting attempt.

Lump has a SIZ of 24. Pushing him over requires a successful Brawn roll; rolling him requires a successful Athletics roll and counts as Strenuous activity for Fatigue purposes: Lump squeals and struggles, although is too massive to do anything about being rolled like a barrel. Rolling Lump *once* across the pen requires two Athletics rolls with Fatigue being accrued for each failed roll. Nevis has Brawn 80% and Athletics 65%. The pen is also caked in slippery mud which makes the Athletics skill one grade more difficult. Failing a roll not only accrues Fatigue, it lands the character in the mire, covering him from head to toe in very smelly mud and excrement.

If Nevis succeeds in his boast, he stands to collect 21 Founders - unless someone can beat him. None of the locals are up for the attempt, but if a character succeeds, rolling Lump four times across the pen wins them the bet. Nevis fumes for a while but is good natured about the defeat unless the characters cheat in some way (or use magic), in which case they make an enemy of him, and, potentially, the locals.

Zoona the Soothsayer

Zoona is the local wise-woman. She is an expert in herbalism and claims to speak with the spirits. She has no true magical skill - only the ability to convince the superstitious locals of her particular gifts. She stumps into the inn while the characters are relaxing, glances around with her beady eyes, and settles on the characters. After a pause she approaches them. Zoona is wild-haired, wild-eyed and toothless. Her hair is caked in bird droppings and her rags barely conceal her emaciated form beneath. "For a Founder I'll reveal your fate as the spirits see it," she declares. "For two Founders I will brew you a potion of Good Fortune."

Saying No to Zoona is difficult. The locals respect and fear her; offering insult attracts withering glances and may provoke hostility - an Insight roll to gauge the reactions of the inn's locals easily determines this. If the characters persist in declining Zoona's offer she takes deep offence and curses the characters in this way: "The spirits are offended! They tell me of misfortunes in your path and the wrath of the dead! I see the raggedy man waiting for you with pain in his mind and blood on his hands. I see your suffering and fear. I hear the lamentations of your loved ones and many graves to be dug!"

All this is rather nebulous and is in no way connected with what lies ahead - Zoona is merely adept in scaring those who are superstitious. But, if so cursed, the characters may believe that Zoona does have the power of foresight when they reach Aylesford, and wish they had paid that Founder.

If the characters agree to Zoona's offer, she takes the character by the hands, stares deep into his or her eyes and speaks in a monotone. She says she sees long years of prosperity ahead, but days of hardship and doubt. She sees love and comfort, but also nights of loneliness and heartache. If a character asks for specifics she dismisses the question: "The spirits have spoken!" She wails. "It is wise not to question their revelations!"

Any character who pays 2 Founders receives the soothsaying and the promise of a Potion of Good Fortune. Zoona takes a pouch from within her rags and empties the contents into the character's drink. The smell is obscene: sickly sweet, like rotten chicken. She stirs the drink with her finger, spits into it, and declares it ready. "Pour this into a flask. When you consume it, you will be assured Good Fortune for a day and a night. No harm will come to you. The spirits have spoken!"

For once she speaks the truth. This vile concoction has the effect of granting the drinker one additional Luck Point for the session. It tastes vile and requires an Endurance roll to successfully swallow, but the extra Luck Point is granted immediately.

I Am The Passenger

The characters are approached by a young woman. She acts furtively and takes some time to pluck up the courage to approach their table. She is, perhaps, 14 or 15, very pretty, and calls herself Dalla. "You are travelling to Aylesford and I would go with you," she says. "I have money to pay for my passage, and I can cook, clean and sew." Of course, the characters need to consult with Jhonen about accepting additional passengers and needs to talk with him first. Dalla, if persudaded with a successful Influence or Insight roll, reveals a little more about her reasons for leaving Thorsen.

"My father plans to marry me to Brok. He is a good swineherd and will inherit twenty sows, but I do not wish to marry him." She sighs and dabs at a tear gathering in the corner of one eye. Dalla, it transpires, loves another. A young man from Aylesford who passed through Thorsen a year ago on his way to Cylder for the city's Great Market. A woodcarver and musician, he swept the impressionable Dalla off her pretty little feet and her yearning has grown daily. Now she has managed to scrape together enough for passage to Aylesford where she hopes to be reunited with her love.

Any character who has a Love Passion that is unrequited, or similar in vein to Dalla's must roll against, and *fail*, his or her Passion to remain unmoved by her story. Characters who are moved feel compelled to plead her case to Jhonen and take her side. Indeed, some characters may actually fall in love with Dalla themselves: she is an undoubted beauty with a beguiling innocence. During the course of the trip they might try to woo her. Success is treated as a Social Conflict task (see MYTHRAS page 287) with either Influence or Seduction being the active skill for wooing her. Dalla resists with her Love Hannen (her Aylesford beau) of 85%.

Naturally enough, Dalla's plight comes with strings. Her father, Rorke, is a determined and possessive man. A marriage between his daughter and Brok will advance his family's standing in Thorsen. When he realises she has run away he gives chase, accompanied by Dalla's four older, and quite strapping, brothers, intent on bringing his daughter home and punishing anyone who helped her leave.

Convincing Jhonen requires an Influence roll. He is grateful for additional money and she has the coin required, but if the Influence roll is failed he expresses doubts about helping a young, promised woman, escape her fate. Utuk also signals his disapproval. If persuaded, her tells the characters that they will be responsible for her - and must deal with any consequences. Jhonen denies, vehemently, any knowledge of her true status.

If accepted Dalla says she will meet the caravan a little way down the road after it leaves Thorsen, sneaking out of the village when the attentions of her father and brothers are elsewhere. She makes good on this promise - although this is an opportunity for the characters to help Dalla with her plans, perhaps arranging a diversion or other scheme to smuggle her safely out of the village.

It takes a day for her father to discover her absence, put two and two together, and organise a pursuit. But Rorke and his sons can move faster than the caravan and soon catch-up, leading to a confrontation. Rorke only wants his daughter back, not bloodshed, and the characters should be able to talk or intimidate their way out of the situation. Dalla pleads with her father, but ultimately is afraid of him and relies on the characters to support and defend her.

Rorke and his sons are not above attempting to kidnap Dalla back, stage an half-hearted ambush or offer a direct challenge. These situations need to be planned by the Games Master and adjudicated as circumstances play-out.

Should Dalla remain with the caravan, she is heartbroken when they reach Aylesford and she witnesses for herself the devastation. However, after frantically searching all the bodies she declares that her beloved Hannen is not amongst the dead: perhaps he is still in Cylder? If so, she uses her wiles to get the characters to help her reach Cylder so she can carry on her search (and this would form a good reason for travelling to Cylder in preparation for the scenario *Shadows Behind the Throne*, starting on page 55).

If Dalla is taken captive later in this scenario, she can also be used as a substitute for Bria (see Beneath the Black Water and Reckoning at Distaff's Peak): she is certainly a Pure Beauty.

The Hog's Trotters

The Hog's Trotters is the sole inn of Thorsen village. It is a two-story structure with a tavern on the first floor and private rooms and a common room on the second floor. The tavern isn't frequented much during the mornings and afternoons. But, at noontime, and in the evenings, it gets packed full of pig farmers and random travellers.

There is one regular patron present regardless of the time of day. A depressed pig farmer, by the name of Glun, is drowning his sorrows in ale throughout the day. Glun shares – to anyone who pays him any attention – that his brother, Daek, sister-in-law, Mathilde, and a good friend left Thorsen yesterday. They had plans to settle north in the hamlet of Aylesford, and Glun is quite unhappy with their decision. Glun's mood brightens if he learns that the characters are travelling north. He asks them to share his best wishes if he encounters the group in Aylesford.

DISGRUNTLED CUSTOMERS

Jhonen has stopped in Thorsen before, and on his last visit, he made an enemy of a local shop owner. Jhonen forced a hard bargain, and this led to strained trade relations and hurt feelings. Marquat, a Thorsen merchant, felt slighted during their transaction and vowed revenge. He has recruited a few friends and a family member to teach Jhonen a lesson – by way of a cudgel.

Marquat, and his thugs wait until the late afternoon before they take action. By this time, the crowds have cleared and Jhonen and his men are packing up and securing their supplies. Marquat's group walks brazenly up to the caravan and begins beating Jhonen and his men with cudgels. Marquat feels confident that he can teach Jhonen a painful lesson, but he won't expect the characters to intervene in his revenge.

THE HOG'S TROTTERS DIAGRAM

This inn can also be used as the basis for any generic inn Games Masters might need. It conforms to a standard design and layout commonly found throughout The Realm.

They may hear the cries from surprised villagers when the tussle breaks out. The sounds are muffled, though, if they happen to be indoors at the time – a Perception roll is required to hear the commotion.

Utuk escapes just as the melee breaks out, and runs to find the characters. He goes to the Hog's Trotters first. He does his best to mime the conflict and then rushes back to the caravan, hopefully with the characters in tow.

They arrive to see that the melee is definitely swinging in Marquat's favour. Jhonen bears a bloody mouth and visible bruises, and one of his men is prone on the ground. They were initially taken by surprise, but have drawn their short swords to defend themselves. Marquat, and his thugs, number eight men.

It won't take much effort to dissuade Marquat's men from keeping up the fight; they are no match for seasoned warriors. In MYTHRAS terms, Marquat's group can be considered Rabble. If any of Marquat's men suffer damage they cease fighting and flee in fear. If three or more are taken out of the fight (killed or injured) the remainder rout.

When the melee is over, Jhonen suggests that they retire to the inn for the night. His men need some rest from their injuries, and he would prefer to leave by daybreak. If the characters press to intimidate or murder Marquat, Jhonen turns, spit out a bloody tooth, and say: "No, don't bother. I think he'll have learned his lesson. Let us not waste our time with filth of his kind."

The evening passes without further incident. Most of Jhonen's men rest in the inn's common room; Jhonen pays

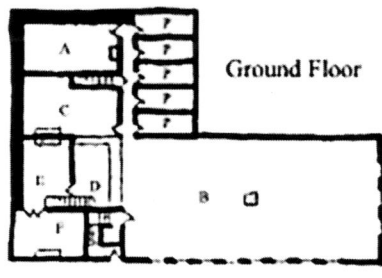
Ground Floor

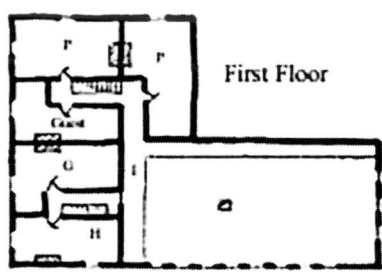
First Floor

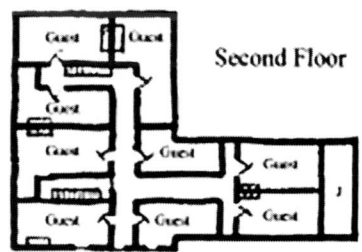
Second Floor

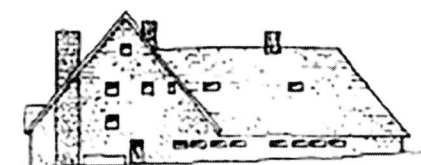

Key
A: Cellar (trapdoor access)
B: Hall
C: Saloon
D: Bar
E: Kitchen
F: Store
G & H: Proprietor's Rooms
I: Balcony/Gallery
J: Store (access via ladder from Balcony)
P: Private Rooms
Guest: Guest Bedrooms for rent

for separate rooms for the characters if they choose. The caravan departs early the next morning.

Road Hazards

The following events are intended to take place between Thorsen and Aylesford. Use some, or all, of these to punctuate the journey between the two settlements.

Rockslide

While the sun is high in the sky, the characters ranging ahead of the caravan spot some trouble. A rockslide has shifted earth and large stones across their path, covering it in raised mounds of debris. Two trees lean precariously in the direction of the roadway, their root structures weakened by the shifting soil. It is apparent that this is a natural occurrence; rainfall from a few days prior has weakened an earth embankment close to the roadway.

Horses can easily navigate through the obstacle, but the wagons risk damage if they are driven through it. A Hard Drive test is required to safely cross the unsteady terrain. Failure can lead to: wheels stuck in the debris field, damaged wheels or axles, or, with a fumble, the overturning of a wagon. Any of these events lead to Jhonen barking insults and threats of reduced pay.

The safest course of action is to spend time clearing the roadway of rocks and then smoothing over the earth with the carried farm implements. Have the characters make Brawn tests to move the larger rocks to the roadside. A fumble results in light injury; that character sustains 1d3 hit points of damage to one of two hit locations. Roll a d10 – on a 1-5 the chest (back) is affected; on a 6-10 the abdomen (lower back) is affected. A failed test delays their road clearing, and one of the leaning trees falls directly into the roadway. Characters participating in the road clearing must make Evade tests to avoid the thick trunk. The tree's "skill" is 35% and inflicts 1d8 damage to a random hit location.

The leaning trees can be easily felled before the work on the road begins. Or, they may try to secure them with ropes and stakes – or use some other form of precaution.

Kidnapping

Four hours before dusk, the riders may catch sight of a subtle disturbance on the eastern side of the road. A successful Perception roll allows a character to notice a large number of cracked tree branches and downtrodden plants just beyond the roadside. It appears that a group emerged from the roadside, moving partially out onto the road. Closer inspection reveals many footprints, and hoof prints, pressed into the soft soil. A failed test bypasses this scene, as the caravan rolls by too quickly.

A Standard Tracking roll provides more detail. A pair of horse tracks leads north on the roadway until they reach this point of conflict. Six sets of horse tracks emerge from the underbrush, and woods, from the roadside. It can be judged that this struggle took place about a day and a half ago. On close inspection, fragments of hemp rope can be found beyond the roadside, indicating that bound captives were taken. From there, the entire group heads northeast through the underbrush. There are no signs of bloodshed to be found.

Searching the underbrush reveals torn and tattered bags and backpacks tossed haphazardly four metres from the road, their contents scattered. Shredded bedrolls and damaged camping gear can be found with just a few seconds of searching. A brass locket on a chain – inscribed to a Mathilde – is found if the characters spend five minutes digging through the underbrush.

The tracks can be followed, and eventually lead 15 kilometres to the barbarian encampment. The back country, through which this trail leads, is navigable by horses but it is much slower going than by roadway. However, Jhonen does not appreciate this kind of distraction. He urges the caravan to press on, and tells the characters to be alert for bandits in the vicinity. If they are resolute in their desire to follow the trail they risk dismissal from service.

> ### Kidnapping – Alternative
> If Dalla is with the caravan, this would make a good place for the characters to encounter Rorke and his sons. Details will need to be adjusted, but the signs of passing the characters uncover belong to Dalla's father and four brothers. They have managed to overtake the caravan, using little-known pathways, and are staging an encounter further down the road.

Wolves in the Night

As dusk approaches, it becomes clear that the caravan will not reach the hamlet of Aylesford that evening. Jhonen directs the characters to advance on horseback and look for a suitable site for a camp – a widening of the road, or a clearing that can be navigated by the wagons.

It doesn't take long to find a suitable spot. In a half a kilometre, the road widens significantly, providing an adequate spot to pull the wagons off the main thoroughfare.

Once the wagons are situated, campfires are lit, tents are assembled, and a meal is prepared. Afterwards, Jhonen assigns watches to the guards; Jhonen and his men do not participate in watches.

As night deepens, watchmen hear the howling of wolves in the vicinity. Torch or lamplight reveal glittering eyes on the edge of wood and underbrush. A pack of wolves watch the camp intently but won't muster the courage to attack. The wolves can be convinced to flee if a group of watchmen approach and make a lot of noise, or wave flaming torches. They are really only a threat if an individual wanders off into the woods; in which case, the wolves will be upon them, knock them prone, and attack.

Ambush

A small group of barbarian tribesmen have set an ambush for any caravan that takes the North Road. A kilometre north of the Wolves in the Night stopover, the caravan comes upon the trap that has been set. The barbarians have split into two groups. One group, of four barbarians, is a short distance down a side trail from the main road. The second group, of three barbarians, is set up on the road, prepared to lure the characters away from the caravan after peppering them with arrows.

In the morning, the caravan proceeds down a winding section of the north road. The leading outriders notice a side trail and could choose to investigate it, if they desire. If they pause and make an Easy Tracking check they see a number of hoofprints that head down the side trail. Following them leads the characters into direct conflict with the first group of barbarians, who wait a short distance down the trail, listening for the passing of the caravan. If the characters disregard the side trail, they proceed further

down the road until they face missile fire from the second group. This group of three barbarians lets loose a short volley before turning and mounting their horses. They flee and attempt to lure the characters to chase them.

The general plan of the barbarians is to distract the characters into pursuing the archers to the point of abandoning the protection of the caravan. Once the second group hears the caravan pass, they spur their horses into fast pursuit. The barbarians attack any characters who remain behind, subduing them as quickly as possible. They ride in tandem on the horses, the passenger hacking opponents with an axe, or leaping on to the wagon and then scrambling up to the drivers. The barbarians slay the drivers if they get the chance, picking off the wagons sequentially. If the bait is not taken, both groups converge from opposite directions and do their best to slay or disable the characters and the caravan drivers.

This could be quite an active battle, with combat and movement occurring at a healthy gallop. Be sure to call for Riding tests for maintaining speed, and for complex mounted manoeuvres. The wagon drivers try to evade the barbarians, but the wagons slow if the road conditions become too treacherous.

If two or more barbarians are killed or disabled the rest flee, riding off down a trail towards their encampment. Their hope is that the force remaining at the encampment is enough to discourage the characters.

The Devastation of Aylesford

The caravan encounters additional signs of trouble around mid-day. The wagons arrive at the edge of the hamlet of Aylesford, three hours travel north of the ambush. As they round a bend in the road, and approach a bridge, they spot the body of a villager, face down, in the roadway. The body is slashed with horrific lacerations; dried blood stains the clothes, and the earth is damp where it has laid. Beyond the squawk of crows, there are no sounds of activity from the hamlet, and no smoke visible from chimneys.

As the caravan proceeds into the hamlet's square it becomes clear that something horrible has occurred. Corpses litter the place, all bearing the same ragged wounds. Some are missing limbs or heads, and appear to have been gnawed by wild animals. Bodies can also be seen outside the tight cluster of buildings – along the northern road and scattered in the pastures.

Doorways yawn open and no light is visible from within the buildings. It appears that any surviving inhabitants have either fled the town or hidden themselves well enough to escape detection.

Aylesford has suffered from the violent rampage of a chaos hybrid. Manuun has unleashed this foul beast on the hamlet as a vile experiment – to test the hybrid's abilities for the time when the barbarian hordes raid the villages of the Vale in full force. The horror was set loose in the very early hours of the day, to kill, destroy, and devour.

Page 31 shows Aylesford and its environs. The North Road bypasses the town, with auxiliary paths through the woodland leading into its centre from both north and south points. Aylesford is large by local standards, although only about a third of the size of Lurien. Its large, circular market area hosts regular fairs for the surrounding villages and this is where Jhonen intends to trade. The plentiful supply of good quality timber makes Aylesford a centre for excellent timber and wooden goods, including very high quality charcoal.

Notes concerning major buildings in Aylesford are as follows.

The Mill

Aylesford's water mill stands beside a redirected stream from the Gatharis River. Wooden bins line the walls, some filled with flour, and others containing raw grain to be processed. The water wheel spins, and the internal gearing creaks and groans.

A half-dead farmer can be found, prone, near the entrance. He bears the same vicious injuries as the corpses found throughout the hamlet. The farmer coughs raggedly if examined, and briefly convulses. He only has time to utter "…the beast…" before expiring.

The Chapel

The Aylesford chapel is a peaked-roof structure with a central prayer hall, and two adjoining chambers. One chamber is the modest room for the local priest; the other serves as a storage room for various ceremonial tools. The chapel serves the cult of Aliya, which is the prominent religion in the region.

The central hall contains a number of low benches facing a table against the opposite wall. A variety of idols cover the table, all representations of the goddess. The roof of the hall is supported by a number of evenly spaced pillars.

The chaos hybrid rests dormant in the priest's chamber when the characters arrive at the hamlet. It has spent the past few hours sleeping off the exhaustion of its violent rampage and the pounds of human flesh it has devoured. It is very perceptive, however, and hears anyone entering the chapel. For more on the monster's tactics, see the boxed section on page 30.

THE GENERAL STORE

Aylesford's general store has been the site of a serious battle. The front doors have been beaten down – practically torn from their hinges – and a large number of corpses can be found within. It appears that a number of the villagers fled into this structure for safety, and tried to defend themselves from the chaos hybrid. Judging from the gory scene found within, they had little success.

THE WELL

The well is covered, and has a bucket and winch attached to it. It descends 30 metres. A character could be lowered by rope down the well, but the shaft would be a very tight fit, and would take a great deal of time. It would also be for naught because there is nothing below but the accumulated water.

THE FARM HOUSES

A few farmhouses are located close to the hamlet's square, but most are spread out across the neighbouring countryside. They are all single-story structures built of stone with thatched roofs.

The houses closer to the square are all vacated and many have corpses littered throughout. Some of the doors show signs of being forced open.

A few of the more distant houses are occupied by terrified families that have shuttered windows and barred any entrances. The people can be calmed down if they are told that the threat has been eliminated, but otherwise they remain indoors, terrified. Once they can be assured that all danger has passed, they assist in the cleanup of the hamlet, and can aid the characters in any other tasks they require.

JHONEN'S SUGGESTIONS

Once Jhonen has had the chance to survey the situation he asks the characters to search through the buildings

HANDLING THE MASSACRE

Aylesford is an exercise in wanton carnage. Few will have ever encountered such a terrible scene before - and even those who have witnessed battlefields will still be unprepared for the dreadful scene awaiting them in the town.

Ever character must make a Hard Willpower roll. Those who succeed are able to function with a relative semblance of normality, although their mood is likely to be grim for some days to come, and sleep disturbed by images of the carnage.

Those who fail the roll are caught in a state of shock. They immediately function at the Exhausted Fatigue level, and the effects endure while the remain in Aylesford, and for 6 hours after leaving. Nightmares are assured.

Those who fumble the Willpower roll simply cannot function. They suffer the Debilitated Fatigue level which endures for as long as they are in the town and for 18 hours after they leave. They require some form of healing or counselling if they are to overcome the horrors they have witnessed.

---

around the town square. He suggests the general store first, because he would like move his men to a safe location if a threat is still out there. Once the characters have cleared the store, Jhonen has his men dismount and hole-up there until the characters check the rest of the hamlet. Jhonen and his men assist them once some level of safety has been assured.

One of Jhonen's men recommends that they deal with the great numbers of corpses scattered across the hamlet. He suggests that a mass burial would be a decent course of action; Jhonen agrees.

Excavation can occur on the north edge of the chapel's burial plots, extending in to a nearby pasture. It takes a great deal of effort to accomplish, but the remaining locals can assist. It is terrible work and takes hours to complete, even with locals assisting. Burying the dead cannot be accomplished in a single day. Jhonen, and his men, recite prayers to Xalgith and Aliya and observe a period of silence for the memory of the slain.

ENTER THE SHAMAN

Jhonen suggests that they camp in Aylesford that evening. He has no interest in leading his caravan in darkness, especially with the threats that they have faced so far and Aylesford's devastation to deal with. He even hints that it may be in their best interest to return to Lurien tomorrow.

There is room in the chapel to occupy most of the caravan's people, though the characters can determine where they want to set up a camp, and whether they want to prepare any defences. Utuk suggests a watch.

During the night a small group of barbarians return to Aylesford to retrieve the Hybrid. Manuun, the shaman, and two of his tribesmen sneak up to the edge of the surrounding woods to observe the state of the town. They are immediately suspicious if the wagons are visible, or if there are

THE HYBRID'S TACTICS

The Chaos Hybrid has been bred by the Ophidians of the Gartharis Mountains with one aim only: to kill. It is large, strong, fast and cunning. It shows no mercy. Its recent efforts have weakened it, meaning it must recuperate and the monster has sought rest in the crypt of the chapel. It only requires a few hours though, and by nightfall of the day the caravan arrives it is ready for more slaughter.

The Hybrid uses shadows, cover and rooftops. Having indulged in relatively easy slaughter already, it now seeks a different approach and intends to stalk and ambush, using the town's layout to full advantage. It therefore bides its time, hides, and then plays a long game of cat and mouse with those still alive in the central town, picking-off stragglers one by one, butchering them and then going in search of the next.

But the Hybrid is no mindless killer. It employs a variety of different combat Special Effects to Trip, Disarm, and incapacitate foes. Those it can render helpless it does so and then leaves them, intent on returning to finish them later. The Hybrid knows how to use a sling, and has a ready supply of missiles to Stun opponents before moving in with more immediate weapons.

The atmosphere to strive for is one of the lone, inhuman, stalker/slasher. The Hybrid uses every part of the environment to aid it, retreating when it has to only to return later to continue its spree. It is quite prepared to move to the outlying houses and murder the terrified locals who have locked themselves in. While it lives, no one is safe.

Aylesford and Environs

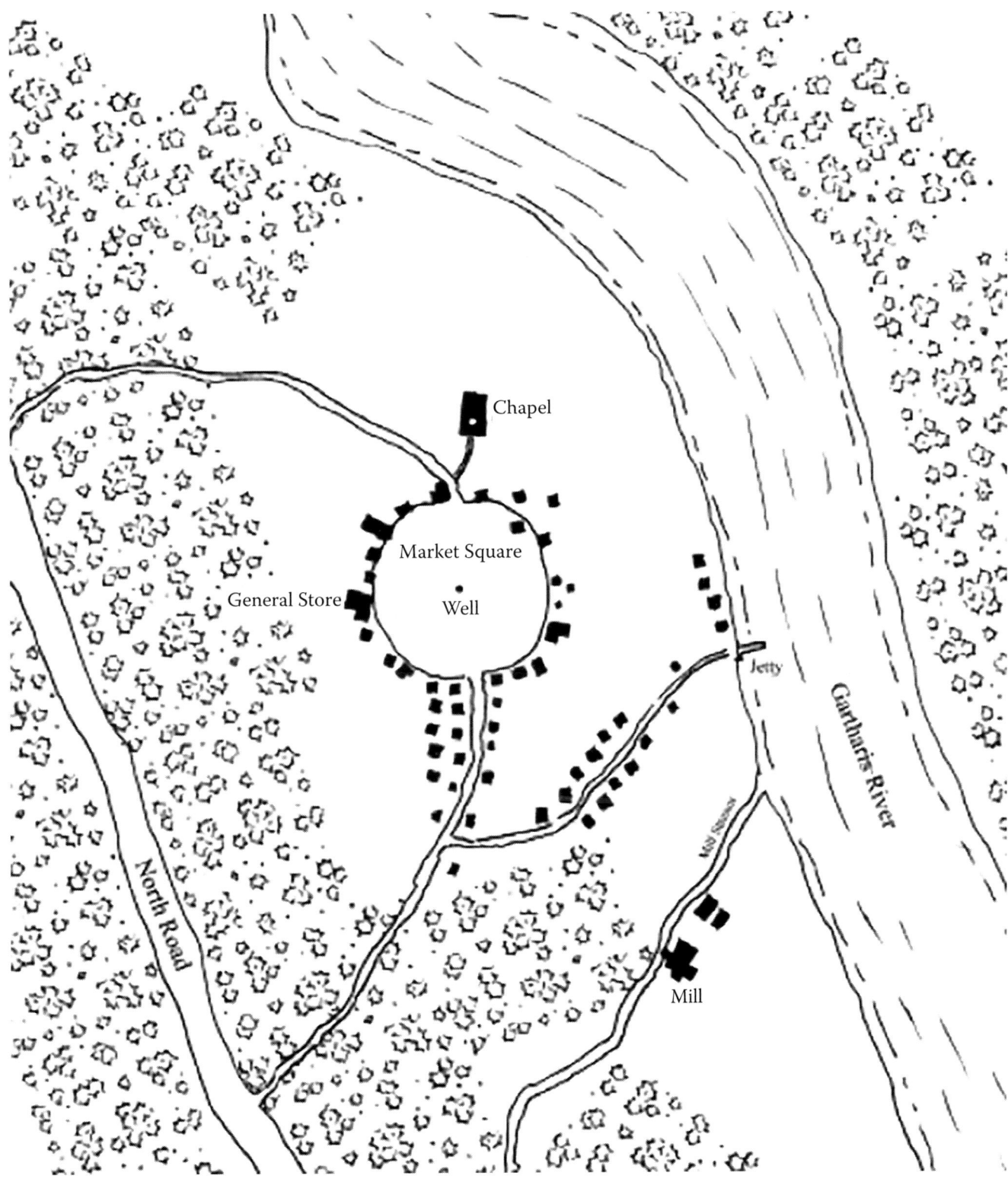

any fires lit in the building hearths. Manuun orders his men to advance into Aylesford to determine what has occurred.

The barbarians cautiously sneak into the Aylesford, hiding in shadows, and using the buildings for as much cover as possible. They are alert to any posted sentries, and try to retreat back to the woods rather than face a confrontation. The Hybrid, also loose in the town, does not attack these barbarians, whom it recognises as its masters. If the characters have posted sentries, and can win an Opposed Perception vs. Stealth test they'll be able to detect the barbarians and can try to eliminate or capture them, if they wish. If a combat occurs the barbarians do their best to disable the characters so that they have the opportunity to flee back to their encampment. Manuun flees at the first sounds of conflict, returning to the encampment to muster his forces to assault Aylesford the following day.

Manuun is the only one who can command the Hybrid, having been taught the skill by the Ophidians who bred the beast. He must have sight of the Hybrid and must succeed in an Influence roll to direct its activities, which included making it retreat and return to the barbarian's encampment. These verbal commands are in the Ophidians' native tongue: hisses and whistles that approximate simple commands: "Cease," "Follow me," "Attack that one," and so forth. If Manuun fails an Influence roll then the Hybrid simply ignores that command. If a roll is fumbled, the Hybrid does the opposite. Manuun, being a shaman, has his own command of spirits - see his description on page 37.

The Old Stone Bridge

Two kilometres north of Aylesford stretches the Old Stone Bridge, a sturdy structure spanning the raging Gartharis River. The bridge was built more than 100 years ago, and is rarely used by travellers. On the eastern side, a stone watchtower stands disused, with a yawning doorway and vacant windows. In years past, the watchtower served as a defensible position against the raids of the barbaric Gartharis tribes. Now, it is simply roadside scenery.

The North road shifts close to the river as it nears the Old Stone Bridge. The banks of the river decline at a sharp angle, and there is three metre drop from the shore to the surface of the river.

The Old Stone Bridge is easily crossed on foot, and can be crossed by wagons travelling single file. It is not wide enough for two wagons to pass, or travel side-by-side. It is well-built and is a safe route to travel.

This location could be the site of a final assault by Manuun's warband if they muster their numbers for a greater assault on Aylesford. The bridge is defensible and Aylesford has plenty of materials that can be used to blockade one end of the bridge, decreasing the barbarians' chances of crossing the river. The Gartharis River is strong and wide here; swimming across is always at a Formidable level of difficulty. Few of the barbarians can swim and so they need the bridge to pass between the civilised lands on the Aylesford side, and the wilder lands to the north east.

The Barbarian Encampment

The shaman's warband has established an encampment in a clearing one kilometre to the north east of Aylesford, on the far side of the Old Stone Bridge. Their animal hide lean-tos are deep in the woods. A few smouldering campfires are dotted across the clearing. See page 33 for a map of the encampment.

In the morning and afternoon hours, barbarians are located on the spots on the map marked with an 'x'. During the evening hours, barbarians are found at the locations marked with a 'y'. Bound hostages are held in the cage which is also used for transporting the Hybrid. Hidden in the eastern edge of the wood is a cart that is used for transporting the monster back into Garthari lands. The barbarians' ponies are tethered out of sight. There are none lean-tos in total, the largest belonging the Manuun, the shaman.

The barbarians always post sentries, regardless of the time of day. The encampment is most active in the morning and afternoon, while the barbarians tend to their horses, eat, and sharpen weapons. There are four barbarians active in the evenings, on watch. Two are posted by the horses, near one of the trails exiting the camp, and the other two are spread out keeping an eye on the other trails.

Manuun's warband consists of 16 barbarians, including himself. The characters could face a challenging fight if they tried to take on the entire group. But it's likely that the barbarian forces could be halved if the characters have already faced some during the Ambush encounter and the Dead of Night encounter at Aylesford.

There are two captives currently in the camp. A traumatised husband and wife are currently bound in one of the lean-tos. Daek and Mathilde, Thorsen villagers, were captured prior to the Kidnapping scenario on page 26, and have been subjected to beatings. One of their friends, Serg, was captured as well, but has since been fed to the chaos

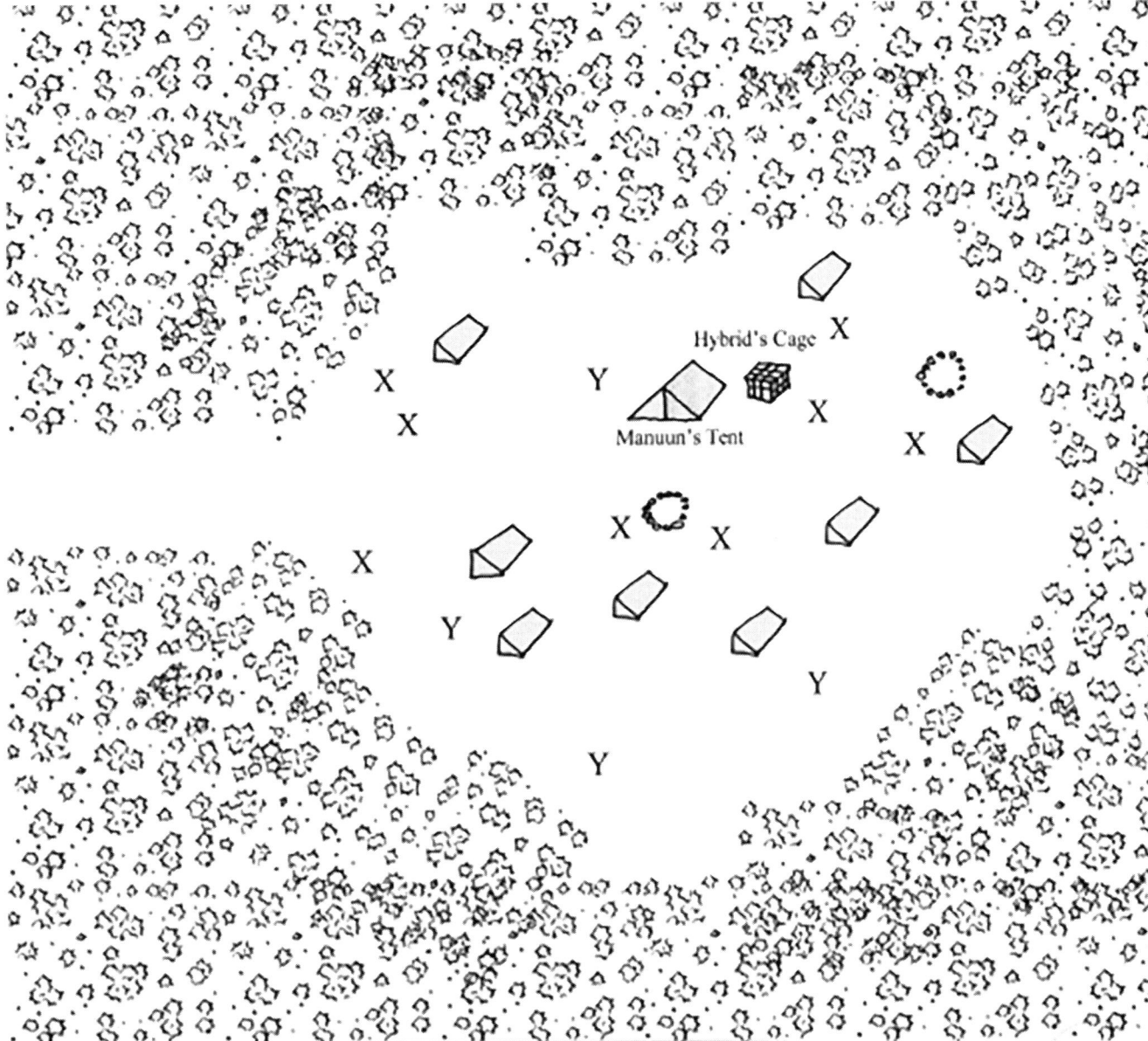

hybrid. Human bones, and animal excrement, can be found near the shaman's lean-to.

slaves (see *Reckoning at Distaff Peak*, beginning on page 192) or used in dread rituals by Jedakiah and the Ophidians.

ENCAMPMENT TACTICS

The barbarians are very well organised and confident in the presence of Manuun. If the sentries are engaged, their first action is to fight defensively and make enough noise to alert the camp. The barbarians initially attempt to screen Manuun from any attacks, allowing him time to call upon his spirits. Once they have determined how many opponents they are facing, they advance and attempt to surround or flank the enemy.

The barbarians will not slay the characters outright. If given the chance, they try to disable them and take them hostage. They will be taken to Distaff Peak and made into

CONCLUDING THE SCENARIO

The scenario has many possible outcomes. Some of the most likely are described below. The end of the scenario is left deliberately vague because it depends greatly on the actions taken by the characters. They should, at least, be able to collect enough information to find the location of the barbarian encampment. And, launching an assault, ignoring Aylesford altogether (if the characters trace the camp first) is a possibility.

If the characters do not take the fight to the barbarians, they waste no time retaliating. Manuun lays siege to Aylesford at an opportune point after his first reconnaisance.

Capturing Manuun, alive, has serious ramifications for this scenario. His tribesmen may try to rescue him, of course, but he would be an immense a bargaining chip for the characters. If Manuun regains his freedom he does not stop until he has seen the death of all the characters. In that case, he seeks immediate revenge if he has a number of surviving tribesmen to aid him. Otherwise, his group retreats back to Gartharis, and Manuun plans to strike back at a later date. The Games Master could use him as a reccurring foil for the characters.

POSSIBLE OUTCOMES

1. Jhonen and the characters see-sense and flee Aylesford, returning to Lurien. Jhonen intends to inform the local duke of what has happened in Aylesford and alert him to the likelihood of more, and more ferocious, barbarian and monstrous assaults. The Chaos Hybrid is proof that chaos is rising once again in The Realm - and clearly something commanding considerable power is behind it. If Manuun is captured and brought before the duke of Lurien, he remains resolutely silent about who her serves. Torture makes him talk and he names Jedakiah is 'The Master' and 'Servant of the Chaos Mother' but says no more about the sorcerer's power.
2. The characters manage to kill or capture the Hybrid and some, possibly all, of the barbarian advanced guard. If Manuun is also captured or killed, then they have achieved a small victory: the remaining barbarians return to Jedakiah to inform him of the situation. This would mark a good point to flee Aylesford, taking evidence of a new threat from Chaos with them.
3. The barbarians amass and descend on Aylesford to capture the Hybrid and complete the massacre. There is an opportunity for a heroic stand at the Old Stone Bridge, house-to-house skirmishing in Aylesford's streets or, more sensibly, fleeing as fast as they can from the devastated town. If the barbarians recapture the Hybrid they may let the characters and others escape: their experiment was successful. Jedakiah can breed many more of these vicious Hybrids, train others to control them, and send an army of Chaos against The Realm, taking control of it for himself and the Chaos Mother.
4. The barbarians are defeated entirely. Some no doubt reveal that they serve a sorcerer who dwells in the mountains of the far north and that his power is unmatched in The Realm. Manuun remains stoic, revealing little. If the barbarians are defeated in this way, then the characters can return and alert those who hold power in The Vale.

In particular there are a number of ways that locating the barbarian encampment could work. The characters could follow the trail from the Kidnapping scene all the way to the camp; also, trails lead from the Ambush scene, and from Aylesford, back to the clearing. If the characters take a barbarian prisoner during any part of the adventure they can intimidate/interrogate him into revealing the location of the camp. It takes Tracking rolls to navigate woods without overly slowing pace.

The true purpose of this scenario is to introduce the characters to Jedakiah's evil and expose them to the kinds of forces and creatures he has at his disposal. The characters' survival leads to further adventure, as described in the rest of the scenarios in Book of Quests. Their death or capture serves little purpose other than to satisfy Jedakiah's villainy.

NON-PLAYER CHARACTERS

JHONEN

Jhonen is a Valeman who has worked the caravan routes for the past decade. He is a very capable merchant who has made a modest fortune with his hard work and ingenuity.

In the past year, Jhonen's attention has drifted from his quest for profits, alone. He has fallen in love with an inkeeper, named Gisal, in the city of Nyren. He longs for her but his social brusqueness forces a barrier between them. This frustrates him no end, and he has found it hard to accept that this obstacle isn't as easily resolved as a trade negotiation.

Jhonen is fervent member of the Xalgith cult. He believes strongly in the principles of his faith and frequently recites the blessings and doctrine of Xalgith.

Characteristics	Attributes		1d20	Location	AP/HP
STR: 11	Action Points	2	1–3	Right Leg	1/5
CON: 12	Damage Modifier	0	4–6	Left Leg	1/5
SIZ: 13	Magic Points	13	7–9	Abdomen	2/6
DEX: 10	Movement	6m	10–12	Chest	2/7
INT: 14	Initiative Bonus	10	13–15	Right Arm	1/4
POW: 13	Armour	Leather	16–18	Left Arm	1/4
CHA: 14	Abilities	None	19–20	Head	1/5
	Magic	None			

Skills: *Athletics 59%, Brawn 62%, Commerce 86%, Deceit 67%, Drive 89%, Endurance 62%, Evade 56%, Locale 66%, Navigate 81%, Perception 64%, Survival 67%, Unarmed 59%, Willpower 62%*

Passions: *Loyalty to The Vale 80%, Love Gisal 90%, Hate Laziness 70%*

Combat Style: *Valeman Merchant (Shortsword, Dagger) 75%*

Weapon	Size/Force	Reach	Damage	AP/HP
Dagger	S	S	1d4+1	6/8
Shortsword	M	S	1d6+1	5/7

UTUK

Utuk hails from the steppes of the Long Riding. He has lived in the Vale for eight years, employed by Jhonen the entire time.

His tribal scars across his face, arms and chest mark him as a member of the Scaled Crane Tribe, a barbarian people who worship Feyr. His tongue has been cut-out for crimes against his people: his exile is self-imposed and he will not return to the Long Riding until he believes he has atoned for his crimes.

Although mute Utuk has developed an eloquent vocabulary of grunts, gestures and expressions. It is not difficult to understand what he means or intends even though he has no voice.

Despite his imposing appearance, Utuk has a thoughtful demeanour and a general calmness about him. He greatly enjoys games of chance and sleight of hand, parlour tricks. He will often entertain his compatriots with sleight of hand by the campfire.

Characteristics	Attributes		1d20	Location	AP/HP
STR: 12	Action Points	3	1–3	Right Leg	1/7
CON: 17	Damage Modifier	0	4–6	Left Leg	1/7
SIZ: 13	Magic Points	13	7–9	Abdomen	2/8
DEX: 15	Movement	6m	10–12	Chest	2/9
INT: 15	Initiative Bonus	12	13–15	Right Arm	1/6
POW: 13	Armour	Leather	16–18	Left Arm	1/6
CHA: 14	Abilities	None	19–20	Head	1/7
	Magic	None			

Skills: *Athletics 59%, Brawn 62%, Drive 70%, Endurance 62%, Evade 56%, Locale 66%, Perception 64%, Ride 90%, Sign Language 90%, Survival 67%, Unarmed 59%, Willpower 62%*

Passions: *Loyalty to Jhonen 80%, Atone for Crimes 90%*

Combat Style: *Long Riding Barbarian (Spear, Shield, Sword, Bow) 74%*

Weapon	Size/Force	Reach	Damage	AP/HP
Shortspear	M	L	1d8+1	4/5
Shortsword	M	S	1d6+1	5/7
Target	L	S	1d3+1	4/9
Short Bow	L	-	1d6	4/4

JHONEN'S CARAVANEERS

The rest of Johnen's group are Valemen who have worked the caravan routes for a varied length of time. They are skilled horsemen, but they are not warriors, and will not fare well in combat against trained opponents. They are a boisterous bunch and will happily converse with the characters – and anyone else willing to receive an earful.

Attributes	1d20	Location	AP/HP
Action Points: 2	1–3	Right Leg	1/5
Damage Modifier: 0	4–6	Left Leg	1/5
Magic Points: 11	7–9	Abdomen	2/6
Movement: 6 metres	10-12	Chest	2/7
Initiative Bonus: 9	13–15	Right Arm	1/4
Armour: Light Leather	16–18	Left Arm	1/4
Abilities: None	19–20	Head	1/5

Skills: Athletics 35%, Brawn 42%, Drive 59%, Endurance 42%, Evade 28%, Locale 65%, Perception 30%, Survival 35%, Unarmed 25%, Willpower 32%

Passions: Loyalty to Jhonen 50%
Combat Style: Valeman Driver (Shortsword, Dagger) 55%

Weapon	Size/Force	Reach	Damage	AP/HP
Shortsword	M	S	1d6+1d2	6/8
Dagger	S	S	1d4+1+1d2	6/8

THORSEN THUGS

The thugs are friends and family members of the tradesman, Marquet. They are unarmoured, equipped only with cudgels, and are no match for skilled combatants. Their numbers are their greatest advantage, and they do their best to surround and overwhelm individuals. They flee at the first instance of injury, or surrender if cornered. Use these statistics for Dalla's father and brothers

Attributes	1d20	Location	AP/HP
Damage Modifier: 0	1–3	Right Leg	0/5
Magic Points: 10	4–6	Left Leg	0/5
Movement: 6 metres	7–9	Abdomen	0/6
Initiative Bonus: 10	10-12	Chest	0/7
Armour: None	13–15	Right Arm	0/4
Abilities: None	16–18	Left Arm	0/4
Magic: None	19–20	Head	0/5

Skills: Athletics 40%, Brawn 43%, Endurance 38%, Evade 23%, Locale 66%, Perception 34%, Survival 20%, Unarmed 30%, Willpower 21%

Passions: Loyalty to Thorsen 75%
Combat Style: Village Thug (Cudgel) 35%

Weapon	Size/Force	Reach	Damage	AP/HP
Cudgel	M	L	1d6	4/4

WOLVES

The wolves of rural Vale are a mangy lot. They only fear men in groups, and aggressively drag down lone travellers.

Attributes	1d20	Location	AP/HP
Action Points: 2	1–3	Right Hind Leg	2/5
Damage Modifier: 0	4–6	Left Hind Leg	2/5
Magic Points: 11	7–9	Hindquarter	2/6
Movement: 10 metres	10-12	Forequarters	2/6
Initiative Bonus: 10	13–15	Right Front Leg	2/5
Armour: Fur and Hide	16–18	Left Front Leg	2/5
Abilities: Night sight	19–20	Head	2/5

Skills: Athletics 80%, Endurance 52%, Evade 55%, Perception 60%, Stealth 55%, Survival 40%, Tracking 70%, Willpower 43%
Combat Style: Wolf Pack Pounce 45%

Weapon	Size/Force	Reach	Damage	AP/HP
Bite	S	S	1d8	As for Head
Claw	S	S	1d3	As for Leg

MANUUN: CORRUPT SHAMAN

Manuun serves as one of Jedakiah's many agents, and has been thoroughly corrupted by the influence of the Chaos Mother. Manuun, like others, fell under the Chaos Mother's power many years ago and has been compelled to seek-out and free trapped spirits of Chaos, Disease and Curse ever since. He was probably destined to become one of the sorcerer's minions.

Manuun bears many scars and is covered in an assortment of tattoos. Most notably, he bears a tattoo that covers part of his forehead and scalp, which is an odd combination of the chaos and fertility runes. This tattoo appears fresh and leaks a pus-like solution that gives his face the appearance of being coated in a discoloured sweat.

The shaman is an intimidating figure, and his barbarian tribesmen do not question his commands. Manuun has proved to be ruthless, unforgiving, and prone to violent outbursts. He has promised a great deal to his men; he has told them of the great wealth, and power, they will possess when the towns of The Realm burn.

Manuun has been gifted a fetch; Uurungun, the Vermin Spider. The fetish holding Uurungun is a ring of black crystal Manuun wears on his left, little finger. Anyone who watches the ring sees its subtance writhe and pulse from time to time, as though alive.

The shaman is also capable of controlling the Chaos Hybrid using his Influence skill and employing the hissing, whistling language of the Ophidians. On a successful Influence roll the Hybrid obeys, and acts to, Manuun's simple commands. On a failed roll it ignores him; on a fumble it does the opposite.

Characteristics	Attributes	1d20	Location	AP/HP
STR: 12	Action Points 3	1–3	Right Leg	1/7
CON: 13	Damage Modifier 0	4–6	Left Leg	1/7
SIZ: 13	Magic Points 15	7–9	Abdomen	2/8
DEX: 11	Movement 6m	10–12	Chest	2/9
INT: 15	Initiative Bonus 10	13–15	Right Arm	1/6
POW: 15	Armour Leather	16–18	Left Arm	1/6
CHA: 10	Abilities None	19–20	Head	1/7

Skills: *Athletics 50%, Brawn 48%, Endurance 55%, Evade 50%, Influence 70%, Locale 66%, Lore (Chaos Mother) 102%, Perception 64%, Survival 67%, Willpower 62%*

Passions: *Loyalty to Jedakiah 80%, Love Chaos 90%*

Magic

Animism: Binding 68%, Trance 77%

Spirits
Uurungun - Allied Chaos Fetch
INT 15, POW 16, CHA 9
Spirit Bite 75%, Lore (Chaos Mother) 130%, Willpower 82%
Abilities: Manifestation, Possession

Uurungun is an allied fetch that once served the Chaos Mother. Its form is that of a huge, black and grey spider with the head of a rat. It can manifest physically and acts to defend Manuun if he is attacked. For this purpose it has 2 Action Points and 16 Hit Points. Its bite causes no physical damage - the victim feels an icy chill - but a bitten victim becomes possessed by Uurungun until such time that it wishes to release the victim. A possessed victim is forced to protect Manuun physically and lay down his life, if commanded. A possessed victim is effectively a Chaos Mother slave and gains Loyalty (Chaos Mother) 82% for the duration of the possession. Manuun can command that Uurungun maintain or release a possession as he feels fit.

Combat Style: *Gartharis Shaman (Axe, Dagger) 52%*

Weapon	Size/Force	Reach	Damage	AP/HP
Hand Axe	M	L	1d6+1	4/8
Dagger	S	S	1d4+1	6/8

COMMANDING THE DEAD

With so many dying an unexpected, violent death in Aylesford, it is inevitable that the sundered souls of the townsfolk become malignant spirits, still tied to the town. Aylesford is therefore a place where Haunts take root, and Manuun knows this. Entering the Spirit World around the town he can see, and commune with, those souls that have the potential to become Haunts and curse them into doing so (see MYTHRAS page 150).

Manuun can awaken 1d4 Haunts if he needs to. These Haunts have the following characteristics and abilities:

Intensity 2, INT 10, POW 8, CHA 10
Locale 80%, Influence 40%, Willpower 66%
Miasma, Glamour

The Haunts want the living to share in their pain and suffering and re-enact their terrible deaths. The Chaos Hybrid appears as a barely-visible, wraith-like form that tears at the Haunts body, which howls its grief and despair. The Miasma ability then takes effect upon all those who witness the Haunting

MANUUN'S BARBARIANS

Manuun's barbarian tribesmen are capable warriors and skilled horsemen. They are not foolish, however, and will flee any conflict where they are greatly outnumbered or suffer a number of losses. They will prefer to retreat and antagonise the characters at a later time than fight to the death, to the man.

Attributes	1d20	Location	AP/HP
Action Points: 2	1–3	Right Leg	2/6
Damage Modifier: +1d2	4–6	Left Leg	2/6
Magic Points: 11	7–9	Abdomen	2/7
Movement: 6 metres	10-12	Chest	2/8
Initiative Bonus: 10	13–15	Right Arm	2/5
Armour: Hard Leather	16–18	Left Arm	2/5
Abilities: None	19–20	Head	2/6

Skills: *Athletics 59%, Brawn 62%, Endurance 62%, Evade 56%, Locale 66%, Perception 64%, Ride 85%, Survival 67%, Unarmed 59%, Willpower 62%*

Passions: Loyalty to Manuun 80%, Love Battle 70%

Combat Style: *Gartharis Barbarian (Axe, Short Bow, Shield, Dagger) 58%*

Weapon	Size/Force	Reach	Damage	AP/HP
Battleaxe	M	M	1d6+1+1d2	4/8
Dagger	S	S	1d4+1+1d2	6/8
Target	L	S	1d3+1+1d2	4/9
Short Bow	L	-	1d6+1d2	4/4

CHAOS HYBRID

This horror is a hybrid of man and bear, covered in patches of fur and crowned with wicked, curling horns akin to those of a mountain goat.

It has been specially bred by the Ophidians who are in league with Jedakiah. It is an experiment in ferocity: the Ophidians have carefully manipulated its psyche and physiology to make it strong, fast, resilient and utterly merciless. However, it needs to be controlled and the Ophidians have been concerned that, consumed by blood-lust, such hybrids will be uncontrollable. So, the Aylesford experiment was devised. Manuun and a small force would take this hybrid into the field, command it to slaughter, and then attempt to regain control. The experiment has been horribly, horribly successful.

The hybrid has been conditioned for limited, single-purpose sapience. It can use cunning, plan strategies, employ tactics and is self-aware. In terms of intelligence it is akin to an alpha male wolf (indeed, parts of its brain were taken from Gartharis wolves). It can use weapons and is armed with a sling, a longspear, and its own formidable weapons. It enjoys raw flesh and, like a bear, will feast on its prey from time to time.

Its only weakness is its singularity. It can be overwhelmed by greater numbers. This matters little to Manuun and the Ophidians. If the hybrid is killed they will simply breed more: the intention is to determine the extent of control by someone like Manuun - and he *is* capable of controlling it.

Characteristics	Attributes	1d20	Location	AP/HP
STR: 18	Action Points 4	1–3	Right Leg	3/8
CON: 26	Damage Modifier +1d4	4–6	Left Leg	3/8
SIZ: 17	Magic Points 15	7–9	Abdomen	3/9
DEX: 27	Movement 10m	10-12	Chest	3/10
INS: 13	Initiative Bonus 20	13–15	Right Arm	3/7
POW: 15	Armour Tough Hide	16–18	Left Arm	3/7
CHA: 1		19–20	Head	4/8

Abilities

Blood Sense, Chaos Feature (Leaper), Formidable Natural Weapons

Skills: *Athletics 90%, Brawn 90%, Endurance 90%, Evade 80%, Perception 65%, Survival 80%, Unarmed 80%, Willpower 70%*

Passions: *Killing 110%*

Combat Style: *Chaos Bastard (Unarmed, Sling, Spear) 80%*

Weapon	Size/Force	Reach	Damage	AP/HP
Claws	M	T	1d4+1d4	As for Arm
Bite	M	T	1d6+1d4	As for Head
Horns	M	S	1d4+1d4	As for Head
Longspear	L	VL	1d10+1+1d4	4/10
Sling	L	-	1d8	1/2

The Hybrid's general tactic is to disable a foe from range using its Sling, with a Stun Location effect. It then closes-in to stab with its spear, and then use natural weapons to finish the opponent. If faced with a straightforward melee, it looks to Impale with its spear, leaving the weapon in the wound, and then to continue attacks with claws, teeth and horns. The claws can Sunder and the horns can Bash.

Scenario 2: Beneath the Black Water

Overview

The characters are asked to recover the abducted niece of a local ruler. Their journey takes them to a dismal swamp where they witness a ritual to an ancient evil, discover a lost city, and escape from the clutches of a debased race of frog men. At the end of the scenario they will prevent the destruction of a farming community, and uncover vital information concerning Jedakiah's plans.

Non-Player Characters

- Lord Drystan - a respected minor lord of The Realm, renowned for wisdom and impartiality.
- The Handmaiden - The maid of Lord Drystan's niece Bria - currently a prisoner of the Toad People.
- The Batrachians - primitive toadmen who worship an ancient demon in their home swamps.

Key Points/Timeline

The scenario is set to run in a more-or-less linear fashion. The general progression of the adventure is as follows…

1. Meet Lord Drystan, learn of the raid, prepare, and set out for the swamp. Once there, encounter the Batrachians and learn of the sacrifice.
2. Encounter the Batrachi Village and witness the ritual summoning of She Who Dwells Beneath the Black Waters. Enter the Forgotten Outpost.
3. Explore the Forgotten Outpost, find the Chieftain's House, free the prisoners, and destroy the Egg of Hylar.
4. Escape from the Forgotten Outpost, Evade/Fight and Pursuit
5. Endgame.

Running 'Beneath the Black Water'

This scenario can be used in a number of ways.

- As a self-contained rescue mission to find and release the captives from Lord Drystan's domain. If used in this way Games Masters can easily ignore all references to Jedakiah, The Hooded One, and place Bria, Drystan's niece, as one of the captives. The Batrachians are little more than upstart troublemakers who have unearthed the Egg of Hylar and want to extend their territory.
- As a further deepening of the extent of Jedakiah's plans, and a vital twist with Bria's capture and transportation to Distaff Peak
- As an introduction to Jedakiah's extensive influence in The Realm, if the previous scenario, Caravan, is not being used, or is being used at a later point in the campaign.
- As a way of gaining a powerful friend, patron and ally in the form of Lord Drystan.

Areas to be Covered

- Lord Drystan's Fief - A small, well-kept demesne where the adventure starts and information is gathered.
- The Frogfens - a large area of swampland close to Lord Drystan's fief, home to the primitive Batrachians.
- Batrachian Village - Home to the horrid Toad People and worship site of She Who Dwells Beneath the Black Water.
- Forgotten Outpost - A lost complex of the Ophidians, now home to the Batrachian Chief, and the Batrachian's new weapon against the dry-landers: the Children of She.

Background and Introduction

The characters can be drawn into the recent events occurring in Lord Drystan's fief in several different ways.

- They can discover, through use of appropriate skills (such as Streetwise and Locale), and any other creative means at their disposal, that the demesne of Lord Drystan borders a swamp reputed to be a stronghold of a primitive race of Toad People, and may shed some light on their recent mischief.
- Any large town or city is abuzz with stories of a recent, devastating attack by Chaos on the northern town of Aylesford (see the previous scenario, Caravan). As a ranking member of the Order of Truth, Lord Drystan is keen to talk with those who witnessed what happened in Aylesford. His own domain has also been the subject of disturbing events and Drystan suspects a link between the two.
- Lord Drystan is looking for people to investigate recent events in the swamps brodering his lands: he is offering a good reward for information.
- Any inquiry into recent events involving Chaos gets a strong referral to the recent unpleasantness at Lord Drystan's fief.

Lord Drystan's home is a semi-fortified villa a day's ride south of Senholm. The lands around here consist of many small farms and hamlets. On the southern edge of the lands, almost where the Long Riding starts, is the swamp region known as the Frogfens. Drystan's villa is a day north of these swamps.

Lord Drystan meets any adventurers that report to his small, solid stronghold with open arms. Lord Drystan is renowned for his intelligence and even-handedness: a popular lord to his people. He sees to the comfort of any group that appears sincere in their desire to help, offering them refreshment and a place to rest up from the road. Once the party's needs have been seen to, Lord Drystan explains the circumstances...

"My lands border the Frogfens. Many before me have held this swamp as being of little worth, but I have grown wealthy in the discovery and harvesting of the herbs and plants growing there, which, coupled with the richness of the soil for farming, has been a boon to Senholm.

"There is a drawback to the location of my lands, however. The Frogfens were not named for their abundance of hopping creatures, although they do teem with these beasts. No. They were named for their more sinister denizens. A race of creatures, remnants of the Chaos Mother's foul domination, calls these swamps their home. I have named them Batrachians, but the common folk have dubbed them the Toad Demons. These degenerate beasts are barely intelligent, have little or no knowledge of fire, and work only with stone tools and weapons. In the past, they have raided my lands, but these pitiful forays were unorganized, and easily repelled by my men-at-arms. For many, many years the Batrachians have remained in their swamp and bothered no one. That is, until recently.

"Several nights ago the Batrachians made the first raid in over two decades, displaying an unusually high organization and numbers. In the assault, several of my townsfolk were captured. Among these captives were my niece and her handmaid, who were attending a local celebration. Last seen, the captives were being dragged into that loathsome swamp by the Batrachians.

"I urgently need someone to enter the swamps and return to me my kinswoman and any other townsfolk that remain alive. My men at arms are good guards, but ultimately are superstitious locals who are not prepared for the action that might be needed. You will be well paid for this task, with an extra sum if you can discover the reason the last assault was so much more effective than the others, so that I can take the proper measures to defend my people."

Lord Drystan is more than willing to open his stores for any supplies the group needs, within reason of course.

The Real Story

There is indeed a new force behind the latest Batrachian raids on Lord Drystan's fief. Jedakiah has determined that Bria, Lord Drystan's niece, renowned for her beauty and purity, is the perfect vessel for his sacrifice in the creation of the Chaos Daughter. Like many others, the sorcerer knows of the old raids by the Batrachians, but, unlike most, he knows of the powerful demon the Batrachians worship as their god. Jedakiah sent an emissary to the leader of the strongest of the Batrachian tribes. The emissary, known as The Hooded One (see *Reckoning at Distaff Peak*, page 207) gifted the chieftain with a powerful magical runestone called the Egg of Hylar. This gives the Batrcahians mastery over She Who Lives Beneath the Black Water. Now in control of the monster, the Batrachian Chief (under Jedakiah's instruction) plans to unite the Batrachian tribes and invade Lord Drystan's fief and take many prisoners to sacrifice to their Goddess.

For his part of the bargain, the Batrachian chief agreed to raid Lord Drystan's fief and capture his niece unharmed. Once this was done, Jedakiah has arranged for Bria to be brought to his mountain stronghold in the north, while the chieftain uses the remaining prisoners for sacrifice. The Batrachian Chieftain has summoned together the other leaders of the Toadman tribes to witness the sacrifice of the human prisoners to their goddess. Jedakiah has convinced him that, once they have seen his control over the Goddess, they will fall in line with his invasion plans.

Into the Frogfens

Assuming the characters agree to help Lord Drystan, he promises them payment of 1,000 Founders if his niece is returned and 500 if they simply manage to determine what has happened to her. Half is paid in advance with the remainder upon completion of the task. The characters need to act quickly, travelling to the Frogfens and beginning their investigation.

The trip through the fief is relatively easy. Drystan maintains decent roads, even if they are merely well tended dirt paths. The fields that make up the majority of his realm are wide and well tended – at least until the characters reach the areas closest to the swamps. These lands show signs of having recently been assaulted. Large swaths of the fields show signs of having been trampled by many feet. Numerous daub and wattle huts that form the majority of buildings in this area have collapsed, as though herds of large cattle had been driven through them.

The people that live in Lord Drystan's domain are of peasant stock: tough, honest hard-working folk with a strong sense of duty and a healthy respect (and fear) of the supernatural. Due to their recent difficulties, they are naturally hesitant to speak with strangers, but if the characters can convince them of their sincere desire to help (a successful Influence roll), the inhabitants eagerly tell their tales of how, during their annual spring celebration, they were suddenly assaulted by the Toad Demons who live in the Frogfens.

Their stories are heartbreaking, frightening, and more than a little contradictory. Several items of information can be gleaned. Unfortunately, it is mixed with some misinformation that has to be sorted through and considered. Some of the rumours that emerge are as follows:

- "The Toad Men were led by a hooded man with terrible magic powers." This is true – The Hooded One is an Ophidian sorcerer who oversaw the assault lent his magic to the attack.
- Lord Drystan's niece, Bria, was last seen being dragged into the swamp by the hooded magician. This, too, is true
- "Those Toad Demons all have magical powers too! I saw them ensorcel strong men so that they staggered around helpless to even defend themselves!" This

is not true – what was seen were the effects of the Batrachians' venom.

- "Any women captured by the Toad People are used in unnatural breeding rites. The offspring of these unholy unions look human, but have the unclean soul of a Toad Demon!" Not true – such a union would be as distasteful to a Batrachian as to a human.
- "The half-human half-Toad Demon offspring are often used as spies. I bet one was here before the assault, telling them what to do and where to go." This is half-true – Jedakiah has human spies in Lord Drystan's fief gathering intelligence, but they are not Batrachian half-breeds.
- "The invaders had among them some kind of huge demon-monsters that smashed houses and swallowed people whole!" Again, another half-truth. This rumour refers to the Children of She, who accompanied the raiders as a test of their battle-usefulness.

The Frogfens begin at the south western edge of the fief, a day's ride from Drystan's villa. The well-kept fields end abruptly at line of twisted willow and alder trees, tall, limp grasses, and slippery black mud that oozes out between pools of oily black water. Even at this distance, a stray breeze brings with it the odour of rot and sickness. The passage of the Batrachians is obvious even to the untrained eye. The passage of numerous feet, bent rushes, and broken branches leave an obvious starting point for the characters' pursuit.

Entering the fens increases the unpleasantness. Saw grass slaps at exposed body parts, leaving behind red welts and sores. The weather, formerly that of a cool day, becomes warm and humid the further the characters venture into the swamp. The stinking black mud sucks greedily at their boots, tugging, as though trying to stop their advance. Shortly after their entrance into the swamp, the trail becomes less obvious, necessitating a successful Track roll.

For every day spent in the Frogfens, at least one party member must make a successful Survival Roll for the party to get any rest at all, find suitable water, and so forth (See the "Team Roll" section on page 52 of MYTHRAS). Failure results in all party members incurring a level of Fatigue for the next day.

ENCOUNTERS IN THE FROGFENS

The following are possible encounters whilst traipsing through the fens. Games Masters should choose an appropriate situation according to the characters' progress.

GIANT SPIDER

A huge trapdoor spider has made its lair beneath an inviting hummock of raised, dry, ground. It lurks beneath the surface, waiting for an opportunity to lunge upwards, seize the nearest warm, soft, blood-filled object, and drag it back into its cramped burrow for a leisurely meal. The burrow is very constricting (not for the spider) which makes the skill rolls for any character grabbed Herculean, and the skill rolls for any attempting a rescue from outside Formidable. The spider can retreat to a distance only reachable from the surface by weapons of Very Long reach, making rescue very tough indeed. Characters are allowed a Hard Perception roll to spot the lair and avoid it. Otherwise the spider strikes from ambush, surprising the characters (see Surprise on page 105 of MYTHRAS).

QUICKSANDS

A patch of firm-looking ground turns out to be quick sand 1d6+1 metres deep. It requires a successful Willpower roll to avoid panicking and being sucked deeper into the quicksand pool. If the Willpower roll is successful, then the character can make an Athletics roll to relax and allow their body to float in the quicksand and resist being sucked down further. If three such Athletics tests are passed in a row, then the character breaks free and climbs out.

If the Willpower test fails, the next roll is at a Hard difficulty grade as the power of the quicksand takes hold and sucks the character down. For each failed roll the quicksand sucks-down one third of the victim's body mass. Thus, if three Willpower rolls are failed, the character is sucked beneath the surface and starts to take Suffocation damage as outlined on page 71 of the MYTHRAS rules.

Companions can assist with Brawn skills which augment the stricken character's Athletics roll - but only once the victim has stopped struggling, which increases the suction and chances of sinking deeper.

INSECT SWARM

The characters disturb an insect nest if an Evade roll is failed as they pass by an overhanging tree or covering of bushes. The swarm (see MYTHRAS, page 251) has a SIZ of 12, possessing 3 Action Points and sting damage of 1d3. The stings cause painful blisters, red and angry, that develop into debilitating sores if not treated by First Aid within a number of hours equal to half the victim's CON. These sores inflict a level of Fatigue until healing (with a Heal skill) can be obtained.

Batrachian Patrol

A Batrachian patrol, scouting for food, herbs or other swamp commodities, is active nearby. There is one Batrachian for every character, plus a leader. These Toad Men hail from the Black Water settlement. If captured and interrogated then a Batrachian can act as a guide. Bear in mind they do not speak the human tongue. Unless they have suitable magic the characters are limited to the use of hand gestures and body language, requiring a successful Insight roll to understand what is being communicated. Captured characters are taken to the village to become a sacrifice: see *The Ritual* later in this scenario.

Marsh Viper

This rotten serpent thrives in the clammy fens, feeding on rodents and other small prey. They are expert swimmers and like to lie just below the surface of the water, waiting for something opportune to swim or wade by. Exposed ankles, calves and knees make for a good striking point for the viper's keen fangs.

The Village

Located deep in the Frogfens, the village where the Batrachians raiders live - and where the human prisoners have been taken - can, eventually, be found. The trails leading to it are obscure and difficult to follow but, after searching, a trail does become clear. Indeed, the characters may even observe, from a distance, other Batrachians heading in small groups, towards a common point.

Following the trail through the chill black mud and stagnant pools requires a Formidable Track roll. The swamp becomes waist-deep reducing movement by half. The misty swamp gas occasionally grows thicker, obscuring the ground ahead. After several hours of strenuous progress the characters see the dense foliage of the intermittent trees, vines, and endless tall grasses recede. Finally, upon parting a particularly thick patch of grasses and cattails the party can see its goal.

In a clearing is a large pool of still, black water, a dark glass of motionless void. On the west side of this disquieting pool, atop a small hill that rises slightly above the water's surface, are numerous shelters, rounded constructs of grass and leaves woven together with strong swamp vines. These brown domes are dispersed irregularly. The combination of the domes and the deeper ochre of the ground suggests the warty skin of the Batrachian inhabitants.

The village is home to about 150 Batrachians. Their homes are the huts scattered to the south of the Forgotten Outpost. Each hut houses between one and three Batrachians. Inside each hut is a waist-deep depression filled with water brought from the black pool. Here the Batrachians wallow and sleep, keeping their skins moist. The venture out when summoned by the chief or attending to the routine chores of catching food, patrolling the area, or attending the sacrifices of The Ritual.

Despite the sight of this atavistic village and its grotesque denizens, two other things attract the characters' attention. On the banks of the misty bog rises a series of ruins, its walls choked with thick vines and moldy growths. One end has partially sunk into the swamp, giving the ruins an odd tilt. Just beyond the Batrachi huts, a pair of tilted gates provide the only break in the lichen-covered walls.

The other interesting sight are three large stakes protruding a metre and a half from the dark waters of the motionless pool. Bound upright by thick vines, visible from the waist up, are three figures, one to each stake. Three burly men, (peasant laborers, judging by their tattered clothing), slump motionless. All display signs of abuse: scratches, bruises, and insect bites covering their skin.

Should the characters decide to explore the ruins, rather than waiting to see what happens, they could miss valuable clues regarding the events unfolding at the pool's edge. They have approximately 30 minutes of watching before the Batrachian Chief and his entourage approach the stakes for the ritual. The loud drums, rhythmic chanting, and screams of the terrified victims can be accentuated to add to the characters' apprehension.

The Ritual

Fifty or so Batrachians emerge from their wart-like huts, and gather in a silent group at the edge of the black pool. Their huge, unblinking eyes are fixed on the still waters and the men bound to the stakes. From the far side of the village, in the direction of the stone structure, approaches an assembly of more Batrachians - important members of the community, judging by their garb. Leading this company is a short, bent Batrachian, stooped and wrinkled. Perched atop its broad head is a strange head-dress of vines dangling about its bulbous eyes. A crude sack of scaled hide is clutched in its webbed claws.

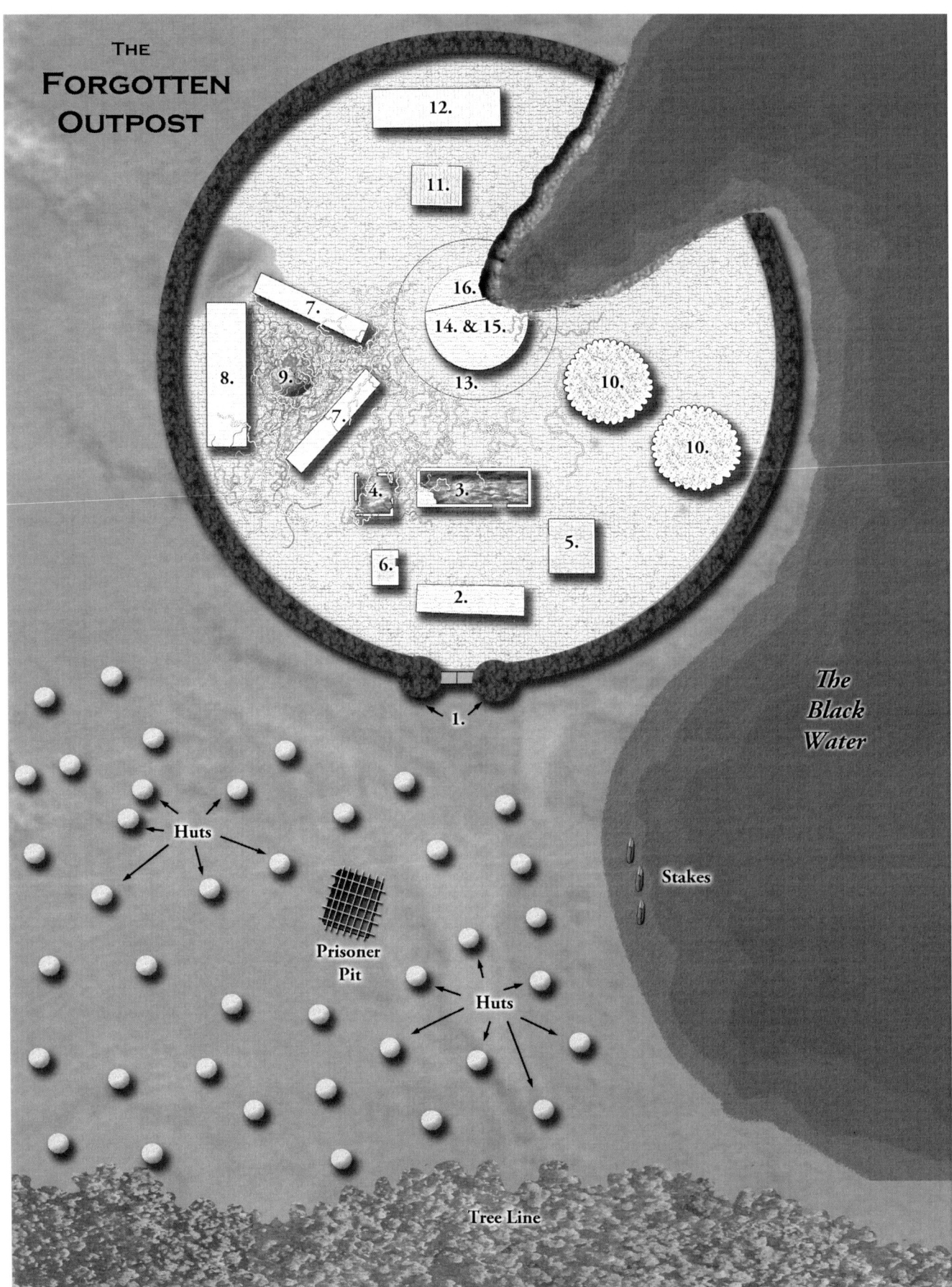

As the leaders reach the edge of the pool and stop, the elder Batrachian continues. It waddles into the pool and takes a position at a point between and behind the staked captives. The Batrachian reaches into its pouch and draws out a strange, irregularly shaped, white stone. Raising both its wattled arms, it holds the stone aloft and begins a deep, rhythmic croak. Others slowly and steadily join in, creating a drum-like reverberation that echoes in the suddenly silent twilight. Awakened by the noise, the three captives stare about them in fear, and struggle uselessly against their bonds.

A bulge appears in the pool, ten metres from the staked victims. A vast bulk rises from the water, towering six or more metres into the night sky. Its horrific, squat head is roughly toad-shaped, but disfigured and distended in a vile parody of the Batrachians. Three huge eyes blink from writhing eye-stalks, focusing on the terrified prisoners.

The creature surges forward, stopping short of the captives, (who scream in terror and increase their struggles against their bonds). Suddenly, the gaping maw opens and a long, flat tongue shoots out, striking one of the captives: he is torn from the vines with a rending of flesh and snapping of bones and dragged, shrieking, into the drooling maw of the nightmare, gulped down in two, hideous swallows. Seemingly satiated, the monster submerges, leaving no trace of its coming but for the splintered, empty post.

As soon as the water resumes its placidity, the aged Batrachian wades ashore, replacing the peculiar stone reverently in its pouch. Another Batrachian steps forward and raises a crude spear clutched in a muscular taloned arm, to the frantic croaking of the assembled Batrachians. Others come into the pool and untie the terrified prisoners from the stakes, marching them deep into the village. With a successful Perception Roll the characters can determine the general direction taken. If the roll is a critical success, the character see them prisoners suddenly disappear, as though swallowed up by the earth.

The Forgotten Outpost

This outpost was one of several raised by the Ophidians, the race of Serpent People that live in the Gartharis Mountains. This mysterious race abandoned these swamps for the Gartharis Mountains a long time ago. Still, some of their long-forgotten outposts remain intact enough for others to make use of them.

The Prisoners

The pit holds six captives: five males and one female. The woman is Neura, handmaiden to Lord Drystan's neice, Bria. She is 19 years of age, terrified, and deeply traumatised by the sacrifices she has witnessed (and survived). It requires a great deal of time - at least one full day - and care to coax the truth from her. Treat this as a Social Conflict Task (see page 287 of MYTHRAS) using Influence as the active skill. The men, too, are traumatised and can offer little help.

When they were captured by the Batrachians, Neura, Bria and the men were dragged back to the chieftain's hut and paraded before him and another, tall, thin, hooded man. Neura never saw his face. The hooded figure singled-out Bria even though Neura pleaded to be taken in her place. Neura was silenced with a stinging slap. Bria was gagged and bound: the others were hauled to the pit. Neura has not seen Bria since.

Before being dragged away the Hooded One spoke something to the Batrachian Chief and Neura heard a few words of the human, common tongue, that she remembers: 'Staff', 'Peak' and 'Akiah' (or something similar). She has no idea of the meaning.

These words are clues to Bria's whereabouts: Distaff Peak and Jedakiah's stronghold at Dark Child's Tower. The Hooded One has magically transported Bria there for the Dread Rite described in Reckoning at Distaff Peak, where she is destined to become the Chaos Daughter...

Captured and Frog Marched

The Batrachians always seek live captives - more sacrifices for She Who Dwells Beneath the Black Water. If captured, the party is disarmed and tossed into the pit along with the other captives. Guards are quadrupled and they remain attentive to escape attempts. The following evening find one of the characters bound to stakes along with a farmer and the female, in reenactment of the ritual. Only this time, She Who Dwells Beneath the Dark Waters takes the woman. It is suggested that Games Masters play up the suspense of the ritual…perhaps simulating dice rolls as though her selection is random. At the ritual's end, the character is tossed back into the pit for further sacrifice. Once per day, buckets of the disgusting food the Batrachians eat are tossed carelessly into the pit, along with buckets of fetid swamp water.

Eventually, the Batrachian Army leaves the village on their way to conduct their war on Lord Drystan's lands. At this time the village is practically unguarded – only a handful Batrachian warriors remain behind.

The latticework covering the pit is strong, requiring a Formidable Brawn roll to break it. There is always at least a single Batrachian warrior guarding the pit.

The open area beyond the gates is a vast compound of crumbling ruins and empty building shells gathered around an open courtyard, now overgrown with swamp grass, snaky vines, and bent, twisted trees. The circular wall surrounding the outpost, although ancient, is thick and surprisingly sound, except where it collapsed many years ago.

1. Gatehouses

The walls from which the massive gates once hung are tall and made of a mottled, red stone. (A successful Locale roll notes that the stone is not native to this region). On either side of the ruins of the gates is a tall, two-story cylindrical tower. Entrance is via a lone large door set on the far side. Inside, the bottom floor of each tower is full of debris - leaves, rotting wood, and fallen stone and mortar. The second floor, reached by a decaying wooden ramp, is much the same. If anyone with a SIZ greater than 10 attempts to climb the ramp, it collapses, dumping the victim three metres onto the cold stone floor below. The top of the tower is flat and weatherworn, but it does give a view of the outpost's remains and a commanding view over the nearby fens.

2. Bunkhouse

A large, flat low building, the top is still almost completely intact. It is reached by a low ramp that twists to one edge. The roof holds many flat stone shelves; sunning ledges where the cold-blooded Ophidians enjoyed basking in the sun's rays. The ground floor is an open room full of blocks of perfectly cut stone surrounding several large stone fire pits. More disturbingly, however, are the numerous bones scattered across the room's interior. Most are smallish animal bones; some though, are much larger. A successful Standard Healing or a Hard First Aid roll reveals them to be Batrachian.

3. Mess Hall

Opposite the bunkhouse, this building is of similarly cut stone. Inside it is full of rubble, all that remains of the roof, and numerous stone tables with downward-curved tops.

4. Kitchen

This building is slightly smaller than the other two. Amongst the vines curling around the half-fallen walls, and vegetation that litters the inside area, are the remains of waist-high stone tables, and what appear to be either cupboards or animal hutches along the outside walls. The cupboards are extremely long and low – about one metre wide by two metres long, but only a few centimetres thick… surely not tall enough to store any type of food container. They are all empty.

5. Officer's Quarters

This smaller building is in a sorry condition. Inside are several stone tables of waist height, covered with rotten vegetation and rain-soaked leaves.

If the debris from the largest table in the room's center is moved, it disturbs a nest of marsh vipers, one per character. The ill-tempered reptiles attack as they try to slither from the room. If their target merely Evades or leaves them alone, the serpents slither away without further attempts to harm. When the debris is removed, the top of it can be seen to be a topographical map of The Realm. On a successful Lore (Geography) or a Hard Locale roll, it can be noted that the map appears to predate the known history of The Realm. Cities such as Cylder and Nyren do not exist, indicating that the map is many, many centuries old. Indeed, the Ophidians were here long before humans arrived to settle the region, and they remained secretive even when the Founding Four came to defeat the Chaos Mother.

6. Armoury

This building is considerably smaller, but in better repair than the others. The solid bronze door's lock is rusted and fused, making any unlocking attempts one grade harder. Inside are several racks of decayed wood that obviously once held weapons. Some still hold huge two-handed swords, elaborately designed battle-axes, and halberds on rotting handles. The weapons all have an odd, alien twist to them – bizarre curves on the blades, disturbing hooks, serrated edges, or inexplicable holes that should make the metal weaker but are obviously part of the design. Though rusted, they are still usable but at a one grade penalty due to their alien design. On a successful hit that scores maximum damage, the weapon breaks.

7. Dormitories

To the left of the military compound, three buildings form a rough triangle around an overgrown stone enclave, open to the sky but shadowed by a thick canopy of vines. Two of these buildings are long and low, and are surrounded by stone benches, some eight feet long. Inside, each building is divided into three parts. The largest is the central area, defined by woven (but now decayed) sleeping mats, once decorated with bright colors and of fine workmanship. The right-hand side is full of marble tables, about one and a half metres tall, discoloured with age. The left side of the building is a large pool of murky, stagnant water. Beside this pool is an odd mechanical apparatus of metal rods and pipes feeding into the water. A successful Engineering Roll helps determine it to be a heating apparatus of some sort.

8. Stables

The third part of this triangle is the largest building in the quadrant. Its interior is divided into several stalls. Lying about the vegetation-littered floor are chunks of metal and scraps of a leather-like material for a very large creature. If these scraps are studied, a successful Locale or Ride roll identifies them as saddles for a huge lizard-like beast. Overhead is a loft-like structure, reached by a long ramp running the length of the building. It is empty of any goods, but is now home to a pair of *Meatsheets*. These creatures attempt to leap upon anyone who separates from the group. Meatsheet are described in more detail in the Pens section.

9. Hatchery

The area between the buildings is overgrown and difficult to traverse (requiring a successful Combat Style or Brawn roll to hack/push through the undergrowth). If a path is cleared to the centre of this vine festooned thicket, a strange sight is encountered. The vines have grown around the remains of a dome made of a glass-like substance, now almost opaque with grime. The top has been shattered, exposing the inside to the harsh swamp elements. Inside are large, leathery eggs. Approximately the size of a cabbage, the ivory orbs are inert and lifeless. These are ancient Ophidian eggs. Although lifeless, an Ophidian laboratory, such as the one found in Yagelan's Bluff (see *Raid on Yagelan's Bluff*, starting on page 160) has the ability to reactivate them, creating newly born Ophidians. Otherwise the eggs have no other value or interesting properties.

10. Pens

To the right of the gate are two pens, partially covered with a fallen roof and close-set, three-metre high rails. Each has, at its centre, a large pool of stagnant water. On the edge of the water is a stone trough. Should either of these pens be entered, on a successful Perception Roll, a soft, slithering sound can be heard from the roof above. If not, the attack is a total surprise...

Dropping from the partial roof are flapping sheets of skin. Amoeboid in shape, they are the size of a blanket; a sickly pink and hairless. They resembles nothing more than a sheet of human flesh, some five centimetres thick. At first appearance, their surface is perfectly smooth, but a closer glance reveals many small, sucker-shaped mouths lining the bottom. The tops of the creatures display remnants of their human origins – a wide, staring eye, the tip of a finger, a vestigial ear, or other human-like body part.

The *Meatsheets*, as the Batrachians name them, are the result of genetic and magical manipulation by the Ophidians centuries ago. The vile Reptile Folk bred them as a source of food, optimised for maximum nutrition, easily stored, flexible and malleable. In the intervening years these unnatural creatures escaped their bondage and learned to thrive in the food-rich environment of the swamps. Their metabolisms are designed for unnaturally long-life: they do not require water and can sustain themselves from airborne bacteria, small insects and, to a point, photosynthesis.

But, living food sources are attractive to them - especially warm blooded ones. They avoid the Batrachians whenever another food source presents itself: the warty skin is unappealing. The meatsheets look forward to a fresh, unexpected meal.

11. Infirmary

The infirmary door is intact, closing it off from the damaging elements. Inside, it is one large room. The centre holds a three-metre long marble table, equipped with a series of levers and gears that, until they rusted solid, allowed the table to tilt up, down and to either side. Metal cabinets nearby contain rusty surgical instruments designed for non-human hands.

12. Food Breeding Pens

The last building on the west side is also closed to the elements. Once past the unlocked doors, vast shelves of glass-like material line both sides. The far side of the room, opposite the door, has wooden cupboards that are falling apart. These contain long, pitchfork-like tools and large tongs. There is also a large sealed vat containing a putrescent, protein-based sludge. This sludge was sealed ages ago by the Ophidians and preserved by magical arts. The Serpent People genetically tailored the meatsheets to be attracted to this food, more so than any other, as a means of controlling the strange creatures. If this is opened, it sounds the dinner bell for a pack of meatsheets hiding atop the tallest shelves and in the dark corners of the building. There are six in total and are attracted to the slurry, attacking anyone getting in their way.

13. Courtyard

This large tract was once a well-tended garden of exotic, alien plants. Now it is an overgrown jungle of grasses, weeds, and long trailing vines. In the centre of this feral garden fetid water still trickles from a vaguely humanoid shaped fountain. The bowl and figurine of the fountain are encrusted with layer upon layer of rock-hard minerals. Time has worn away the features of the model, but a disturbingly reptilian caste to the features reveals it to be of obviously non-human origins. Elaborately carved stone benches, now covered in purple clumps of phosphorescent fungi, surround the fountain in an artful array. This fungus, if consumed, acts as a powerful hallucinogen if character fails an Endurance roll. The victim falls to the ground as visions of She Who Dwells Beneath the Black Water invade his mind – along with further visions of smaller, shadowy figures lurking behind her as though waiting for her command. The hallucination lasts for 1d6 minutes, after which the victim regains consciousness. The victim suffers no ill effects, although they will believe they have lost several hours of time, such is the vivid nature of the hallucination.

Chieftain's House (14 & 15)

Bottom Floor

The house of the Batrachian Chieftain has been established in one of the larger stone buildings. It is set in the exact center of the outpost and has a strong tilt to the back of the outpost wall. The rear of this round building, a portion of the outpost, and part of the wall beyond has fallen apart, and now lies under the foul black water of the swamp. A large, leafy bough covers the only entrance. The lower floor is now a single chamber: the ground here is a slippery, foul-smelling mud inclining towards the brackish water of the swamp. In the centre of the floor a crudely built ladder juts from a pool of vile-smelling water leading to an opening in the floor above. Should the water be disturbed in any way, it suddenly erupts, spraying in all directions, as several horrific monsters heave from its depths. These are several Children of She, miniature versions of the nightmare that is She Who Dwells Beneath the Black Water and there are six in total. They share her nightmarish, toad-like features and the same trio of black eyes staring from their warty skin. They waddle forward on muscular, oddly-shaped legs that end in long curved talons, dragging vestigial tails behind them.

These Children of She are the true source of the Batrachians' power. She Who Lives Beneath the Black Water has pledged the aid of her offspring in the destruction of the land walkers. With these monsters as shock troops, the strength of the unified Batrachian army is increased. Once the dry lands are conquered, surely other suitable habitats for her children can be found, spreading both her cult and the growth of her family. The Batrachian Chieftain has commanded these monsters to act as his guards against interlopers, but the depths of the Black Water hold countless more. Once the assault on dry land begins, the power of the Egg of Hylar will be used to command the rest to join in the attack on Lord Drystan's fief.

Top Floor

This floor is reached by climbing the stout ladder protruding through the trap door from below. Hanging in odd intervals from the thatch roof are crude wooden cages containing an odd assortment of phosphorescent bugs, creating just enough light for the party to see the details of the interior. A large bed of swamp grass covered in filthy blankets (the treasures of earlier raids) lies on a slightly raised dais at the far end. At the foot of the dais squats the wrinkled form of the Batrachian Chief, the pouch containing the Egg of Hylar in its lap. Although its eyes stare straight ahead in an eerie, unblinking fashion, it should become apparent (on a successful Insight roll), that it is in a trance, its mind far away – perhaps even communing with its goddess. The Chief is deep under the influence of the purple fungus growing in the courtyard. Any sort of disturbance, such as the noise of combat, allows it a Willpower roll to snap back to reality. At any time there are six Batrachian warriors guarding the precious Egg of Hylar and its owner. Should the Chief be slain, or the Egg of Hylar liberated from its grasp, control over She Who Lives Beneath the Black Water is broken: the she-demon resents being controlled by mere mortals and intends to have her revenge for their audacity.

If freed She erupts from the confines of the lagoon - released from bondage and insane with vengeance. She heaves her bulk into the village and begins to lay waste to it. Her Children join the carnage, slightering from the depths to murder and feast. The chaos caused is the perfect distraction for the characters to gain a head start against any pursuit or get to the pit where the prisoners may still be held.

16: Treasure Room

Beyond the dais is a partially closed door. A faint gleam is visible in the room beyond. The room holds many items looted from the raids on Lord Drystan's fief. Among the loot are coins, jewellery, tools, and other valuables worth a total of around 2000 Founders. The crafty chieftain recognizes the value of money to the land dwellers, and plans to use it for bribes and mercenaries.

Also among the valuables stashed here is one other, less inviting treasure. Propped against a wall is a human leg bone, its end capped with a cup of some scaled, leathery hide. This gruesome item is hollow, and contains a sheet of human flesh that has been dried and cured like leather. Upon its surface is an array of pictographs, drawn in too fine a detail for the clumsy talons of the Batrachians. The drawing depicts a horde of Batrachians, humans, and some strange snake-like creatures under the leadership of a tall, menacing man. At the rear of this strange army hops a horde of the Children of She, wreaking havoc among lands filled with terrified humans. And, looming over this army is a gigantic, shadowy, spider-like figure emanating a menace and fear palpable even from this rendering. Above this ominous gathering is a night sky, full of stars, planets, and other heavenly bodies. This picture, drawn by The Hooded One, depicts the rise of Jedakiah and the Chaos Mother in ways the Batrachians can understand. It inflates the Batrachians' importance in Jedakiah's schemes, but that is of little consequence.

This hideous scroll is yet another indication that Chaos is returning to The Realm. Lord Drystan understands its meaning - the spider-creature is a popular representation of the Chaos Mother in her World-Spider aspect. That one of her servants is seeking to command an army in the south (and, if Drystan has heard about the events in Aylesford, more monsters from the north) is hugely concerning and causes Lord Drystan to travel to Cylder to consult with the Order of Truth and petition the King for action. The King's condition - and true nature - is explored in the next scenario, Shadows Behind the Throne.

Rescue

The prisoners have been tossed into a pit (see the diagram on page 44). It is covered by a latticework of stout tree branches bound together by swamp vines. The pit itself is in the approximate centre of the Batrachian village, surrounded by their domelike huts.

Following the ritual the village descends into an orgy of religiously-inspired festivity. The Toad Men dance to the frantic tattoo of tribal drums and guzzle a black liquid from plentiful gourds. Soon, many of the Batrachians begin to drag themselves into their crude dwellings, exhausted from their overindulgence.

Stealth attempts are one grade easier at this time. Should anyone peek into a hut, they see that it contains a bed of slimy swamp grass, a couple of flint spears, and several woven vine baskets containing worms, grubs, fish parts, and other Batrachian edibles.

A lone Batrachian Warrior guards the pit. It is wide awake and diligent in its duty. Should it be alerted in any way, it sets-up a loud croaking of alarm, drawing four more warriors from nearby dwellings who arrive within two rounds. For every two rounds the party is in proximity to the pit, three more Batrachian Warriors arrive from the surrounding hovels and attack fearlessly. There are three dozen warriors currently in the village and they use poisoned blowgun darts to incapacitate intruders. If the characters are captured or surrender, they are disarmed and thrown into the pit to await their turn to be sacrificed (see the "Captured!" section below). Of course, if the party manages to free the prisoners without raising an alarm, they can slip away without further hindrance.

In the event that the party actually manages to overcome half of the Batrachian Warriors, the rest retreat, unsure how to handle such potent foes. If the party successfully evades capture and escapes the Batrachian Village and its environs, they can soon hear the sounds of pursuit by a number of warriors. Then, from the muck to either side of the party's exit trail rise four of the Toad Folk, flint-tipped spears clutched in taloned hands. Their task is to slow the group down, so they rely heavily on their blowguns.

This brief skirmish allows the Batrachians time to close the gap. Soon their short, burly forms can be discerned behind the party, either swimming gracefully or hopping awkwardly in their haste. The air is resounding with their excited croaking war cries. On a successful Lore (Military Tactics) or a Hard Insight roll, an adventurer can see that they are forming a rough 'V' shape, as though herding the party in a certain direction. Unfortunately, should anyone veer off, they are confronted by four to eight more warriors, thirsty for blood, while the ones who follow draw even closer.

A fleeing party can, on a successful Perception roll, spot signs of pursuit – a blocky figure gripping the heavy branches of a drooping swamp tree, its warty grey throat sack expanding and producing a shrill call close to a human scream. On another occasion a successful Perception roll reveals the bumps of two eyes, breaking the scum of a nearby pool, observing the party in unblinking silence.

Eventually, the party hears the sounds of something larger than the Batrachians behind them. The Batrachian Chieftain has loosed the Children of She on the trail of the characters as a desperate move to keep them from reaching safety and reporting what they have seen. The Children (one per character), fight to the death to destroy the party. If the party has already dealt with the Children or the Chieftain in the Forgotten Outpost, this attack obviously does not take place.

Escape & Pursuit

If the party manages to leave the village without pursuit (and hopefully with the prisoners from the pit), they still have the task of escaping the swamp. A Navigate or Hard Locale roll is necessary to determine the right direction to take to begin the trek to Lord Drystan's fief. At best, the trip back to safety takes an entire day and night, so any further time needed should necessitate another Survival roll as outlined in the Frogfens section earlier. The prisoners, if rescued, slow-down progress and the characters need to encourage them to keep moving.

Unless all the Batrachian Warriors were killed in the village, the characters should take steps to evade pursuit. Several skills should prove useful to avoid further contact. A successful Conceal roll may cancel out any attempts by the Batrachians to track them. The Mechanisms skill could come in handy to set traps against any pursuers, if the characters feel they have time to set them. A successful Track roll reveals any pursuers that manage to set up an ambush. Lore (Tactics) could be used to flank any ambush, or avoid areas that the Batrachians favour for combat.

Should the party emerge without much injury or loss of resources (or if the Games Master desires more excitement), one, final encounter below can be added.

The swamp ends in a large reed bed. On the far side, the trees break, revealing dry, open land beyond. If the cold water is entered, its icy grip soon closes about the characters' waists, while the chill mud below tugs at their waterlogged boots, cutting their movement rate in half.

At this point, up to eight pursuing Batrachians break from the trees behind. Shrilling in excitement, half leap into the water, while others continue their odd hopping gait along the sides. Warriors that suddenly appear from ambush on the pool's far side beset anyone attempting to skirt the pool. If the Chieftain has survived, he may be with this pursuing force, intent on revenge. Children of She also accompany him.

This part of the scenario is intended to be a grand melee, a suitable end fight for the heroic adventurers. Should anyone make it to the tree line they find themselves in the open fields that set the boundary between the Frogfens and Lord Drystan's domain. No Batrachian patrol will break this boundary, and should the party make it through the trees, the attack ends as the sullen Toad Men slip silently back into their homeland. If at any point the party is in danger of being overwhelmed, a generous Game Master can have Lord Drystan arrive with a party of men-at-arms to drive the Toad Men back into their swamp.

Conclusion

If the party has captured the Egg of Hylar, the Batrachian Chieftain is no longer able to control She Who Dwells Beneath the Black Water. He loses the respect and alliance of the other Batrachian tribes, and Jedakiah has lost a powerful force in his bid for domination of The Realm.

If the party returns to Lord Drystan, he is grateful for the handmaid's return and the prevention of the invasion, but is understandably upset at the loss of his niece. He wastes little time in convening the Order of Truth to gather information on where Bria has been taken and will, eventually, identify Distaff Peak as the likely location. The characters will be given the opportunity to rescue Bria, journeying north to infiltrate Jedakiah's sanctuary and prevent the Dread Rite of the Chaos Daughter.

Lord Drystan can also act as a friendly and grateful patron in several of the adventures in Book of Quests, providing information, help and well-placed influence if the characters require it. He may also offer membership of the Order of Truth to the characters (see page 17), involving them further in The Realm's security.

The Egg of Hylar

The Egg of Hylar is an ancient orb, some twenty-five centimetres across. It is an uneven sphere shot through with odd, swirling designs of a disturbing nature. A Successful Lore (Magic), Lore (Chaos) or Hard Insight roll reveals the curious markings on the stone to be Chaos Runes. Discovered by Jedakiah in the travels of his earlier years, this orb is a powerful magic item that allows its bearer to communicate with and control certain kinds of demons. The bearer of the egg can, by concentrating, create a Telepathic bond with a target, as per the Sorcery spell. It also carries the Enchantment Enslave (Amphibian). The egg casts the spell at an Intensity of 100%, with a Magnitude of 12.

Non-Player Characters

BATRACHIANS

Anthropomorphic toads, the Batrachians detest dry land, prefering murky, secluded swamps. They loathe humans - dry-landers - who reclaim marshlands and use them to supplement their own resources, but otherwise keep to themselves.

The Batrachian tongue is incomprehensible to humans and they lack the vocal facilities for human speech. They communicate in croaks, creaks, groans and whistles, their throat pouches distending. They move with an odd, wobbling gait: their upper bodies are stocky and wide, whilst the lower body is relatively thin, save for the powerful lower limbs.

Their cultures are distinctly primitive: hunter-gatherers, they rely on stone and wooden tools and weapons, and lack the ability to develop metals. Batrachian diet is a combination of small animals, insects, fish and birds. Like their smaller cousins, females create spawn, filled with dozens of eggs. Males act as spawn carriers and protectors during the spring breeding season, carrying the spawn on their backs.

Batrachian venom is secreted from glands located along their warty backs. Batrachian warriors rub the tips of their spear or blowgun darts in the venom for added injury. The venom has a Potency equal to the Batrachian's Endurance. Once the victim is poisoned, he must win an Opposed Roll of his Endurance versus the Potency of the venom or suffers dizziness and heart palpitations beginning 1d3+1 Combat Rounds after introduction to the system. These conditions result in a penalty of one Difficulty Grade to any attempted Skill, due to lack of concentration and co-ordination. This condition lasts for 1d2+4 hours. It does not stack. The poison can be either injected or ingested.

Batrachians use the average statistics provided opposite. The Batrachian Chief has slightly different statistics.

Characteristics	Attributes		1d20	Location	AP/HP
STR: 2d6+4 (11)	Action Points	2	1–3	Right Leg	2/5
CON: 3d6+3 (14)	Damage Modifier	0	4–6	Left Leg	2/5
SIZ: 1d6+6 (10)	Magic Points	11	7–9	Abdomen	2/6
DEX: 3d6 (11)	Movement	6m	10-12	Chest	2/7
INT: 1d6+7 (10)	Initiative Bonus	11	13–15	Right Arm	2/4
POW: 3d6 (11)	Armour	Warty Skin	16–18	Left Arm	2/4
CHA: 2d6 (7)	Abilities	Cold Blooded, Hold Breath, Venomous	19–20	Head	2/5
	Magic	None			

Skills: *Athletics 59%, Brawn 52%, Endurance 48%, Evade 58%, Swim 74%, Perception 61%, Survival 67%, Unarmed 55%, Willpower 42%*

Passions: *Loyalty to Swamp 80%, Hate Dry-Landers 80%*

Combat Style: *Swamp Warrior (Spear, Club, Blowgun) 60%*

Weapon	Size/Force	Reach	Damage	AP/HP
Club	M	L	1d8+1	4/5
Longspear	L	VL	1d10+1	4/10
Blowgun	-	-	Poison	1/4

Chief	Attributes		1d20	Location	AP/HP
STR: 13	Action Points	2	1–3	Right Leg	2/6
CON: 15	Damage Modifier	0	4–6	Left Leg	2/6
SIZ: 12	Magic Points	10	7–9	Abdomen	2/7
DEX: 12	Movement	6m	10-12	Chest	2/8
INT: 9	Initiative Bonus	11	13–15	Right Arm	2/5
POW: 10	Armour	Warty Skin	16–18	Left Arm	2/5
CHA: 9	Abilities	As above	19–20	Head	2/6
	Magic	None			

Skills: *Athletics 65%, Brawn 58%, Endurance 52%, Evade 60%, Swim 75%, Perception 63%, Survival 69%, Unarmed 57%, Willpower 52%*

Passions: *Loyalty to Swamp 80%, Loyalty to She 100%, Hate Dry-Landers 80%*

Combat Style: *Swamp Warrior (Spear, Club, Blowgun) 73%*

MEATSHEETS

Bred by the Ophidians as a foodsource, meatsheets are horrible, vat-grown mutations based on human bodies. They lack sapience and are driven by the simple appetite of hunger, even though they are incredibly long-lived.

They move via a series of rapid convulsions rather like the bodily contortions of a centipede.

Meatsheets attack by rearing up and seizing a random location with their several small, sharp-toothed mouths. Digestive juices are then regurgitated to break down tissue into a slop that the meatsheet is capable of processing, much in the manner certain insects feed. Treat juices as weak acid, causing 1d4 points of corrosive damage. The acid is capable of eating through metal armour, bypassing its Armour Points and inflicting damage directly to Hit Points.

Breaking free of a meatsheet attack requires a Brawn roll opposed by the meatsheet's Combat Style.

Chief	Attributes		1d20	Location	AP/HP
STR: 2d6 (7)	Action Points	2	1-20	Body	0/16
CON: 3d6 (11)	Damage Modifier	+1d2			
SIZ: 6d6 (21)	Magic Points	11			
DEX: 2d6+3 (10)	Movement	4m			
INS: 2d6 (7)	Initiative Bonus	9			
POW: 3d6 (11)	Armour	None			
CHA: -	Abilities	Life Sense			
	Magic	None			

Skills: Athletics 62%, Brawn 42%, Endurance 53%, Evade 48%, Perception 43%, Willpower 42%

Passions: Eat 90%

Combat Style: Nasty Little Mouth 65% (Teeth and Acid)

Weapon	Size/Force	Reach	Damage	AP/HP
Teeth	S	T	1d2+1d2	0/3

A meatsheet is capable of Entangling potential prey, if an attack generates a Special Effect.

MARSH VIPER

Growing to about a metre in length, with dark brown and green reticulations, the marsh viper is a close relative of the moor viper (see page 142). Its details are as follows:

Action Points 3, Initiative Bonus 15, Move 3m, Hit Points 2

Abilities: venomous

Skills: Evade 60%, Perception 65%, Stealth 85%

Combat style: bite (S/T 1 Hit Point damage or inject venom) 75%

MARSH VIPER VENOM.

Application: Injected

Potency: 70

Resistance: Endurance

Onset time: 1d6+4 minutes

Duration: 1d3 days

Conditions: Agony followed after 1d6 hours by gross swelling and loss of all feeling in the location bitten. The numbness spreads to one adjacent Hit Location per hour. When it reaches the head (throat) the victim starts to asphyxiate as their throat swells shut. Successful First Aid or Healing (piercing a hole into the character's throat and placing a tube to allow breathing) does 1d6 damage to the head and allows the character to breathe normally. If performed using First Aid or Healing, piercing the throat only does 1d3 damage. The hole in the throat will not heal naturally.

THE CHILDREN OF SHE

She Who Dwells Beneath the Black Water has many offspring. They resemble the mother: large, bloated, amphibians with a vaguely Batrachian head surmounted by three appendages each holding an eye. They can function out of water, but prefer to remain within it, and propel themselves on four, stunted, clawed legs that still make for effective weapons. They are carnivorous, malignant, and utterly devoted to mummy.

She Who Dwells Beneath is a powerful, demonic creature. For purposes of combat, treat her as one of the Children but increase Her Action Points to 3, Damage Modifier to +1d12 and double her Hit Points. Increase the Size and Reach of her natural weapons by 2 steps. If She suffers a Major Wound she retreats back to Her pool and recuperates within 1d6 hours.

Attributes	1d20	Location	AP/HP
Action Points: 2	1–3	Right Leg	2/7
Damage Modifier: +1d4	4–6	Left Leg	2/7
Magic Points: 11	7–9	Hindquarters	2/8
Movement: 4m	10-12	Forequarters	2/9
Initiative Bonus: 11	13–15	Right Front Leg	2/7
Armour: Warty Skin	16–18	Left Front Leg	2/7
Abilities: Swim	19–20	Head	2/7
Magic: None			

Skills: Athletics 57%, Brawn 63%, Endurance 62%, Evade 42%, Swim 76%, Perception 48%, Unarmed 55%, Willpower 42%

Passions: Loyalty to She 100%, Hate Everything Mummy Hates 100%

Combat Style: Bite and Tongue-grab 67%

Weapon	Size/Force	Reach	Damage	AP/HP
Bite	M	L	1d4+1d4	As for Head
Tongue	M	VL	1d2+1d4	As for Head

The tongue is capable of Gripping and is used first to ensnare prey which is then drawn towards the Child's mouth.

GIANT TRAPDOOR SPIDER

The size of a large dog, these arachnids are thankfully rare, but still devastating marsh predators. Their burrows are long, angled tunnels masked from surface view with reeds, grass, leaves and other debris cunningly webbed together to form a trapdoor over the burrow's opening. Their tactic is to grab prey and rapidly retreat into the burrow to then paralyse it and feast at leisure.

Trapdoor spiders are not to be kept as pets.

Attributes	1d20	Location	AP/HP
Action Points: 3	1-2	Right Rear Leg	4/4
Damage Modifier: +0	3-4	Left Rear Leg	4/4
Magic Points: 11	5-6	Mid Right Leg	4/4
Movement: 10m	7-8	Mid Left Leg	4/4
Initiative Bonus: 15	9-10	Fore Right Leg	4/4
Armour: Exoskeleton	11-12	Fore Left Leg	4/4
Abilities: Adhering, Earth Sense, Grappler, Venomous	13-14	Abdomen	4/5
	15-16	Front Right Leg	4/4
	17-18	Front Left Leg	4/4
	19-20	Cephalothorax	4/6

Skills: Athletics 80%, Brawn 69%, Endurance 60%, Evade 80%, Stealth 76%, Perception 53%, Willpower 48%

Passions: None humans can readily comprehend.

Combat Style: Eight Legged Horror (Legs and Mandibles) 70%

Weapon	Size/Force	Reach	Damage	AP/HP
Legs	M	L	1d3	As for Leg
Mandibles	M	T	1d4	As for Head

Scenario 3: Shadows Behind the Throne

Overview

The characters thwart an assassination attempt on Princess Alynoor. She sets them the task of saving her brother, King Myur, from the clutches of his advisor, the petty sorcerer Gul-Azar, who controls the monarch through magic and rules the land from the shadows.

As they search through the city of Cylder for a way to enter the palace, it becomes obvious that the king is not as innocent as his sister would believe; Gul-Azar is, himself, a pawn of Jedakiah, who seeks to plunge the kingdom into civil war so he can conquer it with greater ease, and the magic being used on the king is far more powerful than Gul-Azar's ability to control it. The kingdom is on the brink of disaster, and saving the king from the sorcerer turns out to be less important than saving him from himself.

At the end of the scenario the characters will have learned of Jedakiah's plan for the coming invasion of The Vale. They may have gained a great ally, or a great enemy.

Non-Player Characters

- Princess Alynoor: The king's sister. She is the only one who has noticed that the changes in the king's behaviour are caused by magic, and is blaming Gul-Azar. She wants the king out of Cylder in the hope that once beyond of his advisor's reach he will return to his former self.
- Lord Athanax: Duke of the East Vale and a former member of the Order of Truth. A direct descendant of the leader of the Order that led the armies against the Old Empire. A scapegoat in Jedakiah's plan to weaken the Vale's forces prior to the invasion. He has been wrongfully accused of sedition and treason.
- Kardash Weathervane: The owner of the Theatre of Shadows, a thief and an information broker. He is untrustworthy, wickedly smart and ready to sell anything for the right price.
- Dagmar Shield-Biter: an ex soldier out of East Vale. He is the owner of The Sweetwater Squid Inn and the leader of the local Eastvaler enclave. A soldier to

Book of Quests — Scenario 3: Shadows Behind the Throne

How to Run This Adventure

Shadows behind the Throne is an urban sword and sorcery scenario. Even though it can be run as pure hack and slash, the most rewarding experience results from the actions of inquisitive characters who try to piece together what is really going on prior to stealing into the palace. The adventure is for the most part linear, but the free form approach to what the characters can do once they enter the city will add spice to it.

The greatest challenge for the Games Master in running this adventure is in presenting the textured back story, and close attention should be paid to fully familiarising with all its aspects. Due to its complex nature we have decided to put in the historical background section only that information widely talked about and known to all the citizens of Cylder, while different versions of events, and knowledge specific to certain characters, are retained until that character is met within the story.

There are two major points of concern – investigation and fighting.

There are several different ways to pick-up on important clues, so there is little chance of a major clue being lost due to poor rolls.

the bone, he is honest, pragmatic and enraged by the false accusations against Lord Athanax.

- **General Mencios**: The tragic, heroic general of the Vale's armies who returned the crown of the Old Empire from Gartharis and gave it to the king. He fell from favour after accusing King Myur of an unspeakable deed. No one really knows what the accusation was and gossip abounds. He is imprisoned and awaits execution.
- **Gul-Azar**: the advisor to King Myur and the secret apprentice of Jedakiah. He is smart and resourceful, but his desire to wreak vengeance against his people's enemies have got the better of him.
- **King Myur the Third**: The ruler of the Vale. Once a warrior king, Myur is an aging monarch of a realm beset by troubles. He has been drifting in and out of consciousness, fighting the magical domination that controls him, but is now almost at the end of his strength and in peril of losing his soul forever.
- **Chandanar**: A past king of The Realm whose malign spirit has possessed Myur. He was mad even in life but since being released from his imprisonment after century and a half, Chandanar is drunk with freedom and seeks to satiate his twisted appetites. While Jedakiah and Gul-Azar both have ideas on how to use the deranged spirit, the Old Emperor clever, despite his madness, and has plans of his own.

Key Points/Timeline

1. Princess Alynoor is ambushed on the Cylder road
2. The princess pleads with the characters to save her brother
3. Investigation by the characters; facts at odds with the princess's story come to light
4. The characters infiltrate the palace and find General Mencios in the dungeons
5. The characters search the palace in an attempt to reach the king
6. The characters are confronted with the final threat in the attempt to save both the king's life and his soul

Areas to Be Covered

- **Cylder**: The royal seat and the capital of The Vale. Aside from the scenario's beginning, the whole adventure takes place within the city and is focused on rescuing the king from the palace.
- **The Palace**: The seat of King Myur the Third.
- **Sweetwater Squid Inn**: the owner Dagmar Shield-Biter is an Eastvaler and a staunch supporter of Lord Athanax.
- **The Plaza of Kings**: The Great Cylder Market is situated here and the unoccupied house with the entrance to the secret tunnel is close to the Plaza.
- **The Theatre of Shadows**: A shadow puppet theatre that serves as a front for a brothel, chance house and a drug den led by Kardash Weathervane, who is

also responsible for the black market in the city
- The Plaza of Gods: The great square in front of the Temple of the Founding Four where executions are held.
- Temple of the Founding Four: The greatest temple of The Realm. It has a great library with over 20,000 books and scrolls.

INTRODUCTION

The kingdom of Vale was never a quiet one. Wars with barbarian tribes to the north and south were always a seasonal habit and feuds among the various noble houses were as common as rain. The towns and cities are a hotbed of treachery and deceit, but no town can match Cylder, the Red and Black City.

The power to rule people is such that few can escape its lure; but a wise man knows that true power lies not with the person on the throne, but with the one standing in the shadows behind it. Throughout the ages there have always been people who dreamed about reuniting The Realm into a New Empire that would overshadow even the wildest legends of the old one. However, none of those rulers came even close to fulfilling that dream. Gul-Azar is different.

The main advisor to King Myur is ambitious and has also done something no pretender to the title of emperor ever did. He has embraced the secret worship of the Chaos Mother and, through letters and envoys, become apprenticed to Jedakiah. This shadowy figure, high priest of the Chaos Mother, initiated Gul-Azar into the cult and helped him achieve his goals by teaching him dark sorceries. Jedakiah also gifted Gul-Azar with a Jade Sceptre - a symbol of the Goddess and, some say, a powerful magical artefact.

Once firmly enmeshed in his webs, Jedakiah told Gul-Azar some of the legends regarding the Old Empire and its last ruler, Chandanar the Mad. Aware of the crown's last resting place, Jedakiah used Gul-Azar to recover it and achieve another stage in his strategy to destabilise The Realm in preparation for his apotheosis and ultimate return as a living god. Gul-Azar is unaware of his true role, and secretly plans to claim power in The Vale for himself.

Gul-Azar, under Jedakiah's direction of his, manipulated the king into sending an expedition into Gartharis, to punish recent barbarian raids. Under the guise of a chance discovery, the trusted advisor revealed rumours of the Crown of the Old Empire, a perfect trophy for the king of Vale. Ripped from the barrow in which it had been secreted, the general leading the expedition brought back the crown which was placed upon the head of King Myur. The king has suffered increasing nightmares and whispered promises of absolute dominion over the entire Realm. He is often seen late at night, wandering his palace in a waking dream in the company of his most trusted advisor.

Gul-Azar aims to rule through the spirit of Chandanar the Mad once it has taken full possession of the king. In return he has promised Chandanar all the twisted pleasures he wishes. However, Gul-Azar does not know that Jedakiah has a different plan for the wraith. As time goes by, Chandanar becomes stronger and more overt in his twisted acts, wrestling free from Gul-Azar's control. Jedakiah's ultimate plan is for Chandanar to plunge the kingdom into anarchy and civil war so that he can conquer the land with greater ease.

The princess, Alynoor, has seen this change in her brother and, after initial denial, she has started to pay more attention to it. She has seen with her own eyes Gul-Azar commanding her brother and fled the city just moments before he sent assassins to dispose of her.

HISTORICAL BACKGROUND

Two years ago, raids from Gartharis became more frequent. King Myur ordered General Mencios to lead an expeditionary

Further to this, some information is either well known or several Non-Player Characters have knowledge of it, so there should be no problem if the clue is missed.

As this is a sword and sorcery scenario we strongly advise that all opponents aside from the major ones should be treated as underlings or rabble. The large number of fighters among Non-Player Characters would make the scenario extremely hard to complete should they be treated the same as the characters. Games Masters should also read the advice given concerning combat on pages 284 and 285 of MYTHRAS.

RUNNING THE SCENARIO AS A PART OF THE CAMPAIGN

If Games Masters wish to run this scenario as part of the campaign, they should have little difficulty linking it to other adventures. Some links are already built in as background detail, while others must be filled in by Games Masters themselves. When bringing the scenarios together, care should be taken with regards to previous events characters may have witnessed, and knowledge they acquired, that may require some modifications to the scenario. Some of these have been mentioned in the scenario already, but Games Masters should consider the repercussions of a character's previous actions and take them into account when deciding on the strength and capabilities of the opponents and availability of allies.

If the scenario is being incorporated into an existing campaign in a homebrew setting, further modifications will be required.

Any large city can substitute for Cylder although the central Non-Player Characters will require some adjustment to fit with the plot. Games Masters are advised to look for thematic similarities within their own settings and place the adventure in an environment where power struggles and the exploitation of power are inherent to the story.

force into Gartharis to bring the raids to a halt.

A year later the general returned victorious. On his way back, however, barbarian guides led him through a forbidden valley where the mound of the last king of the barbarians lay. Within the mound was the long-lost *Crown of the Old Empire*. Mencios knew it would make a royal gift that could raise his status in the eyes of the king; so he dared the taboos and the protective spells and brought the crown south to Cylder.

The king was greatly pleased with the gift and declared that the crown of his ancestors had finally returned home. From that day on it would be the crown of the Kings of The Vale. In a great ceremony the king was recrowned and proclaimed that a new rule was beginning in Vale. Soon it was proved that the king spoke the truth.

In a matter of months new taxes were raised, and laws against thievery and banditry sent many to the rack or worse. The king became fascinated with the lore of the Old Empire. He sent expedition after expedition across The Realm to find artefacts left after its fall, and he became more and more obsessed with arcane lore. Steadily Cylder sank to its present gloomy, decadent state: then came the war with Lord Athanax.

Eight months ago King Myur accused Lord Athanax, Duke of East Vale, of high treason alleging he had plans to seize the throne for himself. The duke protested his innocence but the king put his armies into the field. The real reason was, of course, different. Not only did Gul-Azar see an opportunity for revenge, but the paranoid nature of Chandanar (now in control of King Myur) himself had begun to hold sway. Athanax was a descendent of the man who trapped his spirit in the crown, and so craved vengeance. Once again, Mencios led the King's armies. While he waged war against the Eastvalers, barbarian raids from Gartharis started again.

Two months ago General Mencios returned victorious with the Duke of East Vale as his prisoner. The king imprisoned the duke and declared his life forfeit. Both Princess Alynoor and Mencios tried to reason with Myur, but to no avail. To compound matters another tragedy befell General Mencios.

Mencios's sister, Lady Gallana, committed suicide. Mencios grieved at first, then, in a fit of rage, and for no explicable reason, held the king responsible. He to was imprisoned but faced a much different fate to simple execution.

There is now a patina of gloom upon Cylder. Doomsayers on every corner proclaim that the barbarian hordes will shed rivers of blood across the kingdom. Seers and curse workers offer their false services for high price. Bizarre blood sports are found everywhere - from the lowest dens to the most rarefied salons in the Upper Cylder (if a man knows the proper words to gain entry). There are rumours of a demon snatching people off the streets in the middle of the night, and worship of the Chaos Mother is on the rise. The city sinks into decadence and despair.

AMBUSH AT DAWN

The characters are approaching Cylder from the road winding along the the River Southvale. It is large enough for wagons to pass each other but is otherwise little more than a dirt track. Occasionally, remnants of the Old Empire road appear, with road marks to forgotten cities and slabs of stone paving, telling of old glories and the momentary nature of all things built by humans.

It is early in the morning and the characters expect to arrive to the city by noon. The last day of the journey is proving to be just as bad as all the previous days. The mists roll off the river, it is a cold and grey morning and it seems that the drizzle will last forever. The road, what can be seen of it, is a muddy path than sticks to boots and hampers movement just enough to make walking a slow affair.

Chandanar and the Crown

Chandanar became king at a very young age, following the coup that saw both Chandanar's father and his father's usurper brother ripped apart body and soul in a terrible, sorcerous attack. Witnessing these dark powers left Chandanar with the belief that the old legends of obscene rituals were true and that the Chaos Mother and alien snakemen were going to return to plague the world of men once more. Chandanar's uncle was, at best, a petty sorcerer who meddled with knowledge he couldn't understand. But in his efforts to seize the crown and save the empire from its steady decline he opened himself to ophidian influences. They orchestrated his failed coup in an elaborate ruse that saw the downfall of the most glorious empire The Realm had ever seen.

The Ophidians continued their manipulation through the young Chandanar. Through the use of their sorcerous mirror machines they sent terrible visions to him in the guise of dreams. Night after night, Chandanar would wake screaming, sweating, crying, terrified of what the future held.

The Ophidians then executed their master stroke: they sent Chandanar a false vision of Sayalis the Bright. The ancestor guardian had soothed the young emperor's mind and convinced him that he was chosen to do what Sayalis himself could not: destroy the Chaos Mother. Sayalis told him that the only way to destroy the World Spider trapped in her spirit maze was to take the Chalice, an ancient artefact that held the Chaos Mother's power within The Realm, to the Great Temple of the Earth Mother where it would be ritually destroyed. Wearied by the constant nightmares, guided by ophidian-sent visions of Sayalis and aided by a few trusted friends who, unbeknown to him, were secret followers of Chaos, Chandanar sought the Chalice, and brought it to the Earth Mother's temple.

The subsequent defilement and corruption of the temple broke Chandanar's mind. Everything he wanted to avert came to pass. Worse of all, in their twisted delight, the Ophidians revealed to him that all he had done to stop the return of Chaos was actually part of their scheme. Faced with his unwilling treachery, Chandanar was undone. Accepting the inevitable return of the World Spider, he embraced Chaos, screaming that if he could not prevent the destruction of the world, he would rule it. So came Chandanar the Mad, the high priest of the Chaos Mother. The decades of his terror started with the war against the Ophidians. He never forgave them for making him what he was. The war forced the Ophidians to return to the depths of their mountains, not to be seen for centuries to come. Chandanar prosecuted the devoted followers of the Founding Four until he thought he had destroyed all of them. As the beginning of the Empire was the brightest age of human development, so its end was the darkest.

The coming of Aliya in her aspect of The Vengeful Sister had signalled the beginning of a war that finally saw the end of the Mad Rule of King Chandanar. The Order of Truth rode at the head of the rebelling armies in their moment of glory and destroyed thousands of hybrid soldiers of the emperor. Chandanar was defeated, and the order invoked a punishment. His spirit was imprisoned within his own crown – to live forever, close to power but never to rule again.

Chandanar became a malicious spirit intent on possessing anybody wearing the crown. After decades of petty wars for the remnants of the Old Empire, barbarians from Gartharis took the crown as plunder. In their mountain homeland one chief after another waged war with his neighbour for possession of the crown. Finally, a chieftain strong and wise enough killed the last holder of the crown but did not claim the cursed item. He buried his enemy with the crown, built a mound over the grave and cursed it so that the crown was left alone; and after the passing of an age it was finally forgotten.

As the characters get closer to the city an Easy Perception roll alerts them to a fast-approaching coach further down the road and around a bend, coming from the direction of Cylder. A few seconds later they hear a loud crack, the crashing of a falling tree and the neighing of horses followed by human cries and sounds of fighting.

With another, this time Formidable, Perception roll, the characters hear over the din of the fighting a yell: "Protect the princess!"

Whether the characters rush to help the ambushed party or creep closer to check the situation they see that, across the road, a great oak tree has been felled. The horses have stopped dead, causing the driver to lose control and the carriage to turn over and crash. Dragged by the tumbling carriage, both horses have fallen, one breaking its neck in the process, the other breaking a leg. From both sides of the road, crossbowmen (four of them) loose bolts into the princess's escort and the carriage itself. Four more assassins have charged with spears from the woods toward the six warriors protecting the princess.

Depending on how long the characters take to approach the ambush, two of the warriors fall to crossbow bolts leaving a tally of eight attackers against four defenders. Once close enough to see the fighting, the characters hear one warrior yell to the princess to stay inside the carriage as he charges the closest spearman. If the characters do not aid the princess and her guards, then the guards defeat the assailants on their own, although only two of them survive, one of them heavily wounded.

The assassins are members of the Chaos Mother Cult and servants of Gul-Azar, sent to murder the princess. But, the ambush failed and the princess is alive - although the situation is grim. Her lady in waiting lies dead in the carriage, a piece of wood from the window frame protruding from her belly. The coachman has a broken arm, but is otherwise fine. The leader of the princess's guard, Bandor, has a crossbow bolt sticking from his shield arm and requires first aid. The other warrior, Vanek (who is Bandor's nephew), has a few light wounds but nothing serious. The rest are dead.

If the characters stayed out of the fight, Bandor is suspicious of them and considers them accomplices in the assassination attempt. He approaches them with his nephew, ready for another fight, but the princess commands him to stop. She has reasoned that the characters were not part of the attack. Had they been so, the princess and all her retinue would be dead, and while she knows these are hard times and understands their unwillingness to fight other people's fights, she would appreciate some help with the carriage, the wounded and the dead.

"Know that I am the Princess Alynoor of Vale, and even though I am running from rogues infesting my own house I am still able to reward good men willing to offer a hand."

While the characters and the princess's guards tend to their wounds, Alynoor remains aside, alone with her thoughts. Unless she is approached by a character who is at least of Gentile rank, and addressed in the formal manner, she avoids any conversation, politely but with the finality befitting royalty. While she seems regal and serene, an Insight roll reveals that the princess is actually deeply dismayed by the ambush.

The characters can help with getting the carriage off the road and hiding it (the axle is broken beyond repair and the princess intends to continue on horseback), as well as with disposing of the corpses. Moving the carriage is a Hard "reverse" team roll of Brawn, while burying the dead requires an Endurance roll if it is to be done in a hurry. During this time Bandor talks to the characters, asking them of news from the road and matters that can affect their journey.

Any surviving assassins try to kill themselves by cutting their own throats, throwing themselves onto the blades of the characters' weapons, or drinking suicide potions they each carry in a small gourd. If the characters anticipate or halt these suicide attempts, the assassins prove to be a poor source of information. Getting any information requires

THE DEADLY DANCE

Although this episode is constructed so that the princess survives, even the most reluctant characters, if they do enter the fray, Games Masters are faced with a problem of narrating a fight that potentially has more opponents than player characters.

MYTHRAS is famous for its blow by blow combat system, and statistics are provided for both the assassins and the princess's guard, but it is not necessary to go through the actions of all involved. Games Masters should restrict the combat procedure only to those engagements in which the characters are involved, resolving the rest through pure narration and eliminating assassins and guards as needed.

persistence. An opposed roll is needed of the assassin's Willpower against the interrogator's Influence skill at a Formidable difficulty grade, but this can be improved by one grade or more if torture is applied. Bandor is more than willing to assist: Princess Alynoor turns away if torture is used, but makes no attempt to prevent either Bandor or the characters from extracting as much information as possible from her would-be killers.

If the characters or Bandor succeed in extracting information from the assassins, they learn the following:

- Assassins work for Gul-Azar.
- They are all devotees of the Chaos Mother Cult - as is Gul-Azar.
- They wear a tattoo on their breast, above the heart, which is proof of their membership of the cult. The tattoo is of a black spider crouched over the Chaos Rune - the mark of the World Spider and her Spirit Maze.

If the characters search the assassins they find around 150 Founders, the aforementioned suicide potions and tattoos of the Chaos Mother's cult oozing bloody pus. Whether the characters know anything about the cult depends on appropriate cultural background and relevant skills such as Customs, Locale, Lore (History) or Passions If the characters have had any prior dealings with the Chaos Mother cult, identifying the assassins' membership is a formality.

At an opportune time the princess takes the characters to one side for a secretive discussion. Her trust in them is much stronger if the characters helped prevent the assassination attempt and especially if they are from noble backgrounds. She tells them her story, as described below.

The Princess's Story

For the last two months the king has been sleeping little, always walking by himself at night or, sometimes, with Gul-Azar. Then his memory began to lapse, even other simple things such as names or places. Princess Alynoor remarked about this to Myur and he blamed the lapses on fatigue; he was, he claimed, studing The Realm's ancient history and the work was taking its toll.

Yet the odd behaviour continued, and in worrying ways. The king raised the taxes and made war against Athanax, the Duke of East Vale. At first Princess Alynoor thought he was just raising money for another expedition against the Gartharis barbarians but when she overheard Gul-Azar telling the king *not* to act against new raids from the north she became suspicious, and started paying close attention to the relationship between her brother and Gul-Azar.

After General Mencios returned from the war with East Vale, with the duke as a prisoner, the King Myur declared the duke's life forfeit. Alynoor tried to reason with her brother and she might have changed his mind but she witnessed, in secrecy, Gul-Azar commanding the king to proceed with the execution. Gul-Azar appeared to use his Jade Sceptre to command and control the king, an action she has seen the advisor previously use on guardsmen. Alynoor confronted Gul-Azar and he made vague threats that were so menacing she fled for her life, using the old escape tunnel leading between the palace and the Plaza of Kings. Her personal guards came with her and blocked the tunnel after their escape; they hired the coach and fled Cylder. Now they are making safety, although Alynoor does not say where.

The princess wants the characters to infiltrate the palace and either rescue the king or kill Gul-Azar. She hopes that, with Gul-Azar's influence broken, her brother will regain his senses. If not, she can search for a cure. She tells them that even though the tunnel is blocked, it shares a wall with an unoccupied house near the Fountain of Sayalis on the Plaza of the Kings, so they can certainly gain access to it enter the palace unseen. If the characters are willing to help Alynoor describes the palace. She stresses that this is not just a case of a sister's love for her brother: if Gul-Azar has, indeed, made a pact with barbarians and cultists, how long before they seize the country completely? Or the Founding Four are replaced by the cult of the Chaos Mother? If the characters are willing to help her, The Realm will be in their debt and she will see that they are amply rewarded.

If the characters agree Alynoor summons Baldor and explains what she has told them. Baldor is quiet while he digests this news but eventually agrees that there is no other course. "Cylder is rife with spies and informants working for Gul-Azar," he says. "But a few knowledgable men can be trusted. You will need help. I recommend two people that I know respect the Princess and will offer some aid, even though it might come at a cost. Dagmar Shield-Biter owns the Sweetwater Squid Inn and is loyal to Duke Athanax: he would want revenge on those who have falsely accused him of treason. The other is Kardesh Weathervane, owner of the Theatre of Shadows. Little happens in the city that he does not hear about, and I know he has no liking for Gul-Azar. Seek out both. But keep your wits about you be careful who you trust and talk to."

With this agreement made, the Princess and her remaining guards continue their escape from Cylder. Alynoor tells the characters that if they need to make contact with her, word should be sent to Lord Drystan of Senholm: he will convey any messages. She wishes each character the Luck of the Four and again promises a substantial reward for either Gul-Azar's death or the king's rescue.

> ### GUL-AZAR'S PURSUIT
>
> As an optional scene for the characters, following their meeting with the princess, Gul-Azar has sent loyal guards to make sure that his assassins have done their job. These guards, dressed in the Royal Livery, are met on the Cylder road. They are hunting for Alynoor or looking to meet the assassins and so do not automatically pay the characters much heed. This is an opportunity for the guard captain to pause his horses and question the characters: who have they seen on the road? Did they encounter a carriage? Have they met anyone else? How about bandits? This is a chance for the characters to use Deceit skills to counter the captain's Insight of 64% and, perhaps, through him and his retinue off Alynoor's trail. If the captain's suspicions are aroused in any way, he can have the characters arrested, shackled, and dragged back to Cylder. here they are thrown into the palace dungeons to await further questioning by Gul-Azar himself. It would certainly be one way of gaining access to the palace - although escaping the dungeons would not be an easy matter...

THE GREATEST SLUM OF THE REALM

As the characters continue their way to Cylder they pass people who started out late for the market day. Even though it is late afternoon when they arrive at the gate, the crowd is large and the going is slow. The characters are forced to wait for a long time in the cold, bone-numbing drizzle.

The guards make it difficult for them to get in, asking the characters where they're from and their business in Cylder. If the characters are lying they must succeed in an opposed roll of Deceit versus Insight. If the guards decide not to let them pass, they can try again at the East Gate on the opposite end of the city. It takes about half an hour to reach it.

The guards also inform them that it is forbidden to bear arms within the city walls unless a fee is paid. The fee is based on the size of the weapon and amounts to 50 Founders per size category. Characters who are unwilling to pay must leave their weapons at the gate and collect them once they leave the city.

There are several ways for belligerent characters to avoid paying the fee, though most of them are not worth the effort. Smuggling the weapons in is possible with a successful opposed Conceal versus Perception roll for every weapon they try to hide. The difficulty grade of the roll depends on the size of the weapon. Small weapons are at a Standard difficulty, Medium at Hard while weapons with size Large and Huge are impossible to hide unless characters have a vehicle of some sort with them, in which case difficulties are Hard and Formidable respectively. Smuggling weapons also requires prior knowledge of the law through either making successful Customs (Vale) or Culture (Vale) rolls; overhearing the guards while waiting to get to the gate; or hiding the weapons before reaching the other gate.

Climbing the walls is impossible during the day due to their size and the number of guards patrolling them. At night it requires a Hard Athletics roll and a Formidable Stealth roll to avoid detection. Both rolls are downgraded by one step if the characters have suitable equipment. Detection, however, sees them seized and imprisoned if they do not manage to evade the wall guards.

Trying to persuade any of the waiting peasants to hide them in their carts is not a viable option for sneaking into the city. Even in times of peace, let alone when the kingdom is beset by constant raids, people are suspicious of strangers. Approaching any peasant with a proposition of concealment is a sure way to a swift ending to their adventuring careers (frightened peasants do, of course, accommodate the characters if threatened, but use the first opportunity to alert the guards).

The river traffic is also too heavy for characters to sneak into town by swimming. Whilst the river is slow moving, whirlpools are common. The characters must pass a Hard Swim roll in order to get to the docks. Once the characters are at the docks, a Hard Stealth roll is needed to leave the water undetected. Characters need a dry set of clothes if they are to remain unnoticed.

Once inside, the characters are faced with the full stinking, grimy glory of the greatest city in The Realm.

The City of Red and Black

Cylder is built from local black granite and roofed with red tiles. The city is built on the confluence of Rivers Cylder and Southvale, and the surrounding land is marshy. A couple of kilometres north of the city, dry land starts in earnest and farmland abounds. These marshy surroundings provide Cylder with plenty of fog, mists and oppressively high humidity levels in the summer months.

Cylder was once only a border fort. When the Old Empire fell Valelanders moved increasingly southward. Being on the confluence of two rivers (of which Southvale is still deep enough for ocean vessels), Cylder became more of a trade town than a military outpost. Real wealth came only after silver was found in the hills north of the city. At that time the third king of Vale took his court east from the West Vale and made Cylder the capital.

A golden age ensued. New land was cleared and the city was extended. Buildings were founded, of stone and tile and red-veined black marble facades. The great temple of the Founding Four was raised and became a pilgrimage spot bringing even more wealth to the city.

With wealth came crime. Even though slavery was officially banned in the Vale, indenture due to debt or some form of petty crime was commonplace. Corruption made it possible to have the punishment made permanent through fake records.

The drug business also thrived. Exotic opiates, both from across the sea and from the Forest of Sorrows fetched good prices with the nobles while cheap alcohol catered to the destitute. While the purpose of the City watch is keeping the peace, those who can afford it hire the members of the watch for thief taking – retrieving of stolen goods and hunting down thieves, if they can, in order for the employer to exercise private justice. More often than not, members of the watch steal themselves the items they are paid to return.

The city consists of four quarters: Upper and Lower Cylder, the Harbour with its shipyards and the Trades Quarter encompassing the marketplace on the Plaza of Kings.

The Palace

Commanding a view over the entire city and the surrounding area, the Palace was once a mighty border fortress. A large slab of granite with four corner towers, it is still a formidable keep. Situated on the promontory projecting into the Southvale River, the Palace's famous Hanging Gardens extend over the cliff on the terraces built into the rock and connected by small wooden bridges. The palace is detailed in the maps beginning on page 71.

Sweetwater Squid Inn

If Games Masters require floorplans of the Sweetwater Squid Inn, then use those provided on page 25: the inn conforms to the standard Vale design.

Many people recommend Sweetwater Squid Inn as the best place in town when considering value for money. This inn is in the Harbour district and is owned by Dagmar Shield-Biter, an ex-soldier from East Vale and the leader of the small Eastvaler community in Cylder (and loyal, still, to Lord Athanax). Room and board is 10% cheaper than the standard price for any soldier of Vale (see MYTHRAS, page 58 for standard rates).

The inn is always busy. Dimly lit, but warm, dry and welcoming, there is a constant hubub of conversation, laughter, good-natured cursing and the clink and clank of goblets and tankards. The food is homely Vale fare: stews, roasts and good, hearty bread.

Dagmar Shield-Biter is the owner. he has staff to serve and tend bar, and he is usually found close to the fire, chatting with his cronies - all of them East Vale veterans. He is approachable but is gruff with those who appear to have led soft lives: he can appraise a veteran in a heartbeat and can smell bullshit from several kilometres distant. He likes news and sharing it - especially if he, and his six or seven cronies, are bought a drink as well.

If the characters ask for news they learn that Lord Athanax's execution for high treason is being held in the Plaza of Gods at sunset. The king himself will be present. If talking with Dagmar directly about this, characters see he is stricken by the fate of his liege lord, a fact that can be used to persuade Dagmar and his followers to help them with their mission. However, while Dagmar and his friends are bitter about the fate of Lord Athanax, they are not traitors to the kingdom, especially since, as veteran soldiers, they are well aware that the kingdom is threatened by a foreign force. Any suggestion that sounds too close to treason is declined immediately and potentially causes Dagmar to alert the town watch.

Gossiping with the patrons, a Standard Customs or Culture (Vale) roll, lets the characters pick-up on local events and discover out that, five months ago, people started disappearing from the streets. Some twenty people are missing, both men and women. They vanished without trace; no one heard or saw anything.

Cylder

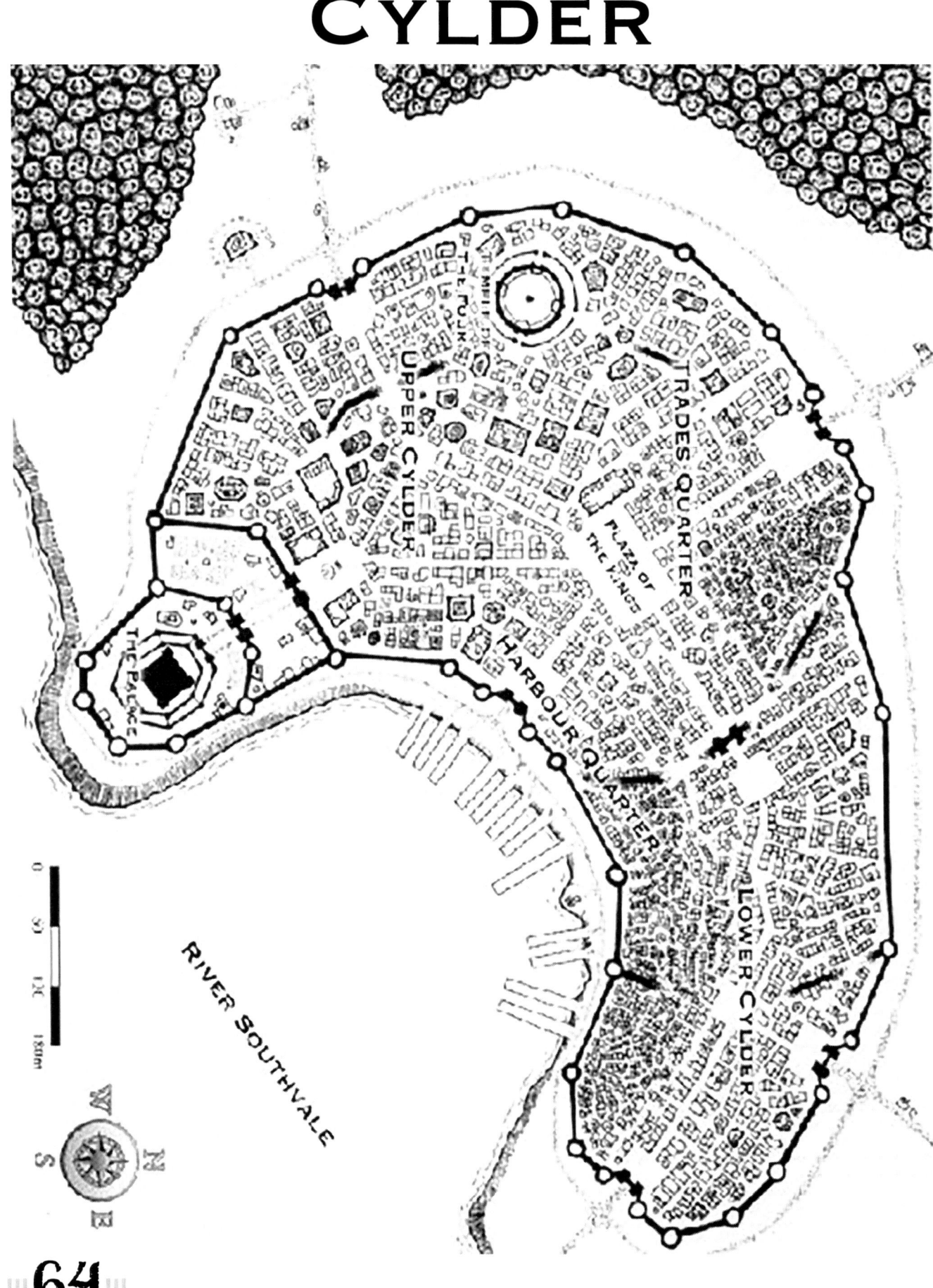

The Great Cylder Market

Situated in the Plaza of the Kings, with the opulent Sayalis Fountain in the centre, the Great Cylder Market is the biggest of the half-dozen marketplaces in the city. Anything can be found here for the right price – the more exotic a product the higher the price. This is the best place for gossiping with merchants and acquiring all the necessary equipment for the mission.

The prices for goods in Cylder are higher than elsewhere in The Realm - up to 50% more in some cases. Attempting to gain a discount requires use of the Haggling rules from Mythras on page 55. Talking with traders about current events revolves around the rumours that the Gartharis barbarians are better equipped and that business in the north is faltering. Some fear that the barbarians are uniting; others have heard tales of chaos monsters on the loose in the Gartharis borderlands, terrorising caravans and raiding settlements. The events in Aylesford have reached Cylder, and these contribute to local fears.

If any loose-mouthed character boasts of being involved in events from previous scenarios, he becomes the centre of attention for the locals. This is a double edged sword, however: while everybody loves news and good stories and, the character is treated respectfully (even gaining one grade bonus on social rolls in the presence of those who heard the tale, as well as few free drinks), such news can also spread panic, and draw unwanted attention from the Chaos Mother cultists (who are Gul-Azar's ears on the street) in Cylder, alerting them to potential enemies within the city walls.

It is left to Games Masters how far to develop such sub-plots, but, at the very least any mention of thwarting the Chaos Mother Cult alerts spies on the characters, jeopardising the mission. In order to avoid this, it is suggested that characters are given ample opportunities to notice that they are being watched and to lose their tails in the maze of Cylder's streets.

The Theatre of Shadows

This shadow puppet theatre is situated in Lower Cylder. It is, besides being a theatre, a chance house, a drug den, and a first-rate brothel with services for every pocket.

Learning of its location and reputation is easy enough. Baldor recommended it and just about everyone in Cylder has heard of it. Streetwise rolls confirm that it is owned and operated by the shady Kardesh Weathervane; some say he is just a chancer; others claim he manipulates the entire city through his contacts, bribes and blackmail schemes.

The Theatre is a three-storey building with a basement serving as a gaming floor, the ground floor being a puppet theatre, a brothel on the floor above it and the drug den in the attic, with a separate stairs reserved for the most notorious customers. It is heavily decorated with silk and bead curtains, wall paintings of sexual acts and incense burning to mask the smell of sweat, river mud, stale air and bodily fluids.

Its proprietor is Kardesh Weathervane, a shady figure if there ever was one. He always sits at a private booth on the gaming floor. A successful Perception roll reveals that, from time to time, people approach the booth, sit and talk with Kardesh, leaving small parcels or gifts when they depart, which are promptly taken upstairs by a large barbarian from the Long Riding.

The mood in the Theatre is far more lively than in the rest of the city, as if patrons feel a small measure of protection and respite here. A Hard Customs or Culture (Vale) roll reveals that most people believe Kardesh is paying the watch to stay clear of his theatre.

If the characters ask after Kardesh a successful Hard Streetwise roll uncovers that he is an information broker. Whether or not the roll is successful, questions lead to the characters being politely, but firmly, invited to join the proprietor at his booth. The theatre's bouncers (a group of massive, musclebound, bald-headed thugs) can be bribed into securing a private audience with Kardesh, if the characters feel bold. It costs a minimum of 50 Founders to secure such an audience.

Weathervane is polite, civil, but savvy. He barters information, asking the characters for news, immediately recognising them as outsiders. His eyes are always judging. He can tell the characters about any of the following for a price of 100 Founders per item (Haggling can be used, but all attempts are at Hard difficulty):

- The king has imposed harsh new laws. "We have seen the like since the rule of Chandanar the Mad," Kardesh observes. "Even innocent thieves are flayed. Some disappear for good. There are rumours of monsters held in the palace dungeons..."
- There are rumours too about Vale weapons and goods being smuggled into Gartharis. "Gul-Azar turns a blind eye to it," Kardesh remarks. "He even bribes some merchants to do the smuggling."
- Mencios's imprisonment is a surprise and has something to do with his own sister and something to do with the King. "Mencios was Cylder's hero. I would

pay well to learn why the Good King Myur has turned on one of his champions."

- Members of the palace guards are being replaced with new people loyal to Gul-Azar. "He brings them in from outside Cylder. Some are no better than mercenaries. Others hail from Westport and Senholm, lured here by promises of fat bribes."
- "In the last five months an expensive black carriage has made several rounds of the city, snatching people from the street. Witnesses tell me there's always a sickly-sweet perfume coming out of the thing - like rotting chicken. It could be slavers; it could be something worse. I'd pay well to learn more."
- "Princess Alynoor has fled Cylder. I've heard that her brother made advances. I've also heard that she was General Mencios's lover. Someone also told me that she tried to murder Gul-Azar. Who knows. All the information coming out of the palace is contradictory. One cannot separate lies from facts these days…"

Kardesh is in a position to offer the characters illegal goods such as weapons and poisons, but as with any black market his prices are very high and getting some items, like poisons, takes time. The price depends on how well Kardesh appraises the characters, but as a guideline it is suggested at least a five-fold increase on the prices listed in the MYTHRAS Economics & Equipment chapter. Poisons start at 200 Founders for a dose of a sleeping draught and go up to 400 Founders for a dose of a venom that kills outright. Kardesh can have any such narcotics ready within a day, and he needs payment in advance.

THE TEMPLE OF THE FOUNDING FOUR

The characters may try and seek help from the priests of the greatest temple in The Realm. The Temple was built three hundred years ago and is in sore need of renovation. Tiles of the dome are crumbling and the statue of Aliya has been missing a hand for more than half a year. Even in such a sorry state the Temple and its sixteen bells (four for every god) draw respect and awe from everyone who visits the Plaza of the Gods in the Upper City. The Temple also boasts the biggest library in the kingdom, holding more than 20,000 books and scrolls on any topic imaginable. People even claim that there are forbidden books of sorcery in the temple vaults.

Here, with the help of High Priest Ulgan and Chief Librarian Sorsta, the characters can discover the meaning of the tattoo found on the bodies of the assassins, and their relevance to the cult of the Chaos Mother. The tattoo has been used for centuries as the symbol of the Chaos Mother and is part of an initiation ritual claiming the bearer as Her property and under Her protection. A successful Hard Perception or Standard Bureaucracy roll may reveal, in the parchments of the Annals of the Order of Truth, a passage describing Gifts of the Chaos Mother: Chaotic Features and hideous mutations 'gifted' to Her most devout followers. If the characters persuade the High Priest of the necessity of their mission (a Formidable Influence roll adjusted by the arguments presented and any proof of their involvement with Princess Alynoor) the temple can offer them helpful blessings from the Founding Four. The precise miracles that can be offered depend on their prayers, sacrifices and the circumstances of the plan the characters have made for the rescue attempt. The priests have access to the miracles outlined on pages 10 and 11.

Note: some Games Masters may wish to eschew such help - in traditional Swords and Sorcery fiction miracles from the gods are conspicuous by their absence. Instead the temple might be able to offer information about the layout of the palace, equipment, or useful aid in the form of diversions.

If the characters want to find out more about the rise of the Chaos Mother's cult, the High Priest can provide much more information. "There have always been those in Cylder who dabbled in her worship," he says. "For decades they were no more than fools or disturbed minds. The cult's worship began to expand perhaps ten years ago and each city of The Realm saw similar rises in worship. Members of the cult are secretive, conduct their rituals in well-hidden shrines, and go to great lengths to protect their existence. Cylder is no different. But the Chaos Mother's power was broken by Sayalis the Bright centuries ago and, even though the Chaos Mother is worshipped, there is no evidence of her sorcery. At least, there wasn't. We have heard of the terrible things that happened in Aylesford. We have heard the rumours of the beast-men abroad in Gartharis. Her power is growing again, and it must be stopped."

THE SEVEN BLADES

The only chance the characters have to see the king and Gul-Azar in person before infiltrating the palace is at the execution of Lord Athanax. This takes place at sunset in the Plaza of the Kings.

The Plaza is a large semi circle of red marble, 100 metres across, surrounded by black buildings. It is dominated by

a massive statue of Sayalis the Bright and it is in front of the statue that the execution occurs. A wooden platform has been erected at the statue's feet and an iron contraption - a suspended cage and screws with blades attached to it - set in the platform's centre: the machine is known as The Seven Blades of Sormund and it has not seen use for more than fifty years. The plaza is teeming with people: stalls have been erected; food and beverages are being sold, as well as various things to throw at the traitor.

The dreary weather takes a turn for the worse: drizzle replaced by chill, biting rain. Guards appear at the far end of the Plaza, twenty of them, carrying spears. After them comes the executioner, followed by Lord Athanax astride a magnificent elk-like beast, half as big as a horse, with splendid white fur and towering set of gleaming black antlers. The beast is sacred to Sormund the Judge of the Dead, and will be sacrificed at the end of the execution. Lord Athanax holds his head high, despite his impending death. The crowd starts to jeer and throw rotten vegetables at the duke as he is led to the platform. After him, another

contingent of soldiers follows, this time the royal guards. If the characters are close to the procession, once the royal guard passes them, a successful Formidable Perception roll makes them aware of a faint, but distinct, sweet, rotting smell mixed with perfume. As soon as the guards pass the smell is overpowered by the general stink of the city and all the rotten vegetables around them.

After the royal guard, and followed by another twenty soldiers, come the king and Gul-Azar riding huge, black geldings. Gul-Azar is robed in crimson and gold; he is tall and handsome with the distinct, heavy features of someone from the Forest of Sorrows. King Myur, on the other hand is short and broad-shouldered, but there is an unmistakable aura of power surrounding him. He was once known as the Warrior King, but those days have passed. He wears the Crown of the Old Empire - the crown General Mencios brough back from his campaigns. It is an unassuming band of red gold with an inlaid pink diamond in the centre, making the king look as though he has a third, sorcerous eye. A successful Insight roll tells the characters that, while

> **FOOLHARDY CHARACTERS**
>
> If the characters by some chance happen to try to stop the execution in hopes to acquire an ally in Lord Athanax, they should think twice. Even Dagmar, if asked, tells them that is folly. The first problem is the crowd. There are so many people on the plaza and in the alleys that effective use of weapons is extremely hard invoking herculean difficulty for melee weapons. Ranged weapons cannot be used at all unless the character is high up above the plaza, and then only with proper modifiers for firing into the crowd. Most importantly there are lots of soldiers between the crowd and the execution platform. There are twenty men of the royal guard in addition to forty regular soldiers. They are all armoured and equipped with spears, shields and short swords and trained in formation tactics. Should any problem occur they execute extreme force without mercy, pressing the mob away from the execution platform, killing efficiently anyone who doesn't back away. If this happens, the crowd stampedes to the alleys trying to save themselves and probably stomping over the characters in the process.

Gul-Azar has a perpetually calculating look on his face, the king is hard pressed to conceal a look of disdain.

As the procession reaches the platform the cloud cover thickens, casting an oppressive darkness across the crowded plaza. The king raises his hands and addresses the audience.

"People of Cylder! Hear your king. Before you stands Athanax, Duke of East Vale. In our hour of need he fomented rebellion in order to supplant us, the Godsent ruler of the Vale. In order to do this he aided the barbarians in their raids from Gartharis in hopes we would look away from his foul treachery. We know all Eastvalers are little more than half-civilised barbarians so it is little wonder their duke helped the foul scum kill our subjects and plunder our towns and villages. But no more! Here ends his life and our trouble from his dealings with the demon barbarians."

Allow the characters Hard Insight rolls following the king's rhetoric. If successful the characters realise that these words are not the traditional words of a King of The Vale, who has always sought unity and co-operation with the East Vale dukedoms: something has clearly changed in King Myur, just as princess Alynoor indicated. Also, despite the gloom, the king is casting a faint shadow: he should cast none. Anyone who rolls a critical success notes that Gul-Azar is whispering to himself, apparently reciting the king's speech, the Jade Sceptre firmly in his hand. This might lead characters to believe that Gul-Azar is controlling the king directly; he is not - it is an unfortunate impression. Gul-Azar is, though, aware of Chandanar's spirit controlling the king's actions.

The king turns to the executioner and calls to him. The executioner approaches the middle of the platform while two royal guardsmen seize Lord Athanax and lead him to the device. Halfway to the cage, Lord Athanax starts to shake, and tries to free himself. Characters of noble status or with appropriate Customs or Culture skills notice that a breach of etiquette has been made. Nobles, even when traitors, are allowed to take a potion that numbs the sense ensuring they go to their ancestors with dignity. Athanax is being denied the potion to be given him. In the crowd, his supporters start to shout Athanax's name in support - until the royal guards trying to maintain the peace silence them. Dagmar Shield-Biter and his comrades are amongst those screaming for justice.

The protests fall on deaf ears and the guards haul Athanax into the lowered cage and fasten him to its frame so he cannot move. The cage is then raised and the executioner approaches the device. He takes hold of the screws and starts to turn them. As he does so, one by one, the slender blades start to penetrate Lord Athanax's flesh. The screams drown the Plaza. A good executioner can impale the victim with all seven blades in such a way as to avoid internal organ damage, leaving the criminal alive for days after the deed. Lord Athanax succumbs to the device after fifteen minutes.

King Myur and Gul-Azar watch impassively. Athanax's screams are terrible and many faint as he is sliced and punctured to a slow death. Once the execution is over, the king, Gul-Azar and their entourage return to the palace while the people on the plaza proceed to the Temple of the Four for the sacrifice. Some remain behind in the plaza; others drift away to their homes. Dagmar Shield-Biter is amongst those who stay, talking with his supporters. here is an opportunity for the characters and Dagmar to connect once again. If the characters do not approach him, he approaches them.

"An act of murder was committed here today," Dagmar says. "No duke of the Realm deserved that fate. That man who wore the crown is no king. You have our help if you need it. Someone has to *pay*."

Gaining Dagmar's help should be a boon to the characters' plans. His men can create diversions, offer extra swords and help arrange an escape route for the characters from the city. Allow them time to plan. Once prepared, and with all resources assembled, the characters are ready to infiltrate the palace using the secret tunnel Princess Alynoor described.

The Tunnel

The unoccupied house the princess told the characters about overlooks the Plaza of Kings, but the main doors are actually in the alley just off the square. Finding the right house is easy as it has a rose carved above the door. Getting inside is a different matter. The doors are locked and the windows all have closed shutters.

Picking a lock on the door is at a difficulty grade of Hard if done during the day when the plaza is filled with stalls and shops; and it requires an Acting versus Perception roll to mask the fact that the characters are actually breaking in, not simply unlocking the door. If a character does not possess the Acting skill it can be replaced by Deceit but the roll is then at Hard difficulty grade. Other characters can help in this by covering the alley entrance or in any similar feat of deception, adding a bonus to the original character's opposed roll. Use the Augmenting Skills rules on page 50 of Mythras.

If any of the characters circle the house prior to trying to break in they also find, on the side opposite the front doors, a small basement window. A successful Stealth roll is required to time the shutter's breaking so it isn't detected (if this is done during the day) and an Athletics roll to squeeze through and enter the basement. If done during the night the characters have enough time to dismantle the shutter piece by piece so no check is necessary unless they do wish to break it on purpose. In this instance the Stealth roll is at Hard difficulty grade – the night time is usually quiet and violent breaking into houses causes enough noise for the guards patrolling the streets to hear. Breaking the shutters on any larger window causes too much noise to be an effective way to enter the house.

Once inside the characters need to find the basement and commence digging their way to the tunnel. If they wish to search the house it takes no more than half an hour – the house is not large and while there is furniture in the rooms there is nothing of value or any kind of personal possessions left.

The house itself is simple enough: a single-storey townhouse with a steeply gabled roof of red slate. The main floor is divided into a bedroom and living room/kitchen by a thick drape of heavy, dark cotton. The access to the basement is in the bedroom; underneath the bed is a tradoor concealed by a threadbare rug. Lifting the trapdoor is easy enough and a ladder leads down two metres to the dark, dank, basement beneath. It is used for general storage and so there are old crates, sacks, pots and a few dried herbs turned rotten with the moisture. As the princess described, the escape tunnel linking to the palace is found on the left hand wall of the basement: it is filled with rubble (the result of Bandor's closing the tunnel to prevent swift pursuit). Proper equipment and at least half an hour's work (and three successful Brawn rolls) is needed to make an opening for a man to pass through. If they work during the day, the noise is somewhat drowned by the ruckus of the market and overhearing the works requires a Formidable Perception roll. However, if they work after dark there is a 30% chance during every Brawn roll for the guards to pick up the sound and come to investigate. If they do, they arrive in 10 minutes (one Brawn roll). If the characters haven't finished breaking through the wall, a fight ensues. If they have already gone through the escape tunnel, the guards follow them. The characters realise they are being followed through opposed rolls of Perception versus Stealth.

Games Masters are invited to judge for themselves the number of guards according to the number of players, their strength and health, but at least three guards should arrive on the scene. As mentioned earlier, treat the guards as rabble or underlings.

The escape tunnel is a straight affair as tunnels go. It runs between the palace and the house in a straight line. The tunnel terminates in a staircase beneath the palace at the far end. The tunnel is made of packed earth with supporting beams every ten metres and is too cramped for any meaningful combat. Characters that succeed at an Engineering roll can predict where to cut the beams in order to further cave the tunnel should the need arise. The tunnel is 360 metres long and terminates in the staircase, which ascends for a hundred metres to its entrance into the palace dungeons.

The Dungeons

The dungeons consist of the torture chamber, the dungeons proper and the guard's room.

From the top of the stairs a small hallway leads to the ladders, above which a trap door leads into the dungeons (see the Palace Basement diagram on page 71). A successful Hard Perception roll reveals a voice, obviously screaming but muffled by the distance and the doors. While they cannot understand what the voice is saying the characters recognise swearing, the king's name and exclamations of vengeance.

The Torture Chamber

The characters have to pass an Easy Stealth roll to open the trap door without being noticed. The door opens into a small torture chamber. From this side, the trap door looks like any other slab of stone. If none of the characters made a successful Perception roll they can hear a voice screaming in the dungeons beyond. Along one wall are assorted torture devices: a rack, a torture wheel and an iron maiden. There is a table with various knives, hammers and nails as well as knee splitters, head crushers and eye-gougers. All are meticulously clean but closer inspection proves that they are also put to frequent use. The floor of the chamber is uneven, the centre being its lowest point and ending in a large drain.

Aside from the torture equipment, almost a half of the room is occupied by a large device made of brass. It comprises of two vats, one smaller and one large enough for a full grown person to enter. The smaller one is etched with numerous runes in an ancient script. Below is a wood-fired heater covered with etched runes. From this a series of tubes and valves lead to the larger vat.

On top of the vat is a lid. If the characters open it they gag from the acrid smell of the contents. The vat is filled with a white, semi- translucent mucous. Inside the liquid is a human body (or bodies), and various body parts whose origins cannot be discerned unless they are taken out of the vat. Putting a hand in the liquid is an act of extreme courage – or folly. The liquid in its current state acts as a concentrated acid - see MYTHRAS page 68.

Characters passing a Formidable Lore (History or Legends) or Hard Lore (Ophidians) roll identify the device as a fully functional Ophidian mutation tank and the runes as an ancient Ophidian script. Ancient Ophidians used these tanks to produce Cjaos Hybrids, used as labourers or soldiers. Legends say that some Sorcerer-scientists among the Ophidians melded more than two creatures into horrifying shapes, trying to express their esthetical sensibilities.

The characters also find the remains of some 15 people, probably those who were whisked off from the streets in the previous months. They were tortured and mutated in strange rituals. Some of the remains are so mutated that there is no sense of what their ultimate function might be. If the scenario is played as part of the campaign than it is clear that these are remains of something akin to Chaos Hybrids bred for war, otherwise a successful Lore (Legends, Old Empire, Chaos, Gartharis or similar) roll must be passed to summise this information. Markings in blood are painted along the floor and the walls. Characters with proper knowledge can discover on a successful roll that the rituals are connected to the Chaos Mother cult, but even if they cannot manage this, they see among the symbols one that they have seen before – tattooed on the breast of assassins.

The Dungeons

The dungeons have a dozen cells and a side door leading to the guard's room and the palace beyond. By the door to the guard's room is a large water bucket with drinking water for both the guards and the prisoners (if the gaolers are feeling generous). Screaming from a far dungeon provokes the gaoler to come and threaten the prisoner, though a successful Easy Insight roll reveals fear in the gaoler's voice.

The Guards' Room

Aside from the gaoler there are two guards and another gaoler in the side room playing dice. The room has a side door on the left wall leading to a similar chamber with bunks for gaolers. The guards do not sleep in the dungeons and change shifts at four hour intervals.

Dealing with the guards

While the characters have to go through the guards' room to reach the upper levels of the palace, fighting them is not automatically necessary. Clever characters can use an array of tactics to avoid combat; from casting sleep spells if they are available and sneaking by the guards, through poisoning the water bucket with the poison found on the assassins' bodies at the beginning of the scenario (the poison so diluted produces unconsciousness), to luring them one by one and locking them in the dungeons. Games Masters should note that some of the ways suggested here may have had far reaching consequences, and should incorporate them into the events further on (new guards reporting

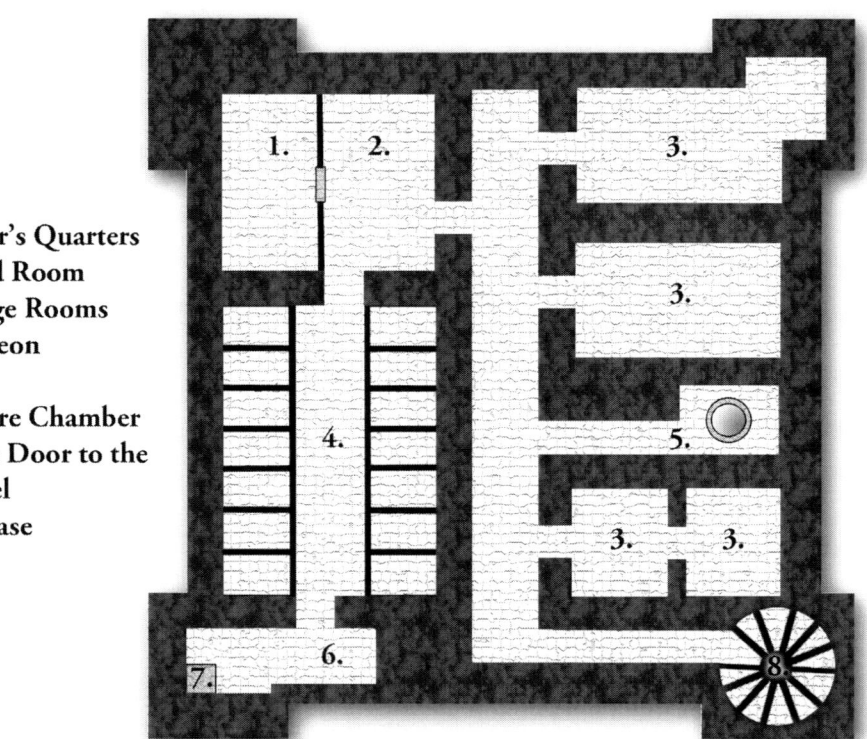

1. Gaoler's Quarters
2. Guard Room
3. Storage Rooms
4. Dungeon
5. Well
6. Torture Chamber
7. Secret Door to the tunnel
8. Staircase

PALACE BASEMENT

for duty, for example, finding their comrades locked in the dungeons, or dead, will raise the alarm throughout the palace.)

THE GENERAL

Once the guards are dealt with, a voice calls to the characters asking for freedom. General Mencios is in one of the cells. He has been magically altered into a hideous monster comprised of several body parts that were not his in the first place and mutated further with no other function than for a totally alien aesthetic. He is three metres tall and bloated beyond belief. He has seven arms, four of which are rotting stumps on his torso. One healthy arm is attached to his back. His eyes have been fused into one and his legs have grown a veil like tail that sweeps behind him. He oozes thick brown liquid from small pustules criss-cross inghis face and exudes a miasma for one metre around him that causes everyone who fails an Endurance roll to vomit violently. He also has two, large, downward protruding tusks. He begs the characters for water and freedom. Freedom that comes with an edge of the knife.

A further three of the cells are occupied by two women and a man in different, terminal states of maltreatment. They have been beaten, tortured and one of them has been transformed as Mencios, but to a lesser degree. No sane man could have performed these transformations, and characters should be now aware that the princess's version of the events is not the whole of the story.

Mencios is eager to talk. Despite his terrifying appearance he has some vestige of sanity left. He tells the characters how he has unwittingly served a monstrous tyrant for years. If they tell him about the princess's belief he counters that she would say anything to make her brother look innocent. She told the same to Mencios after his sister committed suicide. Gallana witnessed one of the king's escapades which earned her a place in the torture chambers – not as a victim but as a witness and accomplice, albeit an unwilling one. In the end, her mind snapped and she sought the only way she could to appease her guilty conscience. He tells them what the king does to his "love interests" when he comes to the torture room to "play". The only reason Mencios still lives is because the king likes him to listen and imagine what his sister had to witness.

He tells them know that Princess Alynoor's story is false, as he knows Gul-Azar does not control the king; at least not in any sorcerous way, because Gul-Azar is no sorcerer. Mencios witnessed a showdown between Gul-Azar and the king when the advisor threatened to send King Myur 'back where he came from': the king simply threw back his head and laughed. Mencios does not know what that

meant, but reasons Gul-Azar knows more about the royal dynasty than anyone else. Mencios further explains that, had he known what the future held, he would have taken the ruby from the crown before he gave it to the king, sold it and made his way over the sea, taking his sister with him. This should make the characters aware that the crown (or, more precisely, the stone set in it), is special. Should any of them ask Mencios about the finding of the crown, he describes how he and his troops found a gathering of megaliths surrounding a barrow carved with strange symbols. One of his men translated them as a warning against plundering the grave as a great evil was imprisoned inside. Mencios ordered the barrow opened anyway. They found the grave with a small treasure hoard and the crown. The crown was made of red gold with a great, red ruby set in the centre. This is the crown the characters saw King Myur wearing at the execution.

The characters can attempt to persuade Mencios that the king is being controlled, just not in the way the Princess suggested; and ask for his help in completing their mission. This requires opposed Influence, Passion and other appropriate rolls versus Mencio's Willpower (which is augmented by his Hate Myur Passion). Mencios may well agree - but he is now a creature driven by hatred for the king and, rather than help the characters rescue him, will kill King Myur, irrespective of Chandanar's possession, for what happened to his sister, to him, and to the innocents plucked from Cylder's streets. Nothing the characters say or do can dissuade Mencios from this goal - and it may result in a showdown with the mutated general as part of the scenario's climax.

The Palace

The palace has five levels. From bottom to top these are:

1. Basement. The floor is divided by a straight corridor into two sections: dungeons and cellar. The cellar has four rooms with stocked goods, one for food, one for beer and wine, one for cloth, and one for weapons. The Palace's well is also in a room here. Aside from the secret tunnel there is only one staircase exit leading to the ground floor.
2. Ground floor. This is the main and largest section of the palace. Servant's quarters are here, as well as kitchens and the great hall for audiences and feasting. There is also a guard room and a small salon for more intimate audiences. A royal shrine to the Founding Four is also on this floor. There are four exits: the main entrance to the palace, the door to

the cliff gardens, the staircase to the upper floors and the small staircase to the great hall gallery.

3. Guard floor. This is where the royal guard is quartered. There are sleeping quarters, a training room, armoury, mess hall, captain's office and a shrine to Sormund. Also from this floor are doors that lead to the gallery of the great hall. The staircase and the gallery are the only ways out.

4. Administrative floor. Administrators of the palace are on this floor: Seneschal, steward, advisors and so forth. This floor consists of five offices and sleeping rooms for dignitaries, visitors and nobles. About one third of the floor is occupied by Gul-Azar's rooms. This is also the place where the official stamps and paraphernalia of the kingdom are stored, so this floor always has five guards on duty, one of whom always remaining in front of the doors to Gul-Azar's chambers.

5. Royal apartments. There are four suites of rooms on this floor. They have been used by the royal family, but now only king uses them. There are also a couple of small rooms for servants, but they have long vacated the premises. The only people allowed on the fifth floor now are Gul-Azar, the guards and those unfortunates lucky enough to be of only moderate interest to the king and not meant for dungeon escapades.

The characters need to reach the royal apartments in order to get to the king. It should also be obvious that Gul-Azar knows more about the king's condition than anyone else and that if the characters wish to learn more, they need to find out what he knows.

Sneaking through the palace

Sneaking to the king's chambers may seem a relatively straightforward task as the palace staircase goes from the basement to the royal apartments directly. However, as it is the major artery between the floors, it means the stairs are frequently used during the day and evenings. Sneaking without any disguise is possible only at night. Even at that time a Standard Sneak versus Perception roll is required for passing each of the lower floors in order to avoid being detected by patrolling guards. Both the Administrative floor and the royal apartments have a duty guard stationed in the alcove just outside the staircase. To pass the fourth floor guard undetected requires a Hard Sneak versus Perception roll. Sneaking through any of the floors is easier due to poor lighting, requiring Standard opposed rolls only when someone is close enough to hear sneaking characters. Again, these circumstances change during the day and in the evening, when many servants use the corridors going about their duties.

Disguise

Disguise is possible. The characters may have planned ahead and acquired disguises through Kardesh Weathervane, Dagmar Shield-Biter or even the temple of the Four. If not, disguises can be found within the palace:

- Servants' liveries can be obtained through theft or even from a servant's quarters.
- Guard uniforms must be taken forcibly.

The poor lighting within the palace does not improve the quality of a disguise, but at night it makes recognition one grade harder.

Climbing the walls

If the characters wish to climb the outer wall of the palace to reach the balcony of King Myur's apartments they'll have to go through the great hall to the entrance of the hanging gardens. This leads them to a large terrace, twenty metres long and ten metres wide. Potted plants abound and small channels from the walls of the palace lead along the terrace floor that pool water into small fountains and fish ponds. The sound of running water joins the ever present bird song coming from dozens of small cages, well hidden in the branches of many potted trees. To the right, stairs lead to smaller terraces built into the cliff below and similarly decorated and designed to offer both pleasure and seclusion to those who would think, meditate or consort with lovers.

Guards do not enter the gardens. It is both unnecessary, as an intruder would have to climb more than a hundred metres to reach the lowest of the terraces or already be in the palace, and it would defeat the gardens' purpose of being a place of seclusion. While the characters need not worry about the guards while climbing, there are still people frequenting the gardens.

Climbing the wall during the night (it should be obvious to characters that doing so during the day, unless they have magical means of obfuscating themselves, is a certain way to end up back in the dungeons) is a Hard Athletics task that can be increased to Formidable if it raining or the characters do not have any climbing equipment (or to Herculean if both conditions apply). A separate roll is needed for every instance of movement. There are 14 metres between the garden and the balcony (so if the character's movement is downgraded to 3 he would need 5 successful rolls to make the climb).

If the characters have dark clothing or any magical means to blend in with the black surface of the wall no roll to stay unnoticed is required unless the Climb roll was a failure.

Diversions

Diversions are probably the easiest way to bypass the guards on the way up, but it also means that everybody in the palace is especially attentive to any out-of-the ordinary happenings unless they are presently involved with the diversion. The best diversions are those that are triggered when the characters are close to the king, while sending the guards and the servants to the lower floors (or outside the palace altogether).

Suggested distraction are:

- Sending Mencios on a killing rampage through the palace.
- Starting a fire.
- Pleading with the members of the clergy for a timely miracle (this requires pre-preparation at the temple of the Founding Four).
- Allying with Dagmar Shield-Biter and his Eastvalers and using their help in the palace.

While distractions are a two-edged blade, they do ensure that a significant portion of potential enemies are busy elsewhere when the characters make their move.

Magic

As previously noted, characters can obtain limited access to magic and miracles which, if timed properly, be of tremendous help in completing the mission. Simple folk magic spells like Darkness or Mimic can be of great use in diverting the attention of palace inhabitants away from the characters or, like Fanaticism, in ensuring that the guards persist in dealing with more violent distractions. Miracles can go even further than that; whether it is a Cloud Call to summon fog in order to hide the climbers on their way to the king's chambers, or Growth to magically age the potted trees in order to climb them to the king's balcony. Practically any spell available can be used creatively to help the characters in reaching their goal. Games Masters should note that the more overtly supernatural the effect, the more suspicious opponents become. So while using Darkness in one crucial spot might go unchecked, using Extinguish repetitiously to put out all the lamps in one corridor provokes cries and superstitious spitting at best, and careful investigation at worst.

Forbidden Knowledge

Getting into Gul-Azar's chambers skill and cunning. The main doors to his apartments are guarded at all times. Nothing short of a palace-wide diversion makes the guardleave his post. A good servant disguise might trick him into letting one or two characters in for a very short time. Killing the guard solves the problem but eventually raises the alarm once the other guards move past his post. Using deceit or magic to lure him somewhere quiet, disposing of him quietly and replacing him with one of the characters solves the problem, but it is risky as it can turn out to be louder than intended and attract other guards. Any kind of deceit in normal circumstances require a Hard Deceit versus Insight roll which can be further modified by circumstances such as diversions. Characters can also go out of the window of one of the offices or sleeping rooms then work their way along the wall to Gul-Azar's quarters.

Once the characters are inside, depending of the time of day, Gul-Azar may or may not be in his chambers. If he is in, there are several things he can be doing: he can sleep (if it's night), hold an audience in the antechamber, read in his solar or even take a bath. Games Masters should decide what would be an exciting choice and tailor accordingly

If Gul-Azar is away from his rooms the characters can search his suite and try to find important information about their opponent. If they manage to find the door into the solar, which requires a Hard Perception roll to spot, they must make a Hard Mechanisms roll to gain access. The solar is at all times protected by a simple alarm spell, causeing Gul-Azar to return with two of his guards at his heels within 1d12 minutes. He is not that concerned with simple burglary, but he fears the king going through his journal. Unless any of the characters have some means of perceiving magic, there is no way of knowing an alarm spell is in place.

Searching the room reveals any number of luxury goods, clothes, jewellery, works of art and money. No precise account is given, as this much wealth is more than the characters have ever seen. It should be clear that looting is out of the question as most of the wealth is in things too large to pilfer. What money there is, amounts to about 500 Founders. This is petty cash: he can, after all, claim much more from the treasury.

Jewellery is another matter. There are rings and gems easily worth 5,000 Founders but anyone with the Commerce skill understands that such jewels, even cut, are not easily sold on the black market.

The solar itself holds a large desk, some shelves with books and a small alchemist's laboratory. There are books on a number of alchemical subjects including poisons and salves, and treaties on various subjects such as acids, incendiaries and truth serums. The desk has two locked drawers requiring a Standard Lockpicking roll to open. Inside, there are official seals of the kingdom and numerous letters and drafts for future edicts. This is standard fare and nothing really interesting can be gleaned from them; but they could be used cleverly to forge a document allowing the characters to trick their way past the upper level guards, if time permits.

Searching the solar for hidden things require a successful Hard Perception roll. With success the characters find a secret compartment within the south wall. The hiding place is booby trapped with acid. The trap requires a Standard Perception roll to see, a Hard Mechanisms roll to deactivate and a Standard Lockpicking roll to unlock the panel.

The trap holds a concentrated acid solution and sprays at face-height, intending to strike the eyes of the victim. Allow a potential victim an Evade roll to mitigate the spray. If failed, an Endurance roll is needed: a fumble indicates permanent blindness; a failure results in full damage (see MYTHRAS, page 68) and a success in half damage. On a critical the spray misses the face. Damage sustained results in temporary blindness (unless the roll was fumbled) for 1d10 minutes.

Inside are letters confirming Gul-Azar's involvement with the barbarians and Jedakiah, from arranging for smuggling of high quality weapons to coordinating the troop movements so the raids can go more smoothly. Also inside is his personal journal which requires a Hard Literacy roll and at least half an hour to decipher (see the handouts on pages 84 to 85).

After either reading the journal or interrogating Gul-Azar, the characters become aware that while the chief advisor is the traitor the princess said he was, he is nowhere near the biggest threat to the kingdom. They can move to the king's chamber for the final confrontation.

SOMETHING ROTTEN AT THE HEART OF EVERY KINGDOM

The royal apartments on the top floor of the palace have guards at all time. There are only three guards but their express orders are never to leave their post unless Gul-Azar

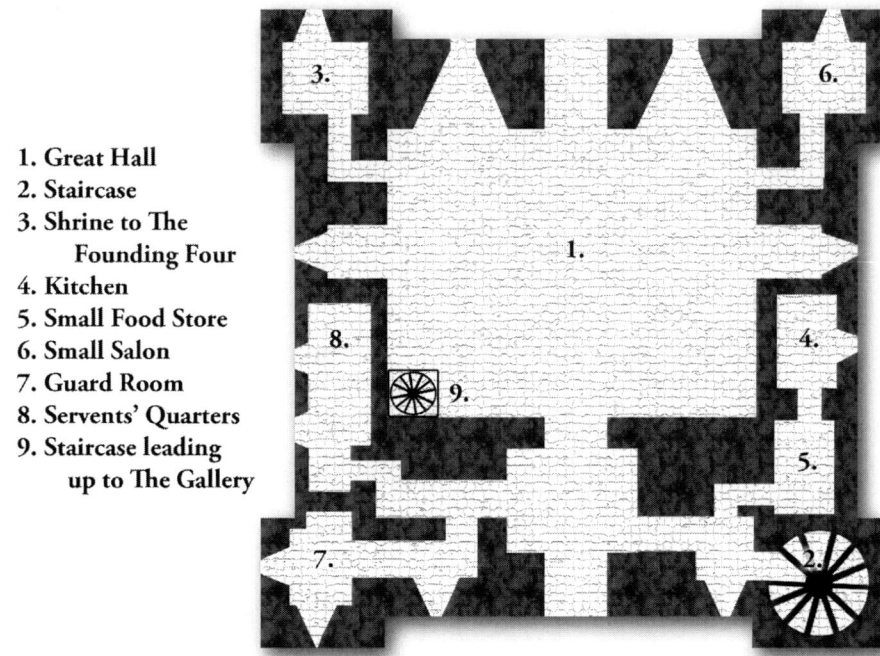

1. Great Hall
2. Staircase
3. Shrine to The Founding Four
4. Kitchen
5. Small Food Store
6. Small Salon
7. Guard Room
8. Servents' Quarters
9. Staircase leading up to The Gallery

PALACE GROUND FLOOR

Book of Quests — Scenario 3: Shadows Behind the Throne

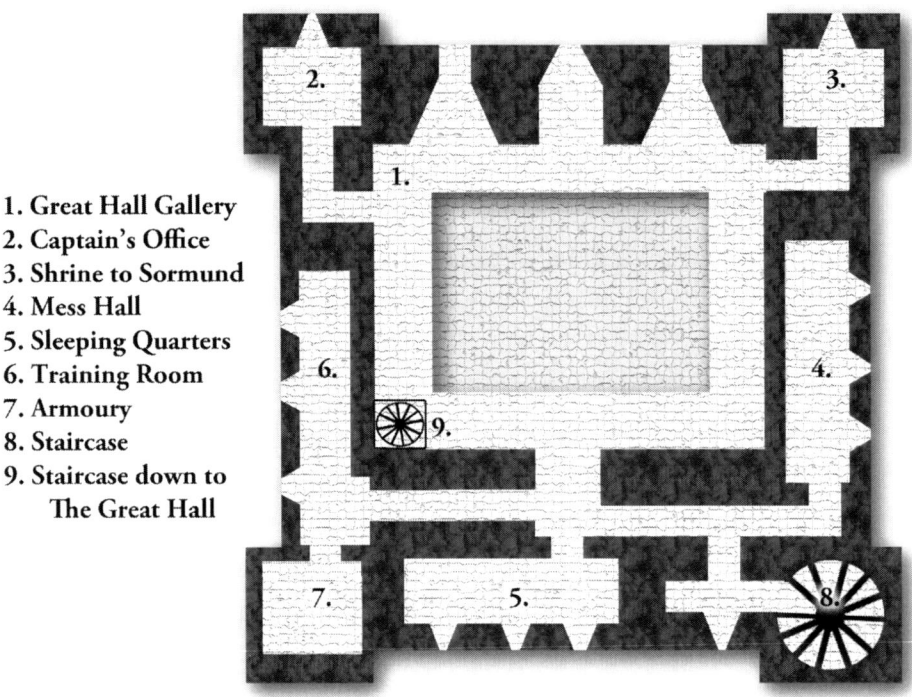

1. Great Hall Gallery
2. Captain's Office
3. Shrine to Sormund
4. Mess Hall
5. Sleeping Quarters
6. Training Room
7. Armoury
8. Staircase
9. Staircase down to The Great Hall

PALACE GUARD FLOOR

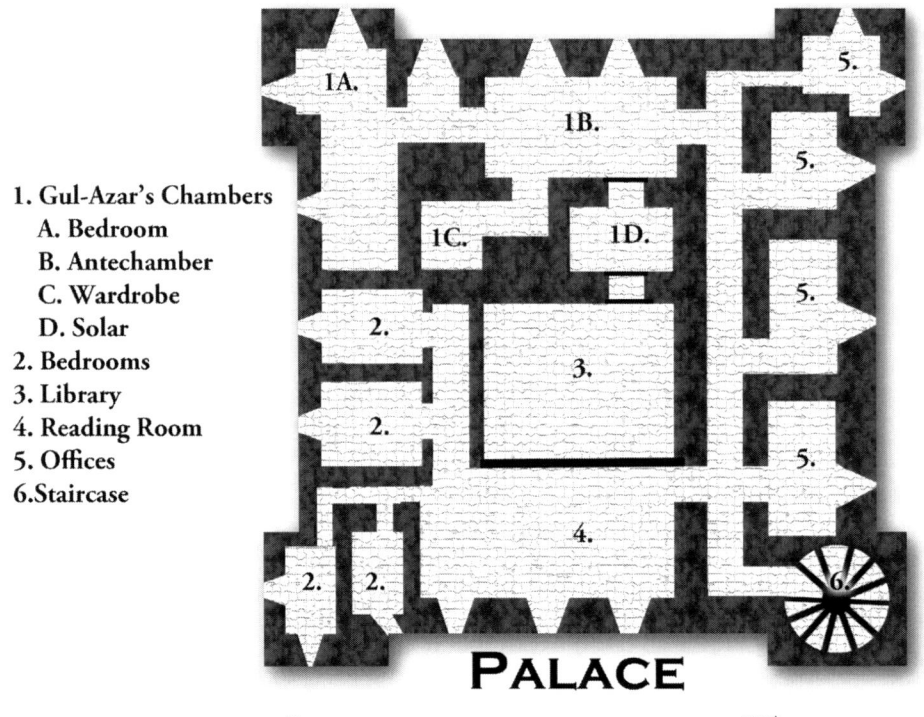

1. Gul-Azar's Chambers
   A. Bedroom
   B. Antechamber
   C. Wardrobe
   D. Solar
2. Bedrooms
3. Library
4. Reading Room
5. Offices
6. Staircase

PALACE ADMINISTRATION FLOOR

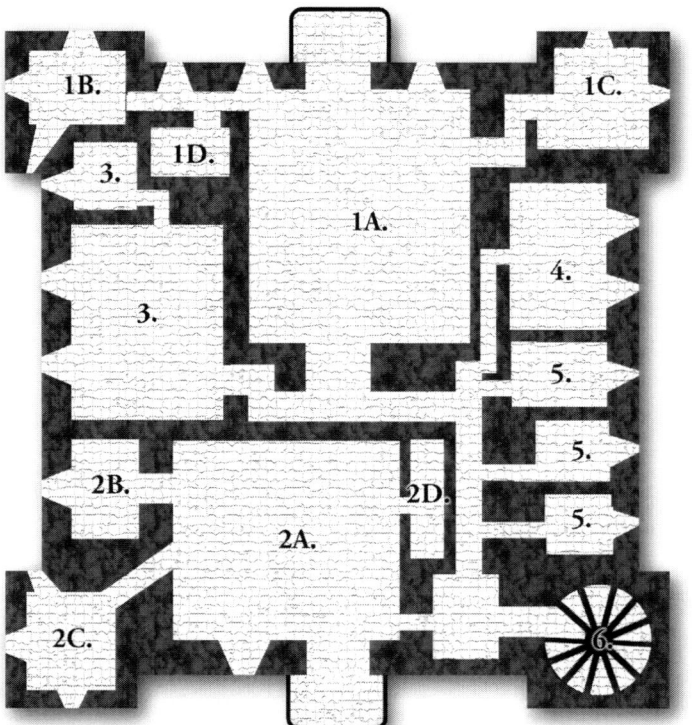

1. King's Quarters
   A. Receiving Room
   B. Solar
   C. Bedchamber
   D. Wardrobe
2. Princess's Quarters
   A. Receiving Room
   B. Bedchamber
   C. Solar
   D. Wardrobe
3. & 4. Additional Appartments
5. Manservant Quarters
6. Staircase

ROYAL APARTMENTS

himself tells them otherwise. No amount of diversion takes them off this floor.

How the characters deal with them and with Myur/Chandanar depends on their previous actions. The circumstances should differ if there was an attack on the palace, if the characters released Mencios to wreak havoc; if they managed to sneak past all of the guards quietly, or if they used any other way to reach the top. For this reason, it is left to the Games Masters to decide where exactly the king is when the characters reach the royal apartments.

Chandanar has almost fully possessed the king. Myur's personality has been subsumed by that of Chandanar the Mad, and this increasing possession is behind the increasingly cruel and vicious rule Myur has imposed on Cylder.

Gul-Azar is powerless to control the malign spirit of the old ruler and, in truth, he fears it. In return for his life (if it is threatened), Gul-Azar can reveal the extent of the possession; when it comes to breaking it though, he is relatively powerless. While Myur wears the crown, Chandanar works through Myur's body - the crown must be seized and taken into safe-keeping, or destroyed. Destroying it would release Chandanar's soul (which can be treated as an Intensity 10 Undeath Spirit (MYTHRAS, page 153), sending it to hell, but this is beyond the competence of the characters.

The Order of Truth and the High Priest at the temple of the Four are the only ones who can assemble the right knowledge and resources to unmake the crown. An easier alternative is simply to entomb it in the temple's crypt or in a secret location known only to the Order of Truth.

If the characters try to take the crown from Myur's head, Chandanar retaliates. Although an insane Undeath spirit he can cast, through Myur, Wrack (Body), Tap (CON), and Transmogrify (Flesh) with Invocation 90% and Shaping 70%. Myur/Chandanar casts these spells with abandon, intending to warp the shape of potential foes, sap their lifeforce and twist their bodies into hideous mutations. If Gul-Azar interferes, he is targeted too. Chandanar despises the would-be sorcerer and cares nothing for Jedakiah's paltry acolytes.

Attacks against the king, if witnessed by the palace guards, are dealt with through extreme force. Although the king has changed, and all in the palace know this, the guards are still loyal to the throne and will not see their ruler harmed. Chandanar cares little for any human life though, and guards may also be targeted by the spirit's sorcery. This may have the effect of turning the guards against King Myur or causing them to flee.

Either way, separating Myur from the crown is the only way to break Chandanar's influence. Under Chandanar's possession the king does not sleep and he never removes the crown: force is the only way to set the king free.

This means a fight - but one that aims to take the crown (a case of Choose Location - Head, Pulled Blows, Grip effects and other, non-lethal manoeuvres) without injuring the king himself. The king can be knocked unconscious, grappled, incapacitated and so forth, but while capable to defending himself, Chandanar uses his magic to assault those who would return him to limbo.

If the crown is successfully seized, Myur lapses into a coma lasting for several weeks. In this time her requires the constant attention of the Priests of Aliya and Xalgith to help him recover from the immense mental and spirtual battering he has taken. Princess Alynoor should be sent-for and she assumes the throne while her brother recuperates. In reality, she continues to rule even when he does; King Myur is left a shell of a man, unable and unwilling to come to terms with what he did to Mencios, Athanax and many others while under Chandanar's spell. Princess Alynoor, assisted directly by the Order of Truth as her council, controls The Vale.

Gul-Azar will, of course, attempt to stop the characters from exposing his schemes. He commands the Chaos Mother cultists in Cylder and, if allowed to escape, or capture the characters, he is easily able to cover his tracks - as long as the characters are silenced. He cannot control Chandanar and, if possible, he plays the role of the innocent, claiming the spirit possessed him, too, driving him to cover the king's increasing evil. Gul-Azar wants to retain power at all costs: if he fails, Jedakiah will take a long, slow revenge.

If Gul-Azar is captured, he refuses to divulge his secrets and true nature - although his letters and journal reveal all. After questioning by the Order of Truth, Gul-Azar is executed in the mechanism used to execute poor Duke Athanax - although this is done secretly. Princess Alynoor approves this final use of the machine and then commands it be destroyed.

Conclusions

Succeeding in saving King Myur is a major blow to Jedakiah's schemes. It breaks his power in Cylder and exposes one of his key apostles. It leads to a fuller understanding of the sorcerer's power, his location, and wider plans. All these, when analysed by Alynoor, Lord Drystan and other ranking Order of Truth members, lead to the conclusion that Jedakiah must be stopped at all costs - a good lead into the scenarios Raid on Yagelan's Bluff and Reckoning at Distaff Peak.

For their help the characters are rewarded handsomely: 1,000 Gold Royals to be divided equally and they are offered membership of the Order of Truth (and roles in defeating Jedakiah once and for all). They are, however, warned never to reveal what they have seen or experienced. If they do, the consequences would be... unfortunate. The gold Alynoor offers them should be enough to buy their co-operation.

Lord Athanax is posthumously pardoned and a statue of his likeness commissioned to stand in the Plaza of Kings, alongside that of Sayalis the Bright. Mencios, if he survives, begs for his own death: the Order of Truth grants it, providing merciful release. As an alternative, the monstrous form of Mencios could be used as a supporting Non-Player Character assisting the characters as the fight is taken to Jedakiah. Mencios need not die. If he does, a statue of his (true) likeness is also commissioned.

Mistaken Identity

Despite what the princess told them, and contrary to all the information they got in the meantime, Gul-Azar is not actually an accomplished sorcerer, nor is he controlling the king with the Jade Sceptre. He is an initiate of the Chaos Mother cult and hass yet to be revealed any more than petty sorcerous knowledge. The Jade Sceptre he received is a purely ceremonial ornament identifying him as the highest ranking cultist in Cylder. The cultists obey Gul-Azar because he outranks them and Chandanar is, at least at first, respectful of his former patron – the Chaos Mother. Gul-Azar likes to carry the Sceptre around with him because it is a sign of his secret compact with Jedakiah. It's a sign of his future success.

NON-PLAYER CHARACTERS

ASSASSINS

The assassins Gul-Azar has sent after the princess are not professionals. They are, however, absolutely loyal to Gul-Azar as part of the Chaos Mother's cult in Cylder. On the short notice that he had, the advisor needed much more reliable men than professional assassins. They are still competent fighters coming from a military background, and the pus that oozes from their tattoos, once ingested, brings a chaotic change in 1d3 turns and lasts for 2d6 minutes. The chaotic change is randomly rolled on the Chaos Feature table on page 275 of MYTHRAS.

Attributes		1d20	Location	AP/HP
Action Points: 2		1–3	Right Leg	2/7
Damage Modifier: +1d2		4–6	Left Leg	2/7
Magic Points: 10		7–9	Abdomen	2/8
Movement: 6 metres		10-12	Chest	2/9
Initiative Bonus: 7		13–15	Right Arm	2/6
Armour: Gambeson		16–18	Left Arm	2/6
Abilities: None		19–20	Head	2/7

Magic: None

Skills: *Athletics 59%, Brawn 62%, Devotion (Chaos Mother) 39%, Endurance 62%, Evade 56%, Locale 66%, Perception 64%, Survival 67%, Unarmed 59%, Willpower 62%*

Passions: *Loyalty to Gul-Azar 75%, Ruthless 80%*
Combat Style: *Vale light infantry style (Spear, Shortsword, Shield) 69% (Formation Fighting); Crossbow Skirmishers (Light Crossbow, Dagger) 61% (Skirmishing)*

Weapon	Size/Force	Reach	Damage	AP/HP
Shortspear	M	L	1d8+1+1d2	4/5
Shortsword	M	S	1d6+1d2	6/8
Peltast Shield	L	S	1d4+1d2	4/12
Dagger	S	S	1d4+1+1d2	6/8
Light Crossbow	L	-	1d8	4/7

ROYAL GUARD

The Princess's Guard are the last remnants of the royal guards still loyal to the Vale king. They are recruited from the best cadets of the Vale army and further trained by Bandor, the captain of the guard himself. All of them are proficient in fighting both on foot and mounted, in close combat and ranged fighting. There are no better fighting men in the kingdom than the members of the Royal Guards.

Note to Games Masters: even though no separate statistics are presented for Bandor, Games Masters who find themselves with players wishing to enter a conflict with Alynoor's guards may increase all relevant combat skills by 25% for Bandor alone.

Attributes		1d20	Location	AP/HP
Action Points: 3		1–3	Right Leg	7/7
Damage Modifier: +1d4		4–6	Left Leg	7/7
Magic Points: 10		7–9	Abdomen	7/8
Movement: 6 metres		10-12	Chest	7/9
Initiative Bonus: 6		13–15	Right Arm	7/6
Armour: Chainmail/ Half-Helm		16–18	Left Arm	7/6
Abilities: None		19–20	Head	7/7

Magic: None

Skills: *Athletics 57%, Brawn 73%, Endurance 70%, Evade 66%, Locale 66%, Perception 70%, Survival 73%, Unarmed 69%, Willpower 77%*

Passions: *Loyalty to The Vale 90%, Loyalty to Monarchy 95%, Hate Chaos 80%*
Combat Style: *Vale men-at-arms infantry (Spear, Broadsword, Mace, Shield) 73% (Shield Wall); Vale Longbow skirmishers (Longbow, Dagger) 69% (Skirmishing); Vale mounted knights (Lance, Battle Axe, Shield) 75% (Mounted Combat)*

Weapon	Size/Force	Reach	Damage	AP/HP
Lance	H	VL	1d10+2+1d4	4/5
Broadsword	M	M	1d8+1d4	6/10
Kite Shield	H	S	1d4+1d4	4/15
Dagger	S	S	1d4+1+1d4	6/8
Sabre	M	M	1d8+1d4	6/8
Mace	M	S	1d8+1d4	6/6
Longbow	H	-	1d8+1d4	4/7

KARDESH WEATHERVANE

Kardesh is the proprietor of the Theatre of Shadows and a superb information broker, though this is not public knowledge. He can be found in his booth of the Theatre's common room. He is tall, thin and bald. Around forty years old, Kardesh is handsome and tanned. He has a piercing look and always seems to evaluate his surroundings or anyone he talks to at the moment. He is of Long Riding stock. Reputedly, he was a raider before a war with the Vale made him a prisoner.

No one knows for sure how he came to be in either of his present roles but all suspect a powerful patron was behind it. Weathervane, though he does not like to be called that, is pleasant and mannered with perfect accent that belies his barbarian origin.

He deals in information and his preferred payment are secrets. If he cannot have them, the price rises exponentially and even small pieces of information cost dearly. Weathervane's minimum price is 50 Founders for small or relatively unimportant information. After that the price rises in increments of 50 or 100 Founders depending on the perceived usefulness of information, and can end in the thousands of Founders range.

Attributes	1d20	Location	AP/HP
Action Points: 2	1–3	Right Leg	0/6
Damage Modifier: 0	4–6	Left Leg	0/6
Magic Points: 13	7–9	Abdomen	1/7
Movement: 6 metres	10-12	Chest	1/8
Initiative Bonus: 12	13–15	Right Arm	0/5
Armour: Leather Jerkin	16–18	Left Arm	0/5
Abilities: None	19–20	Head	0/6

Magic: None

Skills: Athletics 65%, Brawn 43%, Deceit 77%, Endurance 54%, Evade 72%, Influence 79%, Insight 81%, Locale 87%, Perception 79%, Survival 53%, Unarmed 69%, Willpower 71%, Disguise 67%, Sleight 66%, Streetwise 80%

Passions: *Love Secrets 90%, Love Money 80%*
Combat Style: *Dirty Rotten Scoundrel (Club, Chain, Knife) 60% (Hidden Weapons)*

Weapon	Size/Force	Reach	Damage	AP/HP
Club	M	S	1d6	4/4
Chain	M	M	1d4	8/6
Dagger	S	S	1d4+1	6/8

GUL-AZAR'S ROYAL GUARD

Members of the royal guard were once the cream of the Vale army, but that is no longer true. As Gul-Azar placed his own men in the guard, it became a band of well organised thugs. Like Gul-Azar, they are initiated to the cult of the Chaos Mother but they are lay members of the cult with no magical knowledge whatsoever.

Attributes	1d20	Location	AP/HP
Action Points: 2	1–3	Right Leg	5/7
Damage Modifier: +1d4	4–6	Left Leg	5/7
Magic Points: 11	7–9	Abdomen	4/8
Movement: 6 metres	10-12	Chest	4/9
Initiative Bonus: 11	13–15	Right Arm	4/6
Armour: Lamellar and plate	16–18	Left Arm	4/6
Abilities: None	19–20	Head	5/7

Magic: None

Skills: Athletics 55%, Brawn 53%, Devotion (Chaos Mother) 46%, Endurance 62%, Evade 61%, Locale 65%, Perception 69%, Survival 54%, Unarmed 53%, Willpower 77%

Passions: *Loyalty to Gul-Azar 75%, Ruthless 80%*
Combat Style: *Street Scum (Club, Dagger) 53% (Hidden Weapons); Glorified Soldier (Spear, Shortsword, Shield) 64%*

Weapon	Size/Force	Reach	Damage	AP/HP
Shortspear	M	L	1d8+1+1d4	4/5
Broadsword	M	M	1d8+1d4	6/10
Hoplite Shield	H	S	1d4+1d4	6/15
Dagger	S	S	1d4+1+1d4	6/8
Club	M	S	1d6	4/4

General Mencios

General Mencios was once the best soldier in the kingdom. His military victories made him a popular figure among the common people. Once he was tall and muscular with long blond hair and green eyes. There were many women who would have liked to share his bed, but fate decreed that Alynoor was smitten by the general. She declared her love to him but Mencios, although a noble, declined her courtship as she was far above his station. He never took a lover amongst the nobles of the Vale, which only fanned the torch the princess held for him. But the days of the great general have passed.

Chandanar destroyed everything Mencios once was. Now, the general is a nightmare creature that no one in the Vale would believe could exist, though similar abominations appear in Old Empire legends used to scare children. Mencios is slowly sinking into madness, wishing only death for himself and the king.

If persuaded to fight, Mencios has several benefits. First he exudes miasma in a range of one metre around himself that causes violent vomiting. He oozes a dark, thick liquid that is mildly acidic in nature but is a strong adhesive. In a fight, Mencios tries to shoot ooze at his opponents first, favouring choose location - head. Aside from the small damage, the ooze provokes resistance rolls and one grade penalty depending on the location hit:

Arm movement is impeded unless a successful Brawn skill roll is made. Both Brawn roll and any further action using that arm if the Brawn roll was failed are penalised by one difficulty grade.

Similarly, leg movement is impeded unless a successful Athletics or Evade skill roll is made (whichever is higher). Both Athletic/Evade roll and any further action using that arm if the roll failed are penalised by one difficulty grade. Further to this, the character's movement is reduced by the damage value (unmodified by armour) rolled by Mencios.

If a head location is struck, the victim is considered blinded and cannot breathe unless a successful Brawn roll is made. This roll is modified, as are all resistance rolls made to clear ooze, by one grade difficulty.

After this initial attack Mencios tries to trip the target, bind the victim with his tail if he has room and finish off with either tusk or talon; preferring Disarm, Entangle, Stun Location and Impale special effects.

Characteristics	Attributes		1d20	Location	AP/HP
STR: 16	Action Points	3	1–2	Right Leg	2/7
CON: 11	Damage Modifier	+1d6	3–4	Left Leg	2/7
SIZ: 22	Magic Points	12	5–7	Abdomen	2/8
DEX: 10	Movement	8m	9-11	Chest	2/9
INT: 15	Initiative Bonus	13	12–13	Right Arm	2/6
POW: 12	Armour	Thick Skin	14–15	Left Arm	2/6
CHA: 5	Abilities	Chaos Tainted, Miasma, Ooze	16	Rear Arm	2/6
			17-18	Tail	2/7
	Magic	None	19	Dead Arms	1/0
			20	Head	2/7

Skills: *Athletics 49%, Brawn 82%, Endurance 72%, Evade 16%, Locale 66%, Perception 54%, Survival 77%, Unarmed 79%, Willpower 72%*

Passions: *Love (Alynoor) 37%, Loyalty (Family) 67%, Hate (King Myur) 112%*

Combat Style: *Frenzied Abomination (Tail, Tusk, Ooze) 91%*

Weapon	Size/Force	Reach	Damage	AP/HP
Tail	L	VL	1d6+1+1d6	As for Tail
Tusks	M	T	1d4+1d6	As for Head
Ooze (ranged)	S	-	1d3	None

GUL-AZAR

Gul-Azar was born in the Forest of Sorrows as an only child to a powerful shaman. To his great dismay, it was soon clear that he possessed no natural talent for stepping over the boundary to travel the spirit world.

He eventually apprenticed himself to an alchemist from the East Vale, hunting for rare herbs. This was the first time Gul-Azar met a man who didn't obey the spirits and plied a trade that could be learned by anyone and did things he thought only magic can do. He apprenticed himself to the man and learned much from him, even following him to the Vale.

But if he thought the Vale would be the fulfilment of his dreams he was bound for disappointment. No one treated him with the respect he thought he deserved as a learned man. Superstitious folk called him a witch, those with less fear a filthy barbarian. After several beatings, escaping from a lynch mob in a nick of time, he decided to return home. But home was no more.

He returned to his village to find only ashes; Vale soldiers' revenge for an unknown slight. Gul-Azar was in for a rude awakening. He shunned his people because he was not good enough to serve them as he liked. He abandoned them and went to their enemies. The shame was too much. He decided to avenge his clan by destroying their enemies completely and at any cost.

Gul-Azar is a capable alchemist without any scruples. He hates Vale folk from the bottom of his soul, and he doesn't mind selling that soul to achieve his goals, since the spirits of his ancestors never paid him heed. This is the reason he apprenticed himself to Jedakiah, a decision that proved very useful once his master started to disclose sorcerous knowledge to Gul-Azar.

If he must fight he uses his extensive knowledge of poisons to help him even the odds as he is no fighter. All his blowgun darts and steel knives are coated with venom. He also uses two glass daggers with concentrated acid. On a successful hit they shatter dealing no ordinary damage, but splashing the acid on the location. They become useless after a successful hit. When in close combat he prefers special effects that kill the enemy as quickly as possible.

Characteristics	Attributes	1d20	Location	AP/HP
STR: 9	Action Points	3	1–3	Right Leg	0/6
CON: 15	Damage Modifier	0	4–6	Left Leg	0/6
SIZ: 15	Magic Points	11	7–9	Abdomen	0/7
DEX: 10	Movement	6m	10–12	Chest	0/8
INT: 17	Initiative Bonus	14	13–15	Right Arm	0/5
POW: 11	Armour	None	16–18	Left Arm	0/5
CHA: 16	Abilities	None	19–20	Head	0/6
	Magic	None			

Skills: *Athletics 49%, Brawn 82%, Endurance 72%, Evade 16%, Locale 66%, Lore (Alchemy) 80%, Perception 54%, Survival 77%, Unarmed 79%, Willpower 72%*

Passions: *Love (Clan) 81%, Loyalty to Jedakiah 85%, Hatred (The Vale) 78%, Hatred (Chandanar) 98%,*

Magic

Sorcery (The Entropic Revelations): Invoke 45%, Shaping 40%

Damage Resistance, Mystic (Sight), Neutralise Magic, Palsy

Combat Style: *Sorrowful Forest Hunter (Dart, Knife, Club) 49%*

Weapon	Size/Force	Reach	Damage	AP/HP
Dagger	S	S	1d4+1	6/8
Club	M	S	1d6	4/4
Dart	S		1d2	N/A

CHANDANAR/KING MYUR

From the moment he put the crown on his head, King Myur has suffered the gradual destruction of his soul by the ancestral spirit of Chandanar, who covertly possess his body as he did with so many others in ages past.

Chandanar has been trapped in the crown for countless years. In that time, he has been driven completely mad from the combination of loneliness and imprisonment. Now, free once again, his desire to taste everything is both immediate and unquenchable. He craves new experiences, new sensations, even new pains. Once he was first drawn out of the crown, the sensations of having a body, of breathing and eating and drinking were enough. But as time passed he needed more.

First he turned to what he remembered of his old life, worshipping Chaos Mother, torturing his "lovers". But even that is becoming old and stale, and few things exist that he hasn't already tried. The destructive nature of his behaviour cannot last long without eclipsing the whole kingdom.

Chandanar is slowly wresting control away from Gul-Azar, taking over the guards who see a more immediate connection between the king and the Chaos Mother than Gul-Azar has. Once he has the mutation tank fully operational he intends to recreate his old rule. While he is not aware how close to civil war things are, he is certain that his old tyrannical methods of brutal control are sufficient to deal with the most dangerous elements and cowing the rest into submission.

In a fight, Chandanar uses his excellent fighting skills, honed during Old Empire time and over the ages as he possessed one barbarian king after another. Chandanar fights to kill. In one on one combat he goes in quickly, trips or grabs the opponent and finishes him with choose location or impale. If fighting numerous opponents he dances around them using outmanoeuvre and trip, stun location and similar special effects to even the odds. If genuinely threatened, he uses what magic his memory still holds, as a last resort. The Emperors of the Old Empire were accomplished sorcerers in their own right, but the wraith can remember precious few sorcery spells now. Further to this, as King Myur's body has not been conditioned by long study and practice in controlling such energies, any spell Chandanar casts causes him damage to a random hit location equal to the number of magic points he uses to cast the spell, irrespective of any armour he wears.

Characteristics	Attributes		1d20	Location	AP/HP
STR: 14	Action Points	3	1–3	Right Leg	0/6
CON: 13	Damage Modifier	0	4–6	Left Leg	0/6
SIZ: 11	Magic Points	16	7–9	Abdomen	0/7
DEX: 12	Movement	6m	10–12	Chest	0/8
INT: 13	Initiative Bonus	13	13–15	Right Arm	0/5
POW: 16	Armour	None	16–18	Left Arm	0/5
CHA: 9	Abilities	None	19–20	Head	0/6
	Magic	None			

Skills: *Athletics 69%, Brawn 63%, Endurance 52%, Evade 66%, Locale 96%, Perception 64%, Survival 57%, Unarmed 79%, Willpower 72%, Folk Magic 79%*

Passions: *Love (Freedom) 74%, Hate (The Living) 69%, Self Preservation 101%*.

Magic

Sorcery (Chaos Knowledge): Invoke 90%, Shaping 80%

Tap (CON), Transmogrify (Flesh), Wrack (Souls)

Combat Style: *Imperial knight (Rapier, Main Gauche, Buckler) 120%*

Weapon	Size/Force	Reach	Damage	AP/HP
Rapier	M	L	1d8	5/8
Main Gauche	S	S	1d4	6/10
Buckler	M	S	1d3	6/9

Player Handouts

1. Letter from Jedakiah to Gul-Azar

Greetings, Gul-Azar,

Micken arrived with all the goods you have sent me. However, the weapons were not as I expected. I fear I will have to arrange for them myself. I am not pleased. I want you to find me a potential partner in Westport for this business, one who would benefit from our means. I mean to take the weapons from my old country.

Let us return to Micken. Are you certain that he will manage to coordinate the military stationed along the borders with our raids into North and Black Vale? He is truly as ugly as you have described him, but I doubt the intellect you've ascribed to him. I hope you understand that his failure is unacceptable? The expeditionary force must come to Gartharis within six months or a year as planned. You should be in a position to time it well once I send you news of the burial mound. This is crucial in our effort, and in turn to your future progress in the art.

I await news of the king's plans.

J

2. Second Letter from Jedakiah to Gul-Azar

Greetings, Gul-Azar,

The invasion is approaching. We are only waiting for the emperor to claim the king fully. You are quite right about Chandanar's spirit, but he is needed. No hostile actions are to be taken against him. If he returns to the crown or is destroyed, I'll hold you
personally responsible. You understand, I am sure.
Once the invasion commences there will be no turning back and you are free to do with it as you like. I do understand you're concerned for your well being and for that reason I enclose a further spell to advance your knowledge. With it you can make it difficult for any man to act against you. It will be useful for some other things as well, but find those out on your own. It will be a good test.

Soon we will both have what we want. You your vengeance, me my kingdom and my queen.

Jedakiah, Lord of Gartharis

3. Gul-Azar's Journal

12th Flaying, 143rd Year of Return

Finally, everything is in motion. Everything I strived and worked for since my clan was killed is coming to fruition. My spies tell me that the war was won as agreed with Gartharis, and that the general has found the crown. My only fear is that some of those idiot soldiers will try it for measure.

3rd Falsegrass, 143rd Year of Return

The king has declared a feast in honour of Mencios and the return of the crown. After the feast he will be crowned in the Temple. I must admit I am burning with anticipation.

15th Falsegrass, 143rd Year of Return

I am detecting some differences in his behaviour. Some sense of confusion and something akin to contemplative drunkenness. Cautiously optimistic.

16th Falsegrass, 143rd Year of Return

I have had my first conversation with the spirit. It appears when the king sleeps. It has never heard of Vale. It wants a bath. What's that about?

30th Falsegrass, 143rd Year of Return

It is coming more and more often. Yesterday It took over control during dinner. It threw up saying It cannot stand strawberries. There might be some danger from differences in personalities between It and the king.

17th Flowering, 143rd Year of Return

I think I understand how the magic works. Seems like It is bound not to the crown but to the jewel. As Its grip on the king becomes firmer the jewel is losing colour. Where it was the colour of blood before now it is a washed out red.

1st Worming, 143rd Year of Return

I was right. We converse more often. It is drunk on freedom. I cannot imagine how long was It imprisoned. It is obeying my commands though, as It should.

14th Worming, 143rd Year of Return

The king, when he's in, complains about nightmares. He asked me for a sleeping potion. I was only too happy to oblige. Every time he is fast asleep It comes out. It is fascinating. The first spirit I have seen in my life, and It obeys me as if I was a shaman.

12th Sickle, 143rd Year of Return

Everything is going according to plan. New laws, new taxes. The thing from the crown proves to be all I was hoping for. More, even. The only thing It craves is fulfilment of Its base urges. How strange was the Old Empire. It seeks some machine from the ages past. It calls it a creation vat.

5th Redmonth, 143rd Year of Return

The creation vat has been completed, the thing tells me. It is overjoyed. It is in the torture chamber.

4th Falling, 143rd Year of Return

Some of the urges the thing has are difficult to restrain. It has made Mencios's sister watch everything It does. Calling her Its little witness. I anticipate problems when the general returns. It may be something I'll have to sort out.

22nd Falling, 143rd Year of Return

The Princess is showing an interest in me. Does she plot something or is it genuine feeling?

12th Frosting, 143rd Year of Return

The thing becomes even more detached from common sense. Now It has taken to sending guards in a black carriage to the city to bring It lovers. I must put a hold on It.

30th Dimming, 143rd Year of Return

The bitch killed herself. The fool! Worse, she seems to have left a message to her dear brother. We had to throw the general in the dungeon. I did not want this yet. The people love him.

14th Sunreturn, 144th Year of Return

I am horrified! I have seen what the creation vat is for. What it did to the general and to all Its "lovers"! He melds them together into the most horrifying forms! People in the city talk about a demon claiming victims from the streets. I am inclined to agree. I fear I will not be able to control It.

27th Biting, 144th Year of Return

What have I involved myself with? Yesterday It used some kind of a spell on me. It seemed as if my bones wanted to leave my body. I am still weak from the pain. The king's body broke with blisters at the same time. It is beyond my control. The jewel is almost crystal clear. I would destroy the crystal if I had the chance. But It would kill me - either by blade or by magic and most of the guards are Its now.

3rd Flaying, 144th Year of Return

The princess confronted me today. She thinks me a sorcerer who controls her brother. If only she knew the truth. I suggested she leave and sent Marcos after her but she managed to escape. No matter, Denkil will wait for her on the road. Lucky I sent both of them. I wish she was right, though. At the execution It only smiled at me when I tried to remind it of our goals. I wish I have never made the deal with the demon. The city will fall to the mad king and civil war will ensue. The barbarians will overrun us and no one will be there to stand up to them except for the mad wraith in Its crown. I fear this was the plan all along. At least my clan will be avenged, though not as I planned. The gods are fickle and the Chaos Mother most of all... Damn her!

Scenario 4: The Chaos Mother's Chalice

Overview

Jedakiah has learnt the whereabouts of an ancient Chaos Mother temple that holds a chalice of great power. He aims to retrieve the chalice from beneath tons of volcanic debris and use it in the ritual to create the Chaos Daughter.

The characters are tasked with stopping Jedakiah from getting hold of the Chaos Mother's Chalice. Clues from history send them in search of an ancient villa that holds the secret of how to find the temple.

When they finally reach the buried temple they realise that Jedakiah's mercenaries have already excavated the site and have been corrupted by the chalice's malign influence.

Non-Player Characters

- Kalathus: A scribe in the employ of Lord Drystan and a member of the Order of Truth. Both Kalathus and his Lord are loyal to the king and are aware of corruption within the royal court. They seek to thwart the sorcerer and ensure that the king's line continues.
- Lord Drystan: renowned for his intelligence and even-handedness. Loyal to the crown and The Realm, Kalathus the scribe is his trusted right-hand man.
- Karl Pig-Axe: A bandit who operates along the road from Westport to Cylder. He is wily and careful, but prepared to use extreme violence where necessary. He resides in an old villa - a location the characters need to visit.
- Fustilius Slump: A wizened old scholar and the only permanent member of the Guild of Cartographers in Norport. As far as Fustilius is concerned, there is nothing as beautiful as a well drafted map - he dotes and drools over them. Lord Drystan can provide necessary introductions.
- Hanno: A seasoned commander of a mercenary spear troop in Norport.
- Zakar and Mollonius: Two shadowy figures – agents of Jedakiah in the guise of scholars who lead a party of miners and mercenaries into the mountains in search of the Chaos Mother's Chalice.
- Thuk: a Black Vale Barbarian and devotee of the Chaos Mother, sent to Norport to en-sure that no

one follows Zakar and Mollonius northwards. He hates civilised people with a passion and is short on both patience and intelligence.

Key Points/Timeline

1. One of Kalathus's spies learns that Jedakiah's 'scholars' (Zakar and Mollonius) search for the Chaos Mother's Chalice
2. Zakar and Mollonius set off from Norport, heading into the Black Vale Mountains
3. Kalathus hires the characters to seek out the chalice
4. The characters search Duke Lucius's villa and uncover the mural, discovering how to find the buried Chaos Mother Temple
5. The characters travel to Norport and seek out Fustilius Slump, making use of his maps to pinpoint the location of the temple.
6. Zakar and Mollonius find the temple site and start digging. They are subsequently mutated.
7. The characters set off into Black Vale, encounter the miners and hear their story.
8. The characters descend into the ancient temple to try and locate the chalice. There they face a final showdown with the mutants.
9. Either Mollonius escapes with the chalice or the characters recover it.

Background and Introduction

The Sorcerer Plots...

Jedakiah has been questing for the Chaos Mother's Chalice for years. He knows it is essential for the ritual to create the Chaos Daughter (see Reckoning at Distaff Peak, beginning on page 192). Many years ago he instructed one of his servants, Manuun the Shaman, to locate it. Manuun was partially successful in piecing together the whispers and riddles of the dark spirits with whome he communed. However, it also became clear that Manuun's ramblings and visions needed to be clarified with a more scholarly approach.

Acting on the shaman's information, Jedakiah sent two trusted servants, sorcerers by the names of Zakar and Mollonius, to gain information from the Royal Records and Histories Library to pinpoint the temple's location, excavate the chalice and return with it. Jedakiah has even ensured that Mollonius has learnt a sorcery spell to help him find the temple.

The Order of Truth Reacts...

The main requirement for this scenario's opening is contact with a friend or patron. This could be somebody who they met during a previous adventure, or maybe one of the character's Allies or Contacts. Games Masters can determine their own plot introduction; however, for the rest of the scenario it is assumed that the friendly contact is Kalathus the Scribe. He is a member of the Order of Truth, and in the employ of Lord Drystan who is also loyal both to his king and The Realm. He has access to a series of agents, many of which are affiliated to the Order of Truth and range from servants to minor nobility. Lord Drystan, first encountered in Beneath the Black Water, can provide introductions to Kalathus if required.

A few weeks ago information was requested from the Royal Records and Histories Library in Cylder by two hitherto unknown scholars. Such requests are only allowed with the king's permission, but these two provided proof of the king's seal and royal signature. Fortunately, agents loyal to Kalathus were suspicious and investigated further. Both seal and signature turned out to be false. Kalathus feels that the corruption obviously runs deep but the incident has been thoroughly hushed up for fear of the crown looking weak.

Kalathus learnt that the two scholars requested information ostensibly on the location and whereabouts of an ancient temple. Through his studies Kalathus knows that this temple held the Chaos Mother's Chalice. It was buried under ash and pumice by the followers of Aliya.

The two scholars disappeared, only to turn up a week later in Norport heading north with a train of men and supplies. Have they learned the location of the temple? What happens if they recover the chalice?

The characters are tasked with investigating further. It is Kalathus's hope that he can help them find the ancient temple and retrieve the Chalice before the enemy. The reward is 4,000 founders if they recover the chalice. If pressed, he awards the party a maximum of 400 founders up front.

Furthermore, if they prove themselves to be loyal and honest, he recommends them to others for undertaking similar tasks. He may also single out one or more of the characters for introduction to the Order of Truth.

EVENTS AND LOCATIONS

THE SEARCH FOR HIDDEN KNOWLEDGE

The exact location of the Chaos Mother temple has been lost for hundreds of years. Through a scholar or through their own research, the party learns its history (*see page 12 The Mad Rule of King Chandanar*) and, critically, that there is a chance that the mosaic in the Lucius household can be used to determine the location of the temple.

OPTIONS FOR PLAY

This section is optional, being dependent on how the Games Master wishes to run the adventure. It is suggested that for parties consisting of gung-ho fighters, information can just be given to them by the person that is hiring them. However, for those who enjoy some detective work then this information search may be appropriate and part of any contract.

OPTION A: KALATHUS THE ALL-KNOWING SAGE

Kalathus is widely read and is one of the foremost historians in The Realm. He imparts the history of King Chandanar to the party and instructs them to go to Duke Lucius's Villa, although he is not certain exactly where the mosaic is within these ruins.

OPTION B: KALATHUS THE PEN-PUSHING SCRIBE

Kalathus's main task is keeping track of Lord Drystan's revenue. He spends his days checking this and counting that and has no time to delve into historical issues. Part of the contract is to search the historical background surrounding the Chaos Mother's Chalice.

It is well known that the Eastern Empire fell to corruption, and Kalathus can impart some of the history, albeit in a very vague way. It is also well known that Aliya's followers somehow destroyed a great Temple to the Chaos Mother by awakening a volcano. A successful Easy Lore (History) roll is required to know these facts.

The characters then have to use their own imagination and academic skills to uncover more, in particular, the exact whereabouts of a mosaic depicting the location of the temple.

Such information can be found in any number of information depositories but the one suggested here is the archive section in the Temple of the Founding Four at Cylder. If characters stress that they are searching for information regarding the history of the cult of Aliya then they need to make an Easy Bureaucracy, Standard Literacy or Hard Influence skill roll.

SETTING OFF

Whichever method is employed, the characters come to the conclusion that they need to visit Duke Lucius's Villa. If they still fail to work out where they need to go, then they may need to be prompted. This is dependent on the style of play and the types of characters involved.

The general location of the villa is easy to find, (for example, consulting historical maps that show ducal boundaries. These are present in any number of places, including the Temple of the Founding Four at Cylder). The *exact* location is not so easy to decipher on the poor quality maps that are available. The characters need to conduct a better search when they get near to the villa. Goodwool seems to be the closest settlement.

THE RUINS OF DUKE LUCIUS' VILLA

The dilapidated remains of Duke Lucius' fortified villa stand at the southern edge of West Wood, alongside a tributary to the River Southvale. It is best found by following the river road from Westport to Cylder, along which are various small farming settlements and occasional lightly-manned ramshackle forts facing towards the south.

Where the Southvale River is at its closest to West Wood, a tributary leads into it. Here squats the hamlet of Goodwool. It has little to offer and consists of just a few dwellings, a shrine to the Founding Four and the local inn, The Lamb and Plough, where food and lodging can be purchased.

Anyone scrutinising the inn's sign notes that the plough is embossed with the Earth and Plant Runes. A successful

Lore (History) skill test reveals that the combination of plough and the runes relate to Lucius' household. His family once ruled over this and other hamlets in the area.

The locals are not particularly keen to divulge information about the whereabouts of Lucius' villa. They are aware of the bandits residing there and are fearful of reprisals. However, if pressed, the landlord tells the party that the villa is easy to find by following the northern tributary leading upstream from Goodwool.

Note: If the party dawdles for longer than a day, then someone from Goodwool has the time to warn the bandits that they may be receiving company. In this case the bandits are classed as 'alerted' (see below).

THE BANDITS

Currently residing in the ruins of the Villa are a group of 14 bandits led by Karl Pig-Axe – a man local to the southern frontier who makes a living preying on the soft caravans and travellers that pass between Westport and Cylder. He kills when he has to but is not a sadist. He understands that his men must sometimes have their sport with victims but he has never been inclined to join in. Lean and smallish with greying hair, at first glance he does not represent a fearsome adversary. When pressed into combat his features set grim and he fights in a determined way.

Karl is painfully aware that his men are not of very high quality. Morale is low and infighting over scraps of treasure is common. Karl, when stirred into action, is not adverse to killing the worst offenders. He has the assistance of Mad Ester, a self-claimed spirit talker from the West Woods, and Smokefoot, a barbarian from the Moors. Ester is in love with Karl and often talks to the other bandits about his 'rugged charms'. Karl does not love her in return, but he is fond of her. Ester dresses in a fur cape and has many crude tattoos over her body; her red hair is wild and ungroomed. Karl bought Smokefoot as a slave and then freed him: Smokefoot is very loyal to Karl as a result. He wears his dark hair in a top knot, wrapped around a deer jaw. In combat, or when under stress, he tends to shout and swear a lot.

There are eleven other bandits in the group, all of them of poor quality.

Karl has contacts in Goodwool where he occasionally sends men to trade for food and other necessities. He never attacks local farmsteads or hamlets as he knows that this would be his downfall. There is a 500 Founder bounty for him, dead or alive, to be collected at Cylder or Westport.

If the villa is reconnoitred successfully (such as watching from a vantage point) then signs of life are clear; smoke from the fireplaces, occasional sounds of wood chopping; the comings and goings of bandits foraging for apples and firewood in the orchards.

When not alerted, the bandits spend most of their time eating and resting. Readying for another raid equates to an intense period of preparation, involving the repair of weapons and armour as well as the packing of traps and food for the journey. If the party has the villa under surveillance for a long period of time they hear this preparation. Unless the party is very weak - or intent on being non-violent - it is suggested that the bandits do not intend to raid for at least a further two weeks. Bandits do not leave the compound if they know they are being watched.

In the daytime most bandits gather in the main atrium of the villa (A) but on a bright day many rest in the garden (M) - see the map on page 95. At certain times, smaller groups gather in the yard of the villa compound, leave the compound to collect wood and apples, visit Goodwool or even disappear into the West Wood with the hope of catching game (25% chance a day for a group of 1d4+1 bandits to leave the compound per day). In the evening they gather to listen to one of Mad Ester's haunting chants and then sleep in the family hall (D). Karl Pig-Axe and Ester sleep in the master bedroom (H) and Smokefoot, being considered dangerous and insane, also has his own quarters in a family bedroom (G). For the initial contact, Games Masters should determine where the bandits are - an example is provided in the Bandit Awareness Tables. If alerted, Karl positions his men on watch at various points in the villa compound. He gives them strict instructions not to fight the enemy but to report back to him. A small group are lured into the villa and then assaulted from all sides.

THE VILLA'S SURROUNDS

See the Map opposite.

A path follows the tributary north. It is occasionally marked with way-stones but looks disused. A successful Standard Track roll detects occasional human traffic in the last couple of weeks. Roughly five kilometres from Goodwool, characters succeeding in a Standard Perception

Book of Quests ⚜ Scenario 4: The Chaos Mother's Chalice

THE VILLA'S SURROUNDS

THE VILLA COMPOUND

KEY
- River
- Drainage Ditch
- Pond
- Road/Path
- Field
- Forest/Wood

Notes on The Bandits

Games Masters should play the interaction between the characters and the bandits fluidly. A lot is dependent on what the characters do; a frontal daylight assault? A stealthy night attack? Picking off foragers? Or even dialogue? Karl and his men's state of mind are also important. Initially they are cautious until they know how strong the enemy is. If they consider the party to be weak then options include assault or the preparing of an ambush. Karl is not happy about giving up his base and his loot but he is no fool. If faced with a superior foe he runs.

A History of the Villa

The villa was in Lucius' family for centuries, only recently falling to ruin. The original Duke Lucius (the one who married the acolyte of Aliya) added the wall surrounding the compound as the empire neared the end of its long collapse. Throughout the period in which the Chaos Mother dominated, the inhabitants kept themselves to themselves, continuing worship to the 'Goddess-to-be' in secret. The centuries passed and, with the return of Aliya the family's fortune once again increased. Further work was undertaken on the estate over the next 100 years.

This period did not last, and after a few generations and a couple of hundred years, the great Lucius household waned. The last of Lucius' descendants left fifty years ago, selling the remaining herds and family valuables to pay the debtors.

Since then it has changed hands a number of times, being used by squatters, thieves and as a camp by local hunters. Karl Pig-Axe moved in three years ago.

---

roll or an Easy Lore (Agriculture) roll spot that some of the woodland interior has been recently felled.

To the east of the path are a series of fields and irrigation ditches that have been left untended for a few decades. The irrigation ditches have silted-up and are choked by reeds. A few dried-up fish ponds are also dotted along the water course.

The front of the villa is partially masked by a line of ancient chestnut trees and flanked by large orchards. Although the villa is not strictly hidden, its size and grandeur are guarded.

Note: if the bandits have not been warned, one lookout is posted at the corner of the southern orchard. If alerted two guards are at this point and a further two at the back of the villa (in the orchards to the west)

The untended orchards are delineated by weak fences designed to keep out sheep and other livestock.. If they are entered, characters see that some trees near to the villa have had scrub removed around their base and their apples have been harvested (dependent on the season).

The Villa Compound

The diagram on page 91 shows the villa in relation to other buildings within the compound. An old stone wall surrounds the villa; it has collapsed in places and varies from two to three metres in height. It takes an Easy Athletics roll to scramble over it.

There are three gateways leading into the compound. None of the gates have survived but the bandits have made makeshift barricades out of old beams from the ruined barns. These have been propped-up against each archway but are easy to squeeze past – they are there to slow attackers rather than stop them getting in.

Along the south side of the stockade are the shells of a series of old buildings that were once used for barns, stables and storage. Each is in very poor condition and none have surviving roofs. The old stable, which has a partial roof, is used to store wood. The rest lie dormant. A well stands in the centre of the compound; it has a relatively new rope and bucket attached to it. The herb garden along the eastern wall is now overgrown with weeds that reach over a man's height.

Note: In the daytime there is a 25% chance that some bandits (1–4) are in the yard, drawing water, chopping wood and so on.

The Villa

The villa is sixty metres by thirty six metres in size. It is a single storey building built in the style of the old empire – bricks covered by white plaster with bright red roof tiles. The floorplan is depicted on page 95.

Bandit Awareness

Not Alerted: Day time	Not Alerted: Night time
1 bandit posted at the corner of the southern orchard looking out along the track	11 bandits in (D)
4 bandits chopping wood within the compound yard	Karl Pig-axe and Ester in (H)
6 bandits, Karl, Ester and Smokefoot in either (A) or (M) if the weather is good	Smokefoot in (G)

Alerted: Day snd Night
Four bandits watching the front and back (two at each point) of the villa compound ready to retreat to l) if needs be.
Karl, Ester and two bandits waiting in a) the main atrium and watching from out of the b) cubicle windows.
Smokefoot and three bandits waiting in ambush in o) the spare room
The remaining two bandits alongside any that retreated waiting for an attack signal in l) the workshop

The villa is still recognisable as a grand old building. The walls around the garden and the outhouses are four metres high; those around the main house and atrium rise to six metres. The villa walls are still relatively intact. They can be scaled with a successful Athletics roll. The villa's walls are 40 centimetres thick, the inner walls being about 20 centimetres. All the inner walls have been plastered and then painted, although much of this has now faded or has chipped-off over time.

Windows are present throughout the building. All of them are two metres up, defended by corroded bronze bars and some still have shutters. The bars are not difficult to bend, provided the character has a decent Brawn skill (see Breaking on page 39 of MYTHRAS). Each set of window bars has 1d6+4 Hit Points and no Armour Points if being bent; or 4 Armour Points if struck with weapons or tools.

A series of small chimneys sprout from around the edge of the villa, but all are very small and only creatures of SIZ 3 or less could gain access to the rooms below.

The doors into the villa are barred from within making it impossible to pick the door open using Lockpicking. It is possible to break the doors open but this involves using Brawn and creating a lot of noise; due to their rickety nature the once gates possess 4 Armour Points and 20 Hit Points. A combined shoulder charge by two or three burly characters should bring them down in a matter of a few rounds, at the expense of warning the bandits inside.

A: MAIN ATRIUM.

A tall room, 6 metres in height, with a large opening in the centre of the roof directly over a pool set in the floor designed to catch the rain. At the far end, light filters through the remains of a stained glass window. This room is used extensively by the bandits for meetings, planning future attacks and general socialising. A series of makeshift seats, including an old divan and some upturned barrels, stand around its edge.

Note: In the daytime, there is a 50% chance that a large number of the bandits are milling around in this room. Basically, any bandits not present in other rooms are in here.

The atrium was built to impress. The floor is covered in chipped tiles arranged in geometric designs and a series of large flagstones surround the pool. Buckets and wooden bowls have been placed in here by the bandits to trap fresh water as the pool below is filthy with leaves and discarded detritus. Within the buckets are various kinds of cooking and eating utensils.

The stained glass window once depicted a hunting party.

B: CUBICLES.

The cubicles act as storage rooms, containing salted meats, cheeses, cheap wine in wineskins and barrels and various other household items.

C: ALCOVES.

These depict a series of family portraits ranging back to the original owners. A series of stone plinths stand at the intervals between the pictures but the ornaments and statues have long gone.

The southern alcove is piled with 36 bales of wool taken from a recent raid.

The archway to the northern alcove had been bricked up, a pile of plaster lying on the floor below it. Some of the bandits had discovered this doorway and were in the process of breaking into the room when Mad Ester fell into

a trance and then warned them against such folly. They swear they occasionally hear crying from the room.

The only image that has not been defiled or ruined in any way is that of Duke Lucius' wife. It is on the Northern wall of the north alcove. The picture is haunted by Lucius' child; a boy who was strangled to death in the room by an undetected chaos-worshipping servant of the Duke. The ghost now stays close to his mother's image guarding as only a child can.

The boy is a Haunt, and fiercely protects the image of his mother. (Intensity 3, INT 10, POW 22, CHA 10, Spectral Combat 82%, Willpower 94%, Stealth 78%, Spectral Scream 1d10). The boy attempts to scare intruders off using its Miasma ability, trying to instill dread in anyone close by. Failing that, it appears as a ghostly child with a broken neck, assailing people with its scream, which causes physical rends and tears in the skin. If it is left alone with an unconscious or incapacitated character, further attacks are aimed at the neck until this is broken.

D: FAMILY HALL.

This hallway leads to the various private chambers of the Lucius household. A series of bedrolls lie around the room, along with a few half-bottles of wine and some personal possessions and keepsakes.

Note: 11 of the bandits gather and sleep in here during the hours of darkness. If in an alerted state there are fewer here, with guards posted at various stations throughout the night. In the daytime, there is a 25% chance that 1–3 bandits are here.

E: MAIDS' ROOM.

This was once a small sleeping chamber for the maids of the house. It is now empty but is used to house prisoners. In such an instance a wedge-shaped piece of wood is used as a doorstop to keep the hostage secure.

F: FAMILY ROOM.

The bandits have stockpiled a large amount of wood along the western wall. Underneath this is concealed loot taken by two of the bandits and not disclosed to the rest of the group. A Hard Perception roll is required to spot that the woodpile holds a crevice within which is a sack. This contains an ornately decorated silver funerary vase, the top of which has been fashioned into a woman's head. It is worth 300 fFunders. If the family is ever traced (they live in Westport) they pay four times that amount for its return.

G: FAMILY ROOM.

Smokefoot sleeps in this room. He has a collection of scalps nailed above the fireplace and has painted death and storm runes on the other three walls. His bedroll lies to one side of the room. His treasure is collected in a wooden bowl on the mantelpiece (no one would be foolish enough to steal from him). It consists of a collection of bone and wooden dice of different sizes and colours mixed up with coinage – 138 Scraps, 64 Founders and 13 Royals.

H: MASTER QUARTERS.

Karl Pig-axe and Mad Ester sleep in here. They are lovers and share the remains of the double bed in the southern room.

Both have gone to some effort to secure their chamber. Each of the barred windows has also had its shutters nailed closed. This does not make it impossible to break in, but ripping the shutter open causes a lot of noise. The Northern window has had its bars removed. If Karl and Ester really need to, they smash the shutters open to escape.

The door to their room is barred from the inside when they are both sleeping in here. It can be picked (the bar being removed) with the correct tools and a successful Hard Lockpicking roll. It is also possible to break it down but this involves using Brawn, treating it the same as the

COUNT LUCIUS' VILLA

KEY

- ∕ Window
- ▬ Door
- ▭ Fireplace
- ◎ Column
- ⊹ Arch
- ▯ Stained Glass Window
- 🌳 Hedge
- A. Main Atrium
- B. Cubicles (storage)
- C. Alcoves
- D. Family Hall
- E. Maids Room
- F. & G. Family Rooms
- H. Master Quarters
- I. Servant's Quarters
- J. Old Kitchens
- K. Stables
- L. Workshop
- M. Garden
- N. & O. Spare Rooms

Side View

60m

3m

double doors entering the villa. The room is painted a light turquoise and decorated with dolphins and other sea life. Karl has hoarded various items (that he thought had some extra worth) in here from his years of banditry. This equipment is in four trunks and boxes in the centre of the room. They include:

- A large red trunk containing sections of an ancient man-sized corroded bronze statue of an elder statesman of the Eastern Empire. It is missing its left arm and right foot and the head is damaged. Karl thinks that this item is of some worth but it only fetches its weight in bronze these days (400 founders)
- A medium brown trunk containing small, hand-sized rectangular vellum packages. Each one holds a strong dye in powder form. There are 45 packages of red-brown dye (5 Founders each), and 12 of royal purple (20 Founders each). Karl knows that these are of some worth and is waiting for the right buyer.
- A small wooden crate with a lid that holds 12 upright ancient, glazed, clay jars all of which are sealed with wax. Each jar is decorated with mythological scenes, including struggles between heroes, scenes of worship and pornography. Karl has never broken the seals of the amphorae and would be disappointed to learn that the alcohol within has reduced to a sludge. However, the jars are exquisite and fetch up to 200 Founders each.
- A large wooden chest. Inside, wrapped in cloth, is a superb full set of lamellar armour engraved with rearing griffins and a coat of arms. It is bespoke, crafted for one of the leading noble families in the East of The Realm (The Duke of Torin), and fits SIZ 15. Karl knows that it is worth a lot but also realises that it is difficult to sell. He loathes the idea of destroying the art work upon it. It is of high craftsmanship and as such the enc is x0.75 (full suit weighs 15 enc). Its sale value is 4400 Founders.

The southern section of these quarters contain Karl and Ester's personal effects, including their personal armour and equipment when not worn. There is also a ceramic bath sunken in the south west corner. In a hidden alcove within the fireplace Karl and Ester have secreted a bag of coins (446 Founders, 12 Royals) and small purse of 13 gemstones, each one a mere bauble fetching 1d20 Founders. This can be found on a Hard Perception roll.

On the southern wall is a depiction of Aliya, with one curled fist full of writhing snakes and the other hand an open palm, supporting a smoking mountain. The mountain and head of the goddess are surrounded by a halo of mystical sigils. If searched, hand-sized impressions can be found on both the mountain and goddess' head. Initiates and higher ranking Aliya cultists have a chance equal to an Easy Exhort skill to recognise two of the sigils as being the cult runes. If both are pressed then the secret door slides open.

The chamber beyond has stood un-accessed for centuries. It was originally used to stockpile equipment for the long struggle against the Chaos Mother. A pair of sagging old chests stand along the east wall each containing piles of rusting chainmail. In an alcove on the southern wall sits an ancient figurine of Aliya in red clay. It is a small (roughly 20cm high), crudely fashioned figure with unusually wide hips and breasts. Fertility runes run the length of the figurine. It is magical and has a strong affect on fecundity and fertility. Plants within 100 metres of the figurine increase their yield by 25%; animals (including humans) increase the chance of producing healthy offspring by a further 25%.

I: Servants' Quarters.

This dreary room is bare and damp with mould spreading up the walls. It is occasionally used to store wood or other items.

J: Old kitchens.

An ancient fireplace stands along the northern wall but it is not used. Apart from the ovens there is little trace left that this was once a kitchen. A couple of stools and a makeshift table are also present.

K: Stables.

The stables currently house two donkeys which are used to haul loot and equipment when the bandits go out on raids.

L: Workshop.

The workshop has been renovated and is still serviceable. A large forge (marked as a fireplace on the map) anvil and slag tub all show signs of recent use. A pair of new bellows has been fitted onto the forge and new equipment hangs from pegs along the southern wall. Work benches surround most of the room, with half-complete and broken items. The bandits are slack but are to be found mending their equipment in the workshop a few days before they go out raiding.

M: GARDEN.

The garden consists of an ornamental pool flanked by two hedges. The grass in the garden is cropped short by the goats (see below) which free to graze every now and then. The pool has scalloped edges, dropping to a metre in depth. It is now mostly empty, containing a few centimetres of water and wet leaves.

Denoted by columns, the south section of the garden contained what was once a roofed pavilion beneath which was the mosaic. The roof is long gone and a makeshift wooden palisade has been strung up between the pillars to provide shelter for four goats.

Somewhere beneath the straw, goat dung, and other rubbish is the mosaic of the ancient Temple before it was corrupted to become a temple to the Chaos Mother. At the edge of the pavilion is an old stone plaque that now lies face down on the ground near one of the central columns. Anyone searching this area finds the plaque if they succeed a Very Easy Perception roll. It says 'For my beautiful wife, Artesia, that her visions become truth'.

The mosaic (see page 98) can be cleared of rubbish in 30 minutes; this is noisy and involves removing the goats, which are particularly obstinate. They came to join the bandits along with Ester and they are her pride and joy. She claims that they are the pinnacle of 'goatiness' and overseen by a particularly strong and virile goat spirit. They are difficult to control at the best of times; herding them is fraught with complications. They often turn to face the herder and back off, one step at time, occasionally risking a short warning charge. It is also very dangerous to turn ones' back on them as this precipitates a charge (attack 40% inflicting 1d4 damage to the backside/abdomen). In fact, the best way to get them out is to lead them, using a tasty treat as a lure.

If, for any reason the characters are being careful or quiet then it takes up to three hours to clear the mosaic. When uncovered, the mosaic functions as a shrine for Aliya cultists.

N: SPARE ROOM.

A chamber that was used for visitors or family members. It is now in a poor state, having lost half its roof. The bandits do not use it.

O: SPARE ROOM.

Although not in use this room is in a good state of repair (the roof does not leak very much). Sometimes the bandits receive female visitors from the village and take advantage of the privacy.

TRAVEL AND PREPARATION

The characters travel to Norport to see Fustilius Slump and his collection of maps. Buying provisions, they then set off northwards into Black Vale. If they are not careful, agents of Jedakiah attack them.

NORPORT

Norport is a small city-port built up around overseas trade to and from The Realm. It has one harbour; a natural promontory of rock extended by an artificial sea wall that shelters a deep water bay behind. Throughout the day sails of different shapes and colours lie dotted in the open waves, coming and going from the port.

The hills to the south of Norport are dotted with lead and copper mines, small shanty towns and extended family settlements which work the mines. Many of these miners come to town to trade for goods, have a good time or hope to be hired on by one of the larger mining companies.

The city-port itself is crescent-shaped in layout, partially enclosing the bay on either side. Commerce buildings, guild houses and taverns lie along the length of the seafront. In the daytime the seafront is awash with hawkers, the stalls of fishmongers, miners and carts loading and unloading from the merchant ships and the all pervading smell of decaying fish. Behind these an array of smaller houses, huts and hovels wash up against the taller buildings of the seafront. A few small shops can be found in the streets that run through the squalor but they are very quiet and subdued in comparison with the seafront.

Places of interest in Norport include the Boat Builders Association, Norport Sea Trade Guild, Copper and Lead Halls, Hanno's Troop (mercenaries), Lantern Crafters Guild (relying on whale blubber) and the Guild of Cartographers.

The three main taverns in Norport are The Nets and Anchor (mainly frequented by fishermen and local farmers), the Sea Eagle (merchants and ship's crew) and Rory's House (a real dive which doubles as a brothel).

The characters are able to buy all common goods from Norport and there is always a chance that something exotic has just come in from a land afar.

FINDING FUSTILIUS

The Guild of Cartographers consists of one full member, Fustilius Stump, and is situated above a fishmongers shop. The guild's presence is denoted by a sign above the

Deciphering the Mosaic

It is probably dependent on refereeing and game style as to how the mosaic is deciphered. The characters can be left to ponder on the mosaic for a long period of time, requiring them to cross reference the scene with various maps or an appropriate Locale skill roll.

Such a roll identifies the huge mountain in the background as Father's Spike. This indicates the temple is located in the Black Vale Mountains. Maps of the area can be found with Fustilius Slump and the characters have to travel to Norport to see him. On inspecting one Black Vale Mountains map they understand that the beast and water runes and the eels along the river that appear in the mosaic equate to the Eel River. It is then just a matter of locating the river and following it.

fishmongers sporting an image of map, quill and ink. Fustilius can also be found with an Easy Streetwise check by asking questions in any of the taverns or drinking houses. He is a crotchety old scholar who has accumulated a variety of odd maps over the decades. He spends most of the time being hired by miners to pour over old maps in relation to land deeds. It bores him silly. He is stand-offish at first, but if the characters explain where they are heading he becomes animated and helpful, hunting down a variety of old maps. Most are not very useful but they include a map of the Black Vale Mountains.

Actions in Norport

Norport is best used to plan the expedition to the ancient Chaos Mother temple. Games Masters may also want to add some excitement and this should be dependent on the characters actions and motivations guided by the following:

- If characters ask questions at the Copper and Lead Halls, they are told that down on their luck miners turn up every week hoping to be hired by one of the mining companies run by local nobles or entrepreneurs. Asking the right people the right questions (a Standard Streetwise roll), reveals that, a few weeks ago, two scholars (Zakar and Mollonius) arrived promising a good wage for those prepared to travel north and work hard. At least 30 men, guarded by Hanno's mercenaries, took-up the offer despite the apparent dangers.
- Characters seeking information about Hanno's Troop are led directly to the man himself. He manages all aspects of the troop, including hiring, training, dealing with clients and investing the profits.. A fastidious man who pays attention to detail, the troop is his life. For a man who does not panic easily, there is something about his latest two clients that is upsetting. Although they never outwardly threatened him, he got the impression that crossing them would be a bad idea. He has been paid well, but does not divulge any information about where they are going. However, if paid a bribe of at least 500 Founders he explains that he hired out 20 spearmen for at least six weeks work guarding miners in the Black Vale Mountains. If anyone does ask questions (even if Hanno is paid) he reports this to Jedakiah's spies. He certainly won't hire out any of his men to the characters.
- If the characters are not particularly discreet or cautious about their plans to head north and uncover the chalice, then there is a chance that forces loyal to Jedakiah hear about them. Spies are operating in the three main taverns in Norport. These spies are not of high quality, being recruited from the local population of thieves and miscreants. They are present within the taverns 50% of the time and, if present, loud-mouthed characters do not go unnoticed.

The spies report to Thuk, a Black Vale Barbarian and devotee of the Chaos Mother. Thuk lost his wife and five children to an overzealous campaign waged against his tribe by troops from the West Vale. He ardently hates all civilised people and seethes just at being in Norport. On learning of any potential enemies, Thuk leads his men in an assault on the party, either in a hit and run attack in a tavern, or following them out of Norport and ambushing them at night. This assault is dependent on the referee, who should place it at a pertinent point. Thuk is not bright, and his attempts at shadowing the party in Norport prior to any attack are not subtle.

Travelling North through Black Vale

The Black Vale is barren moorland, insipid and bleak. Centuries of grazing has left a rocky substrate that is only good for hardy plants with shallow roots.

The moorland is carpeted by a thin, hardy moor-grass. Occasionally, settlements dot the landscape. These include mud and straw huts that stand at the edge of streams. Many are uninhabited, or used by herders as they pass by, but a few support small family groups. Dry stone forts can also be found standing atop the higher hills of the vale. These are well scattered as they represent the power base for one of the many tribes inhabiting the area. A few of these forts are abandoned – a reminder of the turbulent history of the region.

The Black Vale Barbarians are mostly sheep herders and large flocks roam the moorland. Being the main livelihood of these people, they are well guarded. Threats come from both chaotically warped animals and enemy tribes.

Strangers are shunned; sheep being hurriedly herded away, womenfolk scurrying into their hovels leaving the men to either stand defiantly or turn and run. Approaching a fort is a particularly bad idea and results in the sallying of a war party. It is possible for the characters to get through this land unscathed as long as they are careful in their passing. Successful Stealth, Navigation and Survival rolls mean that the local populace are completely avoided and the Eel River is reached safely.

Travelling to the Chaos Mother Temple

Following the river a few days east into the foothills takes any travellers away from the Black Vale Barbarians. Encounters along the route should be at the Games Master's discretion. It could include fearful shepherds, a war party (use the statistics for Thuk and his men) or, when the party reaches the mountains, a larger and hungry creature, such as a bear.

As the characters enter the foothills the Eel River starts to twist and turn. A few kilometres along the valley steepens even further and threatens to form a canyon. However, there is a seemingly natural path that the characters may follow along the southern edge of the river. An Easy Perception skill check reveals that two stones, one on either side of the route, are way-stones marked with fertility and chaos runes (a plant rune has been chiselled out). Every kilometre, these stones mark the way to the temple and the ancient settlement that stood below it.

After a further day's travel the path turns north then splits, one path leading eastwards, winding up a mountain side, the other continuing north into open woodland. A Standard Perception roll identifies the stone formations (the Stone Men identified on the mosaic in the bottom right hand corner) upon the mountain side along the eastern track.

If the party travels north then they enter the area covered by volcanic debris over 500 years ago. This grey carpet of rock has now broken up and is under an open canopy of pine trees. The path quickly disappears and the going becomes hard. It is difficult to orientate as the land drops and rises quickly, the tree cover blotting out a lot of the landscape.

The Miners

The characters head toward the excavation site through the pine woodland. At some point they hear panicked voices and the sounds of brushwood being crushed under hurried feet. From the general direction of the excavation site comes a group of 10 miners. A couple have digging tools and a few also have some provisions, but they seem ill-prepared. A successful Standard Insight skill roll identifies these men as being very scared and suffering from shock.

If ambushed, they run, scattering in all directions. A calmer approach alongside a Standard Influence roll elicits a friendlier reaction. A humane gesture, such as a warm fire and hot food, and they relax somewhat and tell their story:

- Thirty men were hired as miners and baggage carriers a few weeks ago at Norport by two scholars, Zakar and Mollonius. A unit of twenty mercenaries from Hanno's troop was hired to guard them. They were told that they would travel for a week or so into the Black Vale Mountains and would earn their wage by excavating something. They presumed it was some sort of mining enterprise.
- They travelled up to the stone men and the two scholars checked their maps and drawings before issuing the order to move onto the mountainside they referred to as 'the sentinel'. Upon reaching this they spent three days searching, stopping at various points and undergoing the same ritual: One of the scholars (Zakar) ushered the mercenaries and miners away as Mollonius checked maps and then seemed to be praying. At one point Mollonius became very animated and ordered that they establish camp.
- Under supervision, the miners then started to dig. They uncovered the top of a partially collapsed building. A couple of weeks passed; it became clear that the building was the top of a bell tower. They removed the cracked bronze bell and proceeded to clear rubble from the upper storey until it uncovered a deep shaft below. They could smell brimstone from the depths.
- Once the shaft had been shored up, the sages retired to their tents. On emerging, they had donned robes of red, displaying fertility and chaos runes, insisting that these were merely precautionary. Taking half the miners and escorted by the mercenaries they descended into the shaft. The noise of them coughing and moving about gradually receded and a few hours passed.
- As night descended the sound of distant chanting echoed up from the shaft. This was replaced by screaming and the sounds of men running in panic. Then the ropes that dangled down the shaft became taut. From below, figures came climbing and shouting to be pulled up. Taking strain on the ropes, the

miners initially complied. Then they saw deformed shapes chasing their colleagues up the ropes. Some of these mutations still wore the armour of Hanno's Troop or had other characteristics the miners recognised, but their faces were twisted and hateful. The more quick-witted miners quickly cut the ropes with hatchets and knives. Taking what provisions they could quickly find in the dark, they fled.

After their story has been recounted the miners plead with the characters to return with them to Norport. Whatever was found below ground is monstrous; some ancient demon has been disturbed; the fate of the scholars and mercenaries awaits the characters if they do not flee. If the characters dismiss, or try to assuage these concerns, the miners sigh, offer prayers to Menissa, and shake their heads sadly. At the first available opportunity they take their leave, heading back to the city.

The Excavation Site

Pines have been cleared to make room for firewood and for makeshift lean-tos and supports for tents. There are seven of these huddled around a large fire-pit. These are the sleeping quarters for the miners and mercenaries. Near them, a large canvas has been erected between two trees. A long, rough pine table lined by benches stands underneath the canvas. At one end of this hangs a cauldron over a fire-pit.

One tent stands to one side. It is of much better construction, being supported by bespoke poles. This is Zakar and Mollonius' tent. Their contents have been hurriedly looted by those miners who escaped. Scrolls scatter the floor. Some are hastily drawn, simple images (one of the stone men, one of a bell coloured in brown, many undecipherable) which are visions that have been drawn by Manuun. There is also a depiction of the Chaos Mother Temple in all its glory, just before it was covered in ash. A number of other maps and texts relating to the area are of variable use and worth. It seems to the party that these two scholars have spent considerable time and effort piecing together the various clues to the location of this temple.

Above the camp, on the slopes of the mountains, the excavated bell tower pokes out of a recently dug hole in the ground. The rest of the temple is covered by volcanic debris. The broken bell is half buried amongst this rubble. The bell tower is a five metre square roof supported by large brick pillars at each corner. The roof is sloped and tiled, rising to a spire of corroded bronze. The floor no longer exists and the tower now resembles a well, dropping into the inky darkness below. A large pine log is placed on supports underneath this roof, spanning the dark shaft below. Ropes dangle from it but all have been cut.

The Corrupted Temple

This section is the climax of the scenario. The characters descend into darkness and battle the mutants below. The characters either find and retrieve the Chaos Mother's Chalice, or Mollonius escapes with it. A map of the Chaos Mother temple can be found on page 108.

The Original Descent

Zakar and Mollonius, alongside their mercenaries and miners, entered via the bell tower and started to explore the temple. They made their way to the main hall (room 11) where the chalice sat in an alcove in the statue. In its presence the two sages prostrated themselves, and then recited a chant before picking it up. Molloinus realised that it still contained a white viscous fluid. Overcome with religious fervour he drank it.

Blessed with corruption he vomited the Chaos Mother's milk onto those men within reach and they became marked with mutations. The others ran in abject fear.

LOCATION AND TACTICS OF THE ENEMY

This whole section is not to be played out as a 'dungeon crawl' - characters moving to each room, clearing them out and taking the treasure. The temple is a stage upon which a series of skirmishes take place. Games Masters are encouraged to keep the pace fast and fluid. The fights in the dark should be confusing with the enemy attacking and then melting away. Sometimes the whole temple is alive with a cacophony of sounds and other times it becomes deathly silent.

Mollonius wants to return the chalice to Jedakiah. Mollonius's tactics are to lure the characters into the temple so that he can escape and kill them. On hearing anyone's descent he gathers his mutants and casts his Project Hearing spell, keeping it close to the characters, following them around and coordinating the action of his underlings. Spells that detect magic pick this up as a magical source doggedly following the party. Note that if the characters become quiet, Mollonius may lose them.

Mollonius's chaotic ability means that each mutant follows his orders has a Hate Purity passion of 80%. For the moment, they follow Mollonius' lead. If he is killed, wounded or separated from them, then they lose cohesion.

There are a total of 24 mutants within the temple. This includes Mollonius (Zakar has now lost his mind and is figured as one of the mutants), 7 mercenaries, 10 miners and 6 truly twisted abominations. Since this may present too strong a force for a small or weak group, the actual number capable of fighting should be scaled to the characters. Even with re-scaling, the mutants should still present a fearsome foe and one that should, on paper, hang in the mutants' favour. The characters should certainly not be allowed to run amok in darkness without being seriously tested.

Three options are given for the location of the enemies in the table on page 107. This is dependent on how stealthy the characters are and how much to plan things go for Mollonius and his mutants. Games Masters should use the table as a general guide.

Unaware represents a state where the characters have accessed the temple undetected. This is not very likely, but is possible.

Aware is the state at which the mutants plan to draw the characters in so they can surround them and either get out and/or block the characters exit route. One group waits quietly whilst another create distractions and noises in a far part of the temple.

Endgame is if the mutants are ready to leave but hoping to kill the characters first. In this instance they are all collected back at the bell tower entrance.

Temple Description

This ancient temple was originally dedicated to Aliya. It then became a place of worship for the Chaos Mother before being covered in volcanic debris. It has lain dormant ever since.

The temple is split into three sections, the bell tower (location 1), which once stretched to four storeys, the main building (locations 2 to 23), which is two storeys high, and an adjacent one storey building where auxiliary staff were quartered (locations 24 to 27).

Within the temple was erected a huge statue to Aliya, a towering alabaster monolith stretching up to the domed roof, also acting as a structural support. A variety of other statues, reliefs and giant stone tablets adorned the temple giving it a resplendent, if not slightly decadent, feel. With the coming of chaos and the perversion of the priests, most of the statues and images were altered to mirror the new chaotic nature of the temple. When the volcano known as the Sentinel erupted, blasting away its summit, a pyroclastic cloud swept into the valley. The temple was first purged of life by the heat and poisons and then covered by layers of ash and other volcanic debris. Over the centuries some sections of the temple roof have collapsed, including the central part of the auxiliary staff quarters, and there was an infill of debris through some roof sections of the main hall. In the main, its sturdy construction and multiple-pillared support is still relatively intact.

Most of the internal grandeur has been wiped clean by the influence of the chalice and the passing of time. Some rooms and areas of corridor still display faded geometric designs or fragments of murals, but most of the temple frescos have crumbled or warped into disconcerting patterns. There are windows around the top of the first and second storeys but these only give out onto walls of volcanic ash. Nearly all the organic material has long since decayed although stone furniture and decor still exists in some of the rooms, notably in the main hall (location 11) hall of statues (location 12) and in the meeting room (location 14).

The temple is in complete darkness (except in location 11). If lights are extinguished then inky blackness descends. See the Effects of Lighting table on page 104. Most of mutants are also blind in the dark and rely on Mollonius' light spells, or their few remaining torches and lanterns. They tend to wait quietly and, as such, any light sources are easily spotted.

1. The Bell Tower.

The shaft descends 30 metres in total, although the lower 5 metres are covered in rubble, volcanic ash and debris from the collapsed floors above. Twenty two metres down (8 metres from the floor of the tower) a doorway opens into what was once the second floor. A further three metres down and the characters are standing on a jumble of large rocks and rubble. There is actually a way down through this rubble but it is difficult to see and involves moving some boulders to one side and squeezing through a gap into the darkness below. Characters need to make a Hard Brawn roll to remove the debris that has piled up. Blood, and some human remains, are also to be found on top of the rocks, but the remains of the ropes have been removed.

Effects of Lighting in the Temple

Lighting Type	Change to Difficulty Grade for combat and other visual-based skills
Within the radius of bright light sources such as those caused by light and glow spells.	Standard
At the edge of a bright light source as listed above. Within the radius of lantern light or multiple (more than one) torches.	Hard
Single torch or on the periphery of lantern of multiple torch light.	Formidable
Pitch black	Herculean

Note: If the mutants are aware of the party then they are waiting in the darkness below and grab anyone coming through the crawl space.

2. Acolytes Hall.

Once a grand hall where acolytes and the other faithful would congregate, it is now stripped bare. A couple of large blood smears adorn the wall and a boot lies discarded along the eastern wall. A successful Easy Track roll reveals plenty of traffic passing through.

3. Bath Room.

The walls were originally decorated with images of young maidens swimming in and lounging around a plunge pool below a waterfall. This image was altered at a later date so that fruit and cooked meats can be seen hovering in front of the cascading waterfall. On the cliffs above, a naked priestess can be seen holding aloft what appears to be a dripping heart or other organ. A large pile of corroded bronze washing bowls and chamber pots stand along the southern wall. A fresh human head of one of the miners lies in the furthest bowl from the entrance.

4. Meeting Room.

Four alabaster table legs, magnificently carved into sheaves of barley, stand fastened to the floor. Someone has carved small chaos runes and a smiling face onto each sheaf. The table top has long since gone. A series of shattered clay tablets lie against the western wall.

5. Sleeping Chambers.

Chambers for the acolytes and priests, each one is covered in a thin layer of plaster, pottery shards, the remains of clay tablets and other undecipherable non-organic objects.

6. Sleeping Chamber.

This was once a room for an overseer. It also contains some items collected by the mercenaries. They stashed a leather bag in here hoping to pick it up on the way out. It is hidden in the north-eastern corner under some fragments from an urn. Their treasure can be found with a Standard Perception roll. It consists of one thin yet exquisitely crafted golden chain (1000 founders), a ceremonial silver knife (450 founders to a collector of rare antiques) and a lump of very old silver coins that have fused together (150 founders).

7. Inner Worship Room.

This room was used for smaller worship ceremonies, private functions, marriages, births and other rites of passage. A statue to Aliya has been broken off at the knees and lies on the floor. The head and arms are missing but it is plain to see that parts of the statue have been crudely re-worked in places. Her torso has been hollowed into a bowl-like depression. It is scorched black and contains fragments of bone and human teeth. Corroded bronze braziers lie to either side of the statue.

8. Hallway.

Once a busy thoroughfare for temple life, this large hall was decorated with pictures of forest animals. In front of these stood a collection of large potted plants to give an image of looking through into a forest clearing. The images on the walls are now faded but the eyes of all the animals were re-painted with no pupils by the chaos cultist at a later date. The end result is, in flickering torchlight, an impression of being stared at by hundreds of pairs of empty eyes. In front of this only the line of empty plant pots remain. These are half a metre in height and once held large tree ferns and shrubs. Nine line each wall.

9. Balcony.

This overlooks room 11. and was once used by the off-duty priests and other officials to take part in the ceremonies below, but remain separated from the common worshippers. Nothing remains of the wooden seats that would have lined this stepped chamber. The wooden balustrade is also missing from along its edge. It is a 7 metre drop to the hard stone floor below. On the rear wall a large mural has been painted: onn first inspection it shows a group of priests sacrificing a victim in the Great Hall (room 11 below). Anyone looking closely clearly sees that the image has been re-painted, the blood sacrifice, serene faces of the worshippers and the extra arms on the goddess' statue all being later additions.

10. The Archives.

Each of these alcoves held row upon row of clay tablets that were used for recording the logistics of the temple, the division of the harvests and the service of the people. These tablets now lie scattered across the floor or heaped in broken piles. Anyone scan-reading some of the tablets, and succeeding in a Standard Literacy roll finds the following:

- A series of mostly intact fragments recording increasingly harsh demands on the worshippers of the Chaos Mother, including the requirement of child sacrifices and worse.
- A large clay tablet (the size of a hoplite shield) that explains lost farming methods. Anyone studying this tablet gains 1d4+1% in their Locale Skill. It weighs 7 ENC. It is worth 1,000 Founders to the Aliya cult.

11. The Great Hall.

Once the focus of worship for Aliya, this high-vaulted hall occupies both storeys of the temple. The domed ceiling is supported by lines of pillars and a giant statue that stands with one hand aloft (touching the dome centre and acts as a structural support). The great statue remains, although three of her arms lie shattered on the ground. It is clear that the original statute only had two arms (one of which supports the ceiling) but the chaos worshippers added two more pairs. Of those on the floor one has shattered into many fragments, one has the hand of a snake, and one has a series of eyes running down its length. One of the original arms has its hand replaced with a snake's head. The other is a tentacle that curls its way around one of her huge legs.

Her visage was also defaced many years ago, the eyes being painted golden and a horn being added to her forehead. A hollow has been smashed out of the statue at womb height and the chalice was placed within it. It is no longer there.

Within the hall are mounds of volcanic debris. These formed when the ceiling cracked as the pyroclastic cloud enveloped the temple. The centre of the room has become the main resting area for the mutants. It has been cleared of rubble and scattered with bits of discarded equipment and burnt-out torches.

If the light is dim, or if characters study the statue they notice a tiny chink of light coming from above her outstretched arm. Someone nimble enough to climb to the top of the statue and investigate sees a fissure where the now corroded spire used to be. If the characters are trapped inside the temple this is a possible way of escape. However the climb up the statue is treacherous, being a Formidable Athletics roll. The top of the fissure narrows and only characters with a SIZ of 10 or less can squeeze through. Anyone larger has to start to dislodge rock and rubble from within the fissure, making a Standard Engineering or a Hard Brawn roll. This is very dangerous as the ceiling is close to collapse. A failure merely causes the fissure to become irrevocably blocked, whereas a fumbled roll means that the whole ceiling collapses. Anyone below must make a successful Evade roll to reach cover, or avoid the debris. If the roll is a success no damage is sustained. If a failure then 2d6 points of damage results to upper-body locations (1d10+10 to determine where). If the Evade roll is fumbled the damage increases to 2d6+6.

12. Corridor of Statues.

Once full of towering alabaster statues of heroes and the venerated dead, it is now a dark corridor littered with their shattered remains. All have had their faces repainted. Their eyes are now serenely shut, their cheeks a garish red, Chaos Mother runes carved across their foreheads as if they have now been claimed by the new cult. A couple of the statues (each measuring about four metres in height) have been tipped forwards so that they lean up against the eastern wall. The others present large obstacles within the corridor.

13. Cubicles.

For those not allowed behind the great hall, this series of cubicles was used for undertaking business, having meetings, mediating in disputes and the like.

Within these rooms six of the most deformed mutants wait. They have lost all rational thought and are overcome with hatred for anyone who does not bear the mark of chaos. They shuffle around whimpering and grunting. If aware of the approach of intruders they become silent, listening and waiting to pounce. Once their ambush has been set, or they are revealed, they attack until destroyed.

The two middle rooms contain the piled bodies of those mercenaries and miners who resisted the touch of chaos and were killed whilst escaping: they have been mutilated. If this grisly pile is searched there are a few useable weapons and some bits of salvageable armour (covered in blood and viscera as well as the occasional bit of bone, skin and hair fragment).

14. Reception Hall.

The entrance to the inner workings of the temple for any outsiders, this room was elaborately decorated. What remains is just an echo of its former self; the occasional fragment of mosaic tiles upon the walls; a large marble table that lies along the western wall; a massive shattered stone tablet in the room's centre.

15. Hallway.

This room is blackened with scorch marks upon its walls. It once held a series of large bookcases for scrolls and old tomes. It was torched when the priests mutated.

16. Staircase.

A large set of stairs spiral upwards to room 8 above. The banister has long since gone but the stairs are made of stone and are quite sturdy.

17. Servants Quarters.

The partition walls still survive in this large hall but all the interior furniture has rotted away.

18. Priest Room.

The entrance to this room is blocked by one of the huge torsos from a statue of room 12 as well as smaller statue sections, stones, bricks and other debris. This was hastily erected 500 years ago by the original chaos-mutations to wall-in a priest of Aliya - the only person to have resisted the chaotic nature of the chalice and whose proximity the chaos mutants found disturbing. Rather than face him they blocked up the doorway and continued their rampage through the rest of the temple. He died of dehydration a few days later and the room was never used by the chaos cultist.

The statue is SIZ 75 if the party wishes to shift it, but only three people can combine their efforts (see the Brawn skill on page 39 of Mythras). If the rubble is removed it reveals a chamber, its walls bordered by fierce, red, geometric patterns and a series of small panels painted with mountain and river scenes.

Most of the interior has corroded away but a stone bed lies along the southern wall and there are still the remnants of a wardrobe. Upon the bed lie the remains of the priest – a few bits of bone, a partial skull, an ancient gold necklace (800 Founders) and silver belt buckle (50 Founders). In the centre of this dust is a rather dull-looking, smooth, white stone that is flecked with brown. The stone is an artefact of Aliya and the holder is immune to the corrupting touch of chaos: any chaotic being seeing the stone, or touching the wielder, needs to succeed in a Willpower roll or recoil in revulsion for 1d6 rounds.

19. Priest Room.

A bare room within which lie a series of arms from various statues throughout the building. They vary in size and gender. A faded fresco shows a series of animals being led to market. These have had alterations chiselled into them - the cows have very large udders that drag along the ground, the pigs have humps on their backs and the chickens seem to have their heads totally removed.

20. Storeroom.

An image of a multi-armed goddess has been painted onto the ceiling in some kind of dark resin.

21. Storeroom.

Empty.

22. Storeroom.

Empty

Auxiliary Staff Building (Rooms 23 to 27).

This building has a much lower roof than the main temple and is not so solidly built. As such it has partially collapsed. Anyone wielding a weapon which must be swung, rather than thrust, suffers a circumstantial penalty, making all attacks one grade more difficult.

Note: if the mutants are aware of the characters they are waiting in here, perhaps making noise to goad them in. They lure the party back into room 26 or 27 before fleeing in the opposite direction. This tactic does not work of the characters either decide to split into groups or leave someone behind to guard the way back into the main temple. In this instance, the mutants fight their way back into the temple shouting for help as they do so.

23. Barracks

This was a large barracks for the temple guards. It is now littered in rubble and volcanic debris covers the floor to the extent that a man-sized creature would have to stoop in the room's centre.

Mutant Locations and Tactics

Temple Locations	Unaware	Aware	Endgame
1 to 4	4 mutants, sleeping and talking quietly to themselves	None	All remaining mutants (accept those in 5 to 6 and 8 below) gathered here to ambush the characters or escape.
5 to 6	4 mutants resting in the cubicles	None	Perhaps one or two mutants ready to ambush any returning party that is already engaged with those in 1 to 4 (see above)
8	None but a Standard perception roll indicates noise of chanting can be heard echoing through the balcony (location 9) from the great hall below (location 11)	None	Two mutants stationed here if the characters are below. They either attack if overcome with hate or run back to 1-4 to warn the rest.
9	None present but light shines up from the main hall where a number of them are seen resting / chanting (location 11).	None	None
11	7 mutants and Mollonius dimly lit by a lantern.	None	None
12	2 mutants sleeping in the alcoves amongst the rubble of the statues.	None	None
13	6 of the most twisted and psychotic mutants (Mollonius calls them the 'most blessed') have been coerced into here. They attack non-chaotics on site. If roused into action they go on the rampage but do not knowingly cooperate with other mutants.	6 of the most twisted and psychotic mutations. See unaware.	6 of the most twisted and psychotic mutations. See unaware.
16 to 17	None.	None but anyone reaching these rooms or the corridor between them hears moans and cries for help emanating from 23. To 27, where an ambush is set.	
18	None. This room still has a door and is magically sealed. No mutants have gained access to here.	None. See unaware.	None. See unaware.
20 to 22	None.	10 mutants and Mollonius retreat here if they hear the characters coming down the shaft. They wait until they think the party has moved away from the entrance way and then they slip up through the rubble in the bell tower shaft (below 1).	None.
24 to 27	None	7 mutants have the task of luring the characters into this area as a distraction so that the others can either trap so Mollonius can escape. These 7 are meant to run away when the characters are lured in, but if the Games Master chooses they can be overcome with rage and attack furiously.	If things do not go to plan then Mollonius leads the remaining mutants into this area for a final battle.

Book of Quests — Scenario 4: The Chaos Mother's Chalice

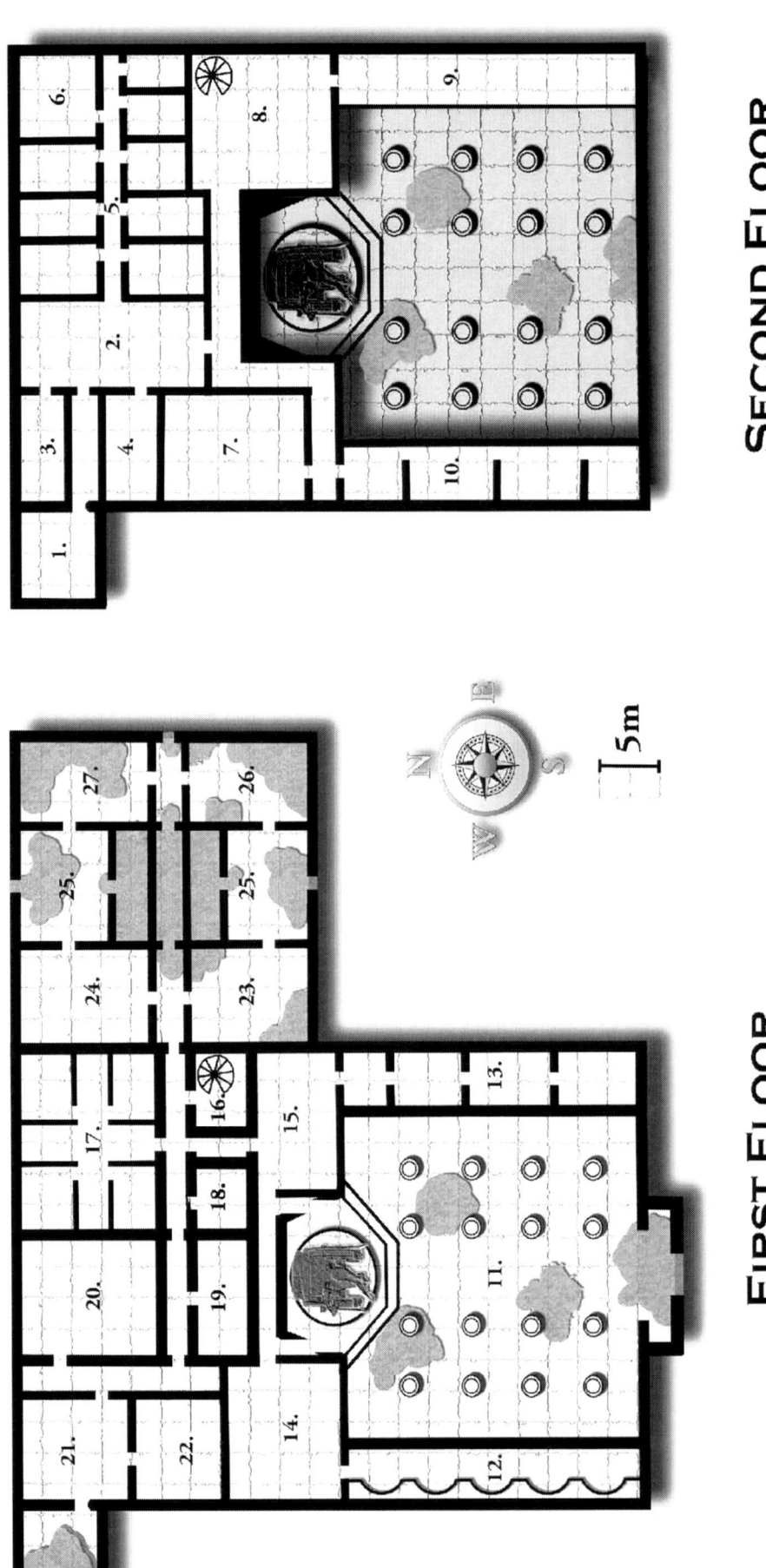

24. Barracks

Another barrack room; this is in the same state of repair as 23.

25. Hallways.

These have both partially collapsed, rock and rubble strewn over the uneven floor.

26. Kitchen.

This room has multiple chimneys around its walls. These are now full of debris and have partially collapsed, throwing bricks onto the floor. The rubble in this room reaches the ceiling (which has also partially collapsed) and the floor is littered in debris, making the channels through the room cramped (between one and two metres in height).

27. Storeroom.

Similar to the room above, dominated by rubble and debris, hindering movement and other action.

Conclusions

Mollonius holds the chalice and keeps it with him at all times (either clasped in one hand or hung around his neck if he requires two free hands). The chalice is both ornate and gruesome. It is an inverted skull of alien origin, hollowed into a bowl-shape. The stem and rim of the cup is of solid gold and studded with rubies.

Mollonius could be encountered at a number of locations in the temple. He and some of his followers could also escape, especially if the characters leave ropes or ladders unguarded at the bell tower (location 1). In this instance Mollonius takes a couple of his most useful followers and heads for Dark Child's Tower, leaving instructions for the others to hunt down and kill the characters in the temple below. At the very least he ensures that the party cannot escape by cutting any ropes – he is happy to leave the other mutants trapped below as well.

Touching the chalice in itself is not very dangerous; but anyone foolish enough to drink from it risks its awesome powers of perversion. In such a situation an opposed of Willpower roll is needed to resist it. Treat the chalice as having a willpower skill of 100%. The chalice contains Milk of the Chaos Mother and drinking it immediately brings about a chaos mutation. STR and CON are raised by 1d6 and INT and CHA are similarly reduced. The victim also develops 1d3 Chaos Features, as described on pages 275 to 276 of the the Mythras rules. The victim also develops the Hate Purity Passion at 80%.

For dramatic purposes, it may be advisable to have Mollonius escape with the chalice. This helps sustain continuity with the remaining scenarios in Book of Quests and provides extra impetus for thwarting Jedakiah's ultimate plan. Mollonius's escape could be secured with the arrival of a Garthari warband who come to offer support, or he may simply allow his mutants to create havoc buying him time to exit the temple with the chalice.

If the characters are successful in recovering the chalice, then Kalathus honours his side of the deal and they are rewarded. They have also struck a grave blow to Jedakiah's plans for creating the Chaos Daughter in the Dread Rite (see Reckoning at Distaff Peak) - although the sorcerer can create, through other means (and the help of the Ophidians) something that will take its place.

Non-Player Characters

Karl Pig-Axe, Bandit Leader

Karl is a survivor. Pragmatic, resourceful, but also realistic. He has survived this long by being careful - with his resources and those he trusts. Although ruthless he is not a sadist: he is tough with his men and with anyone he captures, but he does not see any point in bloodshed if a profit can be turned instead. His relationship with Mad Ester is one of companionship rather than love; he will fight for her, but not at the expense of everything he has worked for.

The name Pig-Axe comes from years ago, when Karl was an apprentice butcher. He shunned the traditional knives used for splitting a pig carcass, preferring a huge, two-handed axe. When he left the life of a butcher behind, the axe went with him and the name stuck. His Great Axe is named Bacon Slicer, in fond memory of those simpler days dismembering meat.

Characteristics	Attributes		1d20	Location	AP/HP
STR: 15	Action Points	3	1–3	Right Leg	2/6
CON: 14	Damage Modifier	+1d2	4–6	Left Leg	2/6
SIZ: 12	Magic Points	12	7–9	Abdomen	3/7
DEX: 12	Movement	6m	10–12	Chest	3/8
INT: 15	Initiative Bonus	11	13–15	Right Arm	2/5
POW: 12	Armour	Bezaint & Pads	16–18	Left Arm	2/5
CHA: 11	Abilities	None	19–20	Head	4/6
	Magic	None			

Skills: Athletics 65%, Brawn 45%, Endurance 45%, Evade 30%, Locale (The Vale) 60%, Perception 60%, Survival 45%, Unarmed 47%, Willpower 30%, Stealth 62%

Passions: Love Wealth 70%, Loyalty (Mad Ester) 40%, Hate Those Who Let Him Down 68%

Combat Style: Banditry (Club, Dagger, buckler) 60%, Heavy Axeman (Great Axe) 75%

Weapon	Size/Force	Reach	Damage	AP/HP
Knife	S	S	1d4+1d2	6/8
Great Axe ('Bacon Slicer')	H	L	2d6+2+1d2	4/10
Buckler	M	S	1d3+1d2	6/9

Mad Ester

Mad Ester hails from the eastern forest and is, by The Realm's standards, a primitive. She is wild-eyed, driven to conversations with herself (in reality with Grandma Goat) and with berating those who displease her. She met Karl Pig-Axe when he fled into the forests, seeking refuge from enemies. Grandma Goat urged Ester to care for him and to become his companion, which she has faithfully done. She does little without Grandma Goat's counsel, which is often contradictory but has never proven false yet.

Grandma Goat was bound several generations ago by a relative of Ester's and passed down through the female line, serving each new mistress as was part of the spirit bargain. Grandma Goat loves Ester the most because she is as obstinate and unpredictable as the spirit itself. The two are almost like sisters - albeit peculiar ones.

Grandma Goat can be called upon to infuse Ester with 'goatliness'. The spirit enters Ester's body and she seems to develop the cloven hooves and slitted pale eyes of a forest goat. Her wild hair seems to take the form of curled horns, close to her head. Possessed by Grandma Goat, Ester bleats insults and curses

Characteristics	Attributes		1d20	Location	AP/HP
STR: 7	Action Points	2	1–3	Right Leg	0/4
CON: 9	Damage Modifier	-1d4	4–6	Left Leg	0/4
SIZ: 8	Magic Points	16	7–9	Abdomen	0/5
DEX: 9	Movement	6m	10–12	Chest	0/6
INT: 14	Initiative Bonus	12	13–15	Right Arm	0/3
POW: 16	Armour	None	16–18	Left Arm	0/3
CHA: 14	Abilities	None	19–20	Head	0/4

Skills: Athletics 25%, Brawn 14%, Endurance 21%, Evade 36%, Locale (The Vale) 45%, Perception 40%, Stealth 68%, Survival 36%, Unarmed 19%, Willpower 64%

Passions: Love Pig Axe 80%, Loyalty to the bandit group 70%, Hatred of nobility 68%

Mad Ester's Magic

Animism: Binding 65%, Trance 63%

Spirits in fetishes:

Grandma Goat - Intensity 2 Animal Spirit

INT 14, POW 20, CHA 13, Willpower 84%, Spectral Headbutt 83% Damage 1d10, Increases Endurance by 25%.

Ember Kin. Intensity 2 Elemental Spirit

INT 2, POW 18, CHA 7, Willpower 70%, Spectral flame 75% Damage 1d8,

Combat Style: Banditry Goat Clubbing (Club) 55%

Weapon	Size/Force	Reach	Damage	AP/HP
Club	M	S	1d6-1d4	4/4

at her foes, lowers her head and charges. Few are prepared the impact of the spectral headbutt that follows.

Ember Kin is less easy to control. A flame spirit, it craves release which Ester has promised but never made good upon. When summoned forth Ember Kin cloaks Ester's arms in pale blue fire that flickers and murmers across her skin. She calls on Ember Kin rarely and even then, only when Grandma Goat suggests it.

SMOKEFOOT

This swarthy Moors barbarian keeps the bandits in-line through sheer fear. A hulking brute, he knows loyalty only to Karl Pig-Axe. Everyone else is incidental.

Smokefoot wears his long, grey-streaked hair in a topknot, secured in place with the arm bones of a slain enemy. He enjoys insults and curses, using them frequently, and likes to taunt his enemies with withering comments about their virility, courage and parents. A common tactic is for him to whip-out the arm bones securing his topknot, hurl them to one side and then reach for his sword, all the while taunting, cursing and swearing.

Most of the bandits consider him insane. He seems to know no fear, rarely shows mercy (unless ordered to do so by Karl Pig-Axe) and never displays pain. His love of violence is clear: he hacks at fallen enemies long after they are dead.

When Smokefoot has killed an opponent, make a Love Violence roll for him, opposed by his Willpower. If Love Violence wins the contest he spends a further combat round hacking at the corpse and cursing it, oblivious to what is happening around him.

Characteristics	Attributes	1d20	Location	AP/HP
STR: 13	Action Points	2	1–3	Right Leg	1/6
CON: 11	Damage Modifier	+1d2	4–6	Left Leg	1/6
SIZ: 15	Magic Points	13	7–9	Abdomen	1/7
DEX: 10	Movement	6m	10-12	Chest	1/8
INT: 11	Initiative Bonus	8	13–15	Right Arm	1/5
POW: 13	Armour	Cured Hides	16–18	Left Arm	1/5
CHA: 6	Abilities	None	19–20	Head	0/6
	Magic	None		

Skills: Athletics 55%, Brawn 52%, Endurance 54%, Evade 20%, Locale (The Vale) 30%, Locale (The Moors) 62%, Perception 53%, Stealth 59%, Survival 65%, Unarmed 57%, Willpower 45%,

Passions: Love Violence 80%, Loyalty to Pig-Axe 83%, Hate soft, lily-livered types 66%

Combat Style: *Moors Warrior (Sword, Javelin and Shield) 75%*

Weapon	Size/Force	Reach	Damage	AP/HP
Broadsword	M	M	1d8+1d2	6/10
Heater	H	S	1d4+1d2	6/12
Javelin	H	-	1d8+1+1d2	3/8

PIG-AXE'S BANDITS

Rough and ready opportunists, these brigands and bandits are thieves but, under Pig-Axe's guidance, have stopped short of being outright murderers. They respect Pig-Axe, are suspicious of Mad Ester, and fear Smokefoot.

Attributes	1d20	Location	AP/HP
Action Points: 2	1–3	Right Leg	0/6
Damage Modifier: +0	4–6	Left Leg	0/6
Magic Points: 9	7–9	Abdomen	2/7
Movement: 6 metres	10-12	Chest	2/8
Initiative Bonus: 11	13–15	Right Arm	0/5
Armour: Quilted Hauberk	16–18	Left Arm	0/5
Abilities: None	19–20	Head	0/6
Magic: None			

Skills: Athletics 38%, Brawn 25%, Endurance 36%, Evade 28%, Locale (The Vale) 40%, Perception 41%, Survival 31%, Stealth 39%, Unarmed 38%, Willpower 19%,

Passions: Love wealth 50%, Respect Pig-axe 73%, Fear Smokefoot 80%

Combat Style: *Banditry (Club, Dagger, Buckler) 50%*

Weapon	Size/Force	Reach	Damage	AP/HP
Club	M	M	1d6	4/4
Dagger	H	L	1d4+1	4/10
Buckler	M	S	1d3	6/9

THUK, BLACK VALE BARBARIAN WAR CHIEF

Thuk is imposing and no-nonsense, amply commanding the respect of his men. His mistress, though, is the Chaos Mother.

Attributes	1d20	Location	AP/HP
Action Points: 3	1–3	Right Leg	2/7
Damage Modifier: +1d2	4–6	Left Leg	2/7
Magic Points: 11	7–9	Abdomen	3/8
Movement: 6m	10-12	Chest	3/9
Initiative Bonus: 10	13–15	Right Arm	2/6
Armour: Linothorax & Padding	16–18	Left Arm	2/6
Abilities: None	19–20	Head	0/7

Magic: None

Skills: *Athletics 72%, Brawn 60%, Endurance 65%, Evade 43%, Locale (Black Vale) 57%, Perception 63%, Stealth 42%, Survival 75%, Unarmed 48%, Willpower 32%*

Passions: *Hate civilised people 95%, Love the memories of his wife and children 86%, Loyalty to the Chaos Mother Cult 78%*

Combat Style:: *Vale Warrior (Battle Axe, Javelin, Heater) 60%*

Weapon	Size/Force	Reach	Damage	AP/HP
Battle Axe	M	M	1d6+1+1d2	4/8
Heater	H	S	1d4+1d2	6/12
Javelin	H	-	1d8+1+1d2	3/8

BLACK VALE WARBAND

Merciless and murderous - all in the Chaos Mother's name.

Attributes	1d20	Location	AP/HP
Action Points: 2	1–3	Right Leg	0/6
Damage Modifier: +1d2	4–6	Left Leg	0/6
Magic Points: 10	7–9	Abdomen	2/7
Movement: 6 metres	10-12	Chest	2/8
Initiative Bonus: 10	13–15	Right Arm	0/5
Armour: Cured Hides	16–18	Left Arm	0/5
Abilities: None	19–20	Head	0/6

Magic: None

Skills: *Athletics 52%, Brawn 40%, Endurance 45%, Evade 33%, Perception 53%, Unarmed 38%, Willpower 30%,*

Passions: *Loyalty to Thuk 80%*

Combat Style:: *Vale Warrior (Battle Axe, Javelin, Heater) 60%*

Weapon	Size/Force	Reach	Damage	AP/HP
Battle Axe	M	M	1d6+1+1d2	4/8
Heater	H	S	1d4+1d2	6/12
Javelin	H	-	1d8+1+1d2	3/8

MOLLONIUS, CORRUPT SAGE AND CHAOS MOTHER CULTIST

Mollonius, whose lips touched the chalice, now speaks in a monotone hypnotic voice. When he breathes or talks, fumes and vapour drift from his nose and mouth. These positively seek out and curl around other chaotic creatures, inducing either fervour or a euphoric trance-like state, depending on what Mollonius wants. Such vapour smells of over-ripe fruit and brings about a mild feeling of euphoria in chaotic creatures. Given time, his chanting imparts certain feelings and passions in such creatures, who cannot help but stop and listen to his sermons and philosophies. For this reason he has near complete control over many of the other mutants in the temple, although this power recedes when he is not in their presence. His CON and STR have been boosted by the chalice. He is also able to projectile vomit if he gets within Touch range.

Attributes	1d20	Location	AP/HP
Action Points: 3	1–3	Right Leg	2/7
Damage Modifier: 0	4–6	Left Leg	2/7
Magic Points: 17	7–9	Abdomen	3/8
Movement: 6m	10–12	Chest	3/9
Initiative Bonus: 15	13–15	Right Arm	2/6
Armour: None	16–18	Left Arm	2/6
Abilities: None	19–20	Head	0/7

Skills: Athletics 65%, Brawn 45%, Endurance 45%, Evade 63%, Locale (The Vale) 75%, Perception 66%, Stealth 47%, Survival 35%, Unarmed 28%, Willpower 70%

Passions: Hate Purity 80%, Loyalty to Jedakiah 60%, Love of the Chalice 78%

Magic

Sorcery: Invocation 67%, Shaping 76%
Intuition, Wrack, Palsy, Enhance CON, Project Hearing, Damage Resistance, Sense Bronze

Combat Style:: Scimitar 52%, Vomit over prone, held or inactive enemy 90% taking one complete turn to perform

Weapon	Size/Force	Reach	Damage	AP/HP
Scimitar	M	M	1d8	6/10
Vomit	T	L	Concentrated Acid: 1d6 Damage lasting 1d3 Combat Rounds	

MUTATED MINERS AND MERCENARIES

These mercenaries have a strong hatred for anything non-chaotic. Their appearance has also changed, being more muscle bound but marked by sores, pustules and small cancerous growths.

The miners who accompanied the mercenaries into the temple have similar statistics but have no armour and carry improvised weapons. Their Combat Style (Improvised Tools) is 55% rather than 65%.

Attributes	1d20	Location	AP/HP
Action Points: 2	1–3	Right Leg	3/6
Damage Modifier: +1d2	4–6	Left Leg	3/6
Magic Points: 11	7–9	Abdomen	3/7
Movement: 6 metres	10–12	Chest	3/8
Initiative Bonus: 9	13–15	Right Arm	3/5
Armour: Linothorax	16–18	Left Arm	3/5
Abilities: None	19–20	Head	4/6

Magic: None

Skills: Athletics 46%, Brawn 42%, Endurance 56%, Evade 30%, Perception 62%, Stealth 32%, Unarmed 48%, Willpower 34%

Passions: *Hate Purity 80%*

Combat Style: Mercenary (Shortspear, Shortsword, Heater shield) 65%

Weapon	Size/Force	Reach	Damage	AP/HP
Shortspear	M	L	1d8+1+1d2	4/5
Heater	H	S	1d4+1d2	6/15
Shortswrrd	M	S	1d6+1d2	6/8

Weapon	Size/Force	Reach	Damage	AP/HP
Spade	M	L	1d8+1+1d2	4/5
Pickaxe	L	M	1d8+1+1d2	6/8

Spades can Bash. Pickaxes both Impale and Sunder.

THE CHAOS BLESSED

The following were those most horribly corrupted by Mollonius after he drank from the Chaos Mother's Chalice and vomited over them. They include Zakar (Mollonius's associate), two mercenaries and two miners.

Their mutations are hideous and vary in terms of their extremes. Those who have never encountered mutated human horrors before - or are of a generally nervous or squeamish disposition - need to make Willpower rolls when first encountering each of the Chaos Blessed, opposed by the Chaos Mutation Intensity score of each mutant. If the contest is a failure, roll on the following chart to determine the effect on the psyche.

1d20	Effect
1-3	Abject Terror: Opponent must flee from the vicinity. If not possible, then the opponent can do nothing but curl into a fetal ball and sob until the mutant goes away or is destroyed
4-10	Revulsion: Opponent's Combat Style is reduced by one grade for the rest of the Combat Round
11-17	Nausea: Opponent feels sick at the sight of the mutant. Next available Combat Action is spent preventing a heaving of the stomach
18-20	Frenzy: Opponent engages in an all-out attack against the creature. The opponent may act defensively, but Special Effects chosen are restricted to those that enhance damage or the ability to kill the creature outright.

ZAKAR (TENTACLE HEAD: CHAOS MUTATION INTENSITY = 80%)

Zakar's head has become a 3 metre long tentacle, his facial features stretched out along it. One eye sits at the tip. He has lost the ability to speak and the transformation has turned him utterly insane. He spies on the characters, and is sneaky up to the point where he attacks, singling out an opponent and trying to throttle them. The tentacle can Grip and Bash and is tough enough to parry weapons. Zakar's lone eye, at the tip of the tentacle watches the victim in fascination as the life is squeezed from them.

Attributes	1d20	Location	AP/HP
Action Points: 3	1–3	Right Leg	0/5
Damage Modifier: +1d2	4–6	Left Leg	0/5
Magic Points: 15	7–9	Abdomen	0/6
Movement: 6 metres	10–12	Chest	0/7
Initiative Bonus: +12	13–15	Right Arm	0/4
Armour: Tough skin (tentacle)	16–18	Left Arm	0/4
Abilities: None	19–20	Tentacle	3/7

Magic: None
Skills: Athletics 40%, Brawn 62%, Endurance 48%, Evade 40%, Perception 74%, Stealth 62%, Unarmed 68%, Willpower 61%,
Passions: Hate Purity 80%
Combat Style: Writhing Tentacle of Horror 68%

Weapon	Size/Force	Reach	Damage	AP/HP
Tentacle	L	VL	2d6+1d2	3/7

THE BLOB (CHAOS MUTATION INTENSITY = 80%)

This labourer is now a gelatinous sack. Its skin is translucent and the organs beneath can be seen. It moves very slowly but can adhere to walls and ceilings and has a long reach with its pseudopod extensions. Its organs are now near redundant and as such impaling weapons have no effect beyond normal weapon damage and crushing weapons inflict half damage. Slashing weapons strike as normal.

Attributes	1d20	Location	AP/HP
Action Points: 2	1–20	Body	2/18
Damage Modifier: +1d4			
Magic Points: 7			
Movement: 2 metres			
Initiative Bonus: 9			
Armour: natural 2 point outer membrane			
Abilities: Adhering, Detect Life			

Magic: None
Skills: Athletics 54%, Brawn 78%, Endurance 96%, Perception 32%, Stealth 63%, Willpower 32%

Passions: Hate Purity 80%
Combat Style: Disgusting Pseudopods of Death, 65%

Weapon	Size/Force	Reach	Damage	AP/HP
Pseudopod	H	VL	1d6+1d4	2/9

The Blob can exude up to 7 pseudopods simulateneously although the rudimentary nervous system only allows the monster to control two at any particular time. It seeks to grasp opponents and then bathe them in secreted digestive juices which act as a Strong Acid, inflicting 1d4 Damage for 1d2 Combat Rounds whilst it maintains contact. If the Blob lashes-out with a pseudopod (which it always does on its first attack), then the digestive juices have no time to make meaningful contact.

HAMMER HORROR (CHAOS MUTATION INTENSITY = 55%)

A labourer whose right arm has increased in size and fused with a stone block he was holding at the time he transformed.

Attributes	1d20	Location	AP/HP
Action Points: 2	1–3	Right Leg	0/6
Damage Modifier: +1d6	4–6	Left Leg	0/6
Magic Points: 11	7–9	Abdomen	0/7
Movement: 6 metres	10-12	Chest	0/8
Initiative Bonus: 12	13–15	Hammer	5/10
Armour: Stone Right Arm	16–18	Left Arm	0/5
Abilities: None	19–20	Head	0/6

Magic: None

Skills: Athletics 54%, Brawn 69%, Endurance 56%, Evade 34%, Perception 62%, Stealth 45%, Unarmed 75%, Willpower 42%

Passions: *Hate Purity 80%*

Combat Style: *Hammer of the Goddess 75%*

Weapon	Size/Force	Reach	Damage	AP/HP
Hammer	H	M	1d10+1d6	5/10

ASH (CHAOS MUTATION INTENSITY = 60%)

A large labourer whose skin has been fused with volcanic ash and stone, and rekindled into life after five hundred years. He smoulders and parts of his skin glow. Anyone coming into Touch range sustains 1d4 damage.

Attributes	1d20	Location	AP/HP
Action Points: 3	1–3	Right Leg	6/7
Damage Modifier: +1d4	4–6	Left Leg	6/7
Magic Points: 7	7–9	Abdomen	6/8
Movement: 4 metres	10-12	Chest	6/9
Initiative Bonus: 8	13–15	Right Arm	6/6
Armour: Stone skin	16–18	Left Arm	6/6
Abilities: None	19–20	Head	6/7

Magic: None

Skills: *Athletics 42%, Brawn 69%, Endurance 76%, Evade 34%, Perception 62%, Stealth 18%, Unarmed 68%, Willpower 34%*

Passions: *Hate Purity 80%*

Combat Style: *Pickaxe 55%*

Weapon	Size/Force	Reach	Damage	AP/HP
Pickaxe	L	M	1d8+1+1d4	6/8

THE WORM (CHAOS MUTATION INTENSITY = 70%)

This mercenary has partially converted into a worm. His body and head are that of a common earth worm but he still has arms with which he holds weapons. He can also make grab attacks with his tail and then continue to cause further crushing damage thereafter, at the cost of one action point. This attack disregards armour once an opponent is grasped.

Attributes	1d20	Location	AP/HP
Action Points: 2	1–3	Tail Tip	2/6
Damage Modifier: +1d4	4–6	Mid Tail	2/6
Magic Points: 11	7–9	Lower Body	2/7
Movement: 6 metres	10-12	Chest	5/8
Initiative Bonus: 10	13–15	Right Arm	5/5
Armour: Skin and Lamellar	16–18	Left Arm	5/5
Abilities: None	19–20	Head	2/6

Magic: None

Skills: *Athletics 26%, Brawn 45%, Endurance 56%, Evade 30%, Perception 62%, Stealth 32%, Survival 30%, Unarmed 48%, Willpower 34%*

Passions: *Hate Purity 80%*

Combat Style: *Mercenary (Shortspear, Shortsword, Heater shield) 65%*

Weapon	Size/Force	Reach	Damage	AP/HP
Shortspear	M	L	1d8+1+1d4	4/5
Heater	H	S	1d4+1d4	6/15
Shortswrd	M	S	1d6+1d4	6/8
Tail	H	L	1d6+1d4	2/6

Scenario 5: Curse of the Contessa

Overview

The characters arrive in Westport where their success in foiling a robbery leads to them being hired by someone they believe to be Contessa Aliana den Solis: the richest and most powerful widow in city. She wishes them to uncover proof that the head of the Contessa's household is stealing from her. What they discover is that their target is an apprentice of Jedakiah and that the Contessa has been blackmailed into smuggling arms and equipment to him. If they succeed in uncovering the Contessa's secrets and learning the true nature of their patron, they can strike a heavy blow against Jedakiah.

This scenario focuses on the MYTHRAS mechanics for investigation. Although there is combat for those who crave it and danger for the incautious, the threats the characters face are more likely to consist of a knife in the back than a horde of slavering monsters. More so than any other scenario in this collection, this one repays a careful read-through first in order to familiarise with the main antagonists, their relationships to each other and the events that may occur.

Key Non-Player Characters

- Contessa Aliana den Solis. Mother of a five year old boy and head of one of the most powerful families in the city. She appears to be the characters' patron. She is enthralled by the demon, Feather Eye.
- Feather Eye. A demon bound by Jedakiah to ensure the Contessa's loyalty. The demon has possessed the Contessa's five year old son, but can also change into other shapes. In the shape of the Contessa, it attempts to manipulate the characters into freeing it.
- Castellan Xhago Garthanian. A cruel, ambitious Chaos Mother cultist and Jedakiah's apprentice. He ensures the Contessa keeps her bargain but, emboldened by Feather Eye's blandishments, is now stealing from both her and Jedakiah.
- "Inch". Spymaster for the city's ruler. He is looking for a means to weaken the former ruling families of Westport including the Contessa's house.
- Krytos den Krytos. A foolish, easily-duped aristocrat who hires the characters in an attempt to win favour with the Contessa.
- Perenge "The Ink Stained" – (formerly Perenge ab Solis). Initiate of Xalgith and former family priest

to the Contessa. He now wishes to find a way to prove his suspicions about Xhago and the Contessa's child.
- Sweggen Nine Fingers. Behind his façade as a simple shopkeeper, Sweggen is a powerful criminal with many contacts.

TIMELINE

SIX YEARS AGO...

1. Jedakiah secretly arrives in Westport looking for an agent to import, discreetly, weapons, equipment and mysterious substances from his old homeland.
2. Jedakiah makes a bargain with the Contessa. He ensures that she successfully gives birth and that her husband is punished for his adultery. She agrees to add, secretly, Jedakiah's shipments to the Solisti caravans heading inland.
3. The Contessa's husband dies as a result of Jedakiah's sorcery, but her son is born safely. Her son has a birthmark in the shape of a rune of the Chaos Mother, revealing his corrupted nature to anyone familiar with the cult.
4. Moving quickly, Jedakiah performs a ritual using Magic Points from his apprentice (Xhago) to bind a demon (Feather Eye) into the body of the Contessa's son.
5. The demon instinctively dominates the Contessa, ensuring that she protects her son with her life.
6. Confident that his gains are secure, Jedakiah returns north and leaves Xhago as the new household steward to monitor the Contessa.
7. Unable to resist the demon's domination and following Xhago's orders, the Contessa starts importing Jedakiah's requirements at great cost to her family.
8. Over the following years the demon becomes increasingly powerful and starts looking for a way to break the binding. It settles on a plan to subtly encourage Xhago to steal from his absent master.

RECENTLY

1. Xhago, who has become increasingly confident of his power, arranges to rob the latest disguised ship from the Contessa. Feather Eye the demon, who is aware of Xhago's plans, dupes Krytos, a noble suitor of the Contessa, into hiring some outsiders to defend the ship from robbers.
2. The characters arrive in Westport out of money and sorely lacking in whisky.

NOW...

1. The characters are hired by Krytos to prevent the robbery and catch at least one perpetrator.
2. Assuming they are successful, Feather Eye arranges a meeting with them disguised as the Contessa.
3. The characters are given a lucrative contract. "The Contessa" is a damsel in distress. Her household has been corrupted, her castellan (Xhago) is stealing from her and many of her family don't trust her. If they can find proof of his crimes she is very grateful.
4. The characters investigate out of chivalry (or avarice) and uncover rumours that, although Xhago is indeed stealing, the Contessa also has dark secrets.
5. The most likely outcome of the investigation is that they discover that Xhago is a sorcerer who leads a coven of Chaos Mother cultists in the Contessa's household.
6. A confrontation at the Solisti compound, probably during the fifth birthday party celebrations for the Contessa's son, provides the characters

RUNNING THE SCENARIO

The scenario is split into four parts

In DOWN AT THE DOCKS, *the characters are hired to defend a ship against robbery and attempt to take at least one robber alive.*

In AUDIENCE WITH THE CONTESSA, *the characters are recruited to try to expose the castellan.*

In the WEBS OF WESTPORT *the characters need to uncover the castellan's treachery before he or the tyrant's agents strike. At the same time they need to see deeper into the web.*

Finally, in SECRETS AND LIES, *the characters have a chance to overthrow a chaos cult and find a way to free the Contessa from the hold that Jedakiah has over her.*

As with all the scenarios in Book of Quests, this can be played as part of a linked campaign. Alternately it can be played as stand-alone or modified to fit your own campaign. Some suggestions for doing so can be found at the end.

The scenario foregrounds MYTHRAS' *strengths in investigation-based scenarios, so you should refresh yourself with the comments in the* MYTHRAS *rulebook on page 282. It is meant to evoke the kinds of urban swords and sorcery of stories that might be found in* Thieves' World *or Fritz Leiber's* Lankhmar *series. The fights are brutal struggles rather than glamorous duels, and hidden beneath the dirt of the city streets and the elegance of the great mansions are deceits and corruptions best left undisturbed.*

with the best chance to strike against Xhago. They need to find a way to defeat Xhago that doesn't result in the death of the possessed child.

Areas to be Covered

- *Westport*: the greatest port of The Realm. This classic Swords and Sorcery city is ruled with absolute power by the Tyrant. The city is a mix of cultures and styles but is gradually falling into disrepair.
- *The Solisti Compound*. A grand complex on Rich Hill in Westport which is home to the powerful Solis family, a demon and a covert coven of Chaos Mother cultists.
- *The Empty Vessel*. A dockside bar in Westport and home of many shady characters.
- *Sweggen's Curiosity shop*. This legitimate shop in Westport's merchant district is a front for Sweggen Nine Fingers, Westport's most successful fence.
- *The Green Dream*. A house of narcotics specialising in "hareesh"; found in the slum area of Westport.
- *Mendrith-Ran's Guest House*. Discreet establishment in the merchant district where Xhago rents some rooms incognito
- *Ash-Dynad's Bath House*. A bath house in Westport's merchant district where Xhago frequently conducts business in secret.

Starting the Scenario

Arriving in the free city of Westport the characters are contacted by a disguised stranger. He is looking for some outsiders to guard a ship against a robbery. He offers to pay well if the robbery is prevented and pay even better for any of the robbers taken alive. He suspects there is a traitor in the crew and he wants to find out who. The characters need to concoct a plan to prevent the robbery and take the robbers alive while not tipping off any of the current crew.

If the characters succeed, their patron soon re-contacts them to let them know that the person for whom he believes he works, the Contessa Aliana den Solis, wishes to meet and thank them.

The Contessa is the most desirable widow in the city. Once a common merchant's daughter she has risen to the head of the Solis family - one of the four great families of Westport. After the death of her husband, just over five years ago, she has striven to maintain her merchant fleet: importing all manner of fine goods from across the sea. She dotes on her only child, Kellan den Solis, who is shortly to celebrate his fifth birthday.

The characters meet with a figure who introduces herself as the Contessa and tells them that she believes that her castellan (Xhago), the head of her household, is stealing from her and was behind the attempted robbery. Xhago has replaced her formerly loyal retainers with his own forces and is now beginning to insinuate that the Contessa should marry him and make him the new count. Worried for the safety of her child and unsure whom she can trust, the Contessa has turned to outsiders. If they can bring her proof of his treachery she may be able to rally those still loyal in an attempt to oust him. The characters are her last, best hope.

The characters must follow the leads that the Contessa is able to offer in order to uncover the Xhago's true agenda. Not only is he stealing from her but he is also dabbling in the black arts. Tracking down ex-employees allows them to arm themselves with some protection against sorcery and a means to penetrate illusions, but it is a race against time. Once the castellan becomes aware that strangers are asking about him he responds violently. What no one knows is that the figure pulling the strings is the demon, Feather Eye. Bound into the Contessa's son by Jedakiah to ensure her obedience, the demon schemes to find release, and has seized on the characters as its best chance.

These events are likely to come to a climax at the Contessa's son's fifth birthday. If the characters are able to unravel the curse of the Contessa they are likely to find themselves facing a moral dilemma. To save her they may need to kill that which she loves above all else, and to thwart Jedakiah's plans they may need to set free an ancient evil.

BACKGROUND

Nearly six years ago, the Contessa encountered the master sorcerer Jedakiah and made a fateful bargain. He was looking for a source of weapons and gold from his old homeland and she was desperate for a child. She had suffered several stillbirths and knew the Count had fathered several bastards in the meantime, so she was looking for a way to bear a child in order to cement her place in the family, and also for revenge against the Count. Jedakiah delivered both. He arranged for her last liaison with the Count to result in a healthy child and, in the process, drained the count's own life. The count finally died just as his son was born. The sorcerer's payment for this was for the Solis family to secretly supply goods from Jedakiah's homeland at rock-bottom prices.

Jedakiah had further nefarious plans for the child. As a result of the ritual, the child was born with a birth mark resembling the rune of the Chaos Mother on his abdomen, signifying the taint in his blood. Using the corrupted placenta, Jedakiah and his apprentice, Xhago, bound Feather Eye, a fully-grown *Cuqulineaen* demon into the child's body, with the apprentice providing the permanent Magic Points for the binding. The demon dominantly possesses the child and by its nature is able to dominate the child's mother – the Contessa. It is bound to serve Jedakiah in whatever way Jedakiah sees fit. It is instructed to obey Xhago's orders as if they were given by Jedakiah.

Once satisfied that the demon was bound, Jedakiah confronted the Contessa with a mixture of lies and truth. The child was cursed and if he ever left the mansion he would die. Xhago would become her new castellan and oversee her compliance. Should she attempt to break the contract, Jedakiah would hear of it and he would activate the "curse of the birth mark." To demonstrate, Jedakiah cruelly cast Palsy on the child that he had held throughout the conversation, leading him to suddenly stiffen in her arms. Panicking, she begged Jedakiah to save her son from this curse and, to show his "mercy" he ended the Palsy. Convinced that the Contessa had no escape from her trap, Jedakiah returned to Gartharis and left Xhago to oversee the shipments of arms and supplies to Jedakiah's clans, and to ensure that the demon could not escape its binding.

As the child has grown, so too has the demon's power, as has its desire to escape the binding. It is able to replenish its Magic Points from its host's life energy, enabling it to start using limited sorcery in secret. The binding has restricted the demon to the area of the compound, but over time it has managed to make several contacts. Most importantly, it realised that Xhago is susceptible to flattery and could easily be swayed by greed and lust. Seeing a chance to pit master and apprentice against each other without breaking the terms of its bindings, Feather Eye has spent the last year subtly flattering Xhago, leading him to believe that he has been insufficiently recognised by Jedakiah.

As the years passed, Jedakiah's demands increased, but his already minimal payments decreased. Now on the verge of bankruptcy, Aliana has taken to smuggling goods past the Tyrant of Westport on disguised ships. Unknown to both her and Jedakiah, the castellan has started robbing her shipments as they enter Westport, seeing a chance to gain riches and power for himself. Subtly encouraged by the demon who whispers dreams of power and glory in the castellan's ear, the castellan has become convinced that he can seize money, power and the Contessa for himself.

Behind the events that are about to unfold is Feather Eye. The demon is a brood parasite. In its natural form it reproduces by injecting a sapient new-born with its own larval offspring. The enthralled parents are quickly dominated by the possessed infant. As the new-born grows, the demon grows with it, consuming the victim from within once it reaches the equivalent of puberty; at which point the withered husk of the host falls away, leaving a fully grown cuqulinaean. Jedakiah discovered a foul, long-forgotten ritual that enabled him to bind a fully adult cuqulineaen into a recently born child. The ritual, a gift from the Chaos Mother, imprisons the demon in the child's body and binds it to the sorcerer's will, providing the sorcerer with a powerful, if dangerous, servant. The demon is able to draw on the child's life force to fuel its own magic, but is unable to

> ### Relationships
> The relationship between the Contessa, Xhago, Jedakiah and Feather Eye is as follows.
>
> - The Contessa is dominated by Feather Eye. She knows this instinctively but is unable to break the domination and is incapable of denying a direct request from the demon. She knows that Xhago reports to Jedakiah and that he has replaced many of her retainers with people loyal to himself but she dare not move against him.
> - Xhago maintains the binding through his Magic Points but does not realise that Feather Eye is capable of sorcery or shape-changing. He believes that Feather Eye is completely subservient and has come to believe the demon's flattery. He dreams of overthrowing the Contessa and establishing his own Chaos Mother cult in Westport.
> - Feather Eye has inspired Xhago's dreams of power. It knows that Jedakiah bound it as part of some greater plan but does not know what that plan is.
> - Jedakiah's modus operandi is the same as ever: have a puppet controlling another puppet controlling a victim.

emerge from the host's body unless the binding is broken (by killing the host) or the sorcerer who has provided the Magic Points for the binding dismisses it. In both cases, the unfortunate host dies from the event.

The demon wants out of this but being expertly bound by Jedakiah, it cannot leave the Solis family compound and cannot act directly against Jedakiah or Xhago. It believes that its best chance to escape is for the castellan to dismiss the binding. Because Xhago provides the Magic Points to power the binding, and he has the power to end it; Jedakiah is paranoid and protective of his own Magic Points which is why he used Xhago's magical energy. It has never occurred to Jedakiah that Xhago – whom he regards as a weak, pitiful and snivelling coward – would *ever* do something as foolish as freeing a powerful demon.

Feather Eye, though, has seen an opportunity. The demon plans to manoeuvre Xhago into a position where he frees the demon in order to save his own life. Due to Feather Eye's constant flattery, Xhago has become so convinced of his own power that he now believes that he can steal from Jedakiah without concern. The minute that Xhago started stealing from Jedakiah, the demon was able to obey the terms of its binding and help Jedakiah. The binding limits what Feather Eye is capable of doing; any direct action against Xhago is forbidden. However by leading some strangers to discover who is stealing from Jedakiah, Feather Eye can act indirectly. Once Xhago is backed into a corner, Feather Eye believes it can persuade the castellan to dismiss the binding in return for Feather Eye saving his life.

Moving secretly through the compound, Feather Eye has perfected a small number of disguises, one of which is that of the Contessa. Appearing to the characters in her guise, Feather Eye plays the role of the damsel in distress, offers riches, glory and the prospect of future favours to play on the characters' hopes and desires. If all goes to plan, the characters confront Xhago with their findings and cold steel. At this point either the characters kill the child to break the binding or Xhago dismisses the binding: either way the demon is free.

Welcome to Westport

Situated at the mouth of the Southvale River between the forbidding moors and the downs of the West Vale, Westport jealously guards its status as an independent city state, granted five centuries ago after the Chaos wars. It is a bustling port, a destination for exotic goods from across the seas and the starting point for many a caravan into the interior. The city itself was once ruled by the 171 Peacock Princes and is home to styles of buildings, names and social customs foreign to the rest of the Vale.

For generations Westport was ruled in turn by one of four noble families but two years ago, a buccaneer now known only as the Tyrant took the complacent city in a daring raid. Now his rule is absolute and the only law is the one enforced by his troops. Punitive tithes make the business of making money honestly so expensive that even the best of men turn to crime.

The Tyrant gambles that the king of The Realm, Myur, is too weak to send an army to Westport, a city that even the hordes of chaos couldn't take. The tithes enrich the tyrant but enough trade still flows that the cost of freeing Westport would greatly outweigh the money saved. Furthermore, the tyrant's pirate fleet is strong enough to significantly reduce piracy by his rivals. At present the king shows little interest in Westport, seemingly more concerned about threats to the east and border wars (see *Shadows Behind the Throne*).

Although the king's advisors worry that the Tyrant is getting richer and stronger, the king's erratic decrees in the last year are of the greatest concern.

With the king distracted, the tyrant has turned his attention to the four families of Westport. Each has a well-defended fortification on Rich Hill and a body of loyal and well-armed troops. Although the Tyrant's men could storm a single compound or attempt to lay siege to it, he fears that the remaining families would band together to resist him. Furthermore, each family has ties of blood and lineage across The Realm, so a direct attack would be likely to force the king to act. Instead, the Tyrant's agents look for indirect means to weaken the families while the Tyrant attempts to exploit age-old rivalries in order to prevent a direct alliance forming. So far this balancing act has kept the peace and the longer the situation remains this way, the more the commoners come to accept the status quo. Still, the prospect of a showdown between the Tyrant and the heads of the four families is a constant source of conversation in the inns and bath houses of Westport

The city is built around two hills linked by the High Bridge from the Tyrant's keep to the city proper at Sayalis Gate. The magnificent structure, with arches reaching over 100 metres above the river dominates the view. Further down river, the Low Bridge provides access to the interior from the main city gate. Sheltered by the keep and High Bridge, the King's docks provide a high quality, secure wharf for shipping. The Old Town Docks are less sheltered and poorly maintained but are the cheapest place for small and independent merchants to land their goods.

The major districts and landmarks in the city include:

THE KING'S DOCKS

This sheltered dock is overlooked by Tyrant's Keep and the Lookout tower. A battery of siege engines at both locations ensure that no invading ship can get to the dock without coming under bombardment.

OLDTOWN DOCKS

Increasingly run-down the further north one goes, these docks are used by independent traders and those lacking the money to moor at the King's Docks

OLDTOWN

Sometimes called Poor Hill, Oldtown is densely packed on a wide, low hill to the north of the city.

MERCHANT DISTRICT

This area contains a mix of more upwardly mobile trade establishments along with many town houses and guest houses: the nearer to the Gardens the more expensive. River Gate – the main gate for the city - is found in the south east corner.

RICH HILL

This is a city within the city. The compounds for the four families can be found here. Temple Gate leads into the temples and parks district while High Bridge Gate connects to the Tyrant's Keep via High Bridge. Guards on Temple Gate monitor who enters and leaves.

TEMPLES AND PARKS DISTRICTS

Also known as the Gardens. As the name suggests this contains many fine buildings and green spaces. The House of the Four can be found here, as is Justice Square.

DOCKSIDE

The pirate heart of Westport. Every street has an Inn, every doorway a whore and every alleyway a footpad. All three contribute to redistributing wealth from visitors to locals.

OLD TOWN SLUMS

This is where those too poor to live on Poor Hill end up. The worst of the hareesh pits are here. Over the years Westport's rulers have varied between neglect, misguided improvement and occasional attempts to raze it to the ground.

MARKETS DISTRICT

This area contains the Market Gate and is home to various food, drink, animal and slave

HISTORY OF WESTPORT

Originally a small fishing village, Westport first came to prominence over 800 years ago when a dynasty of Peacock Princes from the Summerlands invaded. They brought their culture, art, trade goods and technology, naming their new possession Ilan-Den. Despite frequent attempts to expand into the interior, Ilan-Den remained the apogee of Summerland influence in The Realm and, as the decades passed, the city slowly declined, sinking into decadence and disrepair.

When Sayalis led the war against Chaos, Ilan-Den gained a new life. It was besieged by Chaos but did not fall and the four heroes of Ilan-Den were able to break out with a small army and bring Sayalis's forces through a hidden route to secure the city. For the reminder of the war, the city supplied Sayalis's troops with weapons and equipment from across the Summer Sea, enabling him to push the Chaos forces back north.

In gratitude for all the city did, Sayalis renamed it Westport and the new King of The Realm ennobled the families of the four heroes and gave them a quarter of the city each. Newly invigorated, the city became a bustling trade hub and the four families, in conjunction with Sayalis's representative, ruled wisely and well.

Now Westport's glories have once again faded. The stories of the Chaos wars are rarely told and even more rarely believed. Only historians still care enough to argue over the precise location of the mysterious "hidden route." The families' fortunes have withered and, two years ago, the city fell to a pirate leader after a daring raid on the citadel. Proclaiming himself the Tyrant, the pirate seized absolute power and discovered that the king was too weak to touch him. Now all goods are traded only with the Tyrant's permission and his word is law. Westport, a once civilised city, is ruled by thugs and riven by corruption.

markets. The district can change from squalid and criminal to reasonably affluent just by crossing a street.

The Barracks.

These imposing buildings are home to the bands of freebooters, pirates and mercenaries the Tyrant gathered together to take Westport. Half of them lie empty; the other half have been divided into camps where different armed groups claim ownership.

Law and Order in Westport

Order is enforced by the Westport "city guard" - thugs working for the Tyrant who keep a portion of all the fines they levy. They fine citizens for transgression of various laws, real and imagined, and provide 90% of their takings to their lieutenant. Capital punishment is reserved for anyone caught insulting the Tyrant, treason, the practice of sorcery, smuggling weapons and bearing weapons longer than the bearer's forearm (i.e. any weapon of Medium or greater length and any shield other than a buckler) within the city limits. Player characters should be made aware of these rules at a very early stage and encouraged to heed them.

The Tyrant is paranoid, obsessive and utterly without scruples. His various laws against weapons are intended to reduce any chance of a successful revolt against his rule, and to ensure that he maintains a monopoly on importing superior arms and equipment from overseas.

The favoured capital punishment is starvation. The victim is placed in a box with head and hands showing through holes and his mouth sewn shut. The box is placed on a plinth in Justice Square and the victim left to starve to death. Guards ensure that although citizens can abuse the criminals they cannot hasten the process of death. To the locals, this is known as "boxing."

Down at the Docks

In which the characters are hired to protect a cargo.

It starts, as it so often does, in a bar. The Empty Vessel is full to bursting with thieves, pick-pockets, prostitutes, sailors drinking away their last pay, mercenaries gambling away their boots and the kind of bar staff that are as handy with a dagger as a tray of drinks. It's the perfect place to pick-up a hired sword down on his luck: in short it is the place for adventurers to come and maybe make their fortune.

Today, somebody is hiring. Cloaked and hooded, blending in just like a chameleon doesn't, the aristocratic Krytos den Krytos is looking for outsiders for a job. Speaking with the kind of deep, threatening voice that he believes lower-class ruffians speak with, and propped at the bar in a manner he believes makes him look just like a local, he scans the place for a group of tough, capable adventurers.

Assuming the characters take the hint, or at least the offer of a free drink, Krytos explains what he wants. He's responsible for a ship berthed at the Old Town Docks and he believes that a robbery is planned for tonight. For several reasons he doesn't trust the city watch or the ship's crew to protect it and so is looking for some outside help. What he wants the characters to do is to watch the ship and catch the robbers red-handed. In particular he wants at least one robber to be caught and held for questioning. For this he will pay the characters 500 Founders in total, provided nothing is stolen. He pays 100 Founders for each robber captured alive but nothing at all for dead ones.

The characters may wish to haggle for higher payments or may have additional questions. Decide this either through role playing or abstract it as an opposed roll of one character's Influence or Easy Commerce skill versus Krytos's Influence skill. If the character wins,

Krytos doubles his basic rate, and if the character wins with a degree of success, Krytos also doubles his rate for each robber captured alive.

If the characters quiz Krytos further he says little. He is hiring outsiders because he doesn't trust the ship's crew, and says that he is acting as an agent for a respectable merchant. He does not expect the robbers to be heavily armed as they are not expecting opposition. He thinks there may be four to six of them. He won't tell them how he knows this, but insists that his source is completely trustworthy. Should the characters wish to try to discern how truthful he is being, then oppose the Insight of one character versus Krytos's Deceit. If the characters succeed they perceive that he is being truthful (as far as he knows). If they don't succeed they have no reason not to take him at face value.

If the characters agree to the job, Krytos has them to swear an oath not to rob the ship and to behave loyally for the duration of their employment. Once he is satisfied he asks them to meet him at dusk by an abandoned warehouse in the Old Town Docks. If he has been particularly impressed by the characters, he agrees to advance them up to 50 Founders in total for (non-alcoholic) supplies.

When the characters meet Krytos later, they notice two men-at-arms stationed nearby watching the building. These are Krytos's bodyguards. In the warehouse, Krytos stands by a decrepit table; a couple of sacks containing ropes, chains and blindfolds are nearby. He greets the characters cautiously (and a little unsteadily), his breath stinking of wine, as he explains the job.

The ship they are defending is the Man'agan Herald. He expects the robbery attempt to be made during the third watch tonight, in about four hours. He points out the ship which is docked about 100 metres away. He stresses again that he wants at least one robber captured alive and brought back to the warehouse for questioning. If the characters ask any more about what the ship's cargo is, or who they are working for, Krytos clams up. It's their job to prevent the robbery and take at least one ruffian alive: the rest is not their concern.

Defending the Herald

The characters have up to four hours to take up positions from which to watch the Herald. There are plenty of run-down and derelict buildings to provide cover. Broken, empty crates and barrels and other detritus also litter the area. While they are waiting the characters see various dockyard workers passing by, the usual ladies of the night and at least one patrol of city guards. The ship itself has two crew on watch. Sounds of drinking and carousing are clearly heard from the bars. Shortly after the tenth bell is called, a porter walks up the gangplank with a basket of food and drink. He or she talks briefly with the crew, pours out some drinks and then leaves. About 10 minutes later, both crew members collapse unconscious. The same person, who has been lurking in the alleyway, then gestures to a group of nearby thugs and the robbery begins.

There are 1d4+1 thugs and one cultist. One thug stays by a handcart at the end of the gang plank, the cultist keeps watch and the rest of the thugs start fetching cargo from the ship. They seem to be quite particular, only taking some chests and leaving the rest. If the characters don't interfere it takes them 30 minutes to load the handcart, cover the goods with rugs and head off into the night. They take it to a nearby safe house for overnight storage and then meet up with hirelings belonging to a local fence, Sweggen Nine Fingers, in the morning.

It is up to the players to decide how and when to intervene. The longer they wait, the more they may learn but the more likely it is for the robbers to get away with some goods. Should the characters attack, the cultist organise a defence. While the cultist remains in the fight the thugs defend themselves; the cultist is paying them well. None of the robbers are

Healing in Westport

Healing in Westport is provided by the Aliya devotees at the Houses of Mercy in the Temple District. The cost depends on the amount of healing needed and the skill of the healer. Most healers have a skill of 60% to 75% in First Aid (50+3D10) and 50% (40+2D10) in Healing. Use of First Aid costs 10 Founders; generate the healer's skill and then make a skill roll. Use of the Healing skill costs 20 Founders per day of treatment. These payments are made regardless of the success of the skill. Although a small number of the devotees have learned the miracle of Heal Body, such magic is reserved only for the great and noble and is not available to rootless adventurers.

The Four Families of Westport

The SOLIS family, descendants of Solis Evenhand, specialise in trade with extensive contacts in the Summer Lands and also the Vale interior. The Solisti caravans have been a feature of The Realm for five centuries now. Their patron deity was Xalgith until the Contessa severed the family links four years ago.

The KRYTOSI descend from Krytos the Lionhearted. They specialise in the training of martial techniques and weapon-smithing and provided the bulk of the old city guard. With the coming of the tyrant, they have been demilitarised and most of their income now comes from their bath houses. Their patron deity is Sormund.

The QUEOLLISH descend from Learned Quoel. They are famous for maintaining the city lights, music, art and heading the guild of messengers. They are by far the least influential of the four families but thanks to their involvement in preparing the potent narcotic hareesh, probably the richest. Their patron deity is Menissa.

The VES'ENDRI, descended from Ves'End the Magnificent, are builders and architects and are responsible for many properties in Westport. There is a long tradition that the youngest daughter in each generation runs the Houses of Mercy and what passes for a healers' guild in Westport. Their patron deity is Aliya.

---

well-armed, having just daggers and clubs. They flee if facing heavily armed opponents or if the cultist is captured or killed. The cultist (Torech) is a fanatic. He fights to the death or, if seriously outnumbered and facing capture, he commits suicide by slitting his own throat and throwing himself into the water. His fanatical loyalty to the Chaos Mother makes it impossible to use the Compel Surrender Special Effect.

The confrontation shouldn't take long; the only issue is whether the characters manage to capture anyone alive. The real test here is not defeating the foes, but capturing them. Encourage players to be creative in their use of Special Effects. It is unlikely, but not impossible, that they are able to take the cultist without harm.

Various clues may be found. Firstly, all cargo targeted has, on close inspection, been marked with an odd rune. If the characters have had previous experience with it or possess an appropriate Lore skill then the characters recognise it as a the rune of the Chaos Mother. This same rune is also tattooed on the abdomen of the cultist.

Most of the thugs are aware that the stolen cargo is destined for Sweggen Nine Fingers and barter that information for freedom or to prevent a beating. They all finger Torech (the cultist) as the leader. They don't know much about him or any cult and they have never worked for him before. He only wanted the specially marked cargo. They all suspect that it is an inside job.

If the characters manage to capture Torech and interrogate him, then he draws on his Oath to the Chaos Mother to resist torture or threats of it. Should the characters discover his allegiance (through uncovering his tattoo, for example) and reveal that they are already familiar with the Chaos Mother cult, then he curses them and praises the Chaos Mother and her imminent devouring of all non-believers. He is capable of keeping up a stream of profanities for hours on end and kills himself at the first opportunity.

Once the characters get the robbers back to the warehouse Krytos takes over. His two bodyguards tie up the prisoners. Krytos pays the characters their due and then dismisses them. Krytos has his guards beat-up any prisoners brought to him, but the thugs do not tell him much. If he has the cultist he gains nothing and the Torech manages to commit suicide when Krytos becomes careless. Nevertheless, Krytos meets with his go-between later the next day (a street urchin called Meggo), who carries a message to the Solisti compound. Feather Eye meets with Meggo and, seeing his chance, arranges for messages to be sent to the characters involved.

An Audience with the Contessa

In which the characters meet their patron.

Two days after the robbery, just enough time to drink their way through their gains, the characters are invited to a repeat meeting with Krytos. He invites them to the Salubrium bath house on Rich Hill and tells them that his patron wishes them to attend an audience at the Solisti mansion on Rich Hill at dawn to thank them for their help. Krytos is feeling slighted about being treated as a messenger and also because he has not yet been invited to an audience with the Contessa; but he keeps that to himself. From now on, he tasks one of his bodyguards to keep an eye on the characters.

The next morning, the characters are welcomed at the gate of the Solisti compound on Rich Hill. They are asked to leave all weapons and armour in the gatehouse and are then led to the colonnaded courtyard nearest Solis tower. A delightful arrangement of mint teas and candied meats awaits them. The colonnade, like much of the compound, is a study in crumbling grandeur. The exquisite marble columns are cracked, the fine benches are rickety and the floor is covered in leaves and grime.

There is a short delay, giving the characters time to study their surroundings, before a hooded figure arrives. After looking around briefly, she removes her hood, takes a deep breath and says "You don't know how grateful I am that you came." This is Feather Eye using his Shapechange to Human spell and a sight illusion to take the Contessa's form. It is relying on the characters being outsiders who have never seen Aliana close up. Affecting a brave but worried display, "she" introduces herself and explains her problem.

She has discovered that her castellan, a man named Xhago, is robbing her. He is becoming more brazen in his thefts and has hired staff members who are loyal to him alone and spreading foul rumours about her so that many of her old staff no longer know who to believe. Furthermore, he has begun making lewd comments and implying that he feels she should give herself to him. She shudders in horror at the prospect. The problem is getting proof of his activities. If she simply accuses the castellan she worries that he will respond with violence and bloodshed. She cannot afford that because she knows the Tyrant is waiting for a chance to move against the four families to consolidate his control over the city. As the characters have already proven themselves she throws herself on their mercy. Can they find proof of his wrongdoing? If they can, she feels she will be able to sway most of the staff to her side and expel him.

Feather Eye has significantly enhanced his Charisma and tries to play on lust, avarice or chivalry depending on how the characters react. This is an excellent time to take advantage of the characters' Passions and may provide an opportunity to develop new ones (Love Contessa, for instance). Perhaps one character becomes hopelessly enamoured of the Contessa or another finds a burning hatred of the castellan kindled. If nothing else, she offers them 50 Founders a day each plus any expenses to uncover the truth. If they can provide the proof she needs and she can expel Xhago,

they have her everlasting gratitude and 5,000 Founders each from the Solisti coffers. As a down-payment she slips a diamond earring from her ear and gives it to one of the characters. The earring worth the best part of 1,000 Founders and can be exchanged for about 400 Founders locally.

Characters may wish to make skill rolls, such as Insight, to determine if they can trust the Contessa. They have no reason to suspect that this is not the *real* Contessa and Feather Eye is being careful to tell the strict and literal truth. The demon is also genuinely nervous and psychically stressed by the way it is pushing the edges of its binding. Successful Insight rolls thus reveal that she is worried, highly stressed and telling the truth. Should a character make a critical Insight that overcomes Feather Eye's secretly rolled Deceit, the demon has made a slip of some sort which means that when the character meets the real Contessa, he is able to tell that she is not the same woman as the one they met in the compound. Do not tell the player now but make a note for future reference.

The characters may naturally wish to ask questions but, if they do not, Feather Eye does its best to impart certain leads. Again, realise that everything the demon says is true though it chooses its words carefully.

- The Contessa realises now that she should not have dismissed her former castellan, Miguel ab Arranchez. She regrets it bitterly. If the characters ask for more details, the demon tells them that Solisti family jewels were found in Miguel's rooms and the fence, Sweggen Nine Fingers, confirmed that he had been offered them for sale. She heard that shortly after he had been dismissed there was an angry confrontation

Bath House Etiquette

Players are often insistent that their characters go fully armed into any situation, or at least with a knife hidden somewhere unmentionable. Bath house routines prevent this; the guest must fully undress before being presented with their robe. For this reason, bath houses are favoured places for peaceful meetings. Attempts to bypass these rules (by, for example, bribing the attendants to look the other way), will be likely to cause alarm. Make sure the players understand this and adhere to the rules before the meeting with Krytos (and likewise when they enter the Solisti compound) as it is important to get them used to it before they meet Xhago at Ash-Dynad's bath house.

between Miguel and Xhago when he tried to claim that he had been framed. In retrospect, it looks like this was true. As for now, she has heard he has fallen on hard times and frequents drug dens in the slums.
- Although Xhago lives at the mansion he spends many nights away from it. She does not know where he goes but perhaps there are answers there?
- What happened to her husband? She does not want to answer this and she blanches, her eyes welling with tears. She goes no further than saying that the Count was a good man and he did not deserve to die without seeing his son's face. His death was sudden and unexpected and many blame the old family physician who seemed more interested in his drink than his job.
- If the characters ask about the physician the demon tells them that he died some four years ago of a strange disease. His widow lives on a stipend provided by the Contessa.
- If the characters mention selling the earring, Feather Eye advises them *not* to use a man called Sweggen because she has heard that he might have dealings with the castellan. This is reverse psychology. She doesn't trust the dockmaster, Benzaad ab Keffi, as she thinks he may be cooperating with Xhago and he must have been involved.
- She can arrange for a messenger (an urchin called Meggo) to meet with the characters at dawn each day wherever they are staying, and bring messages back to her. Discretion is vital though. Should they need to meet with her, tell Meggo and she arranges it.
- There are things she refuses to answer. She will not talk about what was on the Herald or why she is smuggling goods past the Tyrant. She does not discuss anything to do with the Contessa's personal life nor about her son. Indeed any questions about him lead to a well-simulated display of affronted anger and, if the questions are too probing, to the demon ending the discussion. Finally, she does not mention the priest, Perenge. Feather Eye does not want any Xalgith cultists getting involved, especially if they may be able to use magic. If the characters ask about the Contessa's religion or whether there is a priest they can trust, the demon blankly says 'no.'

Feather Eye is superhumanly intelligent, charismatic and an expert in deceit; yet it is bound to serve its master and cannot leave the compound so there are limits to what it can do and say. Should the characters start to press or ask inconvenient questions, it concentrates on a Sound illusion that it cast just before the meeting. This creates an illusion of someone calling for the Contessa, giving the demon an excuse to end the meeting and plead with them one last time to help her. Feather Eye uses every trick in the book. The Contessa's voice is sultry and seductive, her demeanour frightened yet determined. She is rich, has access to great treasures and capable of great gratitude. She is a fiercely protective mother yet also a lonely widow with a cold bed and a scheming castellan lusting after her. What red-blooded hero could resist?

The Webs of Westport

In which the characters come to the realisation that truth and deceit are habitual bedfellows.

This section of the scenario is a dynamic "sandbox" in which the characters' actions drive the unfolding events rather than being a linear order of events. The characters have free rein to go where they wish in order to find the clues they need. In this section, common knowledge about the Contessa is presented, several key characters are detailed along with what they know, what they might tell the player characters and where they might be found. Several events also occur: some happen regardless of the characters' activities while others are only triggered if the characters take certain actions.

As the characters explore they should come to realise that, five days after the first meeting with their patron, there is a birthday party for the Contessa's son. This is likely to provide the best chance the characters get to penetrate the Solisti compound in order to finally unravel the mysteries around them.

Use the information in this section to help decide how the personalities listed react to the characters. There is no requirement for them to meet every non-player character listed and there are multiple ways for them to uncover enough clues to point them in the right direction. Remember, Feather Eye is doing its best to feed the characters the information they need.

Westport is a living place and the non-player characters have their own agendas and actions which take place both independently of the characters' actions and in reaction to them. However no one person knows the whole picture so their actions should be based on what they can feasibly be expected to know. There are also many more people in the city than mentioned here so feel free to create non-player characters that suit particular needs.

COMMON KNOWLEDGE

Assuming that the characters are not native to Westport, they need to orient themselves and gain a basic understanding of who is who in the city. The brief history of Westport earlier (page 121) can easily be learned by outsiders by buying a few drinks in bars or, for those so inclined, hiring a scribe at the Temple of the Four to provide a history lesson.

The characters' main interest is presumably in discovering what is commonly known about the Solisti family and the castellan. They soon learn that there is little interest in Xhago. Those who have met him rarely have a good word to say about him, but he has kept his secrets well so he is largely regarded as arrogant, foreign (from the north) and bad-tempered. No one has any reason to suspect him of harbouring darker secrets.

The Contessa, on the other hand, is a source of fascination, much of it prurient, to the common folk of Westport. She is glamorous, mysterious, powerful and widowed Naturally the gossip surrounding her focuses on why she hasn't married, the dark secrets that surely must underlie the death of her husband and why it is that her son is never seen outside the compound. Powerful, unmarried women throughout history have been feared, lusted after and seen as unnatural in equal parts. The Contessa is no different. A list of possible beliefs about the Contessa is given below. Hand these out to the character bit-by-bit in the guise of a variety of non-player characters. None of them are wholly true, and many of them are contradictory, yet all are based on true observations.

If any of the player characters are from Westport or its surroundings, assume that they already know the common knowledge about Westport and the Contessa and know 1d4 of the rumours listed below for each 50% (or part thereof) in their Locale skill.

The following is common knowledge about the Contessa and the Solisti that can quickly and easily be gathered.

- She is a widow with just one son who was born five years ago, shortly after the death of her husband.
- Her son has never left the Solisti compound on Rich Hill.
- She is the head of the Solis family who specialise in importing goods from abroad and sending them inland on caravans.
- Each of the four families is a patron of one the cults of the Four. The Solisti used to be the patron of the cult of Xalgith but the Contessa has renounced their support of the cult.

In addition to the common knowledge there is an almost endless number of rumours about the Contessa - some of which are as follows

- She is just a common gold-digger who had her husband murdered.
- She is a barren harridan who refused the count his married rights. When he threatened to divorce her, she had him killed by a sorcerer / lover / family member.
- She is a wanton woman whose many liaisons broke the count's heart. He died a broken man when he found out that her son was sired by another man.
- Everyone knows the old count played around, it's what men do. He was killed by a jealous husband and the Contessa has loyally covered up the truth to preserve his memory.
- Her son is horribly disfigured / weak and sickly so she never lets him leave the compound.
- Her son was cursed at birth by a witch who said he would be murdered by a man who has never seen him so she keeps him locked away.
- Her son is dark skinned / ginger haired / has blue eyes / is inhumanly beautiful

GAMES MASTERING INVESTIGATIONS

A free-form investigation can be demanding to both run and play. Games Masters need to have a good idea of how the plot fits together and how non-player characters react to both the direct encounters with player characters and when they, inevitably, hear about significant events. On the other hand, the players need to be capable of taking the initiative and making choices with often incomplete information. Generally speaking, it is useful to consider beforehand what kind of style best fits you and your group. Two extremes are:

PULP ACTION. *In this style it is assumed that significant clues are easily found and that the interest is in how the player characters put the knowledge to use. As many Swords and Sorcery characters may not have great detective skills, you can make use of Group Luck Points to hand out clues or assume that the most significant elements of each encounter are simply gained by whoever makes most sense or whoever is willing to spend a Luck Point. Some players may regard this as cheating* so you should only hand out enough clues to ensure that the characters have leads to follow.

PUZZLE SOLVING. The emphasis is on clue gathering and characters must succeed at skill rolls to gain them. On failing the skill roll allow Luck Points to be used to either re-roll skills or come up with another opportunity in which the clue may be found. Hard-core puzzle solving would not allow any use of Luck Points. Unlucky or unskilled characters may not gain enough knowledge to understand what is going on, leading to players becoming frustrated. On the other hand, successfully solving the puzzle can be very rewarding.

Of course most groups tend to like styles that are something of a mix; so before the scenario starts you should decide whether clues will be handed out automatically, can be gained through spending Luck Points, through skill rolls that can be re-rolled with Luck Points or only through successful skill rolls. Pulp action styles may seem easier but players who overspend their Luck Points on clues may find themselves exposed when danger finally strikes...

which would give away the secret of his real father if he was seen in public.
- Her son is really a girl and she keeps that knowledge secret so that her daughter can inherit the family wealth.
- The Contessa is having an affair with the Tyrant / king's ambassador / head of the Krytos family / all of them and playing them off against each other.
- The Contessa lies with women / two men at a time / her stallion / demons / travels to the docks in disguise to lie with sailors / no one because her sex was sealed by a curse.
- The Contessa never goes out in public herself any more, a look-alike doubles for her.
- The Contessa has forbidden worship of the Four and now offers sacrifices to a demon from the Summerlands / worships no gods at all / a snake god from the mountains with whom she lies at night.
- The Contessa permanently keeps candles and incense burning in her grief over the count's untimely death.

Naturally Games Masters can add to and embellish this gossip as necessary. Should you wish to broaden out the gossip to more than the Contessa a further selection of rumours are provided in the boxed section on page 132.

CHARACTERS, LOCATIONS & EVENTS

In which the secrets of Westport, great and small, are revealed.

The initial meeting with Feather Eye (disguised as the Contessa) gives the characters several leads that they can follow but there is no set order in which they may choose to explore them. The various personalities of Westport are described alongside what they know, where they may be found, what connections they have to others and what agendas they may have. The direct leads from Feather Eye are given first with the rest presented in alphabetical order. It is for you as a Games Master to bring the events to life depending on the choices the players make.

There are many possible orders in which players can progress through the encounters in Westport so a table showing a timeline of what would naturally happen after the characters' first meeting with the Contessa is given on page 131, along with a list of the characters and their role. Depending on how the characters proceed, some of the events may be moved around or simply not happen.

NON-PLAYER CHARACTERS

The characters are likely to interact with the following non-player characters. There is no set order so they are given in alphabetical order. However, as Xhago is their main target he is detailed first..

XHAGO

The characters may decide to follow Xhago in order to uncover evidence of his corruption. If they do so, they need to make periodic Easy Streetwise (or Standard Stealth) rolls opposed by Xhago's Perception to avoid detection. While on duty, Xhago travels by palanquin carried by two Solisti retainers, with two additional Solisti guards (both of whom are Chaos Mother cultists). This makes him easy to follow but a hard target to ambush. As the days pass he also becomes increasingly paranoid and alert for danger. Of course, the characters are not the only ones with an interest in him.

Xhago's most likely movements over the first few days are as follows:

Day 1 (the day the characters meet with Feather Eye disguised as the Contessa). He spends most of this day at the King's docks. In the afternoon he has an angry confrontation with the Solisti dockmaster, Benzaad ab Keffi, in a private room. He accuses Benzaad of being drunk at his job and of being involved with the robbery. Feather Eye has carefully insinuated that Benzaad might know something in order to get Xhago out of the compound for the day. The characters are unlikely to be able to observe this encounter but may be able to watch both men emerge, at which point a Standard or Hard Insight roll (depending on their vantage point) suggests that a serious disagreement has just occurred and that Benzaad is both extremely worried, and showing signs of several, recent, facial bruises. In the early evening a rough-looking man asks to see Xhago. A Hard Insight roll indicates that at least one of the characters recognises him but cannot place him. A critical success reveals that he is Kantis Yellow Tongue, a regular at the Empty Vessel. Kantis has heard that the Solisti dockmaster might be paying a reward to anyone who knows who was involved in the robbery of the Herald. He fingers the player characters to Xhago and asks for his fee. Xhago has him beaten and thrown out.

Day 2. Xhago spends the day at the compound. He spends a portion of it conferring with Feather Eye and the rest making obeisance to the Chaos Mother. In the evening he travels in disguise through backways to Ash-Dynad's bath house. There he meets with thugs from a street gang and hires them for a job. From day 2 onwards, one of Sweggen's men starts keeping a watch on Xhago. He has a Streetwise skill of 65%.

Day 3. In the morning Xhago sends messengers out looking for the player-characters and inviting them to a meeting at Ash-Dynad's. He spends the day at the compound until his meeting with the characters. After the meeting he heads to Mendrith-Ran's guest house to lie low for a while.

Day 4. If the characters survive the ambush, Xhago flees to the Solisti compound in the morning. He is now beginning to think they may be working for someone important, or may be rivals for his master's patronage. He talks with Feather Eye who agrees that maybe Jedakiah has taken on new apprentices because he is worried about Xhago's growing power. In the afternoon, two of the guards who seem most commonly to be protecting Xhago leave the compound in plain clothes and head to the docks. There they buy two poisonous snakes and return with them to the compound.

Day 5. By this point, Xhago's actions depend on how active the characters have been in opposing him. The Contessa is expecting him to oversee the arrangements for her son's birthday celebration but he leaves this to others and spends most of his time in sending out various cultists to find out more about the player characters.

The Contessa

The characters find the real Contessa hard to approach directly. She spends most of the next few days inside the compound organising the upcoming party for her son. If she leaves, it is in her palanquin with several retainers, perhaps to meet with a tailor or jeweller. The characters therefore need to either gain entrance to the estate and sneak into her private quarters, or arrange for an audience. Naturally, the head of the household, Xhago, dictates who gets to see the Contessa…

If the characters wait until Xhago is absent, the steward – the ageing and slightly senile Imahan ab Solis – will see them and ask for their reasons. Depending on their cover story, the characters need to succeed in a Hard Influence, or Standard Deceit, roll to persuade him to allow them an audience. They are asked to wait for a period of time (1d4 hours). The characters may notice a maid: a sullen, dark-eyed woman who is making only a token effort to clean the corridor outside during the characters' meeting with Imahan. Any character specifically looking around during the conversation who succeeds at a Standard Perception roll notices that she is paying close attention. If Imahan agrees to arrange an audience the maid leaves to tell the highest ranking cultist present that strangers are attempting to see the Contessa. Xhago has left instructions that this is not to happen unless he is present, so shortly afterwards, two cultist guards enter the room, explain that there has been a change of plan and escort the characters off the premises with whatever force they feel necessary.

Despite all these obstacles it is possible that the characters succeed in meeting the Contessa. They find her courteous if somewhat distracted. Generally two handmaids and two guards are present, at least one of them being a cultist. If the characters claim to know her, she is puzzled as she has never seen them before. A Standard Insight roll reveals that she is either a very good liar or telling the truth. If the characters try to implicate Xhago in thieving from her she is taken aback. She knows that Xhago is Jedakiah's man and that many of the staff are loyal to him rather than her but she cannot risk these unknown strangers causing problems. She instantly terminates the audience with an unconvincing defence of Xhago: Easy Insight to realise that she is clearly lying.

If the characters start on an outlandish tale about a demon possessing her child, she is temporarily stunned into silence. Deep in the core of her being she knows that her son is not what he appears, yet his domination of her is too strong for her to admit that to herself. She also knows

Chronological Timeline

Day	Events
Day 1 morning	The characters meet with their patron at the Solisti compound. Xhago uncovers the identity of the people who thwarted the robbery of the Herald.
Day 2	Sweggen discovers the characters' identity through contacts at the Empty Vessel and attempts to set up a meeting. Inch comes to the conclusion that the Man'agan Herald was smuggling goods for the Contessa.
Day 3	Xhago meets with the characters at Ash-Dynad's bath house. Inch discovers the identities of the player characters in relation to the Man'agan Herald's defence and has them followed.
Day 4	Meggo (the characters' messenger) is murdered. Night – an assassination attempt is made against the characters through the "Snake in the night" event.
Day 5	If the characters have not already robbed Xhago's secret apartments, Sweggen arranges for them to be burgled.
Day 6	Count's fifth birthday celebrations

Characters, Locations and Connections

Characters	Where and What
Ash-Dynad's Carnival of Baths & Exotica	A bath house in the Merchant District frequented by Xhago, current castellan to the Solisti.
Mendrith-Ran's Guest House.	An establishment in the merchant district where Xhago has rooms rented under an alias.
The Green Dream	A hareesh pit in the slums where Miguel, former castellan to the Solisti, can be found.
Inch	The Tyrant's spymaster. Believes that the Contessa is involved in smuggling. His goal is to destroy the Solisti family. Can be found anywhere in Westport.
Perenge the ink-stained	Former Solisti family priest. Believes that Xhago is a sorcerer and that the Contessa's child is possessed by a demon. His goal is to prove this. Can be found at the House of the Four in the Temple District.
Meggo	An urchin who runs messages and errands for Feather Eye.
Miguel ab Solisti	Aka "Wormy Mig." Knows that Xhago is a sorcerer and believes that he arranged for the Count's husband's death. His goal is to scrape together enough Founders to pay for his next hit of hareesh.
The widow Mali-An	Widow of the deceased physician to the Contessa. Believes her deceased husband is a songbird. Knows that Xhago has a strange and nasty tattoo. Her goal is to find out which songbird is her husband. Lives in a town house in the merchant district
Benzaad ab Keffi	Solisti dockmaster and Xhago's right-hand man. Knows that Xhago's smuggling operation is losing lots of money. His goal is to pay off his debts before Sweggen gets really violent. Usually found at the King's Docks or the Lucky Puffin.
Sweggen Nine Fingers	A fence who has had dealings with Xhago. Knows that Xhago takes a cut of his smuggling. His goal is to reimburse himself for the losses Xhago has cost him and to send Xhago a message while keeping "Inch" sweet. Usually found at his shop in the Old Town district.

that Jedakiah has some means of killing her child from afar. Without something such as the Eyeglass of True Seeing she refuses to believe the characters and has them thrown out, violently if needs be. Furthermore, this encounter quickly becomes known among the cultists and the characters notice many hostile faces watching them leave.

The Counterfeit Contessa

Should the characters wish to speak with their patron again, Feather Eye puts it off for as long as possible. It knows that it runs significant risks and if it has to spend Magic Points it will not be able to recover them all before the birthday celebration when it expects to need sorcery. That said, it arranges a meeting for dawn by the compound's south postern gate (see page 144) where it normally meets with Meggo's gang. The gate is no longer used and has been blocked up with stones. Feather Eye discovered that it is sheltered and over time has freed some stones around the old grill. Having spent many months looking longingly at freedom it was able to entice a street kid who was panhandling in the area before being moved on. This urchin was Meggo and Feather Eye has since formed a profitable alliance with Meggo and his gang.

Feather Eye meets with the characters here. It has the advantage of making it hard to see the Contessa, and it keeps the conversation as short as possible. The characters may wish to ask about many issues and may suspect her of playing them false. As with the first conversation, Feather Eye is constrained in what it can say, so focuses on trying to manipulate their emotions, offer them more jewellery or whatever it is that seems to motivate them.

If the conversation is going badly for the demon it plays its last card. As with the first conversation it has prepared a Sound illusion which it has been holding. The first part is a rough, coarse voice shouting "Hey! Who's there?" along with the sounds of booted footsteps. At this point, Feather Eye steps back mostly out of sight saying "I have to go. Get out of here before he sees you." If that is not enough, Feather Eye concentrates again. Stepping back a few more paces so that the characters can no longer see, he has the illusion speak again. "Xhago will hear of this. Who are you talking to?" Depending on Feather Eye's reading of the characters, it might have "the Contessa" respond defiantly, or pleadingly or even simulate the sound of a slap. Use judgment of the players to determine what is most likely to convince them - but not to persuade them to try to scale the walls to rescue her there and then.

Inch – The Tyrant's Spymaster

Inch has the kind of face people want to punch. He is wheedling, cowardly, sweaty and grasping. He is also the Tyrant's agent so actually punching him would be a death sentence. It is his job to know what is going on in Westport and to finger those who need *boxing*. It was Inch who arrested the customs agents a few weeks ago and now he's on the trail of the Solis family. Inch may have been tipped off about the characters by Sweggen, or his own interest in the Contessa means that he may have linked the characters to the events on the Man'agan Herald. Either way, he believes that the characters have something he wants.

No meeting with Inch is pleasant and every meeting with Inch requires those unfortunate enough to be involved to pay his "consultation fee." In the tough streets of Westport this has become known as "giving an Inch." He carries a small abacus which he has no idea how to use and at the end of each consultation makes great show of using it to 'calculate' his fee. Generally he picks an amount that he can extort based on his perception of how much money his victims have to hand: roll 3d6+10 for an amount in Founders or pick a value that makes sense in your campaign.

As this is his first meeting with the characters, and they are probably outsiders who have already shown some facility in violence, Inch is likely to choose a public setting and ensure that he has several guards with crossbows discretely present. Inch is cunning and has survived this long through picking his encounters carefully. He will not walk up to a party of armed and violent strangers and simply demand money. His preference is to join the characters at a table in whatever lodgings they occupy. Should they still be in the Empty Vessel, the characters become aware of a sudden dip in the noise level and notice any nearby companions carefully moving away as Inch, a nondescript looking man, comes over to join them. An Easy Perception rolls shows several discreetly armed men nearby while an Easy Insight roll shows that this stranger is making an effort to demonstrate that he means no imminent harm. An Easy Locale, Very Easy Streetwise roll or Standard Lore (Westport) roll indicates that this must be Inch.

Once the prospect of violence abates, Inch quizzes the characters about how they have become involved in the events. He is especially interested to know if they have had any dealings with the Contessa. If they reveal such contacts, Inch has them followed everywhere afterwards. If the characters wish to try to keep a secret from Inch then they need to win an opposed roll of their Deceit against his Insight. This doesn't mean that he believes them (Inch

Rumours, Facts and Other Deceits

Should the characters ask around they may hear several things that are true (T), false (F) or a bit of both (T/F). There are of course more rumours than these doing the rounds; these are the ones that may attract the characters' attention. You may also want to seed some rumours connecting this scenario to others in the Book of Quests.

- Several customs agents were boxed three weeks ago. (T)
- The Solisti trade fleet has been decimated by pirates and storms in the last few years. (T/F)
- The Tyrant once offered to marry the Contessa but was spurned and now seeks revenge. (F)
- Caravan masters are recruiting more heavily than normal for guards because of increased bandit activity. (T)
- A crime boss called "Greeble" has been organising street kids into gangs of cut-purses. (F)
- The Tyrant recently received a jewelled bird that can tell a man the date of his death. (T)
- A formidable blue-faced barbarian has cursed the Solisti caravans in revenge for despoiling his ancestral lands. (F)
- The king's agents in the Order of Truth are infiltrating the city in order to overthrow the Tyrant (T/F).
- The Tyrant keeps vats of boiling oil on the city walls ready to pour it over any approaching army. (T/F)

has never believed anyone in his life and does not intend to start now), simply that he realises he gains nothing else worthwhile at this time.

If the characters are particularly forthcoming, Inch may have a proposition for them. If they can provide proof that the Contessa has been smuggling weapons then they have his unspecified "gratitude." Smart characters may realise that working for Inch is a really, really bad idea. Ask for Locale or Insight rolls if the characters do not realise. If they co-operate, and get Inch the proof he is looking for, then, once the Contessa is safely under lock and key, a group of city guards are sent to arrest any of characters foolish enough to still be in the city on trumped-up charges of treason.

Cunning characters may be able to use Inch to their advantage. His agenda is to weaken the four families enough that the Tyrant can overthrow them without risking too much. If the characters can persuade him that the Contessa, or her family, partake in sorcery or other dark arts, then Inch forms a force of up to 30 of the Tyrant's men to attack the Solisti compound. The characters need to find a way to throw open the main gates and will be expected to lead the force to the Contessa. Naturally the force's commander, a huge and vicious killer by the name of Kubron (use the city guard statistics with +20% to his Combat Style and a Damage Modifier of +1d4) has been instructed to make sure the characters do not get out alive.

Alternately, Inch may be a character who stays largely in the background with the Tyrant. If running further adventures in Westport then keeping Inch out of direct involvement with the characters at this point, while ensuring that he is frequently mentioned, both increases the tension and makes the eventual first meeting more dramatic.

Mali-An – the Physician's Widow

Fredak, the physician who failed to save the life of the Contessa's husband, died of the Bloody Flux four years ago. His widow, Mali-An, now lives in a townhouse in a nice part of the merchant district with her 3 sons, 2 daughters, 21 grandchildren and 20 canaries. One of her sons, Lintle, is a servant at the Solisti compound and is soon to be inducted into the Chaos Mother cult - though Mali-An knows nothing of his new faith. There are various connections to Mali-An. Perenge suggests that she is likely to be the best source of information about the Contessa's son outside of the compound. Miguel claims that the Contessa had her old physician murdered and would murder his widow if she had the chance. If the characters go to the Aliya temple looking for information about the child's birth (on the off-chance that a devotee was present) a novice can clarify that the family physician would have overseen the birth though would not have been present at it. Given a few hours to consult the records, the novice can name the physician and inform them that he is dead though his death record mentions a widow.

Should characters follow up one of these leads then providing they are polite and personable, Mali-An is happy to tell what she knows.

- A seer has told that her husband has been reborn as one of the twenty canaries she keeps but she isn't sure which one.
- The old count sickened and died very quickly just before the birth despite Fredak's best efforts.
- Fredak wasn't present at the birth of the Contessa's son. Mali-An heard that there were rumours that the child was disfigured in some way and that one of the midwives fainted. There was also some sort of argument about a foreign midwife being present. .
- The Contessa seemed to blame Fredak for her husband's death and became very distant to him. She never trusted him to look after her child.
- The new castellan brought in a wet nurse from the Vale who was supposed to have healing skills but her husband accused of the woman of being a witch.

There is something that she doesn't mention at first: she herself used to work at the estate. Like the Contessa, Mali-An comes from merchant stock and one of her daughters, Serra, was a childhood friend of Aliana. (Serra has married and left Westport.) Mali-An was taken on as a housekeeper and met Fredak there. She left the estate when Fredak became ill to help care for him at home and hasn't been back since. Characters with a successful Standard Insight roll realise that her connection is deeper than she admits. If the characters can impress her with a Standard Courtesy roll, persuade her that they know which canary is her husband (Hard Deceit) or simply find a wild canary in the city and bring it back to her she reveals the following

- She once saw a strange and horrible tattoo on Xhago when she surprised him bathing. If asked to draw it she manages something much like the Chaos Mother rune.
- Several of the staff were frightened of the Contessa's son, claiming that he has a cruel and unpredictable temper. He started talking when he was just a few months old and sometimes seems to know things that a young boy should not be able to. If asked further she reveals that only the wet nurse and the Contessa have seen the boy unclothed. Once when the boy fell, Mali-An just happened to be nearest and went to pick him up. Somehow he managed to dig his fingers into her arm and drew blood from deep cuts. She shows them the scars if they ask. Also, she whispers, when he gets angry, sometimes his eyes turn pure black

Miguel ab Solis

Miguel ab Solis the former castellan to Family Solis can be found in a drug den by the name of The Green Dream in the slums of Westport. He is now a hareesh addict with a withered left arm, begging for Founders to enable him to dream the days away. Locals know him as "Wormy Mig" due to his obsession with worms. If the characters follow Feather Eye's information, finding him simply requires half a day trawling the slums. A Formidable Streetwise or Hard Locale reduces the time needed to one hour.

The patron of the Green Dream, Berec the Scowl, is a pinch-faced, sour-tongued type interested only in money. If the characters wish to talk with Miguel they have to pay 15 Founders to provide him with hareesh. They also have to pay Berec an entry fee of 5 Founders each.

Under the influence of hareesh, Miguel becomes lucid for a brief period as the withdrawal symptoms ease before he lapses into hallucinations. It becomes clear that he has no love for the Contessa and blames her and Xhago for everything that has gone wrong in his life since then. He occasionally implies that he thinks she must have been having an

Hareesh

Hareesh is presented here to give characters a minor defence against sorcery in low magic settings such as The Realm, but at the risk of addiction. In other settings it may be preferable to keep hareesh as a simple narcotic.

Hareesh is a highly addictive narcotic that has a side-effect of bolstering Willpower against magic when consumed in its concentrated form. This side-effect is not commonly known but characters with an appropriate Lore or knowledge of sorcery may well be aware of it. The drug can be taken in two forms:

Bubbled though water in which case it causes euphoria and hallucinations;

Ingested as a potion in which case it directly affects the imbiber's Willpower.

Application: Consumed (if bubbled through a pipe the drug has different effects.)

Potency: varies (50-75 usually)

Resistance: Willpower

Onset time: 1D3 minutes

Duration: 1D8 hours

Conditions: If the drug is successfully resisted then for the next 1D8 hours it augment's the imbiber's

Willpower by twice the critical range of its Potency for the purpose of resisting magic. If the drug overcomes the imbiber's resistance then the victim's Willpower is reduced by twice the drug's critical range for all purposes, and the victim becomes listless and demotivated for the duration of the effect.

affair with Xhago. With patience, the characters can gain the following information, not all of which is strictly true.

- Miguel believes he was framed by his successor (Xhago) when goods and jewels which had been stolen from the Solis estate were found in his office.
- A few days later he managed to confront Xhago about it in a guest house. His memory is a bit confused but he remembers Xhago's eyes glowing and then a sudden, agonising pain shooting up his left arm. He thinks he must have run in terror and shame and since then has only been half a man.
- Xhago was previously a caravan master (false) who was appointed to the position of Master of the Docks by the Contessa shortly after the count died.
- The Contessa and the count were unofficially estranged and the Contessa had had several stillbirths.
- Shortly before her pregnancy, the Contessa had secretly met with a mysterious figure two or three times. Miguel hasn't seen him since, but the vague and rambling description he offers approximates with that of Jedakiah.
- A few weeks after his arm was blasted by Xhago, he went to the Solis family physician's house in the merchant district to seek a cure. The physician refused and cast him out. His wife was kind though and came to see him a few times but stopped after a while; he doesn't know why.
- About six months after the count's death, the Contessa started replacing several loyal retainers (he specifically mentions the family priest, Perenge) with outsiders. He thinks these were largely Xhago's men.

Perenge the Ink-stained

The former priest to the Solisti can be found at the temple to the founding four in the Temple District. He is short, short-sighted, mumbles a lot, limps noticeably and rarely speaks to outsiders. He has a frustrating habit of starting sentences half way through and finishing them shortly before the end.

This is one lead that Feather Eye does not want the characters to follow so it is likely that they will have to hunt down Perenge based on conversations with others. Miguel mentions Perenge several times and Mali-An also talks about him. Xalgith is the deity of trade and knowledge so the temple is an obvious place to dig into Solisti history. Any such enquiries will be passed onto the specialist in this area – Perenge. Very observant characters note they have been following leads to ex-employees - yet the Contessa did not see fit to mention Perenge's dismissal despite it being commonly known that the Solisti have turned their back on the worship of the Four. Finally, Perenge's assistant, Ildray, keeps an eye on the Solisti compound for his master. He is likely to become aware of the characters and broker a meeting.

Arranging an audience with Perenge is easy: the run-down temple is rarely busy. He meets with any guests requesting scribe services or expressing an interest in the Solis family. He is wary of any interest in his background but a Standard Insight roll reveals that any mention of Xhago or the Contessa piques his interest. If the characters hint that they have or are seeking information about the Solisti, he asks them to follow him across the weed-strewn cloister to his private chambers. The room is stuffed to overflowing with all manner of scrolls and discarded quills. An Easy Perception roll reveals a locked chest carelessly buried under the clutter. His assistant, a tall and gawky youth by the name of Ildray, is summoned to fetch the guests some honeyed wine and remain on hand.

in a fidgety manner, Perenge asks them about their interest; any mention of the Contessa or, even better, sorcery, sends him into a flurry of confused excitement. There is something he is dying to tell.

Perenge is capable of imparting the following.

- He had previously been friendly with Fredak Sawbone, the Solis family physician, who confided that he felt there was something odd about the child's birth. He has tea once a month with Sawbone's widow.
- After the count's death, the Contessa turned her back on worship of the Four and shortly after her son's first birthday, Perenge was asked to leave.
- Although he doesn't know for sure, he whispers that Xhago has some knowledge of sorcery. He has a knowledge of strange runes and, more than once, Perenge has seen Xhago looking drained in a way that hints that foul magic has been used.
- He became increasingly aware of new staff arriving and noticed the covert use of a rune two or three times. If asked, he can draw the Chaos Mother rune. If he does so, he observes the characters closely to see how they react.
- If the characters show familiarity with the Chaos Mother cult he can reveal that he has been doing some reading and he thinks that maybe the Contessa and the castellan have joined a coven of this ancient and foul cult.

Shortly after her son's birth, the Contessa became distant to Perenge and stopped him from ministering to her baby. The child seemed oddly alert and sometimes it seemed as though his eyes were pure black. When he attempted to make enquiries he was brushed off and then started to notice that some of the new staff appeared to be watching him. Before he could unravel the mystery he was banished from the estate and Xhago made it plain that he was not to return. Since then he has being conducting research and he thinks he knows the truth.

Should the characters show any amount of interest in knowing more, Perenge unlocks a chest and retrieves a huge, double-locked tome and a smaller locked box. After much straining he finally opens it to some cracked and stained pages and lays out the worries that burden him. Characters who are keeping an eye on Ildray notice that he is very uncomfortable with strangers being shown this book, but Perenge is paying no attention.

After a dramatic pause, Perenge lets them see the pages he has opened. Indecipherable scrawls cover the parchment but a woodcut of a foul demon consuming a child and then taking its appearance makes the subject clear. Another image shows a demonic face with huge, black, eyes. Beneath the woodcut, runes are scrawled which Perenge can read aloud. "Should the child's eyes be as black as its soul then it must be put to the mountains and left to die while its mother is manacled in chains."

Folklore talks of demons that once stalked before the chaos wars, impregnating new-born children with their offspring who were then raised as if they were normal until they turned on their parents. Since the war there have been few such accounts and the stories are now dismissed as fairy tales. However, when Perenge was studying tomes about sorcery to see if he could find hints about Xhago's powers; he came across references (and he laboriously and carefully opens a few more pages), to tales of sorcerers binding adult demons permanently into children. The demon possesses the child and as the child grows the demon grows in power. It was a way of binding a more powerful demon than was normally possible for a sorcerer, but it was a dangerous and difficult ritual requiring both a magus and an apprentice.

Perenge does not know who Xhago's apprentice is or how he got into a place where he was able to do this to the Contessa's son; and he has no actual proof but he is absolutely convinced that this is the truth.

At this point he peers anxiously at the characters hoping that they might volunteer their services. If they seem hesitant or appear to want more, he has no money of his own but he does have a great treasure. He was only going to lend it to them but perhaps they want to keep it. Anxious and uncertain he unlocks the small, wooden box. Inside it is a brass and copper telescope. He describes this as an "eyeglass of true seeing" – a relic from the Chaos Wars. Perenge explains that it took him years to find it but now he cannot get close enough to the child to use it. He claims that anyone looking through the eyeglass at the child immediately sees the demon's true form. If they can get to the estate and look at the child through the device, there will, he believes, finally be proof.

Assuming that the characters believe him they are likely to ask him how to free the child from the binding. Unless you are using a "happy ending" option, Perenge cannot offer much help. His tome only mentions infanticide. According to his research, killing a sorcerer sometimes causes his enchantments to die with him but not always. Though Perenge is convinced Xhago is a sorcerer the characters probably have no direct evidence. He does not know how to exorcise the demon or even if such a thing is possible.

He can instruct them in the use of the eyeglass. *"Look, focus and concentrate: you will feel a sharp cold and then whatever you view reveals its true form. As soon as you look away the eyeglass will stop working."* In game terms, the character must spend 1 Magic Point to activate the device.

Finally, the characters may wish to have Perenge accompany them on a mission to the compound, perhaps believing that, as a priest, he has formidable magic powers. Perenge is very reluctant; he is short-sighted, slightly asthmatic and has wielded nothing more dangerous than a paper knife in his life. Still, a Formidable Influence roll or Hard Deceit (flattery) might persuade him. He is likely to be more of a liability than a help and is banned from the compound so needs to be well-disguised or otherwise smuggled in.

Ildray and the Order of Truth

As an optional connection to other scenarios, Ildray is actually a nephew of Kalathus (Chaos Mother's Chalice) and a new member of the Order of Truth. The Order is focused on the gathering threat to the north and the erratic behavior of the king, so Westport has been of little interest. When Perenge started requesting odd documents from the great library, only Ildray could be spared to investigate, as well as deliver some of the requested scrolls. He has begun to believe Perenge's seemingly paranoid theories and wondered if there is some sort of link between the Solisti trading caravans to the north and the strange rumours from the mountains; but no one has responded to his letters. In this case Ildray is the only other person Perenge has talked with, but when he tried to use the telescope he experienced a sharp pain in the temple and passed out so he has been no use to Perenge.

Ildray is now keeping an eye on the Solisti compound in between running errands for Perenge, and the characters pique his interest. He is likely to ask questions about them in an amateur way and start to follow them. He is however trivially easy to ambush. If they encounter him, it is obvious that he is harmless but he does say that he knows someone who may be interested in what they have to say. If the characters are having problems noticing a connection to Perenge then Ildray can provide it.

Meggo and the Street Rats

Feather Eye uses a small gang of urchins, led by a 9 year old named Meggo, to communicate with the characters as well as keep informed of developments in the city. The urchins are well-paid and meet with Feather Eye in his form of a minor noble by the south gate postern door of the compound. More than one of Meggo's gang has noticed something strange about the noble so they call him "The Gribbly Man." Meggo is cheeky, disrespectful and wary, rarely getting within arm's reach of a stranger. He doesn't trust the Gribbly Man but he's been stashing away money and has dreams of setting himself-up in a business with a stall in the rag market. If the characters wish to pay Meggo, treat his gang of urchins as having 75% in the following skills: Locale, Perception, Sleight and Streetwise. Paying Meggo 10 Founders hires the group to perform one task for half a day. For 20 Founders they use Sleight to steal something small from someone not too dangerous.

Meggo knows two things that are significant clues if the characters think to ask. The first is that once, the Gribbly Man got angry over something and his eyes turned black. The other only happens if the characters try to arrange a repeat visit with the Contessa. One of the urchins present tells Meggo that the Contessa smells the same as the Gribbly Man. Meggo does not know what this means and he is unlikely to volunteer this information, after all this job is making him lots of money.

Sweggen Nine Fingers

Feather Eye attempts to lead the characters to Sweggen because Xhago has complained about him several times and tried to come up with a means to teach him a lesson. Sweggen Nine Fingers (he has nine fingers and two thumbs) is a man with many digits in many pies. He is a large, chunky, genial fellow. Cheerfully profane with men, surprisingly courteous with women, he has a certain rough-hewn charisma. His balding scalp is close-cropped and he has strong arms from his time working in the docks; he still speaks like a dock worker. He has come far since and is one of the few former colleagues of the Tyrant to have managed to keep on his good side.

His shop in Old Town is a front through which he sells the items he acquires legally. Most of his business, though, is done in the shadows, connecting buyers and sellers and bypassing city tithes. He has always been careful to keep his business low-level enough not to attract the Tyrant's attention. He has used his profits to buy stakes in several bath houses, gambling dens and hareesh pits.

For the last year he has been working with Xhago and his aide, Benzaad ab Keffi, to smuggle goods through the docks. He is fully aware that this includes weapons but he is being paid well and has a hold over Benzaad should he need it. After the Tyrant acted against customs agents some three weeks ago, Sweggen got the message and when Xhago refused to pay him for the missing goods that the characters intercepted, Sweggen decided that he needed to cut his ties. Should the characters speak with him, Sweggen spots a chance to recoup his losses.

What Sweggen knows.

- Xhago has been smuggling goods, including weapons, through the old town docks for at least a year and in increasing amounts. The goods are destined for the far north but seem to fetch surprisingly low prices. The smuggled goods leave the city and join up with Solisti caravans not far from where the Southvale River meets the Cylder.
- Xhago has started skimming off a percentage for himself.
- Xhago has some rooms in a guest house in the city which he has rented under a false name.
- Sweggen is very careful not to incriminate himself openly and should the characters be interested, he has a proposition. He knows where Xhago's bolt-hole in the city is and he's pretty sure that Xhago has stashed most of his gains there. Recently, Xhago refused to pay for services rendered for a "friend" who has been left out of pocket, so he'll provide the characters with the information if they agree to break-in and split the belongings fifty-fifty. Providing there's an agreement he furnishes them with the address. If they haggle he'll settle for a forty-sixty split, but no lower.

Depending on his judgement of the characters, Sweggen may contact Inch afterwards with information about them. Sweggen's plan is to rob Xhago and use the characters to do it.

What if the characters never visit Sweggen? Keep in mind that he is out of pocket and would like to find out who interfered. Consequently, if they do not come to him, he eventually discovers their names and send a trusted lieutenant (Jorrid Lackhair) to sound them out.

LOCATIONS

MENDRITH-RAN'S GUEST HOUSE

Xhago, under the alias of Kemmal, a "visiting caravan captain" has the top floor of Mendrith-Ran's guest house to himself. He believes that this is a secret but Sweggen Nine Fingers is aware of it and shortly after events start, the Tyrant's agent, Inch, also becomes aware. Both have an

> ### EYEGLASS OF TRUE SEEING
> This sorcerous artefact is a small (30cm long) telescope made of brass and copper with a crystal in the far end. When looked through it acts as an "Abjure Deceit" spell at Intensity 7 and with a range of the viewer's POW in metres times 10. In practical terms it can automatically see through any visual illusion of Magnitude 7 or less. It can also reveal other visual deceits such as written lies, a disguise or even someone pointing in the wrong direction. It cannot reveal non-visual deceits such as a spoken lie. To use it the user must spend 1 Magic Point and concentrate for a whole Combat Round on studying the subject. Unknown to the user, while it is being used, the creator of the eyeglass can study its user. Furthermore, once the user has spent more Magic Points than their POW in total, the creator can perceive that person whenever they wish. At this point the potential victim starts to get the nagging feeling of being watched. In a few months after that, the creator will be able to draw the user to a place far from Westport in which it can consume the victim. The eyeglass is an old and potent trap. The nature of the creator and how the trap is sprung is left to whatever works best for your campaign. If you wish to emphasise the Ophidian threat then this may be a piece of their weird technology: it certainly seems to be made in the same style as the vats in *Shadows Behind the Throne*.

agenda which may lead them to tell the characters about the location. Feather Eye suspects that Xhago has a bolthole in town but doesn't know where.

Xhago never conducts business here; he uses his rooms to stash various items that he does not want Jedakiah knowing about. This primarily consists of what he needs to study the mysterious sorceries of the Chaos Mother as well as a stash of gold and jewellery for emergencies.

Should the characters wish to break into his rooms, then climbing the side of the building is a Standard Athletics roll in daylight with a Formidable Stealth roll to remain hidden. Climbing at night is Hard but the Stealth roll is Standard. Barred shutters cover the windows (4 Armour Points, 10 Hit Points) requiring a Standard Lock Picking roll to open. The door to the main room is locked (4 Armour Points, 25 Hit Points) and requires a Hard Lock Picking skill to open. Naturally, forcing any shutter or the door with Brawn is a noisy affair. In addition, the door to the experimentation room is warded with an Alarm spell.

There are four rooms in total. The main room is a sparsely furnished reception room. This is the only room that any staff in the guest house are allowed to enter. Xhago occasionally uses it to meditate. The other three rooms connect to a hallway at the far end of the room. Both the main door and hallway door are locked with large, clunky locks and an internal bar, when Xhago is present. The other three rooms are a bedroom, a small room used as combination study and bathroom and, finally, a locked room with no windows. This is Xhago's experimentation room. It contains a basket of oiled tarpaulins, has chains and manacles on the wall, various blood - and worse - stains. Should he need to experiment with living subjects, they are taken here, gagged, suspended and the blood carefully caught on the tarpaulins. The room is also enchanted with his Folk Magic Alarm spell to alert him should anyone break in. The runes marking the spell are inscribed on the top right corner of the door jamb. A Lore (Sorcery) roll or Lore (Chaos Mother) roll reveals the spell's identity and that the caster was a sorcerer or Chaos Mother cultist respectively. If running this in a pulp action style, Games Masters may also want the characters to experience the cold, dreadful touch of magic when they enter the room.

In the study is a locked chest containing 150 Silver Founders and 30 Gold Royals. Beneath floor boards in the same room, covered by the desk, is a further stash of 100 Royals and gems and jewellery worth some 2,000 Founders. These constitute his "easily found" stashes. Providing the characters are looking in the right area, an Easy Perception roll shows signs of damage to the floorboards, otherwise a Standard Perception roll brings it to their attention.

In the experimentation room is a small, locked safe bolted into a space above the ceiling. This is carefully hidden so a Standard Perception roll by someone looking at the ceiling is needed to find it (or a Hard Perception roll if no one thinks to study the ceiling directly.) The safe is held in place by a bracket with 8 Armour Points and 12 Hit Points. The wood around the bracket can be chopped or sawn through and has 3 Armour Points and 6 Hit Points. If it can be removed specialist tools are needed to open the box. Sweggen would be delighted to help. A blacksmith or other metal worker can also do the job.

The safe contains figurines of the Chaos Mother, runes inscribed in several, sickly yellow stones, and fragments of various scrolls containing writings that Xhago is consulting in an attempt to increase his understanding of the Entropic Revelations (Jedakiah's grimoire). Jedakiah has forbidden Xhago from the text itself and has only taught him what he wants him to know, requiring Xhago to memorise it. If the characters are able to read, most of the fragments are in a variety of foreign and archaic languages. There are enough visual cues representing parts of the Chaos Mother's maze, images of bloody sacrifices, and elements of the Chaos Mother rune to indicate the general contents. Perenge is able to translate the archaic scroll fragments with an afternoon's work and learn enough to know that they all reference the blasphemous Entropic Revelations.

THE MAN'AGAN HERALD

Unless the characters have been extremely discreet in their defence of the Herald, word has quickly spread of the activities, and the Tyrant's new customs agents have impounded the vessel and seized all the crew they can find. The ship's captain, an Effin Islander named Lekkos One Eye (there are a lot of one-eyed islanders), fled the city as soon as he realised what had happened. When the ship is examined, the smuggled weapons are soon found. The customs agents have no interest in any odd markings on some of the boxes, assuming they are merely some sort of label.

Careful, seemingly casual, conversations (Standard Deceit or Hard Influence) with guards in the area reveal that the Tyrant's spymaster, Inch, is taking a close interest. No one is willing to be bribed as he has been known to try and trap traitors through fake bribes. The characters can learn that weapons have been found and the rumour is that the ship was trading, incognito, for a member of the four families. If the captain has fled there is a bounty of 10 Gold Royals on his head if captured alive, and a reward of 1 Gold Royal for any new information about the cargo.

Although it is unlikely, if the characters manage to speak to the captain, he can tell them that he picked up several items from the Summerlands under commission from an anonymous agent he has dealt with twice before in Westport. The description fits Xhago, though not perfectly. If he is introduced to Xhago he can identify him as the agent, especially if it will save the captain's life. He was not aware that some of the sealed boxes contained weapons (though a Standard Insight roll reveals that he had guessed) and does not know why some of the boxes had odd markings. Throughout the conversation, Lekkos is desperate to find some way in which he may be able to save his ship and his life. He is without scruple and happily cooperates with any plan that might save him.

The King's Docks

Overlooked by the keep and protected by ancient breakwaters, these docks are reserved for the richest merchant fleets and the Tyrant's own ships. The Solis family has its own wharf and several warehouses in the district, though the recent rent increases are proving hard to service. The dockmaster is Benzaad ab Keffi who is often found here. Benzaad is not aware of the Chaos Mother cult but is fully aware of Xhago's smuggling and helps ensure that nothing can be tracked back to the Solisti. He also knows that Xhago seemed to get the job out of nowhere: he knows enough about the caravan business to realise that Xhago was clearly never a caravan master.

There are no direct leads to the docks, although Feather Eye is likely to mention the dockmaster. The characters may decide that they can uncover evidence of Xhago's larceny by poking around, staking-out a building or asking around. They may also follow Xhago here. There is nothing crucial for the characters to find, but uncovering Benzaad's debts may give them some leverage.

Asking around the docks reveals that the Solisti are a lot less busy than previously as business is obviously poor. The last Solisti caravan bound inland left two days before the events started; the Southvale river is not navigable for several days travel from its mouth, so most trade to the interior is overland following the river's course. If the characters spend a lot of time at the docks, Benzaad is likely to order some dockers to rough them up once they come to his attention (1d3+3 thugs are paid to do the task, but remember they are not being paid to kill, just injure). Inch may also take an interest in case they unearth any evidence on the Solisti.

Benzaad is a swarthy, dark-complexioned man with the beetle brow of an Effin Islander. He came to Westport some 10 years ago and has worked his way up in the Solisti business. He knows that Xhago is smuggling goods destined for a barbarian chieftain in Gartharis but that there is very little money in it. He suspects that Xhago must have some sort of deal where he receives a cut of the profits. So far Benzaad has been able to hide the losses but he is starting to worry. Of more pressing concern is that he has run up debts at the Lucky Puffin pleasure house. Luckily for him, Sweggen (a co-owner) has given him extra time to pay, although he did get a beating a few days back. Unluckily for him, he is horribly addicted to cards and drink and cannot stay away. He raided the last of his cash for his last stake and lost it all. If the characters can unearth any of this information they may be able to either blackmail him or pay his debts, in order to get him to tell them all he knows.

Events

These events are likely to happen during the characters' investigations in the following order.

Bath House Brawl

Ash-Dynad's Carnival of Baths and Exotica in the merchant district of Westport is Xhago's normal place to do covert business. He has long since corrupted its eponymous (and immensely corpulent) owner, Ash-Dynad, who is from the Vale but affects the air of an intensely cultured Summerlander. The baths are run-down and decorated with faded murals of all manner of exotic beasts ravaging a variety of nymphs and dyads. Bathers are served by fragrant servant boys.

Two encounters are likely to happen here. The first probably happens without the characters present but they may be able to find out about it afterwards. The day after the characters thwart the robbery of the ship, Xhago meets with Sweggen Nine Fingers. In a tense conversation, Xhago arrogantly refuses to reimburse Sweggen for his losses. Sweggen, as is his wont, smiles outwardly but inwardly starts to make plans against Xhago.

The second likely encounter is between Xhago and the characters. Once Xhago has determined who it is that intercepted his robbery, he sends an invitation to them to meet with an "interested party" at Ash-Dynad's bath house. As is traditional, all patrons of the bath house disrobe in the changing rooms and are presented with a simple sheet that can be wrapped loosely around the body.

If the meeting goes ahead, the characters encounter Xhago in the steam room; Xhago has three heavies present. He demands to know who the characters are working for and why. He implies that he can be a reasonable person and, should the situation seem appropriate, may even offer them the chance to work with him. If the characters are not interested then he threatens them, telling them to flee the city by the end of the day if they value their lives. At this point he makes to leave, telling the characters to enjoy the rest of their time in the sauna as his guests while they think on what he has said. Regardless of his words, he has no intention of letting the characters live. A few minutes later,

hired thugs wielding daggers and chains, and wearing light armour enter under orders to kill the characters.

The bath house brawl is a brutal and dangerous affair. There is a distinct chance that one or more characters will take a Major Wound unless they have Luck Points to burn or are smart in their use of the environment. Remember, the characters most likely have nothing but the robes they are wearing and are facing armed enemies. Their best hope to survive is to use the environment well. There is a brazier of hot stones and some wooden buckets of hot water. Creating confusion in a cloud of scalding steam may be the easiest way to escape. Characters with a swashbuckling Combat Style may find that a towel makes a useful impromptu parrying weapon (Size Medium) and could even be used to Entangle on a Special Effect. A bucket may make a useful club (1d6 damage, Small, Short). Finally, the wall between the steam room and the next is purely decorative, formed of very light wood and plaster. Treat it as having just 1 Armour Point and 4 Hit Points. A burly character could easily burst through it on a charge.

If the characters *do* elect to fight, the heat from the sauna is so intense that at the end of every combat round everyone fighting in the room must make a Fatigue roll. Using Evade to dodge blows is Hard due to slippery conditions. On the other hand, using Evade to slip free of a grip is Easy.

The thugs with the chain and dagger take up position to block the door, the only avenue of escape, while the others flank to either side. Xhago has hired one thug for each character plus the leader with the chain. The thugs themselves focus on maximising their damage with Special Effects. If more than half of the thugs take Serious Wounds, the rest flee. They are vicious and cruel and are well-paid for their pains but in the end they value their lives. If the characters have shown evidence of magical ability, Xhago stays within earshot of the combat for a short time, prepared to use Neutralise Magic or even Palsy in dire circumstances. Remember that Xhago knows that various serving boys are present and any use of sorcery will soon be gossiped about. He is more likely to use Befuddle to ensure that if any characters get past the thugs he can confuse them for long enough to escape the premises.

JUST ANOTHER DEAD URCHIN

This event is triggered either by Xhago discovering who is running messages, or by Feather Eye trying to motivate the characters. Either way, Meggo, the street kid who has been running messages for the characters, is found dead: his throat slit. A tiny, crumpled heap lies in the vicinity of the characters' sleeping place, unconsidered by the few early morning city dwellers who have passed by. If Feather Eye ordered the killing then a scrap of paper or other useful clue can be found on Meggo's body. The precise nature of the clue depends on what, exactly, Feather Eye is likely to think most useful in this context, to provide further information or to motivate the characters to come to the compound. Some possibilities are:

- A blood-stained silk cloth, soaked in the Contessa's perfume.
- If the characters are literate a torn fragment of papyrus with the words ".... Help me. ... knows about you. ... great danger ... birthday..."
- A crumpled invitation to the Contessa's son's birthday celebration.
- A locket. When opened there is no picture but the design shows the Solisti crest and a quiet, whispered plea is heard. "He knows about us." This is a sound illusion. It plays every time the locket is opened until the duration expires (about 30 minutes) or the characters move more than 2 kilometres away from the Solisti compound.

A SNAKE IN THE NIGHT

A random character is awoken by a moor viper: a snake about half a metre in length and poisonous enough to kill a man. It has been abused prior to its release, so is angry enough to blindly bite the first person it finds. This encounter happens for one of two reasons. Either Xhago arranges it after he fails to deal with the characters at the bath house or, if the characters are not being particularly active, Feather Eye arranges it to try to stir them into action. Whoever orders the attack needs to know where the characters are sleeping, so if the characters have gone to ground, this does not happen.

MOOR VIPER

Action Points 3, Initiative Bonus 15, Move 3m, Hit Points 2

Abilities: venomous

Skills: Evade 60%, Perception 65%, Stealth 85%

Combat style: bite (S/T 1 Hit Point damage or inject venom) 75%

MOOR VIPER VENOM.

Application: Injected

Potency: 70

Resistance: Endurance

Onset time: 1d6+4 minutes

Duration: 1d3 days

Conditions: Agony followed after 1d6 hours by gross swelling and loss of all feeling in the location bitten. The numbness spreads to one adjacent Hit Location per hour. When it reaches the head (throat) the victim starts to asphyxiate as their throat swells shut. Successful First Aid or Healing (piercing a hole into the character's throat and placing a tube to allow breathing) does 1d6 damage to the head and allows the character to breathe normally. If performed using First Aid or Healing, piercing the throat only does 1d3 damage. The hole in the throat will not heal naturally.

Choose a character at random to be awoken by a presence in the room. Roll for a hit location; the snake is around that location and is slowly making its way towards the character's face.

On each of the character's turns they must succeed at a Willpower roll in order not to provoke an immediate attack from the snake. Speaking in anything other than a whisper also triggers an attack. Moving very slowly and carefully requires a Standard Athletics or Evade roll (or Easy Acrobatics roll) and allows the character to take actions such as propping himself up slightly, making it easier to attack or defend (Hard rather than Formidable) or maybe reach for a nearby knife.

Resolve this in Combat Rounds with the following special circumstances. The character is lying down and, when woken, counts as surprised. The snake moves 1 hit location closer to the head over the space of each Combat Round. It is ready to bite at the first provocation and remember that it can use its Inject Venom Special Effect on both defence and attack. If a character tries to use an action to grab it, but the snake Evades and gains a Special Effect, then it can Inject Venom to the attacking limb. If a character successfully uses an unarmed parry against the snake's attack then, if the snake's attack is a success, even if it doesn't get a Special Effect, it can use its Inject Venom ability against the parrying limb. This not the case for an armed parry or even a parry with an improvised object such as a blanket or pillow.

Should the character be bitten the Healing temple does have an antidote if the characters can identify the snake (or bring it with them). The potion costs 60 Founders.

Moving On

By the time the characters have faced at least two assassination attempts they should realise that they either need to get out of the city or force a confrontation. As mentioned earlier, if they seem reluctant to do either, Inch can be used to force the issue.

Secrets and Lies

There are many paths that might lead the characters to this section and also many reasons why they might decide to stay away. The characters should have been able to gather circumstantial evidence that Xhago is a sorcerer and that he has been stealing from the Contessa. They should also have become aware that he was involved in the mysterious events surrounding the birth of the Contessa's son. What they probably do not have is any concrete evidence and they may well have doubts about the Contessa's role in the events. At this point they may have conflicting motivations and it is likely that the characters have come to different conclusions about the best way forward. The least risky opportunity for the player characters to gain entrance to the compound is to find a way in during the birthday celebrations for the Contessa's son. This gives them a chance to sneak off during the festivities and possibly, if they have it, use the Eyeglass of True Seeing to study the Contessa's son.

Alternately, they may try to sneak in through various means during the days before the birthday. It is also possible that they may have entered into an alliance with Inch and found a way to storm the compound at the head of a remarkably untrustworthy mercenary force. The following section presents enough information to allow Games Masters to adapt to the characters' plans.

There are also many reasons why the characters might decide not to become involved.

If running a puzzle solving style investigation (see page 128) it is possible that the characters have not uncovered enough information to motivate them to explore the compound. They may also have made enough bad decisions that the wisest is to leave the city before they end up dead or arrested. Games Masters need to decide beforehand how to deal with this: simply let the dice fall where they may and leave the section for another time or look for more lures to entice them to the compound? One thing to remember is that Feather Eye is doing its utmost to bring the characters to the mansion in order to expose the castellan. If it gets desperate it is willing to manufacture unlikely coincidences. If the characters manage to get themselves arrested then Inch may be interested in promising them their release if they can provide damning evidence about the Contessa consorting with sorcerers, or if they can lead a force of men to raid the compound and raze it to the ground.

Even if running more of a pulp action investigation (page 127) it is possible that the characters view the compound as too dangerous or decide that the Contessa is not worth saving. Feather Eye ruthlessly manipulates whatever Passions it can discern in the characters. Inch can be used, as above, to threaten the characters into action while perhaps Sweggen's war with Xhago escalates until he decides to offer a significant bounty if they can kill Xhago. If they do start to leave town (with their tails between their collective legs), perhaps they see Xhago standing and gloating at their failure. Finally, an agent for the Order of Truth may make contact and ask them to continue their investigation for the good of the entire Realm. When it comes down to it, do not be afraid to use the characters' Passions. It is a common trope of swords & sorcery that heroes put themselves in danger because of their beliefs, drives and emotions. Rational calculation usually takes a back seat to rash action.

The Solisti Compound

The Solisti compound on Rich Hill is one of the four complexes that dominate the city. It is surrounded by a sturdy stone wall some 3 metres tall and 30 centimetres wide: good enough to keep out most intruders but not designed to withstand siege engines. The main gate is an impressive double door of thick wood overlaid in heavily ornamented brass (area 4). Watchtowers on the western wall (area 5) provide vantage points for Solisti guards. The tradesman's entrance by the servants' area is a plain, though sturdy, door. The old south gate has been covered up after a collapse over a century ago. Beside each gate is a postern door, allowing visitors to come and go without needing to open the main gate. At night, sconces are lit at various points along the wall, providing illumination for the guards (4 guards per watch, per watch point) although perceptive characters (Hard Perception roll) can deduce a small number of shadowy spots making any attempt at Stealth while climbing one grade Easier than normal.

Inside, the grand mansion combines a mix of the white walls and sloping red roofs from The Realm with the marbled columns, porticos, rounded towers and water features of the Summerlands. The building consists of a public wing to the south and a private wing to the north. The main entrance leads to the great hall while two slim, elegant towers overlook the grounds and provide a view of the city and coast line.

A notable feature of the mansion is the hypocaust. A furnace, three chimneys and a complicated set of vents allow hot air to circulate under all parts of the mansion. The building's floors are raised about two-thirds of a metre above the ground so each entrance to the mansion is reached by several steps. The system is rarely used due to the expense of fuel and maintenance. Children or smaller slaves can access the under floor area through ducts in the kitchen in order to clean and service it. Feather Eye has used this to its advantage to roam beneath the building and listen in to various conversations while everyone thinks the infant count is asleep.

In between the two wings of the estate, a shallow water feature is crossed by raised paths that lead to a central fountain and then into the various entrances. The great hall is reached through a dramatic, raised portico. All of these features show signs of decay and mildew but the exquisite skill of their construction is still evident.

Solisti House Locations

The map key on page 146 provides an outline of the architecture. Some areas are of greater importance and are described in more detail below.

The Great Hall (6).

This grand room is covered in majestic, dark, wooden panelling with a massive fireplace at the far end. Tapestries show mythological scenes and various Solisti heroes, including Solis freeing Westport. Banners and crests adorn the upper walls. Of particular interest to the characters may be several weapons and shields hung on the walls. A mixture of pole-arms, short and long spears and two-handed swords are prominently displayed. None are in a good state of repair (reduce their armour points and hit point by 2 each) and the swords are too blunt to cause the bleed special effect. Otherwise they are perfectly serviceable.

The Family Tower. (13)

The ground floor consists of a suite of rooms occupied by the Contessa's son. They are decorated with scenes showing sailing, martial combat and various adventures – all things to delight a young boy. As with many parts of the house, this section is heated by the hypocaust. Beneath a trunk filled with dismembered toys, Feather Eye has managed to loosen several tiles so that he can sneak into the under floor area and move through the house in secret.

The Family Tower Upper Floor.

This is the Contessa's solar. The beautifully wrought skylights have been covered in heavy fabric giving the whole floor a gloomy air. The four-poster bed has clearly not been used for many years, she usually sleeps in a chair in what would otherwise be the servants' anteroom. Much of the furniture is shrouded and the walls are bare of paintings.

The Guest Tower Ground Floor. (14)

This suite of rooms has been taken over by the castellan and is guarded by 1d3+3 cult members at all times. Xhago uses the upper floor for cult ceremonies and only cult members are permitted access. The rooms contain icons of the Chaos Mother, tapestries and scrawled inscriptions to Her glory, and an altar on which an ornate, gem-encrusted chalice is placed. This is used to mix wine and "milk" to be drunk during rites. The other household members are fully aware that Xhago holds meetings here but do not realise the nature of them.

The South Colonnaded Courtyard (15)

Nearest Solis tower is the one that Feather Eye uses in its meetings with the player characters. It is relatively discreet and only overlooked by the upper floors of Solis tower, so Feather Eye arranges meetings there when it knows Xhago to be absent.

Solis Tower (17)

This slender tower in the Summerlands style has become Xhago's personal tower. He has refurbished it ostentatiously, tastelessly and at great expense. Two cult members guard the doors at all times. There are no signs of cult iconography here but Xhago does keep incense burners active. He regards the top floor as his mage's study. Aware that he is still vulnerable to a crowd storming the tower, he has restricted himself to a library of important books

SOLISTI COMPOUND

KEY

1. Mansion
2. Solis Tower
3. Peruthia Tower
4. Main Gate
5. Watch Points
6. Barracks
7. Servant's Quarters
8. Glasshouses
9. Bricked-up Gate & South Postern
10. Flower Garden

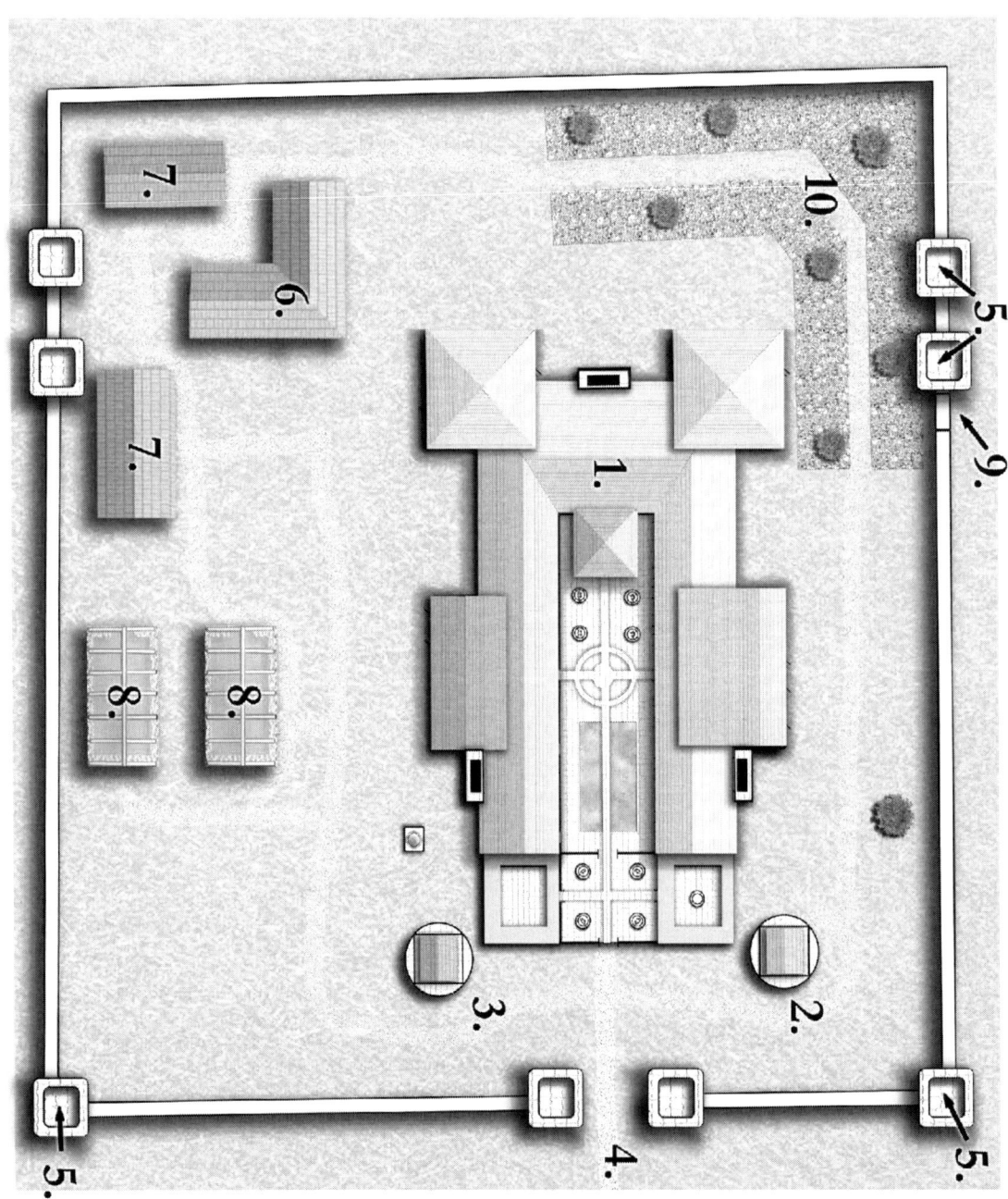

that he never reads (as anyone noticing the dust covering them realises). However, anyone managing to loot the top floor finds various chests containing a total of 4,000 Founders worth of jewellery and coins. As ever, jewels can rarely be exchanged for their face value and treat the value as approximate. Xhago can often be seen on the balcony, fine black cape billowing in the wind, face hooded against the slanting rain, surveying the view of Westport and making plans for his rise to power.

Compound Grounds

The grounds are poorly kept. Of particular note is the walled-up South Gate (9). The wall had collapsed over 100 years ago and rather than rebuilding it was walled-up. The family head of the time (Count Lemnisian den Solis) had claimed that the gate was cursed. Each gate also has a postern door for access when the gate is closed. Feather Eye discovered that it was possible to loosen some of the stones and uncovered the old metal grill. It is through this grill that it communicates with the street kids and, if needs be, the player characters.

The Solisti Family and Retainers

The main characters and factions present at the compound are summarised here.

Contessa Aliana den Solis

Originally a merchant's daughter, the old Solisti count married her for love instead of meeting his expected social obligation. When she proved incapable of bearing him a child, the marriage soured and she found herself spurned. Despite all that has happened she bears herself with grace and courtesy at all times.

Count Kellan den Solis

The five year old child appears to be a quiet, courteous boy with his mother's dark curls and his father's strong jaw. Polite and well-spoken beyond his years, he charms visitors and, if some of servants fear him, they say nothing of it. Certainly no one mentions the strange birthmark on his abdomen or the way his eyes blacken when he falls into a rage.

Castellan Xhago Garthanian

A tall, gaunt man with an arrogant demeanour, Xhago's black eyes and almost black lips mark him as a native of Gatharis. He works as the castellan for the Contessa but his main role is to act as Jedakiah's agent, ensuring that the Contessa keeps her bargain.

Xhago was born with a natural affinity for Folk Magic: a rarity in The Realm. Coupled with his dislikeable attitude and sly cruelty he quickly became friendless in his clan. Unfortunately for him, his talent and attitude bought him to Jedakiah's attention. The sorcerer, recognising Xhago's corrupt nature and natural aptitude, took him as an apprentice to assist with rituals that he couldn't complete alone. Crucially, Xhago assisted in the binding of Feather Eye. Once the demon was safely bound, Jedakiah installed Xhago as the Solisti castellan to oversee the shipment of equipment, weapons and rare materials to Jedakiah's allies.

Jedakiah taught Xhago nothing that could be used against him. However, Feather Eye, spotting Xhago's avarice and pride, has been filling his head with dreams of power and riches. Now Xhago is stealing the goods meant to be shipped to Jedakiah and, with Feather Eye's help, has begun to study some of the sorcerous secrets found in the fragments of the grimoire he has managed to acquire and keep hidden in his townhouse. In reality, Xhago is a pitiful magician but he has been distant enough from his master for long enough to forget this. Still, even an apprentice sorcerer can be a potent threat and what he lacks in power he makes up for in cruelty and ruthlessness.

Feather Eye

An arch manipulator, sensualist and easily-bored cuqulineaen demon, Feather Eye's plans are what ensnare the characters. It was caught off-guard by Jedakiah and bound to this dreary plane. It wants out but it was bound well. It cannot leave the compound, take any action against Jedakiah nor allow any action against Jedakiah to go willingly unopposed.

As a cuqulineaen, Feather Eye is able to use its host's life energy to replenish its own Magic Points. The psychic link nourishes and traps the demon at the same time. As the host has grown, Feather Eye has become increasingly able to perform the physical acts it needs to cast sorcery.

Feather Eye has been able to secretly explore the estate in one of its shape-changed forms. In the form of a lady in waiting it has two stable boys who run errands for it. In the form of a minor noble, it has met with street urchins as well as Krytos den Krytos. Until it arranges its meeting with the characters, it has never let itself be seen in the form of the Contessa. Feather Eye believes no one knows its ability to shapechange.

SOLISTI HOUSE

KEY

- / Window
- — Door
- ▮ Chimney
- ◯ Column
- ⊚ Statue
- ⇞ Stairs Up
- ✳ Spiral Stair
- ⊥ Arch

1. Courtyard
2. Kitchen
3. Family Baths
4. Family Private Rooms
5. Honoured Guest Room
6. Great Hall
7. Statues of Family Heroes
8. Portico
9. Storage Room
10. Gallery
11. Guest Room
12. Offices and Meeting Rooms
13. Contessa's Suite (inc. Nursery for Count)
14. Castellan's Room and Offices
15. Collonnaded Courtyard
16. Walled Courtyard (no roof)
17. Solis Tower
18. Peruthia Tower (3 storeys)
19. Pond with Central Walkway
20. Solar
21. Solar
22. Mezannine

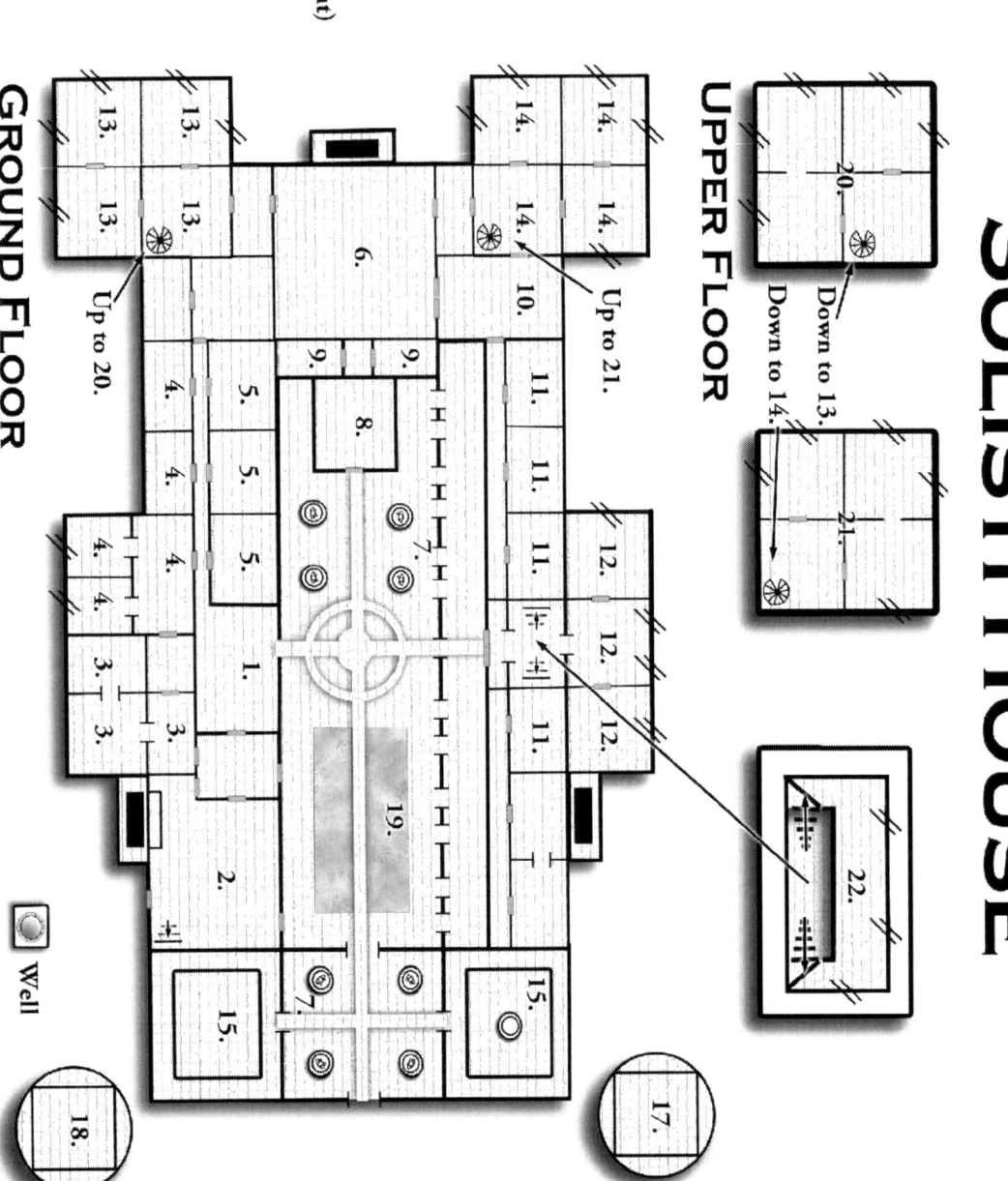

Ever since it first came up with this plan and started to work on the castellan, it has been preparing for this day. The count's fifth birthday is the perfect time for it to bring everything together. It has no strong feelings about the characters it manipulates; if Xhago orders it to kill them to be free, it does so without compunction. However, given a chance, it would happily put them on Jedakiah's trail as it has unfinished business with the sorcerer. The characters may find that Feather Eye appears to be a remarkably generous benefactor - if they find a way to free it.

Feather Eye & Xhago

Xhago frequently consults with Feather Eye; after all he believes that since the demon is bound it must tell him the truth. Once the characters interfere, Feather Eye starts to insinuate that it suspects a conspiracy. Over the next few days, it first attempts to lead Xhago to believe that Jedakiah has hired new agents to overthrow him or even that maybe Jedakiah is growing envious of Xhago's increasing power. Feather Eye's binding prevents it from lying about Jedakiah, but there are many ways to tell a truth and many gaps into which a deceit can crawl unbidden. In particular, Xhago does not realise that the demon is capable of sorcery. Jedakiah did not see fit to tell him and Feather Eye is not going to reveal anything unless Xhago directly asks.

Feather Eye & the Contessa

An effect of the demon's nature and the binding is that the Contessa has become dominated by the demon. She generally does whatever it says and cannot conceive of taking any action that might harm it even though, deep down, she knows that something awful lurks within her son. She is as much a prisoner of the binding as the demon. Feather Eye has occasionally taunted her, suggesting that she should throw herself off High Bridge and end her life, but it knows she can't, because, to do so, would be to forsake her son. Although the Contessa knows something is wrong with her son, she cannot find a way to tell anyone. Should her son be threatened, she tries anything within her power to save him. If the binding is broken, this glamour is dispelled and the Contessa returns completely to her senses.

Miscellaneous family members, staff and servants

A total of 80 people live at the compound. These are primarily servants, along with a force of 20 guards. Another 50-80 come and go on a daily basis. The guards are trained and drilled by the ancient sergeant-at-arms, Lamman ab Solis. Still fiercely loyal to the Solis family and the Contessa in particular, Xhago has been unable to remove Lamman. If it were not for Lamman, Xhago would have complete control of the family guard. Although Lamman distrusts Xhago, he is honour-bound to obey him on the Contessa's behalf, and soon quashes any scurrilous gossip regarding Xhago and the Contessa. The household staff are overseen by the increasingly senile Imahan ab Solis, who happily does as he is told by Xhago.

The non-cult members working at the compound are fully aware that Xhago has created a body of people loyal to him alone and that they hold meetings to some end, but no one realises just how corrupt this organisation is. Those still loyal to the Contessa do not understand why she does not remove him and they have noticed that those who have gone to her with their suspicions are soon fired by Xhago and usually leave the city afterwards. Many have left in despair but most still serve loyally, hoping that the situation will improve.

Worship of the Chaos Mother

Xhago has inducted nearly a third of the staff and eight of the guards into this obscene cult. Of those, 20 have been scarred with the rune of the Chaos Mother, promised power and wealth in the times to come and sworn to the utmost secrecy. The cult's numbers are still small but it is also starting to spread its tendrils to other parts of the city. Currently Xhago only leads ceremonies at the Solisti compound but he is now looking for a secret location elsewhere in Westport in which he could hold meetings with greater numbers but where his identity could be kept secret.

A key sign of the cult is the rune that all initiates are scarified with. This rune never heals and the scar slowly oozes a bloody pus that the cultists call "milk." The more powerful and dedicated the cultist is, the more potent that the milk is. This substance is a key component in ritual sacrifices, allowing the presiding sorcerer to regain Magic Points. Each time a new member is inducted into the cult, they are given a drop of the liquid mixed with wine which provides a glimpse of the Chaos Mother's web and, for a fortunate few, maybe even a glimpse of the power and glory of the Chaos Mother herself.

An inner circle of 6 cultists have been gifted with a sight of the child's birthmark. They believe that this child holds the key to the Chaos Mother's escape from her maze and defend the child to the death. None of them know of Feather Eye's existence.

Events at the Compound

The Count's Fifth Birthday Celebrations

There are two elements to the day's activities: a garden party held in the courtyard during the day and a masked ball held in the great ball during the evening.

During the afternoon, a garden party is held in which the great and the good can mingle. In mid-afternoon the Contessa gives a short speech thanking them all for coming. Drinks and exotic sweet meats are laid out for all to partake and various jugglers, fire-breathers and other performance artists entertain the guests.

Selected guests have been invited to the masked ball to be held that evening. Dances will be held, exotic dishes from across the sea provided and the hall decked-out in all its finery. A competition will be staged to judge the most wonderful mask while acrobats perform stunts.

There are multiple plans that the characters can concoct to gain an invitation to the proceedings. They may pose as labourers, entertainers or simply try to sneak in over a wall. If all else fails, it is possible that Feather Eye manages to arrange an invite. If the characters attend the event then various encounters may occur.

- Krytos spurned. Krytos is drunk and bitter: the Contessa has shown no interest in rewarding him for his actions. If he recognises any of the characters (Hard Perception for him) then he approaches them, accuse them of betraying him or, if the characters are in disguise, alert the guards. Luckily for the characters, he is drunk enough that a sneaky thump on the back of the head knocks him cold for a long time.
- Dance with the demon. If the characters attend the masked ball then, taking advantage of everyone's belief that the Contessa's son is in his bed, Feather Eye adopts one of its shapechanged disguises in order to mingle with the guests. It easily spots the characters if they are there. Assuming they do not recognise this masked figure, he or she may whisper things about them that they would not expect a stranger to know. If necessary, Feather Eye may use this as one last chance to steer the player characters in the right direction depending on what seems most likely to work. It is most likely, however, to use the chance to taunt its puppets in whatever way most pleases its twisted, demonic nature.
  - Explore the house. At any time there are 1d6+6 Solisti guards in ceremonial armour watching the main doors and keeping an eye on the guests. The servants come and go unhindered but no one else gets in unless already known to the guards. The guards are not seriously expecting trouble but any attempt to sneak into the house involves beating the Perception skills of the nearest guards. There are also a further 1d6+3 guards spread around the house protecting the most valuable areas. Remember as well that some of the guards – especially those near the castellan's quarters – are cultists.
- Denounce Xhago. The castellan will be near to the Contessa for the afternoon. It may be possible for the characters to accuse of Xhago of sorcery, theft and other crimes in full view of the guests. This is a great time to use communication skills such as Influence and Oratory. The characters probably lack hard evidence but may be able to panic the castellan into attacking them with sorcery thus sealing his fate. Oppose the castellan's Willpower against whoever is using a communication skill (such as Oratory) to see if he panics. Feather Eye may help at this point, shouting "Use your magic to kill them, uncle!" It may use a sound illusion to effectively amplify its voice. Should Xhago panic, his first step is to cast a Palsy with multiple targets. Once he realises what a mistake he has just made he makes an even worse one and commands Feather Eye "Save me and you're free!" As Feather Eye is bound to the compound, only by releasing the binding can Feather Eye get Xhago out of there to safety.
- Confront the Contessa. The characters may wish to try to persuade her that her child is not what it seems or may suspect her of being a sorcerer. The Contessa is present during most of the garden party, leaving only at the end to change for the evening festivities. Particularly brazen characters may try to confront her in public, others might try and stay in cover and confront her in her solar. Remember that it is likely that she has never seen the characters before, which may lead to some confusion.
- Open the gates. This is probably a terrible time to arrange an attack on the compound as collateral casualties will be high. Still, most of the guards are occupied watching the guests so it is relatively easy to overthrow a side gate and let in a force. The invaders attempt to make for the Contessa as quickly as possible, cutting down anyone in their way. Xhago,

assuming they are coming for him, responds by freeing Feather Eye to defend him.

- Confront the child. If the characters have figured out the role of the demon they may have realised that the quickest, safest way to defeat it is to kill its host, thus breaking its binding. They may have already seen the demon in its host using the Eyeglass of True Seeing or it might be their goal to do so. Naturally they could try to kill the child in public but it is more likely that they try and sneak into the child's rooms. Although the demon wants to be freed, it does not know what would happen should its host be killed and does not really want to find out so it tries to either escape, or if needs be, defend itself with sorcery.

Depending on the characters' actions, this celebration could be the focus of a whole session of intrigue and exploration; equally, it might be a scene of a mass battle, or it might just be a colourful backdrop to other events.

The Final Showdown

Eventually the characters come face-to-face with Xhago, Feather Eye or both. Feather Eye's aim is to have Xhago set it free. Xhago being killed is another viable option for the demon, however it is bound to Jedakiah's service so cannot simply sit back and let the characters kill his apprentice, much though it would like to. The characters may have settled on killing the child - something Feather Eye does not approve of as it is unsure what the after-effects will be. At the very least, it is banished to its plane, crippled and weakened, making it easy prey for stronger demons than itself. If the characters *do* attack, Feather Eye defends itself with every mean possible, including calling Xhago for help if all else fails.

Feather Eye is Freed

If Feather Eye is freed to perform one last service for Xhago, such as saving his miserable life or killing the meddling strangers, the host gruesomely transforms into a fullgrown Cuqulineaen demon over a single Combat Round. During this period it is invulnerable as its flesh bulges out, the air around it swirls in an ice-cold vortex and finally the withered husk of a child's body is cast off. At this point the characters' troubles *really* start.

Feather Eye is an ambush hunter with prehensile feet allowing it to cling upside down from a ceiling. It can use Sight illusions to confuse its true whereabouts, to create clones that copy its movements, or to conceal its hiding place. It is appallingly cunning and utterly without morals. It knows the compound extremely well and for a brief period (about 1 hour) it can still take on the form of its former host: a five year old child. This allows it to easily squeeze through the gaps beneath the floor in the mansion. If it is commanded to kill the characters, it uses every advantage to hunt down and butcher them as quickly and efficiently as possible. The characters have the advantage of numbers and, hopefully, the Eyeglass of True Seeing. Provided the holder of the Eyeglass can keep Feather Eye in sight while the other characters deal with it, the characters ought to be able to prevail.

If the demon is commanded to save Xhago it does so as literally as possible. Xhago can no longer command it so Feather Eye simply slaughters everyone who tries to get in its way. It interprets the command depending on exactly what Xhago says, so you as the Games Master should make Xhago's command as precise or vague as fits the occasion. Of course the characters can just let the demon escape with Xhago if they so wish,

The Host is Killed

The safest, quickest and most morally dubious solution is to kill the host. As soon as Feather Eye realises what is going on it tries to escape, use sorcery as needs be; or if that fails, bargain for its life with riches, power and anything it can plausibly offer. If nothing else, perhaps the characters will balk at killing a five-year old child to achieve their aims. If they do not, the character who performs the act should face some sort of repercussions in a future session.

If the child is killed then, as with the transformation, an intense icy vortex springs up around the body. The body flash freezes then, as suddenly as it started, the vortex vanishes, leaving ice melting from the surroundings. The body falls backwards, shattering into several pieces. What is left is the gruesomely dismembered body of a young boy, some characters and a blood-soaked weapon.

Xhago is Killed

A more morally reasonable solution is to kill Xhago. Unless they are able to ambush him and kill him before he has a chance to react, Xhago is likely to free Feather Eye to save himself. If the characters manage to kill Xhago before he sets the demon free then the binding ends and the demon escapes its host leaving the withered husk of the dead child behind. If they kill Xhago but he manages to command the demon, there are two options. Either Xhago's

The Eye of the Magus - Optional

This is an optional event triggered when Feather Eye is freed. Use it if you are running the scenario as part of The Realm campaign or if you wish to give further clues as to the nature of the Jedakiah.

When Feather Eye's binding is broken Jedakiah instantly feels it. He can tell the difference between a voluntary dismissal performed by Xhago and the binding being destroyed, and reacts accordingly. Within seconds he activates his mark on Xhago. Xhago, terrified and remembering well the touch of his master, holds his left hand out, palm facing outwards towards the event. Disgustingly, an eye appears in his palm and surveys the scene; this is Jedakiah using Mystic Sight to sense the Magic Points of beings in the surroundings via his Mark. What happens next depends on the context. Jedakiah's main concern is to determine why the demon is free and what the threat to him is.

If Xhago has freed the demon, he sinks to his knees and pleads for his life, claiming that the characters were about to uncover all of their plans and this was the only way to stop them. He has no way of knowing whether command dies with him and the characters have survived. Or, if preferred, Xhago's last command persists beyond his death, meaning that Feather Eye will not be free until it kills the characters. Realising this, it may try escape in order to complete its order later. However, with the death of its host Feather Eye can no longer regenerate Magic Points on this plane, meaning it has to manage its magic carefully. Use this option if Feather Eye is to become a recurring adversary - or if a simple, knock-down fight is needed to challenge the characters. Otherwise, assume that if Xhago dies any compulsion dies with him and Feather Eye escapes (or not) depending on what makes most sense.

Civil War

The Solisti compound is divided between Xhago's forces, those remaining loyal to the Contessa and those who do not know what to believe. Many of Xhago's forces are also fanatical cultists. Once violence starts it will spread. Some guards head for the Contessa to protect her and she heads for her son to protect him. Xhago and the inner circle of cultists also head for the child - although for very different reasons. Long-simmering resentments explode, burning braziers are knocked over, and the compound goes to war with itself. If this is in the middle of the birthday celebrations there are also scores of terrified guests. There is no need to run a mass combat, simply use it as a backdrop or as an occasional hindrance (or help) for the characters. If the characters have done a good job of exposing Xhago, then assume that those who are uncommitted side with the Contessa's forces and that they prevail. If not, assume that Xhago's forces win unless either Xhago is killed or escapes with the demon.

Happy Endings?

As in many Swords and Sorcery stories, there is no happy ending. What the characters experience should light a burning passion to deal with the ultimate perpetrator of this crime - Jedakiah. If a slightly more positive outcome is preferred, letting the child survive, then two additional options are presented here.

A Mother's Kiss.

If the characters can make contact with the Contessa, and let her see the demon through the Eyeglass of True Seeing, then the glamour Feather Eye holds over her is broken and she suddenly sees the whole truth. She realises that, as soon as she stops looking, the glamour comes creeping back. She also intuitively understands that there is only one way to save the child. If there is time she confesses her sins to the characters and explains, if they do not already realise, that her son is possessed by a demon. She does not regret the death of her husband – he was a monstrous tyrant – but she regrets the hurts that others have suffered because of her actions. She has learned that the mysterious stranger she made the fateful bargain with is called Jedakiah and is a dangerous sorcerer. Depending on the situation, she begs the characters to help her save her child while palming a tiny, golden dagger. The characters must keep the Contessa safe and take her to her son. If the Contessa acts before Xhago does she addresses her son for the last time.

"I know you, foulness. I know the misery you caused, the hurts you delivered. You have stolen my son from me. But no more." She then kisses a locket and plunges the golden dagger into her breast. As she dies the demon is forced out. It cannot escape nor can it form a body so the vortex grows in strength. The temperature drops to −30C in seconds and the walls around begin to crumble. The characters must grab the unconscious child and make their escape (Standard Athletics roll or Easy Acrobatics roll or take 1d6 damage to a random location with no armour protecting. Repeat 1d3 times each). Perhaps foreshadow this possibility with a passage in Perenge's book, so that it does not seem to come out of the blue.

A Sword to the Heart

When all else fails, a sword through the heart usually works. In this case, Perenge's book claims that if someone kills a sorcerer while he is in the process of freeing a bound demon then the sorcerer's life can be stolen by the demon. The book recounts a story of how by killing the sorcerer half-way through the ritual, the sorcerer's life force saved the child. However it hints darkly that perhaps it would have been better if the child had not lived. (Use that hint as you see fit to add some complications to future sessions.) According to the book the sorcerer needed to draw a complicated rune using his own warm blood to free the demon, a process taking some "three score heartbeats." In that time, the nameless hero ran him through and the sorcerer's life was traded to the child. In this case, Xhago requires a ritual taking 1d6+6 combat rounds to reverse the binding and must kill the child himself at the culmination of the ritual. This gives the characters a chance to kill the sorcerer and save the child with the same act. Of course Xhago has cultists to protect him, but the demon cannot help. It is held motionless from the second the ritual starts until it ends.

Depending on preferences, either or both of these options might be open to the characters. Be aware, however, that the victories of the heroes in Swords and Sorcery tend to be short-lived and often Pyrrhic. If the characters do save the child then it is up to Games Masters to ensure that they do not have long to enjoy the power and patronage of the Contessa. Certainly, if being played as part of The Realm campaign, being unable to save the child should generate a passion to bring to justice the man who is ultimately responsible for the death of the innocent: Jedakiah the master sorcerer.

Aftermath

These three sections provide a chance to wrap up certain loose ends if needs be. They are all optional and could either be added to the start of a future session to link the events together or used as a "cool down" before handing out Experience Rolls and the usual book-keeping that takes place at the end of a scenario. We suggest that you just pick one of the events if you use them.

The Sorcerer's Apprentice

Should the characters capture Xhago alive he knows it is only a matter of time before Jedakiah unleashes some terrifying, sorcerous punishment. Once the initial panic is over he bitterly resigns himself to his fate. He promises to tell everything in return for a quick, clean death; or if he still has a stash of treasure in his safe house promises to reveal its location. If the characters refuse him death, he bargains for high quality hareesh instead in the hope that he won't feel the pain so badly when it comes.

If the characters give him what he asks for he spills out a story laced with recriminations and self-pity. He has realised that he has been manipulated by Feather Eye. He never names his master (possibly making the characters quite paranoid) but is willing to say that he is "preparing for his war against The Realm." Depending on the needs of the campaign, Xhago can give as much detail about Jedakiah's plan as needed, although beware of laying it all on a plate. Xhago is only an apprentice, he knows that Jedakiah is preparing for a ritual and that some of the more exotic substances he helped smuggled were for that end. He knows that Jedakiah has prepared a mountain stronghold but doesn't know *where*. He can also provide clues to other scenarios: for example, he may have had dealings with Manuun, or believe there's something very important on the last caravan. Should Games Masters wish, in good pulp fiction fashion, Xhago may be about to spill the beans when suddenly his flesh begins to burn. As the characters watch, appalled, he melts like a candle,

Jedakiah can hear this but in his abject terror he does not stop to think things through. If the characters have broken the binding, Xhago makes a similar plea but puts all the blame on them and begs for a chance to prove his worth by bringing their flayed corpses back to his master.

At this point the enraged Jedakiah will either cast Sculpt (Flesh and Bone) at Xhago alone for betraying him or Wrack Chaos at everyone, including Xhago, in the area (except the demon). The Wrack spell seems to come from the eye so characters may be able deduce that severing the arm may save them. A side effect of the Wrack Spell is that the magical energies also warp the walls around the targets, causing them to crumble within 1d3+1 activations of it. Remember that Jedakiah has up to 8 points of Shaping at his command and that the range is measured from Xhago.

screaming and writhing in utmost agony for the best part of a minute– a victim of Jedakiah from afar.

Feather Eye One Last Time

If Feather Eye survived the events and has not been ordered to kill the characters then it picks a time to appear to them one last time, probably in the shape of the Contessa (because such trickery delights it). Although it is no longer bound to this plane of reality and can no longer regenerate Magic Points, it does have revenge on its mind and the characters have probably served it well. Feather Eye does not reveal this to the characters. Instead it pretends that it bears no grudges, "nothing personal you understand." It willingly tells the characters that the sorcerer who bound it is called Jedakiah and that although it doesn't know the details, Feather Eye does know that Jedakiah plans to overthrow The Realm. It also suggests that this sorcerer, Jedakiah, undoubtedly knows their names now, if he did not already. Should it be useful for the campaign, it may even casually toss them the best part of 5000 Founders worth of exquisite jewellery. There might well be no way to sell it in Westport as it is a collection of Solisti heirlooms, but there are other cities in The Realm where that will not be a problem.

At this point, the demon finally leaves. If the characters show signs of violence it surrenders to the pull of its plane and disappears. If not, it walks off as it plans to enjoy itself a while before returning home.

Finally, the Contessa

It is likely that the characters never speak to the real Contessa and depending on how events transpire, it is highly likely that they have made an enemy of her through their actions. Although the characters may believe that her child was better off dead, if that is indeed what happened, she most certainly doesn't agree. That said, should the characters find a way to rescue her child she is grateful and more than willing to fund some type of counterstroke against Jedakiah.

In person she is both more ordinary and more appealing than Feather Eye's illusion. She speaks carefully and listens attentively and well knows the power of a shy glance. She is capable of filling in the gaps of her history but, short of blackmail, does not admit directly to what she did. She is consumed with regrets and has told herself that she will put things right for her child. That is now what she lives for.

What Next?

It is possible to play this as a stand-alone scenario. Most of what happened in Westport ought to have been satisfactorily wrapped up and the characters may have managed to net themselves a fair amount of loot. Alternately, the players may have further plans. Maybe they are inclined to try and overthrow the Tyrant, either for the greater good or an even greater store of loot. Or the Solisti may have been weakened beyond recovery by the events and the characters may want to either make the estate their own or take over its trade routes. There are other areas they may want to explore; the Tyrant destroyed the old thieves' guild with just a few, like Sweggen, surviving, so perhaps the characters may find opportunities to explore a life of larceny. There is also the matter of an angered sorcerer to deal with.

If played as part of The Realm campaign or adapted into your own, there are several avenues of exploration left. The characters should realise that they have caused a major disruption to a conspiracy years in the making and that they have probably come to the attention of a powerful sorcerer. Wise characters realise that once one crosses a sorcerer the only sensible options are fight or flight. If played late in the campaign, the characters may have journeyed to Westport because hints in previous scenarios have indicated that Jedakiah had a base there bringing him goods for his allies. In this case they will have been able to expose his plans and gain some indication as to where he can be found. Perhaps they can sign up for a caravan (see the next chapter) and travel incognito further into The Realm. They may have become known to agents acting for the Order of Truth, which needs agents who have proved they can face sorcery and overcome it. Whatever path they choose, death, madness or glory, perhaps all three, await.

Cylder Connections

Characters who take part in the events in Cylder may start to recognise patterns in the way Jedakiah uses puppets and demonic entities to progress his plans. Both the Contessa and King Myur found themselves under the influence of a malign force and, in each case, one of Jedakiah's underlings oversaw the control. Should the characters survive to face Jedakiah in his lair, some of them may begin to wonder if perhaps there is some power beyond Jedakiah who has manipulated him the way he has manipulated others. It is a great tradition in Swords and Sorcery that there is always a bigger threat lurking in the background.

Non-Player Characters

Contessa Aliana den Solis

The Contessa is a porcelain-skinned, raven-haired woman of thirty summers. She was once a beauty of The Realm but what people see is a shadow of her true self. Although she carries herself with bearing and grace she seems much older than her years, has dark rings beneath her eyes, and deep lines across her brow. Her voice is soft, almost to a hush, and is filled with sadness.

The contessa always dresses richly, preferring dark, heavy fabrics with complex embroidery, but her gowns and robes are never ostentatious and she wears little jewellry, save for a tear-drop pearl on a gold chain around her neck.

Her hair is habitually worn long and flowing, sometimes with a single, loose plait that she wears draped across her right shoulder, and secured in place with a simple, silver clasp.

Characteristics	Attributes		1d20	Location	AP/HP
STR: 7	Action Points	3	1–3	Right Leg	–/4
CON: 10	Damage Modifier	-1d2	4–6	Left Leg	–/3
SIZ: 10	Magic Points	10	7–9	Abdomen	–/3
DEX: 11	Movement	6m	10–12	Chest	–/6
INT: 15	Initiative Bonus	13	13–15	Right Arm	–/5
POW: 10	Armour	None	16–18	Left Arm	–/4
CHA: 16	Abilities	None	19–20	Head	–/4
	Magic	None			

Skills: Athletics 18%, Boating 17%, Brawn 17%, Customs 105%, Dance 62%, Deceit 66%, Drive 26%, Endurance 20%, Evade 22%, First Aid 26%, Locale 65%, Influence 82%, Insight 35%, Native Tongue 71%, Perception 30%, Ride 21%, Sing 26%, Sleight 32%, Stealth 26%, Swim 17%, Unarmed 18%, Willpower 25%, Bureaucracy 45%, Commerce 66%, Courtesy 81%, Lore (Solisti family history) 35%, Musicianship 32%, Seduction 51%

Passions: Love (her child) 120%; Hate (Jedakiah) 95%; Loyalty (family) 70%

Combat Style: Shout for a Guard

Krytos den Krytos

A love–struck fool who has proved to be a useful idiot. Krytos has access to his own rather splendid suit of armour but will usually be encountered wearing fine clothes. Although he has had fencing training he has never used a weapon in anger and can be expected to surrender at the first hint of a serious wound..

Flamboyance – New Combat Style Trait

Any uses of the combat style to pose impressively and beautifully are one difficulty grade easier than normal. This trait is often found in societies where actual combat is rare and the intent is to use the combat style more as a highly stylised dance than as an actual fighting technique.

Characteristics	Attributes		1d20	Location	AP/HP
STR: 9	Action Points	2	1–3	Right Leg	5/5
CON: 10	Damage Modifier	0	4–6	Left Leg	5/5
SIZ: 12	Magic Points	10	7–9	Abdomen	5/6
DEX: 13	Movement	6m	10–12	Chest	5/7
INT: 11	Initiative Bonus	6	13–15	Right Arm	5/4
POW: 10	Armour	Ornate Half Plate	16–18	Left Arm	5/4
CHA: 15	Abilities	None	19–20	Head	5/6
	Magic	None			

Skills: Athletics 22%, Boating 19%, Brawn 22%, Courtesy 76%, Customs 72%, Dance 73%, Deceit 46%, Endurance 20%, Evade 26%, First Aid 24%, Gambling 41%, Influence 70%, Insight 31%, Perception 31%, Ride 43%, Seduction 46%, Sleight 33%, Stealth 24%, Unarmed 22%, Willpower 25%

Passions: : Loyalty (Family) 60%, Love (Aliana den Solis) 80%

Combat Style: Noble layabout 57% (Rapier, Main Gauche, Crossbow) – Flamboyance (see Sidebar)

Weapon	Size/Force	Reach	Damage	AP/HP
Rapier	M	L	1d8	5/8
Main Gauche	M	L	1d4	6/10
Crossbow	L	-	1d8	4/5

INCH

Inch has never fought fair in his life and doesn't intend to start now. He generally carries three daggers, all well-balanced for throwing, along with a garrotte. He can use a crossbow but doesn't usually carry it; he has a bodyguard for that. Should he be attacked he surrenders at the first opportunity.

Attributes		1d20	Location	AP/HP
Action Points: 2		1–3	Right Leg	-/5
Damage Modifier: +0		4–6	Left Leg	-/5
Magic Points: 12		7–9	Abdomen	-/6
Movement: 6 metres		10–12	Chest	-/7
Initiative Bonus: 12		13–15	Right Arm	-/4
Armour: None usually, but can access whatever he needs		16–18	Left Arm	-/4
Abilities: None		19–20	Head	-/5
Magic: None				

Skills: Athletics 49%, Brawn 32%, Deceit 71%, Endurance 37%, Evade 66%, Influence 74%, Insight 87%, Locale 110%, Perception 64%, Streetwise 69%, Unarmed 49%, Willpower 52%

Passions: Loyalty (The Tyrant) 90%, Love (Self) 90%

Combat Style: Never Fight Fairly (crossbow, dagger, garrotte) 70% - Assassination

Weapon	Size/Force	Reach	Damage	AP/HP
Dagger	S	S	1d4+1	6/8
Garrote	S	T	1d2	1/2
Crossbow	L	-	1d8	4/5

PERENGE THE INK-STAINED

Perenge's former title of "priest" to the Solisti was a reflection of his role, not his status in the cult. Miracles are provided for use in appropriate campaign settings. Note that Dismiss Magic will not have a significant effect against an enchantment such as Feather Eye's binding because the effect is simply suppressed for a split-second.

Characteristics	Attributes		1d20	Location	AP/HP
STR: 6	Action Points	2	1–3	Right Leg	–/4
CON: 8	Damage Modifier	-1d2	4–6	Left Leg	–/3
SIZ: 11	Magic Points	16	7–9	Abdomen	–/3
DEX: 9	Movement	6m	10–12	Chest	–/6
INT: 15	Initiative Bonus	12	13–15	Right Arm	–/5
POW: 16	Armour	None	16–18	Left Arm	–/4
CHA: 8	Abilities	None	19–20	Head	–/4
	Magic	None			

Skills: Athletics 15%, Brawn 17%, Bureaucracy 60%, Commerce 53%, Courtesy 53%, Customs 60%, Deceit 33%, Endurance 16%, Evade 18%, First Aid 43%, Influence 36%, Insight 61%, Lore (Sorcery) 60%, Lore (History of The Realm) 70%, Native Tongue 83%, Perception 31%, Willpower 72%

Passions: : Loyalty (Solis Family) 30%; Loyalty (The Realm) 60%; Oath (Xalgith) 80%

Magic

Theism (Xalgith Initiate)

Devotion (Xalgith) 64%, Exhort (Xalgith) 63%

Miracles: Dismiss Magic, Lay to Rest

Devotional Pool = 4 (1 available)

Combat Style: Pray and Hope for the Best 80% (Frantic Wringing of Hands and Muttering)

SWEGGEN NINE-FINGERS

Sweggen has no great interest in combat but if pressed he fights as brutally and nastily as he can. He usually carries a dagger and has a chain and hatchet in easy reach at his shop. He is capable of using the chain as a garrotte to choke a victim if he can get behind someone.

Characteristics	Attributes		1d20	Location	AP/HP
STR: 16	Action Points	2	1–3	Right Leg	–/6
CON: 12	Damage Modifier	+1d4	4–6	Left Leg	–/6
SIZ: 17	Magic Points	8	7–9	Abdomen	–/7
DEX: 8	Movement	6m	10–12	Chest	–/8
INT: 12	Initiative Bonus	10	13–15	Right Arm	–/5
POW: 8	Armour	None	16–18	Left Arm	–/5
CHA: 12	Abilities	None	19–20	Head	–/6
	Magic	None			

Skills: Athletics 35%, Brawn 80%, Commerce 86%, Courtesy 45%, Deceit 61%, Endurance 67%, Evade 26%, Influence 74%, Insight 65%, Locale 90%, Perception 55%, Streetwise 75%, Unarmed 69%, Willpower 42%

Passions: Love (money) 85%

Combat Style: Streetwise bruiser (small one-handed, weapons, two-handed club, chain) 65%

Weapon	Size/Force	Reach	Damage	AP/HP
Dagger	S	S	1d4+1+1d4	6/8
Chain	M	M	1d4+1d4	8/6
Hatchet	S	S	1d6+1d4	3/6
Great Club	H	L	2d6+1d4	4/10

XHAGO GARTHANIAN

Xhago's one serious threat in combat is Palsy which he can cast at Intensity 7, enough to affect nearly all humans. Jedakiah refused to teach him the most dangerous spells in the grimoire. His folk magic spells have little use in combat situations though he may be able to use Befuddle to make an escape in some circumstances.

Note that Xhago's Magic Points have been reduced by the cost of maintaining both Feather Eye's binding and an Alarm at his secret quarters.

Although Xhago is an initiate of the Chaos Mother the cult is not yet strong enough to grant miracles to its followers. All this will change if Jedakiah succeeds in performing the Dread Rite (see *Reckoning at Distaff Peak*).

Characteristics	Attributes		1d20	Location	AP/HP
STR: 8	Action Points	3	1–3	Right Leg	–/5
CON: 11	Damage Modifier	0	4–6	Left Leg	–/5
SIZ: 13	Magic Points	12	7–9	Abdomen	–/6
DEX: 11	Movement	6m	10–12	Chest	–/7
INT: 15	Initiative Bonus	13	13–15	Right Arm	–/4
POW: 17	Armour	None	16–18	Left Arm	–/4
CHA: 11	Abilities	None	19–20	Head	–/5

Skills: Athletics 19%, Brawn 21%, Craft (Inscription) 31%, Customs 75%, Deceit 56%, Endurance 22%, Evade 32%, Locale 45%, Influence 52%, Insight 52%, Lore (Chaos Mother) 40%, Native Tongue 66%, Perception 52%, Stealth 26%, Swim 19%, Unarmed 19%, Willpower 94%

Passions: Hate (Jedakiah) 75%, Loyalty (Jedakiah) 25%, Lust (for power) 100%, Oath (Chaos Mother) 85%

Magic

Folk Magic 72%: Alarm, Beastcall (snake), Befuddle, Bypass, Disguise, Pet (snake)

Sorcery (Entropic Revelations)

Invocation 65%, Shaping 57%

Mystic (Sight), Neutralise Magic, Palsy

Combat Style: Desperate measures 39% (Dagger)

Weapon	Size/Force	Reach	Damage	AP/HP
Dagger	S	S	1d4+1	6/8

FEATHER EYE

In its natural form Feather Eye has a body shape somewhat like an orang-utan with four outsized, powerful limbs each as strong as the other. Its forelimbs end in wickedly curved talons while its hind limbs end in strong, prehensile feet with two forward facing digits and two backward facing ones allowing it to cling onto most surfaces. Its skin is wrinkled and baggy, somewhat like an elephant's and just as tough. It has a blunt beak instead of a mouth and eyes as big and soulful as a bush-baby.

Feather Eye has four mastered human forms he can change to: a five year old boy (resembling the Contessa's son), a serving girl, a male noble and the Contessa. Statistics for his boy-form are given below. In the other forms his skills are roughly the same but his attributes change slightly.

- Serving girl (Selaah): Action Points 3, Damage Modifier -1d2, Movement 6. Unarmed 43%
- Male aristocrat (Risyk): Action Points 2, Damage Modifier 0, Movement 6. Unarmed 83%

In its form as a child, Feather Eye has no viable combat styles but should it become unbound it reverts to its natural form in which it has formidably sharp and hard talons. Its sorcery spells are largely non-combative; however Transfer Wound can be lethal. Given a chance, Feather Eye casts a well-practiced sight illusion on itself that hides its natural weapons. Unless a character can penetrate the illusion, this allows Feather Eye to strike with what are effectively invisible weapons. Another favourite trick is to use Phantom Sight with multiple targets to make multiple copies of itself that all imitate the original's movements. In its natural form its prehensile feet allow it to climb surprisingly effectively and it is capable of using its talons like pitons. It can make devastating attacks from ambush while hanging upside down and using illusions to distract attention or to conceal itself. It is perfectly capable of severing a head with a surprise attack from above, using a flurry (MYTHRAS page 97) special effect to attack with two talons in a scissoring motion.

5 Year Old Form	Attributes	1d20	Location	AP/HP
STR: 3	Action Points	2	1–3	Right Leg	-/9
CON: 5	Damage Modifier	-1d6	4–6	Left Leg	-/8
SIZ: 4	Magic Points	22	7–9	Abdomen	-/8
DEX: 4	Movement	4m	10–12	Chest	-/11
INT: 19	Initiative Bonus	12	13–15	Right Arm	-/10
POW: 22	Armour	None	16–18	Left Arm	-/9
CHA: 4	Abilities	None	19–20	Head	-/9

Skills: *Athletics 7%, Brawn 7%, Bureaucracy 53%, Commerce 38%, Courtesy 73%, Customs 113%, Deceit 138%, Disguise 73%, Endurance 10%, Evade 8%, Locale 123%, Influence 98%, Insight 101%, Native Tongue 93%, Perception 96%, Seduction 73%, Stealth 73%, Unarmed 7%, Willpower 109%*

Combat Style: *Tantrums of Impotent Rage*

Natural Form	Attributes	1d20	Location	AP/HP
STR: 17	Action Points	3	1–3	Right Leg	3/9
CON: 22	Damage Modifier	+1d6	4–6	Left Leg	3/9
SIZ: 19	Magic Points	22	7–9	Abdomen	3/10
DEX: 16	Movement	8m	10–12	Chest	3/11
INT: 19	Initiative Bonus	18	13–15	Right Arm	3/9
POW: 22	Armour	Wrinkled, leathery hide	16–18	Left Arm	3/9
CHA: 15	Abilities	Adhering, Formidable Natural Weapons	19–20	Head	3/9

Skills: *Athletics 33%, Brawn 36%, Bureaucracy 53%, Commerce 49%, Courtesy 84%, Customs 113%, Deceit 149%, Disguise 84%, Endurance 44%, Evade 82%, Locale 123%, Influence 120%, Insight 101%, Native Tongue 104%, Perception 96%, Seduction 84%, Sleight 56%, Stealth 85%, Unarmed 83%, Willpower 109%,*

Magic

Sorcery

Shaping 101%, Invocation 98%.

Sorcery spells known: Enhance CHA, Intuition, Phantom Sight, Phantom Sound, Shapechange (to Human), Telepathy, Transfer Wound

Combat Style: *Natural Weapons (Talons)*

Weapon	Size/Force	Reach	Damage	AP/HP
Talons	M	S	1d8+1d6	As for Arms

Chaos Mother Cultists

Use these statsitics for assorted Chaos Mother cult initiates. They fight fantaically, if incompetently. Use the Underling rules for MYTHRAS page 111 if necessary.

Attributes	1d20	Location	AP/HP
Action Points: 2	1–3	Right Leg	-/5
Damage Modifier: +0	4–6	Left Leg	-/5
Magic Points: 13	7–9	Abdomen	-/6
Movement: 6 metres	10-12	Chest	-/7
Initiative Bonus: 12	13–15	Right Arm	-/4
Armour: Faith and Zeal	16–18	Left Arm	-/4
Abilities: None	19–20	Head	-/5
Magic: None			

Skills: Athletics 21%, Brawn 23%, Deceit 49%, Endurance 30%, Evade 22%, Locale 44%, Lore (Chaos Mother) 29%, Perception 35%, Stealth 23%, Unarmed 21%, Willpower 61%, Passions:

Passions: Love (Chaos Mother) 100%, Loyalty (Xhago) 90%, Oath (Chaos Mother) 100%

Combat Style:: Mother's Little Helpers: 46% (Club, Dagger)

Weapon	Size/Force	Reach	Damage	AP/HP
Dagger	S	S	1d4+1	6/8
Club	S	T	1d2	1/2

City Guards

These statistics can also be used for bodyguards and the guards at the estate. Figure that each group is commanded by a more experienced guard who has 75% combat style, 1 extra point of armour per location but still has an adjusted Initiative Bonus of 8.

Attributes	1d20	Location	AP/HP
Action Points: 2	1–3	Right Leg	2/6
Damage Modifier: +1d2	4–6	Left Leg	2/6
Magic Points: 9	7–9	Abdomen	3/7
Movement: 6 metres	10-12	Chest	3/8
Initiative Bonus: 11 (8 when wearing armour)	13–15	Right Arm	2/5
Armour: Quilted	16–18	Left Arm	2/5
Abilities: None	19–20	Head	5/6
Magic: None			

Skills: Athletics 45%, Brawn 59%, Deceit 27%, Endurance 54%, Evade 32%, Locale 40%, Perception 29%, Stealth 21%, Unarmed 55%, Willpower 33%, Gambling 29%, Streetwise 31%

Passions: Love (Money) 70%, Loyalty (Employer) 60%

Combat Style: City Guard 60% (Dagger, Short sword, Short spear, Target Shield, Crossbow)

Weapon	Size/Force	Reach	Damage	AP/HP
Dagger	S	S	1d4+1+1d2	6/8
Shortspear	M	L	1d8+1+1d2	4/5
Shortsword	M	S	1d6+1d2	6/8
Target Shield	L	S	1d3+1+1d2	4/9
Crossbow	L	-	1d8	4/5

THUGS, BODYGUARDS AND SNEAKS

These statistics can be used for a selection of combat-trained individuals the characters might have to face.

Each thug will have a selection of weapons from the list based on their role. If needed, individual non-player characters can be tweaked on the fly by adding or subtracting up to 20% from their main combat styles, adding an Action Point (especially for sneaks) or increasing the damage modifier.

> ### MEGGO THE URCHIN
> A 9 year old urchin living on the streets. He is one of several who have come into contact with Feather Eye and is used by Feather Eye to send messages and also keep him up to date on rumours in the town. The street kids know the demon as the "Gribbly man" because they occasionally spot weird parts of his illusion. Feather Eye treats them well though. During the events he is likely to be killed by either Feather Eye or Xhago. No statistics are provided for him but assume the following skills if needed: Evade 60%, Perception 50%, Stealth 70%, Streetwise 50%.

Attributes	1d20	Location	AP/HP
Action Points: 2	1–3	Right Leg	2/5
Damage Modifier: +1d2	4–6	Left Leg	2/5
Magic Points: 9	7–9	Abdomen	2/6
Movement: 6 metres	10-12	Chest	2/7
Initiative Bonus: 10 (8 when wearing armour)	13–15	Right Arm	2/4
Armour: Quilted	16–18	Left Arm	2/4
Abilities: None	19–20	Head	2/5
Magic: None			

Skills: *Athletics 45%, Brawn 41%, Deceit 38%, Endurance 37%, Evade 31%, Locale 52%, Perception 35%, Stealth 39%, Unarmed 40%, Willpower 18%, Drinking & Whoring 58%, Gambling 30%, Streetwise 41%*

Passions: *Love (Money) 50%*

Combat Style: *All at 55%*

Body Guard (Dagger, Shortspear, Shortsword, Target Shield)
Thug (Club, Dagger, Hatchet)
Sneak (Club, Dagger, Shortsword, Crossbow)

Weapon	Size/Force	Reach	Damage	AP/HP
Dagger	S	S	1d4+1+1d2	6/8
Shortspear	M	L	1d8+1+1d2	4/5
Shortsword	M	S	1d6+1d2	6/8
Target Shield	L	S	1d3+1+1d2	4/9
Crossbow	L	-	1d8	4/5
Hatchet	S	S	1d6+1d2	3/6

NEW CREATURE: CUQULINAEAN DEMON

Pronounced: KOO-cu-lee-NYE-an.

This demon is the product of a perverse coupling of the fertility and illusion runes. It is not known if they are the result of sorcerous invention or of a natural catastrophe. The Realm has several legends of these demons abroad in the world, supplanting human children and giving rise to Changeling myths and horror stories.

The demon has a body shape somewhat like an orang-utan with four outsized, powerful limbs each as strong as the other. Its forelimbs end in wickedly curved talons while its hind limbs end in strong, prehensile feet with two forward facing digits and two backward facing ones allowing it to cling onto most surfaces. Its skin is wrinkled and baggy, somewhat like an elephant's and just as tough. It has a blunt beak instead of a mouth and eyes as big and soulful as a bush-baby.

It is a brood parasite, capable of injecting a larval offspring into a newly born sapient creature. This offspring quickly possesses the host and then is able to naturally dominate the unfortunate parents who will feed, nurture and protect it, oblivious to its increasing demands. At the equivalent of puberty, the demon bursts out from the host, killing it then usually consuming the hapless parents as they sit helpless. Once sated, it emerges into the world ready to continue the parasitical cycle.

Cuqulineans are natural sorcerers, however the sorcery they know is innate from birth and more cannot be learned. Each demon is born with 1d8 spells, selected randomly from the list given in the demon's description, opposite.

Characteristics	Attributes		1d20	Location	AP/HP
STR: 3D6+6 (17)	Action Points	3	1–3	Right Leg	3/9
CON: 3D6+12 (23)	Damage Modifier	+1d6	4–6	Left Leg	3/9
SIZ: 2D6+12 (19)	Magic Points	23	7–9	Abdomen	3/10
DEX: 3D6+6 (17)	Movement	8m	10–12	Chest	3/11
INT: 2D6+12 (19)	Initiative Bonus	18	13–15	Right Arm	3/9
POW: 3D6+12 (23)	Armour	Leathery Hide	16–18	Left Arm	3/9
CHA: 2D6+6 (13)	Abilities		19–20	Head	3/9
	Adhering, Formidable Natural Weapons				

Skills: *Athletics 44%, Brawn 46%, Custom 62, Dance 36%, Deceit 79%, Endurance 44%, Evade 82%, First Aid 35%, Locale 72%, Influence 72%, Insight 61%, Native Tongue 82%, Perception 82%, Sing 37%, Sleight 56%, Stealth 85%, , Unarmed 63%, Willpower 79%, Disguise 54%, Survival 70%*

Magic

Sorcery

Shaping 61%, Invocation 68%.

Sorcery Spells - 1d8 from: Enhance CHA, Intuition, Mystic Sight, Phantom Sight, Phantom Sound, Shapechange (to Human), Telepathy, Transfer Wound

Combat Style: *Natural weapons (Talons, all unarmed attacks) 75%*

Weapon	Size/Force	Reach	Damage	AP/HP
Talons	M	S	1d8+1d6	As for Arms

The talons have 6 armour points when used to parry, and are capable of the Bleed, Flurry, and Impale Special Effects.

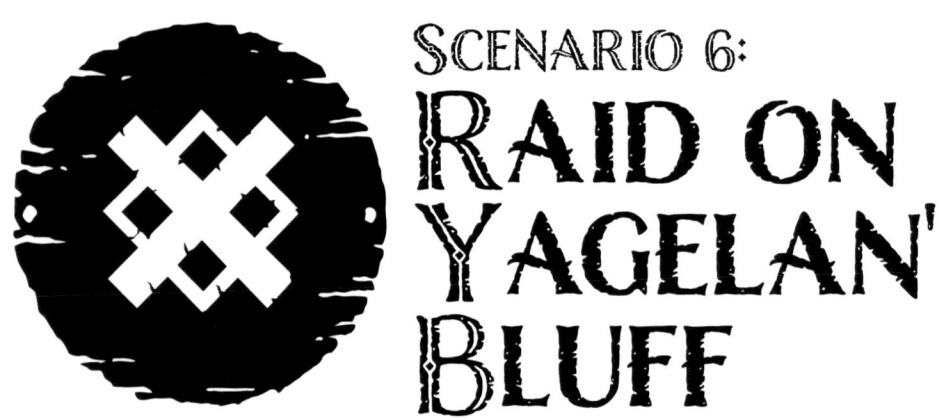

Scenario 6: Raid on Yagelan's Bluff

Overview

This adventure sends the characters on a mission to search out and destroy a new operation involving cultists, the barbarian Garthari and Ophidian serpent men. They travel through the Garthari wilds, avoiding various natural hazards and enemies, scout the Ophidian temple complex and take decisive action against key members of the leadership.

The characters must pass through enemy lands, avoiding patrols, and negotiate natural hazards and inclement weather to find their way to the Bluff. An ally provides knowledge crucial to the task.

The Bluff is surrounded by foes. Careful reconnaissance rewards the characters with possibilities for infiltration and opportunities to eliminate the leaders of one or more of the three factions. When they finally reach the heart of the crag, the characters must destroy the vats and other sorcerous machines. Unfortunately, the act of sabotage imperils their lives and they must flee poisonous gases, enraged Beast-Men and collapsing tunnels.

Non-Player Characters

- Chaos Hybrids, created by Jedakiah and the Ophidians
- Astomvar, Duke of Nyren
- Aganthus, his Priest Counsellor
- Garthari Hunters and Warriors
- Ophidian Sorcerer-Scientists

KEY POINTS/TIMELINE

1. The characters come to the aid of victims of a Chaos Hybrid attack.
2. The refugees, with the characters' help, flee to Nyren.
3. The characters meet with Duke Astomvar and Aganthus, who outlines what is known of the incursions of Chaos into The Realm.
4. Planning and preparation for the journey to Yagelan's Bluff.
5. Travel through the Garthari wilds.
6. A variety of locations and encounters between Demon Horse Overlook and the Bluff.
7. Infiltration and sabotage of the Ophidian complex.
8. Escape!

AREAS TO BE COVERED

The scenario starts on the northern border of the Vale, along the Gartharis River. This is frontier-country, abutting the Gartharis wilderness. Nyren is the nominated town, but Sarshen and Lurien are equally good candidates. Yagalen's Bluff is found in the delta of land between the two rivers, a no-man's land between Gartharis and the North Vale, but with some work it could be moved nearly anywhere that the Games Master wishes, as long as it is remote and it makes sense for barbarians and cultists to congregate there.

Specific locations within The Realm visited during the adventure are as follows:

- The River Gartharis and the road to Nyren. An ancient ruined hill fort, a landmark a few hours' walk from the town.
- The town of Nyren and locations within; The Duke's manor house, the Shrine of Sayalis and other optional scenes in the hostelry and the Temple of the Four.
- The Garthari wilderness.
- Yagalen's Bluff in the north, east of the origin of the River Nyr. Upon and within the Bluff sprawls the Ophidian complex.

BACKGROUND

In his thirst for domination of The Realm, Jedakiah has sent trusted agents as envoys to treat with the barbarian Garthari and the Ophidians under the mountains. The Ophidian tunnel complex is hidden in lands in the delta between the mountain origins of the Nyr and Garthari rivers. Jedakiah has sent a contingent of trusted agents to negotiate with both the Garthari and the reclusive Ophidians. They have begun to produce an army of savage Beast-Men: the Chaos Hybrid encountered in the first scenario of Book of Quests, *Caravan*, is an example of what the Ophidians are capable of breeding. Now, Jedakiah wants more and the Ophidians are obliging. As this force swells, small groups are sent south to sow misery and havoc. This pulls the characters into conflict with Jedakiah's agents.

This scenario does not directly implicate the sorcerer, but if the characters are already aware of his activities, it is only a small leap to link Jedakiah to the Ophidians and the Beast-Men. Obviously, someone seeks to strengthen Chaos in The Realm.

HOOKS

The adventure begins with an encounter with roving Beast-Men near to the city of Nyren. The Duke then implores the characters to discover the origin of these fiends and stop their depredations in The Vale.

Reasons for the characters to travel to Nyren could include their interest in the specialised magic of the Hero cult of Sayalis, a Theistic cult fallen from favour for many generations. Aganthus, a favoured elderly acolyte of the cult who resides in Nyren, is perhaps its last member.

Established enemies of Jedakiah may need only to learn of his involvement with the Garthari, and rumours of a cell of cultists in Nyren, to motivate them to travel there.

The Duke of Nyren, Astomvar, has also let it be known that he seeks "warriors of strong arm and resolve" to help with the Beast-Men roaming the wilderness north and east of the city.

STAND ALONE ADVENTURE

At its heart, this is primarily a cross-country trip and commando raid against the sorcerous Ophidians' base in the wilderness. The snake-men have barbarian and cultist allies that make a frontal assault suicidal. In contrast to a typical dungeon-crawl, the characters don't have time to clear the complex and it is not intended that the enemies

> **ALTERNATIVE HOOKS**
>
> Other possible sources of information that will focus the characters' attention on the Ophidians could include one of Jedakiah's lieutenants, who bears a grudge and has treacherous intent. Even stranger allies could include traditionalist Ophidian or Garthari, who each view the other as interlopers and the alliance as blasphemous. These individuals might seek to employ the characters directly, through a cat's-paw, or by providing detailed information to the Duke. It is also possible that Feather Eye (see Curse of the Contessa) knows of the Ophidian complex and may impart this information to characters.

can be eradicated. Basic requirements are a wilderness of pine and spruce trees, bordered by mountains.

The key to making this mission satisfying for your players is to tailor it to their characters' drives. The quest-giver (the Duke of Nyren in this case) might have secret knowledge, land grants, noble titles, or any number of other potential rewards. Characters bent on vengeance might find the Ophidians allied with their enemies.

NYREN AND THE BEAST-MEN

The characters are travelling to the city of Nyren, pursuing rumoured riches and noble favour, the promise of secret magical power or lost knowledge. Cold drizzle soaks through their clothes as they draw closer to the city. A trail close to the river is nothing but a muddy wound amongst the spruce. The river is swollen and grey with the rain.

The characters may be travelling either by road or by river. About 10 miles from Nyren, they find Beast-Men picking over the spoils from a successful ambush.

A Perception roll allows careless characters to note the danger before they are seen by the Beast-Men. Careful characters do not need to roll.

Smoke hangs in the still air above a wrecked barge, tethered to the shore by several ropes and grapnels.

Two half-human Beast-Men snarl and posture over dead horses and trade-goods spilled across the trail. A short distance away, in the direction of a bloody trail, whoops and howling laughter combine with panicked screaming.

Characters undetected by the Beast-Men may attack by surprise with a Stealth roll opposed by the Beast-Men's Hard Perception roll. River-borne characters could navigate the grounded barge and continue on unmolested, but will need to land if they choose to sneak up on the Beast-Men or investigate further.

The two Beast-Men scouts are distracted by their contest over the horse-flesh. Once aware of the characters, they call out and try to flee to their brothers at the ruined fort. If engaged, they try to safely withdraw unless the characters don't seem to pose a threat.

Shortly after the characters encounter the scouts, horrible shrieking and screaming is heard from the direction of the trail away from the river. A short distance away, the characters find a group of six more Beast-Men scouts surrounding a hilltop ruin. Up ahead a victim held down by one of the Beast-Men, falls silent as a much larger Beast-Man warrior pulls the victim's arm away from the shoulder. This Beast-Man holds the gruesome trophy aloft, bellowing in bloody rage as gore cascades from the dismembered limb. Travellers huddling within and upon the upper floor of the ruined shell of an old tower scream and throw rocks and branches, whatever they can find, at the other Beast-Men surrounding the hilltop. If the characters intervene, the Beast-Men fight, trying to gang up on individuals, but fleeing if injured or if the characters seem to overmatch them. None fight to the death.

The Beast-Man warrior launches himself at the closest enemy. The remaining Beast-Men engage more carefully, dividing equally amongst the characters, bleating warnings to each other.

The Beast-Men do not fight to the death, preferring to flee and later harass the characters with thrown rocks and intimidation. They attack opportunistically or once reinforcements embolden them. Otherwise, the Beast-Men use hit and run tactics throughout the afternoon until the overcast sky darkens towards evening. Horns call back and forth, revealing that many more Beast-Men are out there in the forests, coming closer.

The travellers were headed east from Norport to Nyren until their barge was ambushed by an organised band of Beast-Men hurling grapnels and ropes to pull it to shore. None of the travellers have encountered Beast-Men before. The group is as follows:

Sianas, Priestess of Aliya, is somewhat distant, but authoritative. She acts as spokesperson for the refugees. Sianas travels with her servants and assistants (four young women in all) who are uniformly timid and furtively protective of "The Lady". The Priestess and her assistants lack magic but are skilled healers, aiding those they can while looking to the characters to lead the group on to Nyren. It was the priestess' horses that the Beast-Men slew.

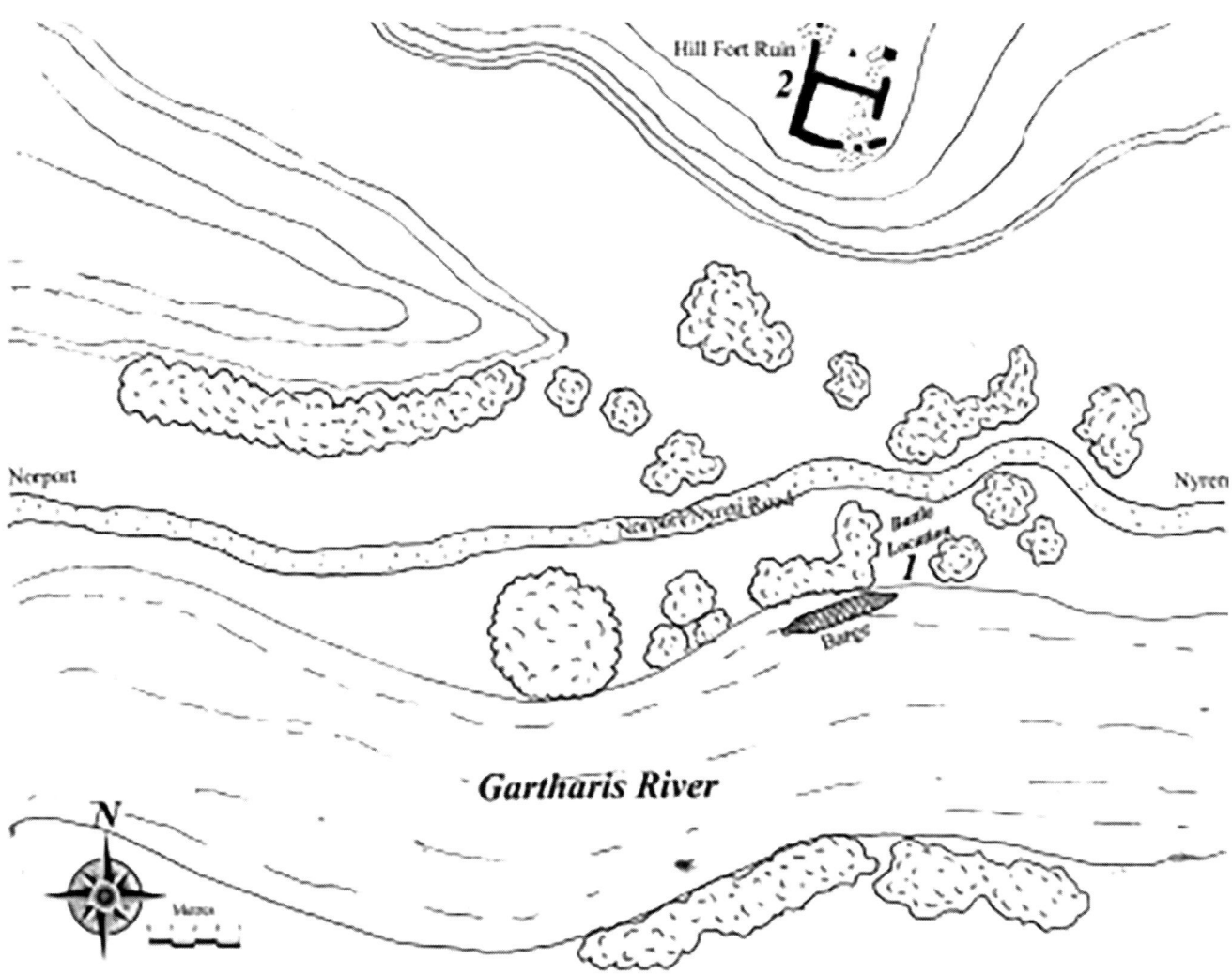

The farmer Sergany and his teenage sons Laganis and Magado, Sergany's wife Desina, fierce protector to her small children Cassa and Jula.

The stonemason Henrig, fond of wine and laughter, has thick dark hair and a full beard. Henrig is strong but has gone to fat in recent years. Henrig's apprentice *Riodro*, a foreigner from the far south; young, smart and good-looking. Riodro knows this and uses it to his best advantage.

Wylin and Bannis both have a chequered past in Norport. Wylin is big, uncomplicated, but not stupid; drawn into conflict between criminal gangs, he left Norport to escape the violence and get honest work logging. Bannis is slim, but with ropey muscles and a dishonest mien, an ex-gang enforcer from Norport. His old gang mates have placed a 200 Founder bounty on his head. Both were working their passage to Nyren by helping Franko, the now dead owner of the barge, and his two sons Petro and Dacci. Dacci was knocked into the water and fled to the far shore in panic. His older brother was the man killed in gruesome fashion by the Beast-Man warrior.

Wylin and Bannis ask for weapons in order to help fight. The others flee further attacks and fight only when in immediate peril. Lady Sianas asks the characters to help the group to Nyren, pointing out that the temple in Norport and the folk of Nyren would be grateful for her safe arrival.

Flight to Nyren

Heroic characters who agree to protect the group of refugees face harassment and repeated feints and volleys of thrown rocks from a group of several Beast-Men shadowing their path. The journey over-land takes almost four hours due to the weather and road conditions and the presence of the farmer's small children. River travel is faster, requiring only two hours.

The characters must watch for lurking Beast-Men, making a Standard Perception roll each hour of travel. Success allows vigilant characters to avoid opportunistic attacks. The refugees provide an additional +25% Augmentation to perception rolls in helping watch for Beast-Men. Six Beast-Men attack randomly-determined targets with thrown rocks if this roll is failed. A fumbled roll allows two of the trailing Beast-Men to draw close enough (perhaps by swimming out to a boat-borne group) to attack one of the refugees with hand weapons.

After any attack, several of the refugees may panic unless the characters make a successful Hard Influence or Standard Oratory roll to retain control of the group. Panicking refugees might try to flee or otherwise behave erratically. Stalking Beast-Men use this opportunity to attack again! Two of their number engage vulnerable refugees in close combat; defeating them permits the characters to attempt again the pertinent roll to restore order to the group.

COWARDS!

Craven or selfish characters may abandon the survivors to their fate. Such characters must make only three successful Easy Perception rolls to reach Nyren in three hours by foot. Those riding or travelling on the river must make only one roll. Note that the augmentation bonus noted is not available.

Any refugees that make it to Nyren publicly denounce them as cowards, which influences interactions with residents of the city.

A HERO'S WELCOME

As the beleaguered group approaches Nyren at last, the city's gates are thrown open and armed guards, outriders and others surge forth to chase off the remaining Beast-Men, assist the wounded and celebrate the characters' arrival. Among their number is the Duke's castellan, Yoreth, who speaks with them once the gates are closed and all are safe within.

Yoreth is a middle-aged man, slight in build, with thinning hair but youthful vigour and an air of competence. He is dressed in a sturdy leather hauberk and bears a heavy, well-maintained sword. He asks the characters to accompany him to the Duke's residence, as their assistance is needed.

MEETING WITH THE DUKE OF NYREN

After a short wait in a warm reception room in the well-appointed, but old, manor-house, servants bring refreshments and water to wash their hands and faces. A tall, bulky man in late middle age, with short-cropped dark hair, enters the room unannounced and impatiently waves the characters back to their seats. He introduces himself as "Astomvar, Duke of this place" and, after listening to the characters' account of the encounter with the Beast-Men, asks if they will help with "these accursed creatures". The Duke does not know their origin, but "more and more of these fiends ravage my people, the farmers and foresters and the pasturelands". Astomvar describes reports of unusual activities possibly linked to the Beast-Men attacks. Various folk, wood-cutters, rangers, scouts, hunters and trappers working the wilds of Gartharis, have observed the movement of supplies, equipment and men north, towards the mountains along the river Nyr. The further north one travels, the more one hears of Beast-Men predation.

A servant interrupts the meeting by announcing the arrival of Acolyte Aganthus, a stooped, elderly man dressed in priestly robes, leaning on an unusual wooden sword that he uses as a walking stick. He walks slowly and with a limp; nodding and smiling at the characters and the Duke before sitting with a relieved sigh at the Duke's gesture. Again, Astomvar ignores protocol and introduces Aganthus as an acolyte of Sayalis, describing the cult as old and honoured, having knowledge of the Beast-Men and where they might originate.

Aganthus explains that he venerates Sayalis, pointing out that the hero is not the one in the story-books and folk tales. He describes old scrolls recording Sayalis' exploits that claim the Beast-Men are soldiers called forth by "degenerate snake-man magic". Aganthus is certain the Beast-Men are coming from the Garthari range "and what's more, I reckon its Yagalen's Bluff". Sayalis led the defeat of the Chaos-worshipping barbarians and discovered their Ophidian allies coiled in the bowels of the northern mountain range.

A servant unrolls a crudely-sketched map on the table (see opposite). Aganthus weights the corners with empty cups, platters and the like. Gesturing at a place on the map near the departure of the River Nyr from the Range, Aganthus smiles: "here is Yagalen's Bluff. And I know how they can be stopped". He offers to provide training in exchange for the characters' help. He also suggests they might be welcome as initiates if they would fight Chaos.

Aganthus describes the old magic of the snake-men, vats made of iron that grow beasts similar to those that plague the lands around Nyren. If the characters have played-through Shadows Behind the Throne, then these vats are all-too familiar.

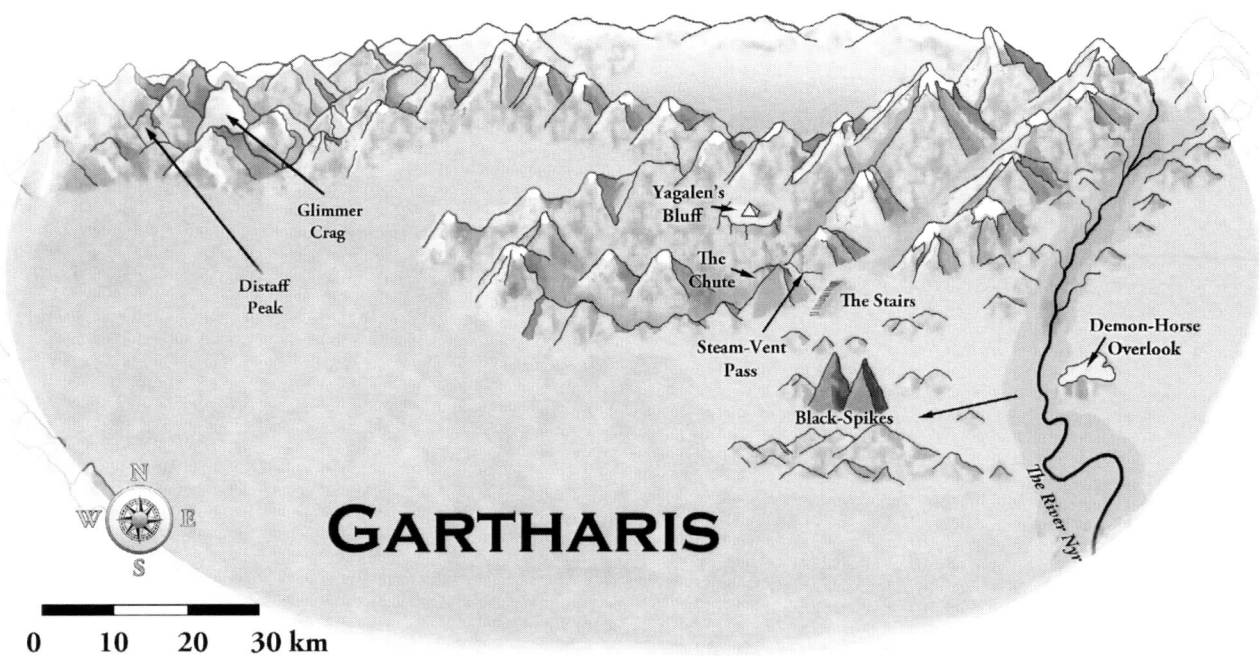

"Sayalis has shown me in dreams that an unholy trinity holds a conclave at Yagalen's Bluff, its slopes darkened by a multitude which shall fall upon Nyren, unless the sorcerous machines which unify them are somehow destroyed. The histories say the cauldrons may be stopped with a special material that I will render for you. The vats will be made useless by Kremathus' Concoction, a little something I have."

Duke Astomvar and Aganthus propose a covert operation to surgically strike at the source of the Beast-Men and the destruction of their leadership. It is important that the Acolyte warns the characters that there will not be time to 'clear' the complex and neither is it possible to do so. The enemies facing them at Yagalen's Bluff are strong both individually and in numbers.

The Duke offers a bounty of 1000 Founders for each character who aids in the destruction of the machinery used to create the Beast-Men and a bonus of 1000 to be shared among the characters if they are able to assassinate the leadership behind the Beast-Men attacks. The Duke can provide mundane equipment and horses. His armourer can provide ringmail hauberks, but a maximum of hard leather in all other locations (equivalent to a maximum total cost per character of 900 founders). Weaponry and other items totalling no more than 500 founders per character.

Aganthus provides the characters with a copy of his map, a sketched route to the east from the river Nyr.

Kremathus' Concoction

Prior to their departure, Aganthus gives the characters three small flasks of unusual construction. He advises great care, for exposing the contents to air or water is likely to 'end poorly'. He advises that they must be completely immersed in the vat-fluid. The flasks are of glass, wrapped in layers of leather and cloth to prevent breaking. They are each placed in a padded wooden box that is strapped-shut.

Breaking a flask outside of the Vats produces an unusual white smoke that spirals rapidly from the exposed fluid, and the fluid itself becomes increasingly hot giving-off a bright white light. The hissing, bubbling and crackling lasts several seconds (1d3+1 Combat Rounds) before the remainder detonates, inflicting 4d6 damage to all locations to characters within 5 metres, and 3d6 to 1d3 random locations to those between 10 and 20 metres away. Immersing the opened flask in pure untainted water causes an immediate detonation whilst "impure" water (such as the Crystal Pool) would cause the flask to detonate between 1-3 rounds depending on the fluid.

BOOK OF QUESTS ✕ SCENARIO 6: RAID ON YAGELAN'S BLUFF

NYREN RUMOURS

1d12	True	Partially True	False
1	Someone is arming the northern barbarians with quality weapons.	Snake-men live among us! They can't eat anything but raw meat (there are some ophidian spies, but they eat cooked meat, too)	An army of sorcerers, trained in the south, has infiltrated the Vale.
2	Twisted magic killed men who were excavating ancient ruins in the Black Vale.	A snake-haired woman has been seen in the Wilds of the Vale. Her gaze turns men into stone.	The Beast-Men cannot cross running water.
3	Slavers have been sighted on the borders of Garthari territory.	The Garthari Ranges are worm-eaten, riddled with tunnels 20 feet or more across.	A village in the Vale has been eaten whole by a great worm!
4	The Garthari don't kill everyone they find in their territory, just almost everyone.	The old Chaos Cults are growing in secret in the towns of The Realm.	A demon lurks in the glacier of Karkan, and the River Nyr has been tainted by blood and the stench of sulphur.
5	There's a trapper in Nyren who is on good terms with the Garthari.	The barbarians mass as an army in the Black Vale, planning to destroy the towns along the River Gartharis.	Blood-drinkers rule each of the towns of the Vale, careful not to kill too many of the human 'herd'.
6	The road between Westport and Cylder is dangerous. Officials from either Westport or Cylder offer rich rewards on the heads of bandit leaders	A sorcerer and his apprentices skulk in Norport and the Black Vale.	Garthari custom prohibits refusal of drink.
7	Someone with great power and influence has been scouring The Realm for information on the whereabouts of an Ancient Earth Mother Temple.	A trader uses a barbaric token that allows him to travel unmolested though Garthari lands.	The sorcerer in the Gartharis Mountains is a complete myth. It's all a ruse by the King to spread fear and so raise levies. In fact, some say the King IS the sorcerer...
8	Someone is searching for the Mermaid; she isn't just a legend.	A demon is snatching children off the streets of Cylder.	People feed on a mountain of corpses hidden underneath Cylder.
9	The bandits in the mountains west of The Long Riding have allies in Locharis, a small town nearby.	The Founding Four punished those wicked Cyldermen: The river took the city – it is now under water.	The end times are coming!
10	They say the Tyrant of Westport is so paranoid that he hired a sorcerer to remove all knowledge of his name. (True but Jedakiah wasn't involved.)	Chaos Cultists stalk Norport killing virgins.	New deposits of gold have been found in the mountains (false, but some of the tombs have had gold in them)
11	They call the cliffs north of Westport the Dragon Bone cliffs because treasure hunters often find the bones of ancient dragons and even larger monsters buried deep within them. (Mostly true. Fossilised skeletons of immense beasts can be dug out of the cliffs.)	The forts that dot the Southern Border are ill-equipped to repel any barbarian invasion (true) and warbands have been seen amassing in The Long Riding (false).	There are undead in the forest north of Locharis, a small town near the mountain range west of The Long Riding (false)
12	Beast-Men have been seen before in The Realm, more than 500 years ago.	There is a family of giants in the mountains (almost true, there is a Cyclops)	The richest woman in Westport, the Contessa den Solis, plans to marry again when her son reaches the age of 5. (Mostly false: she has no plans to re-marry.)

Planning and Preparation

The characters need to decide on either a land or river journey. The river winds over approximately 180 kilometres until Demon Horse Overlook. The characters must charter a boat and crew, or sail a smaller boat themselves. No traders head much past Aylesford. Without complications, such a journey might take a week. Characters travelling by land face a shorter journey (90 kilometres). but also more danger. If travelling by horseback they can count on three days of travel. On foot things progress more slowly, taking about 6 days.

Chaos Mother cult spies may hear of a small group provisioning themselves for travel north, but they will be certain to note a group chartering a boat for travel along the River Nyr to the mountains.

Cunning characters may wish to ask discreetly about contacts between townsfolk and Garthari barbarians or even elements of any Chaos cults in the town. The characters find their activities are being observed if they make a successful Streetwise, Perception or Insight roll. A critical success identifies Eyloi the Hare as having particular interest in them.

Rumours in Nyren

Careful characters can gather rumours by spending silver and talking with the locals. A Standard Customs, Streetwise or Perception roll provides a rumour (see page 166). The difficulty of this task can be reduced to Easy if the characters spend at least 60 Founders. A critical success provides a true rumour, a success finds a partially true rumour, a failure results in a partially true rumour while a fumble provides a false rumour. The Games Master may prefer to roll for the character and conceal the result. One rumour can be found each evening of carousing.

Departure

The Duke and the Acolyte counsel discretion - if not secrecy - in departing for the north. Characters disregarding this advice have many well-wishers and, perhaps, cheering crowds, to see them out the gates, bringing gifts of food and garlands of flowers woven by the local women. Assassins follow shortly thereafter.

If the characters *do* heed the warnings, and make suitable precautions against advertising their departure and purpose, there are fewer difficulties later, but no cheering, no gifts and no infatuated well-wishers.

Travel North

The characters head, either by land or by river, north towards the Garthari Range. Assassins may intervene and the Games Master might introduce any number of chance encounters or diversions at this point.

Assassins!

Eyloi the Hare is a brutal killer. He lives in Nyren and acts as eyes and ears for the Cult of the Chaos Mother. He prefers frank efficiency and minimal risk. Eyloi first sends a group of sell-swords to kill the characters. These men are ignorant of their employer's true nature and believe he is a party wronged by the characters and seeking justice. Eyloi took care to disguise himself and find out-of-town and out-of-luck killers. They are hungry, desperate and have flexible morals. They strike about a day's travel from Nyren, trying to surprise their quarry, if possible.

These men do not fight to the death and flee after taking a Serious Wound. Captured would-be assassins provide little useful information.

Eyloi himself trails the characters north, intending to strike at an opportune time, preferring to attack lone characters. He favours unarmoured locations when aiming to incapacitate. Eyloi disengages after attacking, trying to avoid the other characters, biding his time until another opportunity presents itself.

The Garthari Wilds

The characters follow the map and directions therein, encountering various obstacles and challenges on the way to Yagalen's Bluff.

A River Cruise

Characters travelling with a trader up the river have an uneventful trip to Lurien, sailing in daylight and camping at well-frequented sites at regular intervals along the shore. Unless side adventures in Sarsmen, Lurien or other locations along the way are of interest to the Games Master or the Players, the characters arrive safely in Lurien after six days. Characters piloting their own boat should make a daily Standard Boating roll. Failures and fumbles should lead to delays or difficulties negotiating obstacles along the river. Complications could include injuries, loss of provisions or equipment, damage to the boat requiring landing for makeshift repairs, and so on.

If the first scenario of Book of Quests has been used, *Caravan*, Lurien is filled with gossip of the terrible events that befell Aylesford. Talk of monsters and dread sorcerers abound. Indeed, the characters already know, first hand, of what happened, if they have been through the *Caravan* scenario. For this reason few are travelling north from Lurien and many villagers from the remote settlements have come to the town seeking sanctuary. The characters may well spot people encountered in Thorsen amongst those looking for refuge.

From Lurien, the characters must travel north with the river until they find the Demon Horse Overlook. No traders venture beyond Lurien. Chartering a boat in this town is impossible and any attempt to do so is reported to allies of the Garthari or Chaos Mother's Cult. The response is more assassins and ambushes.

Travel Encounters

1d8	Day	Night
1	Bear	Bear
2	Beast-Men Scouts	Beast-Men scouts
3	Garthari Hunters	Garthari Hunters
4	Lost	Ghost
5	Ravine	Spoiled Provisions
6	Rockslide	The Mother's Kiss
7	Spirit Guardian	Wild Dogs
8	Wild Dogs	Zombie

Bear

A large brown bear stumbles into the characters' path (or their camp, if at night). Attracted by noise and the smell of food, it may be discouraged by aggressive characters, distracted by food offerings or enraged as the Games Master wishes. If the roll that caused this Problem was fumbled at night, the bear is in the camp, rummaging through supplies and potentially scaring horses away. If the triggering fumble was in daylight, the bear comes across a character briefly separated from his companions. The bear flees if the characters wound it or brandish fire.

Beast-Men Scouts

The characters' path intersects that of a small band of marauding Beast-Men. A fumbled roll means they are ambushed. Otherwise, an opposed Perception roll will determine whether both groups are aware of each other. The Beast-Men attack with thrown spears and rocks unless they believe they have sufficient strength to kill the adventurers.

Garthari Hunters

An encounter with Garthari may go peacefully, if the barbarians see no advantage to attacking the characters. This hunting party of three is looking for game, but gear and silver taken from the cooling bodies of trespassers would be a welcome substitute. They may trade. If zealous characters seek information on the Cult of the Chaos Mother or disclose their path towards the Ophidians or Yagalen's Bluff, the hunters will track the group whilst also sending a runner to get reinforcements.

A fumbled roll leading to this encounter means the Garthari are aware of the characters first. They may still choose to parley, if there is advantage to it.

Brutal warriors, cunning in the forests and hills of their lands, the Garthari are extremely aggressive, but not foolish. Like most, they rarely fight to the death, but will flee rather than surrender, as they show no kindness to their prisoners and expect none in return. They prefer guerrilla tactics, striking fast and hard before fading back into the trees.

Ghost

The adventurers have set up camp near the binding object of a Haunt. A woman was brutalised here by fellow tribesmen and then slain. Her spirit became bound to a small love-token she had previously given to one of the men; lucky or clever characters will find a painted clay figurine of a dove hidden in the gnarled roots of a weeping tree. The weeping tree is not commonly seen in the Gartharis region.

A translucent figure of a slim girl with matted hair, dressed in tattered rags. At first, she weeps quietly, but swiftly becomes enraged, using first her Miasma ability and then Wither to strike any remaining characters. The haunt will target males only. She is immune to any attacks made by the characters. A character making a successful Easy Lore (Spirits) roll will recall the haunt's vulnerability to the destruction of its binding object. The clay figure may be crushed easily once found.

Haunt: Intensity 2. INT 11, POW 17, CHA 14
Willpower 84%, Hate Men 134%, Spectral Fists 84%
Miasma, Wither.

Lost

The group has become lost. This day's travel does not contribute to the journey. If the roll causing this Problem was fumbled, the next Survival task is harder by one difficulty grade.

Ravine

A steep-walled, deep, rocky ravine blocks progress. A day's travel is lost in finding another way forwards. Characters on foot may try to navigate the climb, with attendant danger. Ravines encountered after a fumbled skill check have caused the leading member of the group (determined randomly unless specified previously) to stumble over loose rock at the lip of the ravine. A Hard Evade (or Formidable Ride test, if mounted) avoids the 8m fall. Any character that falls receives 2d6 points of damage to two random locations.

Rockslide

The path ahead is blocked by a rockslide, necessitating a dangerous climb or a massive detour. Mounted groups cannot proceed over the loose rocks with the horses. This detour costs most of a day's progress.

When this Problem arises due to a fumbled roll, it indicates the group has been caught in a rockslide. Success on a Hard Evade (or Formidable Ride if mounted) roll preserves life, limb and provisions. Failures here inflicts 1d3 wounds (each 1d6+1 damage, affecting both man and mount), increase Fatigue by one level and a Standard Survival test to avoid loss of 1d2 provisions or an item of equipment.

Spirit Guardian

The characters stumble across a sacred site; they find a circle of crumbling standing stones covered in rust-coloured runes surrounding a central black altar. An ancestral spirit (treat as a Wraith, MYTHRAS page 153), that seeks to possess and kill intruders, guards this place. If the triggering Survival roll was fumbled, the characters are subject to immediate attack, having already entered the warded area. Otherwise, prudent characters may circumvent the danger with a wide detour. Any character with Lore (Spirits) or another relevant Lore skill recognises this place as bad magic and knows the Wraith cannot follow them out of the circle.

Spoiled Provisions

The characters discover Bitterworm spoiling their food, ruining about half the group's provisions. If a fumble caused this Problem, all of the food is rendered inedible. Starvation is not likely to be a factor until the return trip from Yagalen's Bluff. The Games Master may wish to review the Starvation rules on page 82 of the MYTHRAS rulebook, but tests will not be needed until characters are without food for a number of days equal to half CON (which then requires daily Standard Endurance rolls).

The Mother's Kiss

The characters have made camp in a diseased area. A successful Standard Endurance roll means nothing more than a few minor symptoms (shivering, headaches and general aches and pains) incurring an extra level of Fatigue for a day or two. If this Problem was caused by a fumble, the Endurance roll is Hard. Failure on the Endurance roll results in The Mother's Kiss, and for the following 1d6+1 days, that character suffers the conditions of Confusion and Fever (see MYTHRAS page 75). The disease increases the difficulty grade of all tasks by one and the infected cannot perform any knowledge, communication or magic skill – a potentially fatal situation if the entire party succumb to the disease. A repeat Standard Endurance roll can be made each day. Success will end the illness.

Wild Dogs

A pack of six wild dogs trails the group, barking, howling at night and otherwise calling attention to the characters. Seeking an easy meal, the dogs attack a solitary figure, but prefer to try to separate a horse from the group and chase it down. Aggressive characters, fire and distractions of food may deal with them. If the roll that triggers this Problem was fumbled at night, the dogs are in the camp, tearing into supplies and perhaps about to attack a horse (which may then flee). If the fumble was during the day, the dogs attack a randomly determined character who is separated from his companions.

The dogs flee if they haven't managed to bring down their prey after ten combat rounds or if more than two dogs are wounded. The dogs flee immediately if threatened with fire. Use the statistics for wolves (MYTHRAS page 272)

Plague Zombie

A single plague zombie (see page 274 of the MYTHRAS rulebook), roused from torpor by the passing of the characters, shambles into the camp at night. If the roll that caused this Problem was fumbled, the attacking Zombie surprises a lone character. After defeating the zombie, tracking backwards leads the adventurers to a small broken cairn that they passed earlier without note. Those exploring within will find 240 silver coins of ancient manufacture and a small gold medallion (worth 300 founders). Unfortunately, disease has infected the treasure and all who are exposed for longer than four hours may develop symptoms and impairment of The Mother's Kiss (see above) if they fail a Standard Endurance roll.

Cross Country

This more direct route is fraught with much greater likelihood of hostile encounters and other obstacles. Unfortunately, despite having the map, the characters still need to explore to the northeast towards the origin of the River Nyr to find the Demon Horse Overlook. This task can be repeated but each re-roll requires a day of exploration, exposing the characters to further dangers (see below).

Temperature and Other Environmental Concerns

The landscape of the Garthari Wilds is one of rough hills concealed by light forests of pine and spruce trees. The ground varies from flinty stone to marsh and peat. Within the gloom of the trees, there is no significant ground cover save the endless bed of pine needles smothering sounds of passage. The weather is usually still, cold and overcast, with infrequent rain, and sporadic storms. Opposite the

OBSTACLES

1d8	Day
1	Beast-Men Raiders
2	Cliffs
3	Cult of the Chaos Mother Region
4	Gathari Encampment
5	Icy Valley
6	Peat Bog
7	Rapids
8	Tunnels

BEAST-MEN RAIDERS

As the characters enter the region, it quickly becomes apparent that others came this way only to find a gruesome fate. Beast-Men are found along their path amongst dismembered bodies, pulling limbs from their fallen prey, organs strewn about the area. They number six Beast-Men Scouts and a single Warrior in total. On a failure of the original Navigation roll, an opposed perception test will determine if both parties are aware of each other. If the Beast-Men become aware of the characters, they attack and react in the same fashion as described on page 162. If the Navigation test was a fumble, then the characters arrive only to find a scene of dismembered bodies and gore before being ambushed by the Beast-Men. A Standard Perception roll determines if the characters are aware of the Beast-Men before they attack.

At the Games Master's discretion, the bodies may have salvageable loot but anything found should be no better than of poor quality.

CLIFFS

Twisting mountain paths and towering valleys lead the characters to a sheer cliff that they must overcome to continue their journey. They can choose to climb down the cliff by making a Standard Athletics roll, or an Easy Athletics roll if the characters have the relevant tools, but will be subject to dangerous fall damage if they fail causing 4d6 points of damage to four random locations. Alternatively, the characters may spend a day looking for an alternate route. On a failure, the cliffs open out to a scene that gives the characters a good idea of the route they need to take and their next Navigation roll to determine if they reach a Key scene will be easy. However, on a fumble the cliffs open out to nothing but twisting pathways and rocky outcrops and the characters need to make a Standard Navigation roll as per normal.

CULT OF THE CHAOS MOTHER REGION

The characters inadvertently stumble into a region where the Cult of the Chaos Mother is actively operating. A Standard Perception roll leaves characters feeling as though they're being watched and, maybe unnerved, as they catch glimpses of figures peering from behind rocks or trees. Games Masters using the scenario as part of a campaign involving the cult may want to use this as an opportunity for the cult to gain some information or insight into what the characters are doing, or even create a mini scene in which the cult confront the party for some reason. Otherwise the characters pass through mostly undisturbed unless a fumble was rolled for the Navigation roll, in which case they are attacked by sell-swords that have tracked the party and have found the opportunity to strike them. For these encounters, use the same outlines given in the Assassins! section on page 167.

GATHARI ENCAMPMENT

A Gathari Encampment is found along the way to the characters next destination. On a Standard roll, the scene can remain largely uneventful as the characters spot the camp from far enough away that they can easily navigate around it, but may instead try to interact with the Gathari. Be aware, however, that by doing so they are entering their territory and the Gathari attempt to defend their camp and drive off the characters, pursuing them only if they see advantage in it. On a fumble, the characters have unwittingly already stumbled into Gathari territory and they will attempt to drive them off regardless.

ICY VALLEY

The snow and frost have iced-up a valley the characters have attempted to traverse. Treacherous crevasses have formed between the ice and the party needs to tread carefully if they wish to get through in one piece. A successful Survival roll allows the characters to pass the valley safely, whilst a failed roll requires the character to make a Hard Evade roll (or a Formidable Ride roll if mounted) to avoid falling into a crevasse and taking 2d6 points of damage to two random locations. If the characters arrive in the valley through a fumbled Navigation roll, then the lead character (randomly selected unless previously stated otherwise) automatically counts as failing their Survival roll and must immediately roll their Evade/Ride.

PEAT BOG

The path turns out to be a swamp of deep mud, stagnant water and organic mulch, making the route cumbersome, tiring and difficult. Characters must make a Standard Athletics roll to find their way through the bog without any problems other than losing a day's travel, whereas a failed roll still allows them to make it through the bog, but will gain a level of Fatigue. Characters who are mounted must make a Formidable Ride check or are forced to dismount and try again to lead their mount on foot, but will not gain a level in Fatigue for failing their Ride roll. If the characters arrive at the bog from a fumble, then all Athletics rolls become hard and mounted characters are forced to dismount before continuing.

> ### RAPIDS
>
> A swift river crosses the characters' path. Dangerous rapids extend in both directions, making a crossing hazardous and forcing them to abandon any mounts. Heading downstream to find a better place to cross causes a day's delay.. If they choose to walk through the rapids, a successful Standard Athletics roll allows the characters to traverse the rapids without incident, whereas a failed roll increases Fatigue a level and a fumbled roll inflicts 1d6 points of damage to a random location as the character loses footing and catches him/herself on the sharp, jagged rocks below the water's surface! If the characters arrived due to a fumble, then the rapids are a swollen river and are impossible to cross. Characters should spend a day finding a way across the river.
>
> Swimming across the river requires a Herculean Swim roll. If failed, the character is washed 1d3 kilometres downstream and sustains 2d6 damage to 1d3 locations - the result of swallowed water and river-borne debris. If the Swim roll is fumbled, the character has been dragged under by strong currents and drowns.
>
> If the characters reach this scene when nearing Yagalens Bluff, the Game Master may wish to include details of the water having a slightly greenish tint as it washes down from the mountain range (rejected or waste fluids are washed out from the vat chamber and into the local water source). If the party fumbled when arriving, the water is acidic instead of being a swollen river, causing damage to the legs even if they successfully traverse the rapids. Treat this as Weak Acid.
>
> ### TUNNELS
>
> The paths the characters take lead them to the base of some cave and tunnel systems at the base of a mountainous region with no immediately obvious alternate route. They may try and spend a day finding an alternate route, in which case the next Navigation roll is Hard, and a further failure leads to the characters back to the tunnels. In this case they have no choice but to go through them. Either way, the caves and tunnels are dark, requiring a Standard Survival roll to get through without wasting a day. If a fumble was rolled on the Navigation test, then some kind of danger is lurking within the cave system, it may be a Bear, a Beast-Men scouting party, members of the Chaos Mother Cult, Assassins, Gathari Hunters and so on. Game Masters should use their best judgement as to what danger this is depending on their storyline, location or any other factors they may wish to consider.

Characters suffer Exposure after CON hours, requiring hourly Endurance rolls to avoid accruing a level of Fatigue (refer to Survival on page 82 and Weather on page 84 of the MYTHRAS rulebook) until they make camp and build a fire or find adequate shelter.

There are no settlements, the only evidence of men are the old battlefields and stone monuments so decrepit that it is no longer possible to discern who they honour.

Each day and night of travel overland requires the characters to make a Standard Navigation roll. Use the Assistance rules, with one character acting as the primary. Other appropriate skills could be substituted as determined by the Games Master. Success permits travel north without incident, a critical success confers an advantage to the next skill check (reducing the difficulty one step from Standard to easy). Failure results in an increased level of Fatigue (page 78 of the MYTHRAS rulebook) and a Problem that may be selected or rolled randomly on the table below. A fumble also results in a Travel Encounter, but the characters face the problem from a disadvantage (see the description of each encounter).

FROM DEMON HORSE OUTLOOK TO YAGALEN'S BLUFF

Each period of travel between key locations on the map requires the characters to make a Group Standard Navigation roll. Use the rules for Augmenting Skills. Characters with appropriate Lore or Locale might substitute these skills instead.

Success permits the characters to move to the next Key Scene (see below). Failure results in an Obstacle Scene (these two pages). Critical Success allows the characters to start the Key Scene in an advantageous position, whereas a fumble results in disadvantage for the characters entering an Obstacle Scene. If characters are entering an Obstacle Scene, Games Masters may wish to choose the most appropriate one depending on the situation, otherwise roll on the Obstacle table to determine what blocks the party's path.

Key Scenes move the story forward, with the characters closing on their final destination. They are sequential, although of course common sense applies. Obstacle Scenes are optional and usually arise due to bad luck or another incident (reflected by failure of the skill rolls). Astute readers will note that the rate of travel is slowed using this approach. This is a deliberate pacing mechanic, focusing

attention on the increasing dangers and difficulties of the region.

The landscape in this part of The Realm is rugged and bleak. Cold winds, scattered flurries of snow and permafrost higher up in the foothills and mountains themselves. The ever-present pine and spruce continue throughout the foothills but are sparse in the mountains. There are some hardy plants, mainly bushes and scattered grass growing in glimpses of soil between the bare granite and shale. There is little game. There are signs of volcanic activity with steam vents, dormant volcanic caldera, rare hot springs and areas of surprising warmth, as noted in certain areas below.

KEY SCENE 1: THE DEMON HORSE OVERLOOK

The Overlook is a cold, windy place. The characters follow the curve of the River Nyr heading north into the foothills. From about 2 kilometres away they see a high (20 metres) overlook bearing the unusual stone formation above the treeline. This ridge is to the west of the river, about 500 metres away from the shore. The Demon Horse faces due west and has the appearance of a huge, rearing, horse skeleton imprisoned within the rock, with the skull at the apex of the rocky ridge. The stone of the skeleton has a dark, discoloured hue compared to the surrounding rock.

KEREBAS – THE DEMON HORSE

The Demon Horse was a real creature. The stallion Renamos rode into combat, it was killed by the Chaos Mother during the Chaos Wars: in rage for his horse, Renamos drove the Chaos Mother back into her lair in the Gartharis mountains.

The horse's spirit is still tied to the fossilised skeleton. The horse's name is Kerebas and it is an Intensity 8 Nature Spirit. Kerebas loathes Chaos and, if a shaman can communicate with it, it lends its aid if so persuaded. Kerebas can boost the speed of any mounts the characters have by a further 8 metres, the effect lasting for 8 days. Plus Kerebas can summon up to 8 of the shaggy-haired, tenacious, mountain ponies native to this region.

In return for its help Kerebas requires that some beast of chaos is killed or sacrificed in the name of Renamos the Rising Storm

Kerebas
Intensity 8 Horse Spirit
INS 13, POW 46, CHA 13
Spectral Hoof 109%, Willpower 142%
Abilities: Domination Horses (up to 8 mounts)
Bless Movement (up to 8 metres)

Opposite the overlook, the eastern shore of the river is a gentle, pebbly slope to the water - an easy place for landing. On arriving in this area, the characters note some foot traffic and animal droppings. A Hard Track roll reveals many hooved feet, most likely Beast-Men, and evidence that a small boat was pulled ashore recently. Those expressly scrutinising the far shore see a small boat partially hidden behind alpine scrub and lichen covered rock. Three Beast-Men sentries are camped on the overlook keeping watch for boats and, unless dealt with, signal with smoke about an hour after the characters have departed the area. This signal alerts the Beast-Men at The Stairs. Sentries are more vigilant and an ambush is prepared (see below).

The Beast-Men try to avoid engaging the characters in combat, withdrawing if they can. Unfortunately their current position does not afford them an easy escape route. They use missile fire and dropped rocks to try to discourage characters scaling the rocks up to their position (usually a Standard Athletics task, worsened to Hard when under attack. A kind Games Master may warn the characters that a fall here will likely be fatal – refer to Falls on page 78 of the MYTHRAS rulebook – a 20 metre fall (from near the top) causes 4d6 points of damage to four random locations).

Those who climb the ridge and inspect the skull and other exposed 'bones' find the entire surface is carved with tiny runes. Characters with relevant knowledge may note that this stone formation is anatomical. The internal aspects of the skull are not carved, but bear the bony projections, areas of roughness and smoothness that would be expected on a real skull. The hollow vault of the skull can be glimpsed through the back wall of the eye sockets. A chill emanates from this space and observers note a suggestion of a presence within. See the boxed section for Kerebas, opposite.

The instructions from Aganthus direct the characters to travel due west from the Demon Horse Overlook, over the River Nyr. Characters who look find the previously mentioned boat and are able to use it to cross the river.

KEY SCENE 2: THE BLACK SPIKES

The characters probably approach this imposing pair of steep-shouldered mountains from the east (from the Demon Horse Outlook). Despite their height, no snow caps their summits. Characters approaching the spires note the vegetation changes to show species of plant from more southerly regions. It is warmer here, and the characters find they begin to sweat under their cold-weather gear and may need to remove any heavy furs as they draw within two kilometrees of the Spikes. The source of the warmth is under the mountains themselves.

An ancient tower stands crumbling next to a spring about a kilometre from the base of the Spikes. Ivy and opportunistic bushes strangle the stone of the building. Decades past, the top of the tower collapsed to the side, leaving a tumbled pile of stone blocks. Degenerate winged apes hunt from the topmost remaining floor of the building; there are a great number of smaller ruined buildings, of many different ages and architectural styles, scattered in the vicinity of the spring.

A small family group of Garthari came here to bathe in a hot mineral spring. The spring is taboo to the tribe, but known to have healing properties. In desperation, Viduva has broken tribal law to save her husband Lamonis, afflicted with Pyrohoxia (see page 75 of the MYTHRAS rulebook). Accompanying the couple are their children and Laimonis' brothers, Egils and Otomars. Laimonis has entered the manic phase of the disease and is bound hand and foot. Unfortunately, the group has been chased away by the winged apes. They were forced to flee and have abandoned Laimonis, their belongings and their mounts to the apes. The apes recognise disease in the man and have left him unmolested, but ransacked the baggage and killed the horses.

On approaching the Black Spires, the characters see a small group of people anxiously watching three bulky winged creatures hopping and flapping around a pool a short distance away from a ruined tower. Viduva, clearly unarmed (and distraught) and her husband's elder brother Eglis approach the characters, seeking help to rescue Laimonis. She offers payment (a heavy silver necklace worth nearly 400 Founders) or help travelling through the Garthari wilds. She explains her purpose here and knows of the positive properties of the spring. Characters that assess her honesty with the Insight skill sense she is not entirely forthcoming. When pressed, Viduva admits the spring is taboo to her people. More pressure leads her to confess that the waters exact a "terrible price" upon those who bathe.

If the characters rescue Laimonis and he is cured (either by immersion in the spring water or by other magic: mundane Healing is ineffective once mania has developed), he can provide information about the layout of the Valley and the Bluff, the sizeable forces camped there and perhaps provide a sketched map of the major entrance. He was with a warband escorting one of the clan leaders to the Bluff some months ago before he became ill. He refuses to permit his family to accompany the outlanders.

Egils and Otomars accompany the characters to retrieve Laimonis. They help fight the winged apes, but their main priority is to retrieve their bound brother. Their second priority is to deliver him into the spring. Viduva and the children do not fight.

The winged apes are average specimens. Three beasts live in the highest part of the ruined tower, approximately 15 metres up. They are fiercely aggressive but only pursue intruders to a distance of roughly 200 metres. They take shelter in the tower from ranged attacks unless they can change the distance to the attackers. Imaginative strategies could be found to intimidate or distract the winged apes, permitting characters to retrieve Laimonis. Getting him into the spring and away without attack from the winged apes is much more difficult. In combat, the winged apes prefer to use their Diving Strike ability. Any Seriously Wounded winged ape flees back to the tower. If pursued into the tower they fight to the death. The tower contains ancient debris, masses of bones (generations of winged apes and a few human skeletons), refuse, excrement and nests made of plant fibre and shredded clothing. Breaking open one of the nests reveals a gold hand-mirror with shattered glass, worth 480 Founders. A mural shows men being transmuted into winged abominations by the spring.

Key Scene 3: The Stairs

Travelling north from the Black Spikes, the warmth quickly diminishes and the characters once again feel a chill in the air. The gentle ascent to the base of the Stair is unremarkable, although windy. The stony base of the stair is strewn with broken and rotten Beast-Man corpses.

The Stairs are an oversized, natural-looking stairway that curves and winds back upon itself, ascending into the mountain range. The extremely steep ascent and strong winds elevate the risk of a fatal fall. A good level of skill in climbing and sensible precautions such as roping together, using spikes and belaying ropes, help the characters reach the summit safely.

A small unit of Beast-Men is bivouacked a short distance from the summit, in the lee of a shelf of stone that offers a little protection from the unrelenting winds. This is miserable duty and the sentries huddle under layers of furs near to a small fire dug into the permafrost. Unless the sentries have been warned by their brothers at the Demon Horse Outlook, even incautious characters can reach the summit of the Stairs without being discovered.

The Accursed Spring

The spring cures disease and poisoning. The cure requires immersion in the waters. The effect is immediate, but comes at a cost. Those who bathe may be cursed with a desire to remain near the spring and bathe in its water regularly. Over months, bathers become stronger, larger and hardier. Their body hair thickens and intellect declines. The wings develop much later, well after the bestial nature has become dominant.

Characters who bathe in the waters of the spring must succeed in a Hard Willpower roll or be subject to the curse. Any who are cursed must bathe in the spring's water once each day or be subject to further Willpower tests. Failing these results in increasing levels of Fatigue (see page 78 of the Mythras rulebook) only alleviated with immersion in the spring. Death is a potential consequence of remaining separated from the spring for too long.

Beast-Men, alerted to the approaching characters, prepare a deadfall and occupy ambush points with spears and rocks to throw at those climbing the Stair. These Beast-Men resist the characters' drive to engage them in hand-to-hand combat and withdraw, where possible, in order to follow intruders through the Steam Vents Pass and kill them in the Chute.

Scouting the Stair reveals these preparations and provides advantages to ascending characters that plan accordingly. Characters expressing caution and making efforts to ascend carefully, while remaining vigilant for trouble, spot the Beast-Men traps automatically. Incautious characters must succeed with a Standard Perception roll. Awareness of the ambush points prevents surprise but climbing characters are still subjected to attack by Beast-Men scouts.

Deadfall

The Beast-Men deadfall is a precarious woodpile ready to be released on climbers below. It could result in many deaths. Treat it as an attack by the beast-man with a skill of 55% and the advantages of surprise (characters are unable to defend and the attacker receives a bonus special effect). If the attack is successful, in addition to damage (2d6 points of damage to two random locations), the attacker's preferred Special Effect is Bash, knocking the defender back 1m for each 3 points of damage inflicted. Generous Games Masters might permit a successful Hard Athletics or Acrobatics roll to avoid falling. If a limb receives a Serious Wound and is rendered useless, the Athletics and Acrobatics roll to avoid falling is Formidable.

KEY SCENE 4: STEAM VENTS PASS

After ascending the stairs, the characters approach the Steam Vents Pass, an uneven, rocky valley of erratic geysers shooting jets of burning steam into the air, causing the air to become hot and humid. Characters wearing winter clothes immediately notice the difference in temperature and begin to sweat.

The geysers cause damage to anyone caught directly by the jets they produce. At first, the jets seem erratic with no discernible pattern, but a Standard Lore/Locale roll gives the characters enough knowledge of the area that they can time their advance and make it through the valley unharmed. Alternatively, cautious characters can use the day to watch the geysers and mark their locations, advancing only when each jet stops, making their way safely through the pass.

KEY SCENE 5: THE CHUTE

Before the characters reach Yagalen's Bluff, they must descend the Chute, a steep and narrow path heading northwest from the Steam Vents Pass. The path is walled with steep, smooth cliffs ending in flat, rocky surfaces that make the descent seem more like the inside of a fissure than a true path. Characters without any form of climbing equipment find it impossible to scale these walls to reach the top. The air is cold, exaggerated by the drop in temperature during the journey from the Steam Vents Pass, and the deep walls block out much of the sunlight that may otherwise reach the party.

The Chute also poses an ideal spot for an ambush, and any surviving Beast-Men that spotted the characters on the Stairs trail the party to this location, taking up positions on the cliffs to await their arrival. Once the characters begin their descent, the Beast-Men begin to hurl rocks at them. A Hard Evade roll is required to make it through the falling rocks and deep descent successfully. A failure causes characters to lose their footing and tumble down the Chute, sustaining 2d6 points of fall damage to two random locations, but arriving at the end of the descent. This is particularly dangerous if characters at the back of the party fail as the narrowness of the Chute allows little room for other members of the party to manoeuvre and, in turn, may cause them to also lose their footing.

Once the characters have made their way out of the Chute, there is no need to continue rolling Navigation tests; the characters exit out into the Valley.

THE VALLEY AND YAGALEN'S BLUFF

As the characters emerge from the Chute, they find themselves in a large valley filled with ancient ruins that are broken and crumbled with age, overgrown by exotic and unusual plants and trees, giving the scene a very bright, green and alien feel in comparison to the dank, greys of the mountain lining the valley itself. Past these ruins the characters see the bluff in the distance, a giant rock 200 metres high, topped with a pyramid of dark stone. Observant characters notice small glints of light shining from the pyramid as sunlight hits it.

As the characters move further into the valley, they also detect a rise in both temperature and humidity. They begin to sweat and discover pits of steaming mud, layers of volcanic ash and other signs of warmth. Wildlife not common in other parts of the region is also noticeable, including lizards, snakes, and birds of majestic plumages and colours.

Characters should be alert to increasingly common patrols of Gathari Hunters, Beast-Men and Cultists as they get nearer to the immediate area of the Bluff. A Standard Stealth test ensures the characters remain undetected as they hide in the local flora.

If the characters are spotted by any of the patrols, they attack. The main tactic is to overwhelm with numbers, but if inflicted with serious damage, retreat. Unless the patrol is made up of Gathari Hunters, a single member of the patrol breaks away from the rest of their group and heads towards the Bluff itself to warn others of the impending assault. This may cause complications for the characters later on.

THE VALLEY

The valley's strange nature is the result of geographical mutation caused by the Chaos Mother during her long years of domination. Her spittle dropped here, causing the ground to boil. Great pools of the stuff seeped into the rock forming the thermal vents and troughs of hot mud that are still visible.

This energy is valuable to the Ophidians who channel it into their pyramid laboratory to help fuel their experiments, but the strange conditions are not the result of natural geological processes: they are a direct result of the Chaos Mother's influence.

Infiltration and Sabotage

In this part of the scenario, cautious and fearful, the characters risk death and destruction by entering the dangerous lair of the Ophidians to discover the secret behind the Beast-Men forces. Characters should feel uneasy and at constant risk as they make their way into the belly of Yagalen's Bluff.

> ### Patrols
> Games Masters should give some thought to the size of Beast-Men and Cultist patrols. It is recommended that a patrol should consist of a number of members equal to the size of the characters' party, plus or minus up to two additional members. If randomness is desired, roll 1d6:
> 1-2: Party Size minus one or two (as the die result dictates)
> 3-4: Equal to Party Size
> 5-6: Party Size plus one (5) or plus 2 (6).

Infiltrating the Base

Upon reaching the Bluff, the characters learn that the place is constantly patrolled by Beast-Men and Cultists of the Chaos Mother. They need to decide amongst themselves what the best route to take will be - whether they decide to go in stealthily or via a (potentially suicidal) full frontal assault. Astute characters may even find secret passages leading inside.

Scouting Outside.

To successfully infiltrate Yagalen's Bluff unnoticed, the characters have several options. The most direct route is through the Pyramid at the summit of the Bluff, however such a route is not without its dangers as the path to Pyramid is heavily patrolled by Beast-Men and Cultists, but the route is immediately visible to the party. Alternatively, if the characters spend some time scoping out the rocks that make up the Bluff, they discover a cavern leading into its base that is far easier to infiltrate.

The party may still feel this is a risky way to go, and if they look carefully, they discover that there are more ways into the Ophidian's lair than at first glance. If they backtrack and do a thorough search of the ruins, they may find a secret passage into the Bluff. On a successful Hard Locale roll, characters spending an hour looking for the passage find it. Generous Games Masters may allow the party to check again each hour, but this may lead them into straying too close to Beast-Men/Cultist patrols.

If the characters decide to take their time and investigate the north side of the Bluff, they have to continue to make their Standard Stealth rolls or encounter more patrols. Upon reaching the other side of the Bluff, however, they spot water vapour rising out of the rocks roughly 20 metres above the ground. This is the quickest and most direct route to the Vat Chambers, but has the most environmental hazards.

Getting In.

Once the characters have decided on their route, they encounter obstacles and enemies that attempt to stop them. This is the Ophidians' laboratory so the characters should be well-aware that the enemy has every obvious entrance guarded or patrolled: this is apparent to them as soon as they approach the Bluff. Generous Games Masters may wish to create new ways of entering the Bluff depending on how the campaign in progressing (such as a secret door or carefully concealed additional passage).

The Pyramid

The most immediately noticeable route is the pyramid capping Yagalen's Bluff, a temple roughly 60 metres in height and made of dark-hued stone that glints strangely in the sunlight. Down the centre of its southbound facing is a flight of worn, weather-beaten steps that feel warm beneath the characters' feet. The entrance to the Ophidians' lair can be accessed through the pyramid's flat peak. However, the path to the temple is crawling with vigilant patrols of Beast-Men and fanatical cultists, requiring a Hard Stealth roll to reach undetected. This roll is made Formidable if the characters were caught in the ruins by patrols and at least one of the patrol members retreated, as described earlier.

The Cavern

The cavern is an irregular opening at the base of the Bluff. The cavern is not as heavily guarded and characters who make a Standard Stealth roll can make their way inside without detection. This roll becomes Formidable if the characters were caught in the ruins by patrols and at least one of the patrol members retreated, as explained earlier.

As the characters enter the cavern, they find themselves inside the base of the Bluff. The area is dimly lit by torchlight, and numerous human-sized holes pepper the walls and ceilings of the cavern. On one side of the cavern, about 100 metres from the entrance, is a naturally formed basalt

THE BLUFF PROFILE

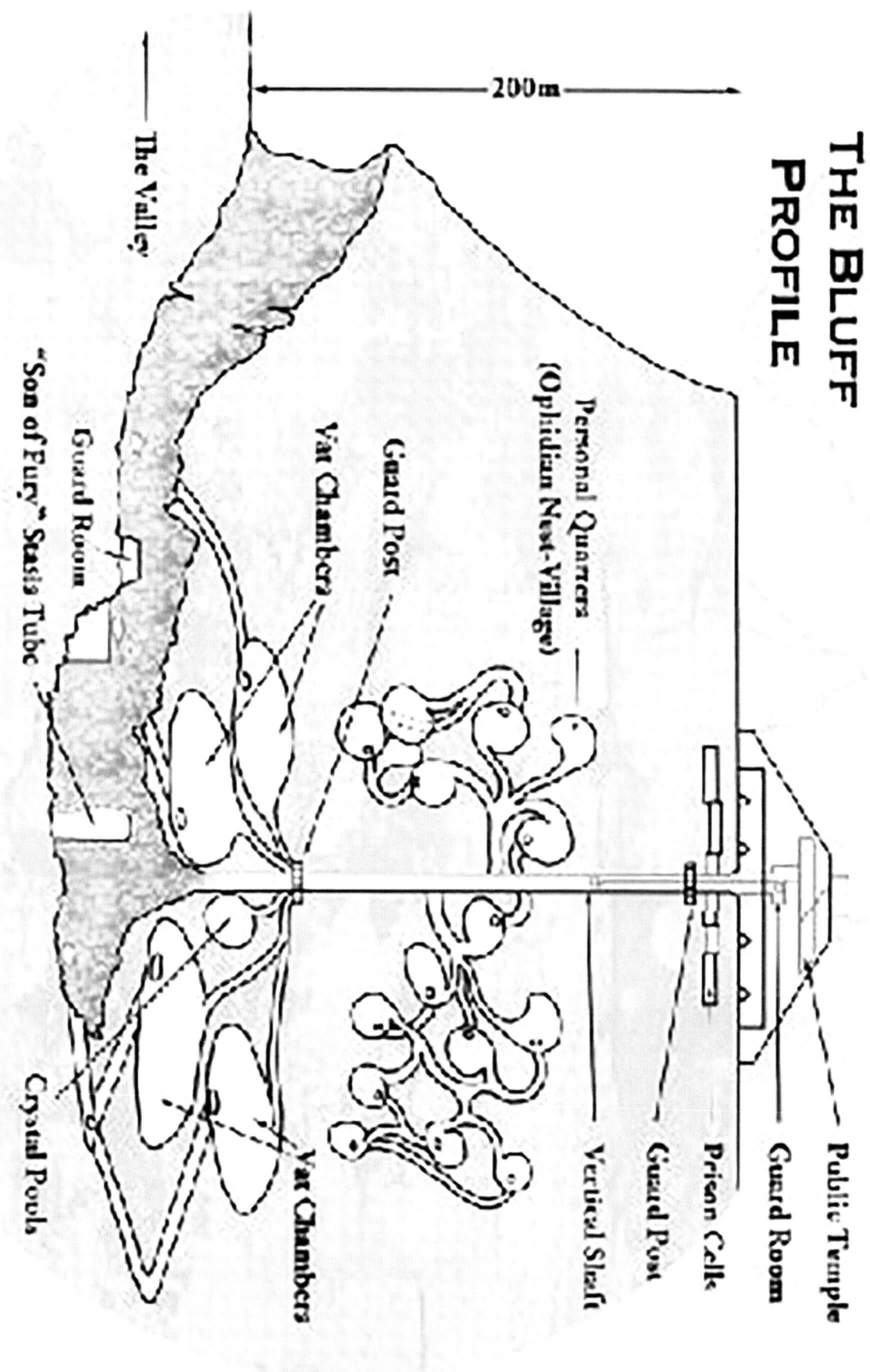

THE OPHIDIANS' PLAN

The Ophidians have been at large in this part of the world for a very long time. They hail from a different dimension where intelligent life developed amongst reptiles rather than mammals. In their world the Chaos Mother dominates and she taught the Ophidians sorcery and how to bend the universe to their will. In time they found ways of moving between dimensions can came to The Realm of Men, finding the Chaos Mother almost (but not quite) as dominant as on their home plane.

The Ophidians served her secretively, establishing bases across The Realm. Eventually the Chaos Mother's power was broken and the Ophidians retreated to two bases in the Gartharis Mountains: this one at Yagelan's Bluff and a smaller base near Distaff Peak.

When Jedakiah came to The Realm he already knew of the Ophidians' existence and sought them out. They recognised his devotion to the Chaos Mother and tutored him more in the sorcerous arts. Over time Jedakiah and the Ophidians hatched plans to seize The Realm and bring back the Chaos Mother's rule. Jedakiah would seed the land with spies, agents and cultists: the Ophidians would breed an army of hybrids to be used as an invasion force.

Their plan is coming to fruition. Jedakiah plans to execute the final ceremony that will create the Chaos Daughter and elevate himself to god-hood. This is described in the final scenario, Reckoning at Distaff Peak. The Ophidians have bred their army, the culmination being the Chaos Hybrids found in the first scenario, Caravan, and the Son of Fury. Once Jedakiah has completed his ritual to create the Chaos Daughter, he and his new wife intend to unleash All Hell against The Realm, ushering-in a new era of chaos dominance.

The Ophidians have a place in all of this. They will be given key territories where reptilian, not human, dominance will be asserted. From there they will explore other dimensions and send Chaos Armies to capture more planes of existence, creating a trans-dimensional Ophidian Empire in the Chaos Mother's name.

bunker occupied by six Beast-Men alert for intruders. Characters using their own light source are automatically detected by these guards and attacked on sight by missile fire. These Beast-Men are armed with light crossbows and use the bunker's protection to defend the cavern system, but do not pursue if the characters escape. They do, however, bellow an inhuman roar to inform other patrols of their presence and any Stealth rolls made afterwards are one degree harder.

THE SECRET PASSAGE

If the characters succeeded in any search for a secret passage, they encounter a crumbled, moss-ridden stone and wood building missing its door and roof. The interior is littered with broken furnishings ranging from rotting beds to smashed vases. If they investigate, a trapdoor is found buried beneath the remains of one of the bunk beds. The handle and hinges are rusted shut and it requires a successful Brawn or Mechanisms roll to heave the thing open. The hinges squeal as the trapdoor is lifted and this may alert patrols in the Bluff area as the grating sound echoes around the valley. Beneath the trapdoor is a passage accessed by a flight of shallow stairs cut into the stone.

The passage is dark, but a sconce at the base of the stairs contains a torch that the characters can use to illuminate the path. The passage, unlike many of the tunnels in Yagalen's Bluff, is walled with smooth stones unlike anything else in the region, with various runes scrawled into them. These runes are of an alien tongue but are poems and paens to the Chaos Mother, celebrating her ever-changing nature and the freedom she gives to those souls who embrace her change. The air is uncomfortably hot and very dry. The tunnel runs in a straight line for 400 metres, and the Game Master may wish to make the characters make a roll for Fatigue as they weary from the heat. As the characters reach the end of the passage another flight of stairs rises towards a stone ceiling. Observant characters see a discreet lever jutting out of the (otherwise smooth) rock of the passage. Once activated, the stone blocking the staircase moves, revealing the passage's exit into the Son of Fury stasis tube chamber and bypassing the Cavern described in the previous section.

THE VENTS

On the north side of the Bluff, a series of vents (at least one per character) expel vapours from the vat chambers on a constant basis. This is the most direct route the characters can take to the vat chambers, but is not without risk and peril. To enter the vents they must first make a Standard Athletics roll to reach the vents 20 metres above, and then make a Hard Brawn roll to pull off the grates covering them.

The vents are tubular in shape, forged of a bronze-coloured metal and sloping down into the bluff. Due to the nature of its construct and the condensation, characters have no choice but to slide down the vent. A Hard Athletics, or Standard Acrobatics, roll can be attempted to control the descent enough to avoid injury; otherwise 1d6 damage is sustained to either one leg or the head, depending on the character's orientation when entering the tube. The damage comes from impacting the iron grate at the far end of the chute, and it is likely that the sound of the impact (and the cry of an injured character) alerts the Ophidians within the complex as the sounds echo and resonate.

The grate at the far end requires a Standard Brawn test to break it down, or an Easy Brawn test if the character failed to slow down on the descent, the impact having weakened it.

Areas within the Complex

The tunnels in the Bluff are a labyrinth of twisting, turning paths from one area to the next. There are no stairs, but vertical chimneys with ridges spiralling along the circular walls which the Ophidians use for ease of movement, able to semi-slither rather than climb using stairs. There is a central elevating platform as a concession to non-Ophidians. Even so, it is warm and humid throughout the complex, and stinks of snake. Lots of rats and other small creatures run free and appear to be encouraged to feed and breed.

The Ophidian complex has several discrete areas: the upper reception area and barracks within the body of the pyramid built for the races of man, the holding cells, the living areas for the Ophidians within the Bluff and, lastly, the laboratories, vats and the energy source for the machines.

Pyramid Level

The pyramid is constructed of basalt. Weathered serpentine images are graven into the surface. There is little light and it is unpleasantly warm. The interior of the pyramid consists of reception chambers constructed for human envoys to the Ophidians. There are secret passages used to monitor visitors. The central area contains the Great Stair descending to the basement Barracks and Pit.

Killing The Envoy

As the characters enter the main reception of the Pyramid, they hear voices coming from the room. Inside is an envoy of the Chaos Mother Cult, sent by Jedakiah, four of his own personal bodyguards and an Ophidian scientist. The characters may enter the room, but regardless of their actions, the cultists spot them. The bodyguards attack on sight and fight to the death whilst the Ophidian and the envoy retreat into the Pit. If, however, the characters stop at the door and listen, they hear the following discussion:

"As you have seen, the experiments are progressing nicely," the first voice hisses. "Every batch we create becomes stronger, faster and smarter." Another voice, human, answers. "As long as they are obedient this is most excellent news. You and your people have done well. I will send word back to the Master, and let it not be said that the Mother does not bless those who show loyalty to her and her people."

The characters hear footsteps coming towards them as the Envoy makes his exit. A Standard Stealth roll allows the characters to surprise the group as they leave, giving them a surprise round or allowing them to pass. Killing the Envoy delays Jedakiah's plans as news of the Ophidian experiments fails to reach him.

> ### Manuun, Again
> If not captured or killed in the *Caravan* scenario, the envoy is the shaman, Manuun, and his bodyguards are Garthari barbarians. See *Caravan* for the appropriate statistics.
>
> The deadly experiment in Aylesford has elevated Manuun in status and Jedakiah has placed him in charge of liaising with the Ophidians for further Chaos Hybrids, hence his presence at Yagelan's Bluff and interest in the work here.
>
> If Manuun was captured or perished at Aylesford, then the envoy is a human agent of Jedakiah's - a would-be Chaos Mother acolyte intent on serving his master's wishes.

The Barracks and the Pit

The Pit is a depressed area in the central part of the barracks surrounding the nearly 10-metre diameter vertical shaft that descends uninterrupted for 200 metres, piercing through the heart of the Bluff. The pit houses a huge mechanical winch, usually powered by scores of slaves pulling the massive chains that ultimately connect to a heavy wooden platform, itself over four metres in diameter. The chains from the platform ascend to the ceiling of the barracks, loop around the geared compound pulleys and descend to a chain housing.

This level contains wells and latrines. The wells offer a means of entry into the complex and share a common aquifer, permitting covert infiltration. The latrines are connected between the Pyramid and Barracks levels, offering a bold, albeit challenging, way of avoiding the guards by the Shaft.

The Shaft

Ten metres wide and 200 metres deep, the walls of the shaft are textured with scalloped shelves that spiral downwards in an anticlockwise direction. There are numerous small tunnels leaving at various strata leading into the Ophidian Nest.

> ### MEAT THE SHEETS
> The Ophidians feed on mice and rats, but also have a specially bred stock of Meat Sheets (see page 53) that are allowed to cling to the walls of the nesting area, hide in shadows, or form sickly carpets upon the floor. Meat Sheets also feed on rodents but do not attack the Ophidians, allowing themselves to be fed upon by the snake men. Games Masters in a sadistic frame of mind may want to scatter Meat Sheets through the complex - handy snacks for the Ophidians - or have a batch available just in the nest area. Naturally the Meat Sheets are capable of attacking warm blooded creatures such as humans.

THE HOLDING CELLS

These are rudimentary rooms dug out from the rock of the Bluff to form a crude, cavernous jail. Jagged stone juts out of the walls and ceilings, rusted bars pierce menacingly into floor and roof to form the walls of each cell. There are Ironwood doors that are succumbing to rot, and crumbling anchor points and chains. Their design suggests they were primary built to house humans.

FREEING THE SLAVES

Inside the holding cells are men and women alike, held as slaves to operate the winches that make descent down the shaft possible without fatality. They vary in age, from mid-teens to old age and wear loose rags around their bodies, chains around their wrists and their ankles tied to steel balls to prevent escape. They appear dirty, unkempt and without hope having spent months, possibly years, in captivity to serve their Ophidian masters, and the sight of the characters does not change this. The odds of the slaves escaping, to them is desperate at best, but a Hard Influence test may raise their spirits somewhat. If the characters are somehow able to free them, they may assist in helping the party reach the vat chambers.

If the characters lack the ability to smash the cell doors down, another way to free the slaves is to take the keys from the Beast-man gaoler patrolling the cells. The characters need to make a Standard Stealth check to hide from the gaoler who is hurling buckets of meat scraps and ruffage into each cell. If the characters fight the gaoler, this is a particularly strong Beast-man who fights using the statistics of a Beast-man warrior.

Once the characters free the slaves, many will still be unconvinced, but are willing to work the winch for them to descend to the vat chambers if the pit is cleared of Ophidians and Beast-Men. A Standard Influence roll can spur the slaves into a rebellious frenzy, and they gain twenty slaves who will help the characters clear out the pit while five of them remain with the characters as they descend the Shaft. Regardless of what happens, apart from these five, the slaves do not leave the pit unless they are told that the way out is clear.

THE NEST

Here are long abandoned nesting capsules and incubator chambers. The characters do not find anything else of interest should they search the nest.

THE VAT CHAMBERS

The Vat Chambers are divided into four large areas that house strange, oval tanks made of glass with bronze tubes snaking into the floor, ceiling and other tanks, all filled with dense, translucent green liquids and strange, grotesque creatures submerged within, all at various different stages of growth. Some resemble infant Beast-Men, whilst other, more disturbing creatures float within the bigger vats. Creatures with chitin type shells of various shades of browns, bulbous heads with varying numbers of small horns and long, lanky arms and legs, all of which have digits resembling hands, curl up and bob in the fluids with hideous part-mechanical umbilical cords attaching them to their vat. The smaller, less-developed creatures have semi-transparent shells where blood and organs can be seen, barely functioning within their bodies.

Scattered around the chambers are other pieces of equipment and sickening experiments. Twitching muscle is spread over beds of crystals and wire. Bellows move rhythmically, fuelling the giant furnaces adorning the walls. The air is humid and warmer than any other part of the Ophidian's lair and condensation clings to the glass of the vats. Human slaves chained to each other heave large levers and tend the furnaces as an Ophidian scientist wanders the chambers, writing notes on strips of parchment as it inspects the tanks and the creatures within.

KILLING THE SCIENTIST

The scientist should pose no problem for the party to kill, assuming they can catch it. A Standard Stealth check allows the characters to get the jump on the scientist and kill him with whatever weapons they may be using. If the scientist spots the characters, it attempts to slink away as quickly as possible, using the winding paths between the vat chambers. Ophidians have the advantage when traversing the passageways and Athletics tests become Hard. If the scientist escapes, it ultimately reaches the cavern and informs the first patrols it sees of the infiltration, which are most likely guards from the guardhouse in the cavern, if they have not already been dealt with.

THE CRYSTAL POOL

This is the source of power for the Ophidian machines in the vat chambers and is the primary focus of the scenario. The crystal pool is a lake of luminescent, bright green liquid that remains unnaturally still. The surface of the pool is highly reflective; characters looking into the pool see every detail of their own reflection with crystal clarity. No torches or artificial lights can be found in this chamber, the light given off by the pool is enough to clearly illuminate everything surrounding it. Three Beast-Men Warriors patrol the edges of the pool, and attack anyone other than cultists, Ophidians or other Beast-Men on sight.

SABOTAGING THE CRYSTAL POOL

Sabotaging the crystal pool is the characters' main objective. To destroy it, the characters must drop a vial of the concoction given to them by Aganthus into the pool itself. As the vial hits the pool, it immediately begins to exude a black smoke as the container starts to crack from the chemical reaction caused by the two substances interacting. As the pool is not pure water, the characters have 3 Combat Rounds until the reaction detonates, flooding the entire chamber with an explosion, destroying everything in it and decimating the pool.

Destroying the pool weakens the physical integrity of the Ophidians' complex. The lift in the centre of the shaft collapses, falling and smashing through the shaft's guard post and into the caverns. Rocks begin to fall from the roofs of the caverns. Tanks in the vat chambers shatter, the creatures within flopping to the floor unceremoniously, squirming as their malformed bodies struggle with their very existence before dying. Characters attempting to escape through the Pyramid exit find it near impossible to ascend the heights without fatal consequences (a Herculean roll of any kind), and insightful characters realise that the party's best chance of escape is down through the caverns.

THE STASIS TUBE

The stasis tube houses an entity called the Son of Fury, a giant beast closely resembling the Chaos Hybrid found in the Caravan scenario, but bigger - roughly 3 metres tall in height - and much nastier. The Son of Fury can be controlled in much the same way as its predecessor, but for now it is held in a Stasis Tube until Jedakiah calls for its release. The Stasis Tube is filled with a greenish gas that acts as a soporphic: if the gas level diminishes by even a litre or so, the Son of Fury emerges from its stupor and, unless commanded, is filled with the urge to kill.

THE SON OF FURY BREAKS FREE!

Releasing the Son of Fury can also be triggered by sabotaging the crystal pool. As the machinery explodes within the Ophidian lair, rockslides begin within the Bluff. In the chaos, the lift section in the central shaft is broken loose from its chains and plummets through the core, smashing through the guard post below and into the side of the stasis tube, where green gas escapes and the Son of Fury awakes. If the characters escape through the caverns, the Son of Fury hunts them. Should the characters run away from the encounter, it continues to track them during the course of their escape.

THE CAVERN

This is a marshalling area for vat products, and the exit point for the Son of Fury, surrounded by many Beast-Men and the Ophidian slave-guards. There is a secret entrance from the ruins encountered previously, exiting next to the stasis tube from under a loose, ornately decorated plate that blends in with the metal work floor. The floor is designed to bolt the stasis tube into place and this section of the cavern has a look more akin to a lab than a cave.

COMPLICATIONS

What are the potential results and complications arising from sabotage of the Ophidian base? Some considerations:

- Naturally enough the characters may feel weak, hunted, and vulnerable. The Ophidians seek their destruction.
- Acrid vapours escape the vat chambers and tunnels collapse around the party, as per the Earthquake table on page 185 of the MYTHRAS rules.
- The Ophidians unleash their stock of Beast-Men, including the Son of Fury to pursue the characters. The characters must flee the complex and evade pursuit through the valley and up to Demon Horse Overlook. The pursuers are tenacious and rabid: this becomes a desperate chase with the characters fighting for survival in hostile territory.
- The Ophidians do nothing. Their complex can be repaired and providing Jedakiah with his army is more important that chasing down these foolish humans. Jedakiah will deal with all of them in good time, in his own way.

Further detail on these complications follows.

EARTHQUAKES AND POISONOUS VAPOURS

The explosion from the crystal pools causes a chain reaction within the Bluff, allowing various deadly gases to escape the machines that snake their way through the complex, and rockslides and earthquakes that shake the Bluff itself, making the characters' escape difficult and treacherous. For the earthquakes, refer to the Earthquake table on page 185 of the MYTHRAS. In addition, characters need to make an Evade roll when escaping the Bluff, unless they are escaping via the pyramid - in which case it becomes a Hard roll as rocks plummet down the shaft making the ascent perilous. If they fail, the characters take 1d6 damage to a random location, with the damage being increased to 2d6 on a fumbled Evade.

Also, if the characters attempt to escape through the caverns, they need to make an Endurance roll as they attempt to fight-off the effects of the gas that has broken out of the stasis tube. If they fail, one level of Fatigue is accrued for each minute they remain in the Cavern area. The gas is not lethal, but it is an anaesthetic.

ESCAPE THROUGH THE WILDERNESS.

Games Masters can structure a pursuit meticulously, tracking movement and routes of the characters and the Beast-Men. This can become a tense series of evasions and combat encounters with different waves of Chaos Hybrids assaulting the characters, wearing them down, and finally with the Son of Fury catching them.

Alternatively, the pursuit and escape can be abstracted to help save time. Members of the group must succeed in three skills tests to navigate the wilderness and arrive safely back in Nyren. Each skill roll represents the key activities for one day of pursuit. The skills tested depends on the characters' strategies to arrive back in the city. Example tasks are noted below, but other suggestions by inventive players should be considered by the Games Master, using the vignettes below as templates. Each failure leads to a complication, any fumbles result in delays that permit the Beast-Men (or Son of Fury if he is chasing) to consolidate reinforcements and launch another attack. Critical successes may bestow an advantage to the next test, reducing the difficulty of the next skill roll by one step according to how the scenario is progressing.

Remember the Augmenting rules on page 50 of the MYTHRAS rules if the characters help one another in the skill rolls below.

A failed skill test results in a complication, ideally one linked to the skill. Complications present the group with an immediate obstacle. Successfully navigating this obstacle allows the characters to make another skill test. Delay or failure leads to another attack (see below).

Example Skill Tests & Complications

Athletics

A character that tries to draw off the pursuing Beast-Men by yelling and running in a different direction from the others may help the group get closer to Nyren with a successful Standard Athletics roll. Failure results in the character gaining a level of fatigue and face to face with two Beast-Men scouts. Defeating the scouts, or escaping them with a successful opposed Athletics roll, permits the character to return to the group and continue the flight to Nyren.

Brawn

A character that tries to block off the pursuing Beast-Men by causing rockslides, pushing over debris (such as rotting trees and so forth) may help the group get closer to Nyren with a successful Brawn roll. Failure results in the character being ambushed as the enemy catches up: the character is attacked by two outrider Beast-Men Scouts. Defeating the scouts or escaping them with a successful opposed Athletics roll allows the character to return to the group and continue the flight to Nyren. If the Beast-Men Scouts are not defeated within six combat rounds, move on to *Another Attack*, below.

Deceit or Track

Some of the more cunning characters may attempt to throw-off their pursuers by leaving false trails or faking tracks (for example riding down one edge of the river, then doubling back through the river to mislead the Beast-Men). This requires time and a Hard Deceit roll confuses the pursuers; but a failure means the characters are caught by a number of Beast-Men Scouts equal to the number of characters in the group. One of these Beast-Men has some means of raising an alarm and, unless preventedwithin six combat rounds, Another Attack occurs. It also occurs if the Deceit roll is fumbled, indicating the party is blindsided by an enemy attack.

Endurance or Survival

A character might attempt to put-off their pursuers by taking particularly dangerous or seemingly suicidal routes, such as sliding down steep hills or frozen parts of the mountains where temperatures are too low to survive without particularly high levels of endurance and/or survival gear. A failure results in the character taking 1d8 points of damage to a random location or a level of Fatigue: the Game Master should decide which, depending on the situation.

A fumble leads to the character needing time to recuperate and Another Attack occurs!

Influence, Oratory or Sing

A character may attempt to boost the group's efforts to shake off their pursuers by either giving a rousing speech or by singing, using the skill most appropriate. The test is Standard and, if made, does not count towards the three skill tests required to reach Nyren, but reduces the difficulty of the next test by a single step (Hard tests become Standard and so on). A fumble increases the difficulty by one step as the characters are reminded of the bleakness of their current situation and begin to succumb to despair.

Insight or Lore (Strategy and Tactics)

A character may attempt to interpret the movements of the pursuing Beast-Men and attempt to take routes that gains them distance. A Hard Insight test allows the character to find an advantageous position, whereas a failure leads to the character making a poor decision. A fumble leads the characters into a path that benefits the Beast-Men and *Another Attack* occurs!

Locale

Familiarity with the local geography might present a character with a helpful shortcut with a successful Standard Locale roll. A failed roll leads to the group becoming lost and in a dead-end ravine, requiring all to run for their lives, or climb quickly up the rough stone of the side of the ravine (either requires a Standard Athletics roll to assist the other members of the group). If this is failed, see *Another Attack*, below.

Perception

Characters keeping close watch for Beast-Men attempting to outflank the group with a Hard Perception roll have an advantage in getting to Nyren without attack. Failure permits a number of Beast-Men scouts (equal to the number of characters plus two) to close with as they cross a rocky stream amongst the dark shadows of the pine trees. If the Beast-Men scouts are not defeated within six combat rounds, move on to *Another Attack*, below.

Ride

A mounted character tries to misdirect the pursuing Beast-Men by riding in a different direction from the others with a successful Ride roll. Failure results in the character becoming Winded, as well as being thrown of his/her horse and coming face to face with two outrider Beast-Men scouts in a small clearing. Defeating the scouts or escaping them with a successful opposed Athletics roll (remember the character is Winded) permits the character to return to the group and continue the flight to Nyren. If the character failed their original Ride roll, the mount rears, throws the rider and disappears, lost forever in the maze of forests and rocky paths.

Stealth

Careful characters might go to ground, double back or otherwise try to throw off pursuit with a successful Hard Stealth roll. Failure leads to discovery by a group of Beast-Men Scouts, equal in number to the number of characters. One bears a horn that it attempts to sound, requiring three combat actions to do so. If it is permitted to sound the horn, move to *Another Attack*, below.

Swim

Upon reaching the river Nyr, a character may attempt to brave the water instead of following the river, putting the group at a distinct advantage in losing the pursuing Beast-Men. This requires a Standard Swim roll. On a success, the character makes it across the river, losing the Beast-Men for the time being. On a failure the characters escapes the pursuing Beast-Men only to run into an encampment on the other side. The group is attacked by a group of Beast-Men Scouts of the same number as the group. On a fumble, the character also gains a level of Fatigue from the swim.

Willpower

If all else fails, characters may decide the best course of action is the most simple – sheer determination to escape their pursuers as they push themselves to gain a bigger lead. On a successful Willpower roll, the characters push on and gain enough distance to get ahead of their pursuers… for now. A failure causes the characters to gain a level of Fatigue and a small party of Beast-Men Scouts, equal in number to the group, to catch up. One of the Beast-Men carries a horn which it sounds within in six combat rounds unless neutralised, causing *Another Attack* to occur. On a fumble, the characters still gain a level of Fatigue but *Another Attack* occurs automatically. The group can use this skill test as many times as they wish towards their required three skill checks, but each time the difficulty of the test increases by one.

Mechanisms

A character skilled with mechanisms may be able to set up traps for their pursuers. This takes time and effort the group may not have before their pursuers catch up with them. To do this the character must make a Hard Mechanisms roll that can be Augmented with the Survival skill. On a success, the character sets a trap that delays their pursuers enough to get ahead, whereas on a critical they not only get ahead but the next Beast-Man attack the group encounters contains two less Beast-Men than normal as the trap causes substantial damage to the pursuers. Failure causes a Beast-Men Scout group to catch up with the characters equal in number to the party. One has a horn which is sounded in six combat rounds unless neutralised, at which point *Another Attack* occurs. On a fumble, *Another Attack* occurs automatically.

Navigation

A character might identify the fastest route to take with a Standard Navigation roll. A success means the group finds a faster route to Nyren through the forests, mountains and trails. On a fail, the group stumbles into a number of Beast-Men Scouts equal to that of the party. On a fumble, the characters navigate their way into a dead end and Another Attack occurs automatically.

Another Attack!

A fumbled skill roll or delay due to complications gives the Beast-Men (or Son of Fury) another chance to attack. In either event, a party of pursuers have caught up to the fleeing group and mount an assault. The site in which this attack occurs depends on the complication or the fumbled skill test.

The number of Beast-Men is equal to twice the number of characters if they were not already engaged in a fight with Beast-Men Scouts, and equal to the number of characters if they were already engaged. Three of these Beast-Men are Beast-Men Warriors and the rest Beast-Men Scouts. Unlike other encounters with Beast-Men, this group fights to the death and the characters have to either defeat them or, if they are able to, escape. The latter is a Hard skill check in most situations but the Games Master may increase this to a Formidable check depending on the nature of the encounter.

Optional Scene: The Son of Fury

If the characters encountered the Son of Fury during the assault on the complex it hunts and stalks the party on the way to Nyren. After the first successful test when making their way back, the Game Master should make a secret Standard Perception roll for the character with the highest Perception, and, if successful, describe strange shapes moving in the scenery, rocks scattering on the floor seemingly on their own, trees rustling and so on. Heighten the atmosphere as the Son of Fury stalks the party.

Afterwards, on the second and third successful tests, the Game Master should make a Stealth roll for the Son of Fury. This should be compared to the character's successful roll. If the Son of Fury wins the contest it ambushes the party aiming to kill as many as possible. For additional tactics this kind of Chaos Hybrid uses, see *Caravan*, page 30.

> **CRAZY HORSES**
> If the characters have obtained Kerebas's help earlier in the scenario, the Horse Spirit can provide further assistance in the characters' escape. It can, of course, boost the speed of their mounts (if they have them), provide them (if they don't), or, alternatively, use its Domination (Horses) ability to draw dozens of the native, wild ponies to the area and causing a stampede against pursuing Beast-Men and/or the Son of Fury.

RETURNING TO NYREN

Outrunning, evading or surviving the pursuers of the Bluff leads to the characters managing to return to Nyren and a meeting with Duke Astomvar and Aganthus. Lord Drystan (see *Beneath the Black Water*) may also be present as the characters meet at the duke's villa to report on their exploits.

Duke Astomvar and Aganthus meets the group in a reception room. Food and drink is offered. The mood is very serious.

"The food is regrettably meagre, our crops and livestock have been in decline and merchants have feared to trade with us with all the activity surrounding the town," Duke Astomvar says in a solemn voice, dabbing his mouth with a napkin. "I am hoping to hear good news now that you have arrived back in Nyren."

The characters are invited to explain the situation at Yagalen's Bluff to Astomvar and Aganthus in its fullest, including the creatures being created, the Son of Fury (if encountered), the cultists working with the Ophidians and any damage the characters managed to inflict on the complex. Aganthus listens intently.

"Indeed, this aligns with research pointing at a greater evil than the Ophidians. I had suspected as much, but to have eyewitnesses to confirm it leaves me with little doubt. I have heard such terrible, terrible tales similar to those you have described; I have also consulted with others, including the Order of Truth, and that worthy agency has confirmed that some darkness looms in Gartharis. It also has a name: *Jedakiah*. If what we suspect is correct, then I fear the worse and this is not the end." Aganthus ponders before continuing. "In fact, now that I think about it, much points to a place known as Distaff Peak. If there is anywhere this sorcerer, Jedakiah, may be hiding and scheming, Distaff Peak would be my guess."

The characters receive 1000 Founders each if the crystal pools were destroyed and 1000 Founders shared between them if they tell the Duke and Aganthus of the envoy being killed in the Pyramid. Before dismissing them, Duke Astomvar speaks to them once more of what has been learned.

"This is grim news. The true evil has not been stopped. I do not feel any more hopeful for Nyren's future at this moment. Before you leave, I have one last proposition for you all to consider. You have seen these creatures with your own eyes; you have knowledge vital to stopping this evil. I ask, for the sake of Nyren and the Vale, for you to consider travelling to Distaff Peak, to destroy this evil once and for all, and be heroes amongst our people..."

AGREEING TO HELP

If the characters agree to one, final attempt to halt Jedakiah, the duke and Aganthus provide as much help as possible in preparing them for an assault on Distaff Peak. They introduce the characters to Lord Drystan and the various parts of the jigsaw from previous scenarios begin to fall into place. If Jedakiah is defeated then The Realm is in the characters' debt and wealth and fame are assured. There is no doubt that this will be a risky mission and, if additional resources are needed, these three patrons are able to call upon with them with no questions asked.

Non-Player Characters

Beast-Men

These are Chaos Hybrids bred by the Ophidians on Jedakiah's instructions. They come in a variety of forms but are all bipedal combinations of human and an animal - typically goats, sheep, bears, foxes, wolves and other wildlife found in the Gartharis mountains. They have limited intellects but are all equally vicious.

Unlike the Chaos Hybrids described in the MYTHRAS rules, they do not carry disease.

Beast-Man warriors are a further development. They are stronger and faster, although resemble their Scout brethren in appearance. The warriors have more developed intellects and can command the Scouts - although the warriors are, themselves, not the brightest of creatures. The warriors have better armour and weapons. In combat the warriors fight with a scimitar in the primary hand and a spear in the off-hand. The spear is used to keep an opponent at bay, for thrusting/impaling and for throwing. The scimitar is a parrying and slashing weapon which the warriors use to inflict Bleeds as often as possible.

Beast-Man Scout	1d20	Location	AP/HP
Action Points: 2	1–3	Right Leg	1/5
Damage Modifier: +1d2	4–6	Left Leg	1/5
Magic Points: 11	7–9	Abdomen	1/6
Movement: 6 metres	10–12	Chest	1/7
Initiative Bonus: 10	13–15	Right Arm	1/4
Armour: Fur and Tough Skin	16–18	Left Arm	1/4
Abilities: None	19–20	Head	3/5

Skills: Athletics 60%, Brawn 36%, Endurance 37%, Evade 31%, Locale 42%, Perception 50%, Stealth 40%, Unarmed 40%, Willpower 18%

Passions: Hate Humans 80%

Combat Style: Beast-Man Scout (Spear, Thrown Rock and Headbutt) 60%

Weapon	Size/Force	Reach	Damage	AP/HP
Shortspear	M	L	1d8+1+1d2	4/5
Thrown Rock	S	-	1d3+1d2	-
Headbutt	S	T	1d4+1d2	As for Head

Beast-Man Warrior	1d20	Location	AP/HP
Action Points: 3	1–3	Right Leg	3/6
Damage Modifier: +1d4	4–6	Left Leg	3/6
Magic Points: 10	7–9	Abdomen	3/7
Movement: 6 metres	10–12	Chest	3/8
Initiative Bonus: 12	13–15	Right Arm	3/5
Armour: Heavy leather hauberk	16–18	Left Arm	3/5
Abilities: None	19–20	Head	3/6

Skills: Athletics 65%, Brawn 52%, Endurance 43%, Evade 30%, Locale 34%, Perception 36%, Stealth 26%, Unarmed 50%, Willpower 21%

Passions: Hate Humans 80%

Combat Style: Beast-Man Warrior (Scimitar, Sword, Thrown Rock and Headbutt) 60%

Weapon	Size/Force	Reach	Damage	AP/HP
Scimitar	M	M	1d8+1d4	6/10
Shortspear	M	L	1d8+1+1d4	4/5
Thrown Rock	S	-	1d3+1d4	-
Headbutt	S	T	1d4+1d4	As for Head

WYLIN, WOLF OF THE NORTH

Wylin hails from Norport. He is a large, uncomplicated man who says what he feels with little regard for others' sensibilities. This bluffness has got him into trouble many times, as has his association with several criminal gangs in his home city. As this trouble (he never discusses it) escalated, it became prudent for him to flee and find a simpler life elsewhere.

He is a big, red-haired, grey-bearded stocky man with a slight stoop and a slight limp. Although blunt, he has a good sense of humour and is a loyal companion to those he trusts.

Characteristics	Attributes	1d20	Location	AP/HP
STR: 18	Action Points	3	1–3	Right Leg	2/6
CON: 14	Damage Modifier	+1d4	4–6	Left Leg	2/6
SIZ: 16	Magic Point	9	7–9	Abdomen	2/7
DEX: 11	Movement	6m	10-12	Chest	2/8
INT: 13	Initiative Bonus	12	13–15	Right Arm	2/5
POW: 9	Armour	Leathers	16–18	Left Arm	2/5
CHA: 12	Abilities	None	19–20	Head	0/6
	Magic	None			

Skills: Athletics 59%, Brawn 74%, Deceit 55%, Endurance 60%, Evade 52%, Locale 56%, Perception 52%, Streetwise 68%, Survival 67%, Unarmed 64%, Willpower 52%

Passions: Loyalty (Friends) 90%, Hate (Beast-Men) 88%, Plain Speaking 90%

Combat Style: North Vale Warrior (Battle Axe and Shield) 72%

Weapon	Size/Force	Reach	Damage	AP/HP
Battle Axe	M	M	1d6+1+1d4	4/8
Target Shield	L	S	1d3+1+1d4	4/9

BANNIS THE QUICK

Wylin's companion, Bannis is also fleeing criminal entanglements in Norport. His are more serious; Bannis carries a price on his head and so he is intending to get as far away as possible from his home city.

Where Wylin is gruff, Bannis is loquacious. Where Wylin is uncomplicated, Bannis is sly. He is, foremost, a self-preservationist and few trust him (Wylin seems to be the exception).

Slender and dark-haired, Bannis has several prominent scars on his hands, arms and neck - the results of knife-fights in Norport's slums. Daggers are his preferred weapon, and he carries six on his person at all times, concealed in various sheathes. He wields daggers in both hands in combat, one held in a reverse grip for downward stabs while the second dagger is used for thrusting.

Characteristics	Attributes	1d20	Location	AP/HP
STR: 11	Action Points	3	1–3	Right Leg	0/5
CON: 11	Damage Modifier	0	4–6	Left Leg	0/5
SIZ: 11	Magic Point	11	7–9	Abdomen	2/6
DEX: 18	Movement	6m	10-12	Chest	2/7
INT: 14	Initiative Bonus	13	13–15	Right Arm	0/4
POW: 11	Armour	Leathers	16–18	Left Arm	0/4
CHA: 15	Abilities	None	19–20	Head	0/5
	Magic	None			

Skills: Athletics 59%, Brawn 42%, Deceit 77%, Endurance 48%, Evade 66%, Insight 66%, Locale 60%, Perception 64%, Stealth 65%, Streetwise 74%, Survival 51%, Unarmed 59%, Willpower 62%

Passions: Self-Preservation 90%,

Combat Style: Street Fighter (Daggers) 69%: Assassination, Hidden Weapons

Weapon	Size/Force	Reach	Damage	AP/HP
Dagger	S	S	1d4+1	6/8

Desperate Sell-Swords

Arem, Nagal, Nils and Paga have poor quality arms and armour. They are, however, experienced warriors.

Use the statistics opposite for all three.

Arern, Nagal, Nils and Paga	1d20	Location	AP/HP
Action Points: 3	1–3	Right Leg	0/6
Damage Modifier: +1d2	4–6	Left Leg	0/6
Magic Points: 11	7–9	Abdomen	2/7
Movement: 6 metres	10–12	Chest	2/8
Initiative Bonus: 9	13–15	Right Arm	0/5
Armour: Heavy leather hauberk	16–18	Left Arm	0/5
Abilities: None	19–20	Head	0/6

Magic: None

Skills: *Athletics 50%, Brawn 55%, Endurance 47%, Evade 49%, Locale 39%, Perception 52%, Survival 37%, Unarmed 69%, Willpower 42%*

Passions: *Self-Preservation 80%, Love Money 85%*

Combat Style: *Mercenary Spearmen (Shortspear) 60%*

Weapon	Size/Force	Reach	Damage	AP/HP
Shortspear	M	L	1d8+1+1d2	4/5

Eyloi the Hare

Nondescript, this unremarkably dressed trapper deliberately assumes a slumped and downcast posture, and rarely makes eye contact. Eyloi trails the characters north, intending to strike at an opportune time, preferring to attack lone stragglers. He favours unarmoured locations. Eyloi disengages after attacking, trying to escape the other characters, biding his time until another opportunity presents itself.

Eyloi coats all his weapons with the Tongue of Lygge poison (Potency 45%, resist with Endurance, onset immediate, duration 1d4 rounds, inflicts Agony on the first location wounded by freshly envenomed weapons). Any skill roll using the affected location must also be less than or equal to the character's Willpower. See page 75 of the MYTHRAS rulebook

Attributes	1d20	Location	AP/HP
Action Points: 3	1–3	Right Leg	2/6
Damage Modifier: +1d2	4–6	Left Leg	2/6
Magic Points: 12	7–9	Abdomen	2/7
Movement: 6 metres	10–12	Chest	2/8
Initiative Bonus: 12	13–15	Right Arm	2/5
Armour: Leathers	16–18	Left Arm	2/5
Abilities: None	19–20	Head	0/6

Magic: None

Skills: *Athletics 55%, Brawn 45%, Disguise 57%, Endurance 47%, Evade 54%, Insight 46%, Locale 39%, Perception 60%, Stealth 55%, Survival 37%, Unarmed 70%, Willpower 55%.*

Passions: *Hate People from The Vale 55%*

Combat Style: *Gartharis Assassin (Sword, Dagger, Bow, Garrotte) 70%, Assassination*

Weapon	Size/Force	Reach	Damage	AP/HP
Shortsword	M	S	1d6+1d2	6/8
Dagger	S	S	1d4+1+1d2	6/8
Short Bow	L	-	1d6+1d2	4/4

Gartharis Hunters

Typical hunters of the wild north, used to spending days in search of prey.

Attributes	1d20	Location	AP/HP
Action Points: 3	1–3	Right Leg	–/5
Damage Modifier: +0	4–6	Left Leg	–/5
Magic Points: 9	7–9	Abdomen	–/6
Movement: 6 metres	10–12	Chest	–/7
Initiative Bonus: 13	13–15	Right Arm	–/4
Armour: None	16–18	Left Arm	–/4
Abilities: None	19–20	Head	–/5
Magic: None			

Skills: *Athletics 50%, Brawn 30%, Endurance 55%, Evade 60%, Locale 50%, Perception 60%, Stealth 60%, Survival 60%, Track 55%, Unarmed 40%, Willpower 25%*

Passions: *Fear (Jedakiah) 80%, Loyalty (Clan Chieftain) 60%*

Combat Style: *Gartharis Hunter (Sling, Shortspear) 70%*

Weapon	Size/Force	Reach	Damage	AP/HP
Sling	L	-	1d8	1/2
Shortspear	M	L	1d8+1	4/5

Brown Bear

The brown bears of The Realm's north are hunters and scavengers generally preferring to avoid human contact. If they feel their territory is threatened, attacks are assured, and guaranteed if the bear is female and accompanied by cubs.

Attributes	1d20	Location	AP/HP
Action Points: 3	1–3	Right Rear Leg	1/7
Damage Modifier: +1d6	4–6	Left Rear Leg	1/7
Magic Points: 7	7–9	Hindquarters	1/8
Movement: 8 metres	10–12	Forequarters	1/9
Initiative Bonus: 13	13–15	Right Front Leg	1/6
Armour: Hide	16–18	Left Front Leg	1/6
Abilities: Nightsight	19–20	Head	1/7
Magic: None			

Skills: *Athletics 74%, Brawn 59%, Endurance 61%, Evade 46%, Perception 60%, Stealth 46%, Willpower 48%*

Passions: *Defend Territory and Cubs 100%*

Combat Style: *Ursine Fury (Bite and Claws) 62%*

Weapon	Size/Force	Reach	Damage	AP/HP
Bite	L	S	1d8+1d6	As for Head
Claw	H	L	1d8+1d6	As for Front Leg

Winged Apes

Winged Apes are extremely rare in The Realm. Where they exist, they are a vestige of the Chaos Mother's corruption stemming back to the time of her domination of the land.

They use their flight to their advantage, dropping rocks from on-high and launching diving attacks designed not to connect, but to force opponents to cower or flee. Once they are satisfied that potential foes have retreated to a non-threatening distance, attacks cease.

Attributes	1d20	Location	AP/HP
Action Points: 3	1–3	Right Leg	2/8
Damage Modifier: +1d8 (1d10 with Diving Strike)	4–6	Left Leg	2/8
Magic Points: 11	7–9	Abdomen	2/9
Movement: 4 metres (land), 8 metres (flying)	10	Chest	2/10
Initiative Bonus: 13	11–12	Right Wing	0/8
Armour: Fur	13–14	Left Wing	0/8
Abilities: Diving Strike, Flying, Formidable Natural Weapons	15–16	Right Arm	2/7
	17–18	Left Arm	2/7
Magic: None	19–20	Head	2/8

Skills: *Athletics 64%, Brawn 74%, Endurance 60%, Evade 54%, Fly 47%, Perception 52%, Willpower 48%*

Passions: *Defend Territory 74%*

Combat Style: *Rip Apart (Fists, Teeth, Wing Strike) 74%*

Weapon	Size/Force	Reach	Damage	AP/HP
Bite	M	T	1d3+1d8	As for Head
Fists	M	M	1d4+1d8	As for Arm
Wing	M	L	1d3+1d8	As for Wing

The Son of Fury

The Son of Fury is a further development of the Chaos Hybrid described on page 38. The Ophidians have made this one larger, stronger, faster and imbued it with Chaos Features.

It resembles a combination of boar, bear and human. Its head is porcine with wicked, curving tusks, and the upper torso is that of a huge black bear. The lower half of the body is human like, but much larger than standard human proportions.

The Son of Fury knows only hatred. Once instructed to hunt something and kill it, it absolutely will not stop.

Characteristics	Attributes	1d20	Location	AP/HP
STR: 20	Action Points	3	1–3	Right Leg	3/8
CON: 28	Damage Modifier	+1d6	4–6	Left Leg	3/8
SIZ: 20	Magic Points	10	7–9	Abdomen	3/9
DEX: 28	Movement	12m	10–12	Chest	3/10
INS: 13	Initiative Bonus	21	13–15	Right Arm	3/7
POW: 10	Armour	Tough Hide	16–18	Left Arm	3/7
CHA: 1			19–20	Head	4/8

Abilities

Blood Sense, Chaos Features (Frightening, Nerveless), Formidable Natural Weapons

Skills: *Athletics 90%, Brawn 104%, Endurance 90%, Evade 86%, Perception 75%, Survival 90%, Unarmed 90%, Willpower 70%*

Passions: *Killing 110%*

Combat Style: *Chaos Bastard (Unarmed, Spear) 80%*

Weapon	Size/Force	Reach	Damage	AP/HP
Claws	M	T	1d4+1d6	As for Arm
Bite	M	T	1d6+1d6	As for Head
Tusks	M	S	1d4+1d6	As for Head
Longspear	L	VL	1d10+1+1d6	4/10

OPHIDIAN SORCERER-SCIENTISTS

These Ophidians are part of the ancient race that has been in the world for countless years, working in secret. They are sorcerer-scientists and researchers, rather than warriors, but are capable of defending themselves when needed. If faced with superior odds, they hide and prepare spells, preferring not to enter into contact.

OPHIDIAN VENOM

Ophidian venom has a Potency of 70%. A victim must win an opposed roll of his Endurance against the Potency of the venom, or suffer the following symptoms: at the start of the round following being poisoned, the bitten location suffers the Agony condition, rendering it unusable for the next 2d6 minutes and possibly disrupting any attempts at concentration or spell casting. One hour later the victim begins to suffer the combined effects of Hallucination and Mania, developing a rabid fear of snakes. This effect lasts 2d6 days, during which time the victim grows increasingly paranoid until they must eventually be tied up for their own safety. After the poison subsides the victim will have no recollection of what bit them or how.

Characteristics	Attributes	1d20	Location	AP/HP
STR: 11	Action Points	3	1-3	Tail	1/6
CON: 13	Damage Modifier	0	4-5	Right Hind Leg	1/6
SIZ: 13	Magic Points	16	6-7	Left Hind Leg	1/6
DEX: 15	Movement	6m	8-10	Hindquarters	1/7
INT: 16	Initiative Bonus	16	11-14	Forequarters	1/8
POW: 16	Armour	Scales	15-16	Right Front Leg	1/5
CHA: 8	Abilities		17-18	Left Front Leg	1/5
	Cold Blooded, Night Sight, Poison		19-20	Head	1/6

Skills: *Athletics 46%, Brawn 40%, Endurance 66%, Evade 60%, Insight 75%, Lore (Alchemy) 65%, Lore (Ophidian Science) 70%, Perception 75%, Unarmed 56%, Willpower 80%*

Passions: *Loyalty (Nest) 90%*

Magic

Sorcery: *Invocation (The Scaled Secrets) 65%, Shaping 60%*

Spells: Animate (Flesh), Enhance (STR and DEX), Diminish (INT), Dominate (Hybrids), Sculpt (Flesh), Wrack (Chaos)

Combat Style: *Unseen Blade (Dagger) 45%*

Weapon	Size/Force	Reach	Damage	AP/HP
Bite	M	M	1d6	As for Head
Claw	M	T	1d4	As for Arm
Tail	M	L	1d4	As for Tail
Dagger	S	S	1d4+1	6/8

ZOMBIE

Reanimated by the insidious influence of the Chaos Mother. Mindless. Dead. Hungry.

Anyone bitten by a Zombie should make an Endurance roll opposed by the Zombie's Willpower. If the Zombie winds the contest the victim contracts the Chaos Aura trait, as described on page 215 of the MYTHRAS rules. If the victim fumbles the Endurance roll, a Chaos Feature, as described in the appendices (pages 275-276) is also contracted. The feature takes 1d6 days to manifest and is accompanied by fevered dreams and painful convulsions. The pain ceases when the feature fully appears, but the fevered dreams of the Chaos Mother continue until a cure can be found. The only cure for either the Chaos Aura and Feature is powerful healing magic from the Temple of Aliya.

Attributes	1d20	Location	AP/HP
Action Points: 2	1-3	Right Leg	-/5
Damage Modifier: +1d2	4-6	Left Leg	-/5
Magic Points: 0	7-9	Abdomen	-/6
Movement: 6 metres	10-12	Chest	-/7
Initiative Bonus: 10	13-15	Right Arm	-/4
Armour: None	16-18	Left Arm	-/4
Abilities: Undead	19-20	Head	-/5
Magic: None			

Skills: *Athletics 41%, Brawn 46%, Endurance 61%, Evade 38%, Perception 40%, Unarmed 61%, Willpower 48%*

Passions: *Eat the Living 100%*

Combat Style: *Unarmed, 61%*

Weapon	Size/Force	Reach	Damage	AP/HP
Bite	S	S	1d2	As for Head
Fists	S	T	1d3+1d2	As for Arm

Scenario 7: Reckoning at Distaff Peak

Overview

The characters are questing to locate and defeat Jedakiah, the insane and ambitious Chaos cultist whose schemes threaten all the lands of The Realm. Dark Child's Tower, the sorcerer's stronghold, is located deep in the harsh and gloomy Gartharis wilderness. The characters must try to win their way through the natural hazards of beasts and weather, whilst avoiding attacks from the savage, Chaos-worshipping barbarians who inhabit the land. With cunning and good fortune, Garthari warriors or foreign slavers questioned or followed to Jedakiah's lair provide valuable information, or a means of getting into the mountain hideout.

Once the peak on which the sorcerer's tower stands is located, the characters face a nerve-wracking approach along a winding trail guarded by terrifying blasphemies of nature. Alternatively, a subterranean route can be used to infiltrate the lower chambers of the stronghold, but it is the lair of a mutated monstrosity. Finally, the characters confront Jedakiah himself, who is guarded by a retinue of fanatical warriors and who has the power to harness the dark, wild powers of the Chaos Mother.

Non-Player Characters

- Jedakiah: An ambitious and ruthless sorcerer whose continent-wide machinations are meant to bring about his apotheosis into a God of Chaos.
- 'The Hooded One': The secretive stranger who advises Jedakiah on the summoning and nurturing of the forces of Chaos. He is actually a cold-blooded, calculating Ophidian named Fisshazz.
- Bria, 'The Pure Beauty': The daughter of Lord Drystan. This young woman has been kidnapped and taken to Jedakiah's lair, as her innocence and beauty make her an ideal sacrifice for his planned invocation.
- Geriss Lortt: A sadistic and mercenary slave merchant who has been selling human goods to Jedakiah for years. He visits Jedakiah in person to conduct his negotiations.

Key Points/ Timeline

1. The characters make enquiries about the location and nature of the secretive and evil mastermind who threatens The Realm and who has kidnapped the Lady Bria.
2. The characters' activities lead them to the foot of Distaff Peak in the interior of Gartharis.
3. The characters find a route to Dark Child's Tower.
4. The characters learn of an imminent ceremony that Jedakiah will conduct to attain Godhood.
5. The showdown between Jedakiah and the characters occurs.

Areas to be Covered

- The borderlands of The Vale: The towns and villages that border the wilderness of Gartharis.
- The Gartharis hill country: A wind-blasted moorland that is home to fierce tribes of barbarians.
- Distaff Peak: A peak sacred to the Gartharis barbarians. It is located in the Pierce Sky Mountains. It incorporates a winding trail known as The Mother's Cord and is riddled with tunnels which connect to the foundations of Dark Child's Tower and the subterranean realm of the Ophidians.
- Dark Child's Tower: An ancient watch castle that has been rebuilt as the loathsome, black-stoned stronghold of Jedakiah.
- The Cavern of Changes: In the foundations of the Dark Tower can be found a resurgent manifestation of The Chaos Tree and the spawning pits of a race of foul beastmen.

A Doom Rekindled

Centuries ago, Distaff Peak in Gartharis was the location for the Dream Tree, a huge, sacred tree that was the focus of a cult of the Chaos Mother. The obscene monstrosity bore hallucinogenic fruits and fungi which gifted those who ingested them with power and madness. When the hero Sayalis led an army against the peak, the defenders were slaughtered and the tree was cut down and burnt along with all the roots that could be unearthed. The ground was sanctified by priests of the Founding Four, and a watch tower known as the Gaze of Saylis was raised to guard against the return of the cult.

Over the centuries the garrison became a place of virtual exile for priests and military men who had fallen out of favour. Starved of adequate support, and finding that their mounts soon sickened, the guardians had little influence beyond a bowshot of the tower. Some hundred and thirty years ago, all contact between The Vale and the tower ended. Scouting parties sent from The Vale reported that the tower had fallen to the Garthari barbarians. Unknown to the folk of the Vale, the priest attached to the tower's chapel in recent years lacked sufficient devotion and diligence to ensure that the Gods still guarded Distaff Peak from Chaos. A dormant root of the Tree of Dreams was reinvigorated and, as it reached the water source of the garrison, it contaminated the tower's water supply. Warped dreams of Chaos drove men to acts of perversion and violence which escalated until all the outbuildings were burnt down; and former comrades murdered each other until only a single madman was left alive to flee the tower. The fugitive was captured by a band of Garthari who spared him as he was apparently touched by Chaos. He gabbled a crazed story foretelling how a Dark Child of the Mother would come one day to restore her power to the lands. The tribesmen looted the tower and desecrated its shrine. One of their shaman declared the tower as a taboo area until the Dark Child arrived to claim his

Campaign Notes for the Games Master

It is envisaged that this scenario will be the last in the Book of Quests campaign. Care must be taken that the sorcerer proves a formidable enough foe to make for an exciting climax. Important henchmen of Jedakiah from earlier adventures may have chosen to report in person to their master, or may have fled to the tower for safety. Either way, they might be present when the characters arrive at the location. Worse yet, Jedakiah might have obtained the occult items he needs to ensure that his sacrifice of the Lady Bria (see Beneath the Black Water) brings about his union with the Chaos Daughter and his own deification. Similarly, potential allies for the characters could be held as captives within the tower, or if free, might be available as advisors or more active participants in the characters' activities. If the characters have suffered misfortune in an earlier encounter with Jedakiah's minions, they might well find themselves reaching the tower as prisoners!

The Games Master will need to consider what, if anything, Jedakiah may have learnt of the characters if he recognises them when they arrive at his stronghold. He is probably arrogant enough to neglect the

defence of the tower, but might have an idea of some of the prowess and abilities of his persistent foes when he finally confronts them.

The scenario is written with the assumption that a party of characters will be making a lone quest into the wilderness. If they are able to call on substantial military assistance or are accompanied by powerful sorcerers, then the Games Master will have to ensure that enough opposing tribesmen, Beast-Men and, possibly, Ophidians are assembled by Jedakiah to negate the expedition's numbers. Care must be taken to ensure large hosts of 'spear carriers' which accompany a party are destroyed, routed or kept occupied so that the decisive heroic actions of the adventure are performed by the characters themselves.

The characters can start from anywhere in The Realm but will need to head for the borderlands of the troublesome land of Gartharis. Unless they have specific information on the lair of their quarry, they will travel through the countryside in a direction of their own (or a hireling's) choosing, searching for clues to their destination. Eventually they should find themselves ascending into the Pierce Sky Mountains. On locating a mountain known as Distaff Peak, inheritance, and the place was left deserted though the entrances to the passes were guarded.

A decade ago, Jedakiah's delving into the history of the Chaos Mother's cult prompted him to locate and visit Distaff Peak. He found the tower in decay and ruin, but on discovering the Dream Tree's root he was able to use its power to commune with the Chaos Mother herself. Making a staff from part of the root, he then went forth from the tower and used his token of favour to demonstrate to the local tribesfolk that he was the prophesied Dark Child. Since then he has used barbarians and slaves to restore the tower, which became known amongst the Garthari as 'Dark Child's Tower'. A few years ago, after consulting with the Ophidians, Jedakiah and Fisshazz, an agent of the hidden folk, have discovered a way of using the mutating powers of the 'Root of Dreams' in the lowest cavern of the tower to spawn Beast-Men with which he can further their ambitions and spread the influence of Chaos.

Now, like a dark spider at the edge of its web, Jedakiah waits in his mountain fastness as his converts, dupes and hirelings further his schemes and power throughout The Realm. Finally, after many years, he has played his hand as his agents are tasked with bringing him the items he needs to ascend to Godhood. Yet despite his patient planning, there are heroes who endeavour to thwart his schemes and who now move inexorably towards a confrontation with the arch-schemer.

OF RUMOURS AND OBLIGATIONS

If the scenario is being run as the conclusion to the entire campaign in this volume, then in all likelihood the characters will have already acquired evidence of Jedakiah's schemes and his lair's location. Various patrons, prisoners or allies will have helped guide them towards this final mission. If the characters have no accurate leads at this point, then an acolyte of one of the sects of The Founding Four receives dire omens and portents in which both a dark soul and the abandoned Gaze of Saylis figure.

Games Masters running this as a standalone adventure can tailor the offered rewards and information needed for a group of characters, selecting an employee from amongst the Non-Player Characters listed in this book.

The characters start the adventure on the borders of Gartharis. Most folk are fearful of the barbarian raiders and stay to the borders and grumble about the inefficiency of the patrols that police them. To locate suitable guides for hire, seekers need to make a Standard Streetwise roll or a Critical Commerce roll to learn the identity of a Valesfolk trader who is permitted by the Garthari tribes to travel through the tribal lands of the northern wilderness. Some of these individuals will have profited from trade with Jedakiah and might decide to warn the sorcerer and lead the characters into a trap.

Characters would be wise to obtain all the equipment and provisions for their journey whilst outside the borders of Gartharis. Tavern wenches who learn of their destination probably suggest that they purchase other comforts that will be lacking beyond civilisation. Shrewd characters who make a Survival roll make good choices of travelling gear and are also aware that sure-footed ponies make better mounts for the conditions ahead. Few maps show anything beyond a day's ride of the frontier, save for a few largely inaccurate maps at Norport's Guild of Cartographers. Detailed charts that mapped the route to

The Gaze of Saylis were once held in official archives throughout The Realm, but have vanished, the result of Jedakiah's network of agents. The Games Master might decide that one map was spared theft or destruction and comes into the hands of a character as a personal heirloom or, more likely, is given to them by a patron or ally.

Beyond the Vales

Even if the characters have obtained a map or a guide from an earlier adventure in The Book of Quests, they are faced with the daunting task of locating Jedakiah's tower. They will not travel too far into Gartharis before they sight macabre warning posts, typically skulls of trespassers located in rock niches. They find themselves in a bleak land of hills and mountains with a scattering of tarns and gloomy pine forests. The tribes of the area are devoted to the Chaos Mother and obey the instructions of her favoured priest, Jedakiah, without question. Settlements are located on hilltops that are close to water sources. Their ramshackle buildings are made with stone, timber and turf. The larger villages are usually protected by a wooden palisade or a low wall of earth or rocks. The rough pasture near the homesteads is grazed by scrawny sheep and small shaggy cattle, usually under the eye of a youth and a gaunt hound. Few crops are grown, save for patches of oats and barley. The Garthari are wary and often hostile to each other, but they are especially belligerent to people from foreign lands. A few traders have been tolerated in the past and some captured foreigners are made to serve as slaves if there are enough resources in a village. The barbarians fear sorcerers and seem especially superstitious to civilised characters.

The Garthari barbarians are unlikely to volunteer helpful information concerning Jedakiah and his whereabouts, though insightful characters might notice that their gaze subconsciously flicks northwards. It takes great cunning or charm to get the elder warriors to talk of Dark Child's Tower and its location. Ruthless inquisitors find the Garthari prove hard men to break through torture or intimidation, although a sorcerer who threatens to cast dark magic against their souls might break their resolve.

If not using deception or guides to traverse the wilderness, characters may try to sneak through the uplands using their Conceal, Stealth and Survival skills to pass unnoticed. Such attempts are always penalised by at least a difficulty level of Hard, considering they are strangers in a strange land and that the barbarians send out frequent hunting parties. Groups without guides also run the risk of straying into areas of bog which can be found below the mountains. These dark morasses of peat are capable of swallowing up unwary travellers, their mounts and overladen beasts of burden (See Quicksands, page 42).

The uplands are home to wary game animals that can be hunted, though hungry packs of wolves may prove a hazard to mounts, beasts of burden and weak stragglers. The moor viper is a lurking danger that is best left undisturbed. Even in winter it might prove deadly if a forager mistakes its dormant form for a stick when rummaging in hollows for dry kindling and fuel. Statistics for wolves are on page 36 and the moor viper is on page 142. Characters who do not ensure that they have waterproof apparel or oils for their equipment may find that some of their gear corrodes or rots.

Garthari encountered in the wild can be rolled randomly on the table below, although the Games Master can always choose to select what encounters best fit into their campaign.

Unless encountered in their home settlements, Garthari barbarians will probably be hunting parties looking for game, or else war bands setting-out to raid the borders of civilised lands or returning from a foray, loaded with the spoils of victory (or limping back to their hearths and scornful womenfolk after miserable failure). Some parties of barbarians include warriors mounted on unkempt, but hardy, riding ponies. Roused by recent events on the borders, they typically prove hostile to most strangers they

they will need to travel up a winding gorge known as The Mother's Cord or else thread their way through the natural subterranean water courses that lead up to the sorcerer's hideout. Dark Child's Tower is a restored keep that has a few small outbuildings The tower's foundations include a dungeon and access to a subterranean cavern.

If the adventure is adapted for an alternative campaign, any remote area of a land that is home to savage tribes can be utilised for Gartharis.

Wilderness Encounters

1D100	Encounter
01-10	1d3 adolescent Garthari hunters
11-40	1d6 Garthari hunters 5% chance of being mounted
41-70	2d6 Garthari raiders 10% chance of being mounted
71-90	Garthari Chieftain and a warband of 20+3d6 warriors. There is a 50% chance the group has 1d6 mounts and a 25% chance they include 1d3 adolescents.
91-95	1d6 Garthari outlaws
96-00	Burial cairn

encounter, though they respect those who bear the mark of the Chaos Mother or who have tokens which shows that they are engaged on Jedakiah's errands. Most captives of the barbarians are taken to Jedakiah after having their wrists bound behind their backs with leather cords.

Adolescents occasionally accompany their elders as scouts and skirmishers. If unsupervised by seasoned warriors, foolhardy striplings might attempt to stalk the characters with the intention of collecting a head or scalp.

Sometimes the barbarians comprise just a few desperate individuals who have fallen foul of a taboo or a blood feud, and now operate as bandits who prey on all and sundry.

Cairns are mounds of stones built over the dead often in areas far away from homes of men. Some of them honour great heroes of the Garthari who were laid to rest with their arms, chattels and a sacrificed companion. Most of these memorials, however, are simply regarded as a means of stopping dead spirits from plaguing the living. Intruders who are discovered dismantling them may well find themselves slain out of hand by the tribe folk of the region.

LOCATING DARK CHILD'S TOWER

If the characters are getting nowhere with their quest to locate Jedakiah, one or more of the following encounters may occur.

VASSALS AND VIANDS

At various times Jedakiah orders tributes of food from various tribes, mostly comprised of cattle. A barbarian envoy bearing a token of Jedakiah leads a few tribesmen from the settlement with the livestock selected. When the trail, known to the Garthari as the Mother's Cord, is reached the sheep aere either tied or slaughtered to facilitate getting them up the trail. A group of characters, learning of this, can attempt to seize a token or might try to covertly follow such a group.

A group typically comprises of an envoy that is treated as a Blessed One without a Chaos gift, 1d6+3 warriors and 1d3-1 adolescents. They also have 3d6 sheep or cattle with them and there is a 25% chance of their having 1d6 slaves as extra tribute.

TRADERS IN MISERY

The characters encounter a group of slavers who are making their way towards the tower. The human goods that are intended for the sorcerer may well include individuals that the characters have encountered in their earlier actions against Jedakiah's underlings. The characters might learn of the slavers and be on a mission to stop them or might merely stumble across them.

The party of slavers numbers four men mounted on sturdy ponies and their leader, Geriss Lortt, who rides a sure-footed horse. Two wagons, each pulled by four mules and driven by a slave, hold some provisions and personal goods of the slavers. A column of 1d6+12 half-starved and weary slaves are roped together and trudge towards their grim destination; any stragglers being urged on by the long, swishing and cracking bullwhips used by their tormentors.

Geriss Lortt has +10% in all the skills listed for his men, and also has Commerce 70% and Deceit 70%. He also has an enchanted medallion that has been inscribed with a Chaos mark by Jedakiah. The slave master wears this openly when he approaches the Screamers, which recognise it.

If the characters seem vulnerable, Lortt may attempt to add them to his stock of slaves; but he is too shrewd to take unnecessary risks. The slavers are a cruel and callous bunch, but they will not fight a battle they feel they will lose. The slavers may be persuaded to divulge what they know of the tower and its inhabitants, either through bribery or significant threats if these are backed up with obvious power. The despicable crew will be openly eager to escape Jedakiah's wrath if the characters have bested them. If compelled to accompany the party to the tower they plan treachery. The slaves are grateful for their freedom, and some may wish to slay their former captors. It is unlikely that they can be formed into a useful fighting force unless they are inspired to fanaticism, or used carefully and shrewdly. If the party wish to pose as the slavers, the guards at the tower are all familiar with Lortt's appearance, though the composition of his henchmen has varied over the years.

Death in the Darkness

If the Games Master wishes to give the characters the option to avoid ascending the part of the trail to Distaff Peak which is guarded by Jedakiah's minions, he may choose to have the party reach Dark Pines Tarn. This is a small lake fringed by huddled conifers into which an underground stream pours. The stream can be accessed as a means of entering the Tower if the characters have good climbing skills and tools for forcing doors. The outlet into the lake can be reached by wading through the shallows, or else by clambering along the rocky slopes. The later route requires an Easy Athletics Skill test.

Learning of the Underground Route

The following plot hooks can be used to get the characters to attempt to negotiate their way through the tunnels.

- The rivers below the mountain are tainted, and cattle sicken. On the approach to the stronghold the characters notice the rocks of a stream bed are filmed with a faint luminous sheen. Further upland, when the Black Pines Tarn is reached, and if it is late evening or night time, the characters detect an eerie, phosphorescent glow coming from a stream that cascades into the small lake. This is from some alchemical waste which has recently been poured down the well of the Dark Tower.
- If examined closely, the vegetation around the tarn is found to be mutated; plants have asymmetrical leaves, and the scales of pine cones terminate in cruel barbs whilst the ground cover includes sickly, lurid toadstools marked by disturbing patterns. Thorough investigation shows that the mutations are more frequent and pronounced near the stream. Small bats are noticed travelling in and out of a cavern on their nocturnal activities.
- During their travels in the wilds of Gartharis, the characters hear a local legend. It mentions the mad survivor of the old watch tower who foretold the arrival of the Dark Child. He was apparently discovered by tribesmen as he floated, half-drowned, in Black Pines Tarn.

Navigating the Caverns

The underground system is in complete darkness. Use the table on page 199 to calculate the difficulty factor for a character's skills if in total darkness or using a light source. Most of the passages have a flow of chilling water which is usually up to mid calf in depth, though from floor to ceiling the height is usually one to two metres. The Games Master can call for Athletics rolls as he sees fit, and Swim rolls are needed for characters who encounter difficulties in deep sections of water.

The following encounters can be used in the caves.

- **Treacherous footing**: Athletics roll or sustain a sprain for 1d2 points to a leg, ignoring armour. Fumble inflicts 1d4 to the location and movement is painful and at third speed.
- **Sink hole**: Unless an Athletics roll is made, the individual who encounters this one metre diameter hole in the ground plunges 2d6 metres into an underground lake with a depth of 2d6 metres. In two metres or more of water he starts to drown unless he can make a Swim roll.
- **Fish**: Sometimes blind, pale fish can be sighted or sensed in the stiller pools. A character making a Hard Locale roll or a Standard Craft (fishing) or Survival roll knows that the species is edible and can also be utilized as improvised torches, the congealed oil burning as well as pitch.
- **A swarm of bats** startles the characters who must make an Easy Willpower roll, or else be forced into dropping a torch or lantern.
- **Flooded passageway**: The length of the flooded stretch of passageway where the water level reaches the ceiling will be unknown to the characters. It stretches for 4d6 metres and requires a Swim roll to

pass through safely, though an alternative passageway that detours it might be located by tracking.

- **Strange rock formations:** Most are harmless geological features which may cause apprehension and distraction until examined closely, although ones near the tower might be bizarre corruptions of human forms.
- **Sudden torrent:** The current sweeps a character off his feet unless he can make a Brawn roll. If carried away by the current the character will suffer 1d6 damage to a random location and will be swept 6x d6 metres downstream.
- **Steep Climb:** The character must make an Athletics roll or suffer falling damage equivalent to a 1d6 metre drop.
- **Alchemical Taint**: Areas downstream of the well might have traces of luminous slime which aids characters seeking the tower. Unless washed off the clothing of a character this substance might make him easier to detect in poor lighting.
- **Giant Salamander:** The effects of alchemical waste and the presence of Chaos that infests the locality warped much of the wildlife of the mountain. The salamanders that inhabited the subterranean lakes and streams had their adult maturity arrested although

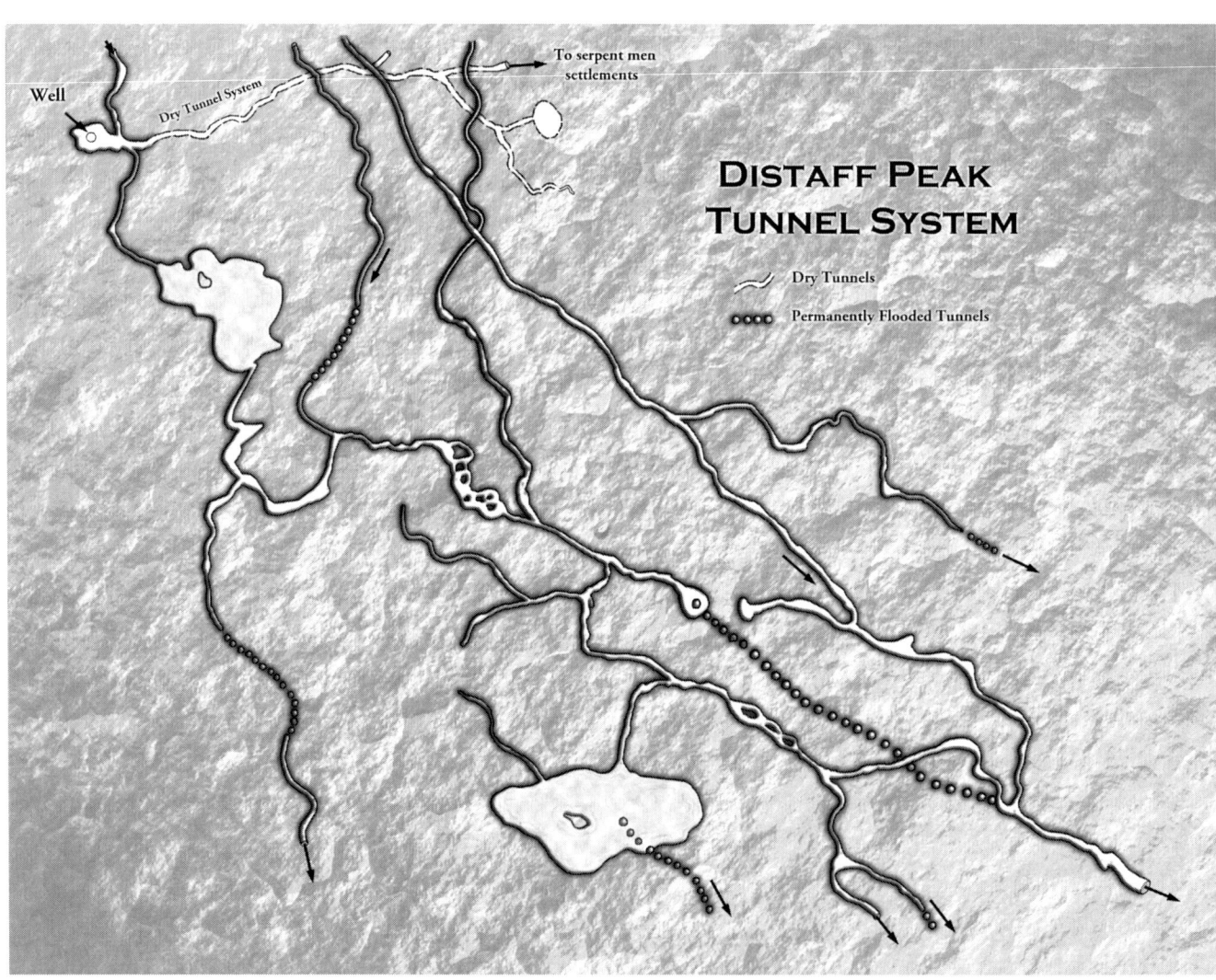

Effects of Lighting within the Caves

Lighting Type	Change to Difficulty Grade for combat and other visual-based skills	Skill Modifier
Within the radius of bright light sources such as those caused by light and glow spells.	Standard	No adjustment.
At the edge of a bright light source as listed above.	Hard	Reduce the skill value by one third
Within the radius of lantern light or multiple (more than one) torches.	Hard	Reduce the skill value by one third
Single torch or on the periphery of lantern of multiple torch light.	Formidable	Reduce the skill value by half
Pitch black	Herculean	Reduce the skill value to one tenth

Note that the negative for grappling and knife-fighting (close combat) is always considered one grade less severe (to a maximum of Standard) as the foe is so close that tactile senses are also used to identify the target's location. Therefore, characters left in the dark may do best by pulling out knives and daggers and feeling out their enemy.

their regenerative abilities were boosted. Many grew to a huge size, though cannibalism has reduced their numbers. One giant axolotl is trapped in part of the subterranean complex because of the huge size it has attained. It has red, branch-like gills, although the rest of its flesh is a ghostly white. No eyes exist in its huge head, but its huge maw has developed strong, needle-like teeth. It preys on fish, though it will eat anything else it can overpower and it is often ravenously hungry. Sometimes the beast has been desperate enough to eat its own tail or a limb, although these appendages have always regenerated.

AT THE WELL

The Games Master must note what precautions, if any, are made to waterproof equipment carried by characters, and decide if any items are damaged or perish. Games Masters can also secretly roll a Conceal or a Survival test for each character; any failures indicating the loss of a small item that was carried-away in a torrent. A second roll can be made using Perception to determine if a character notices the loss.

The water where the well is shaft is located has a depth of 1.5 metres. The cavern's ceiling is three metres above the bottom of the stream and has a shaft of roughly a metre diameter that leads up another seven metres until it reaches the well's cap. The rough hewn walls of the well shaft are slick with moisture on the lower third of their depth. Climbing tests using the Athletics skill will be Formidable on the lower reaches and Hard on the drier surface above. Loud noises echo up into the well room of the tower and are distorted.

A PASSAGE THROUGH NIGHTMARES

If the Characters use the route travelled by Jedakiah's human followers and hirelings they must progress up the guarded mountain pathway as described in The Mother's Cord, below. See the map on page 200.

THE MOTHER'S CORD

Distaff Peak is located alongside a trail that runs through part of the inhospitable Pierce Sky Mountain chain. The upper reaches of the slender mountain are always capped with fleece-like clouds that were once likened by the Garthari to the distaff from which the Chaos Mother creates form from Chaos. The 'Mother's Cord' is the local name given to the narrow, rocky-walled path that winds its way upwards towards Glimmer Crag, where gold, tin and copper can be mined. The mountain's surface is largely devoid of animal life; most mammals and birds have been scared away by a sense of foreboding or by the Screamers. At odd

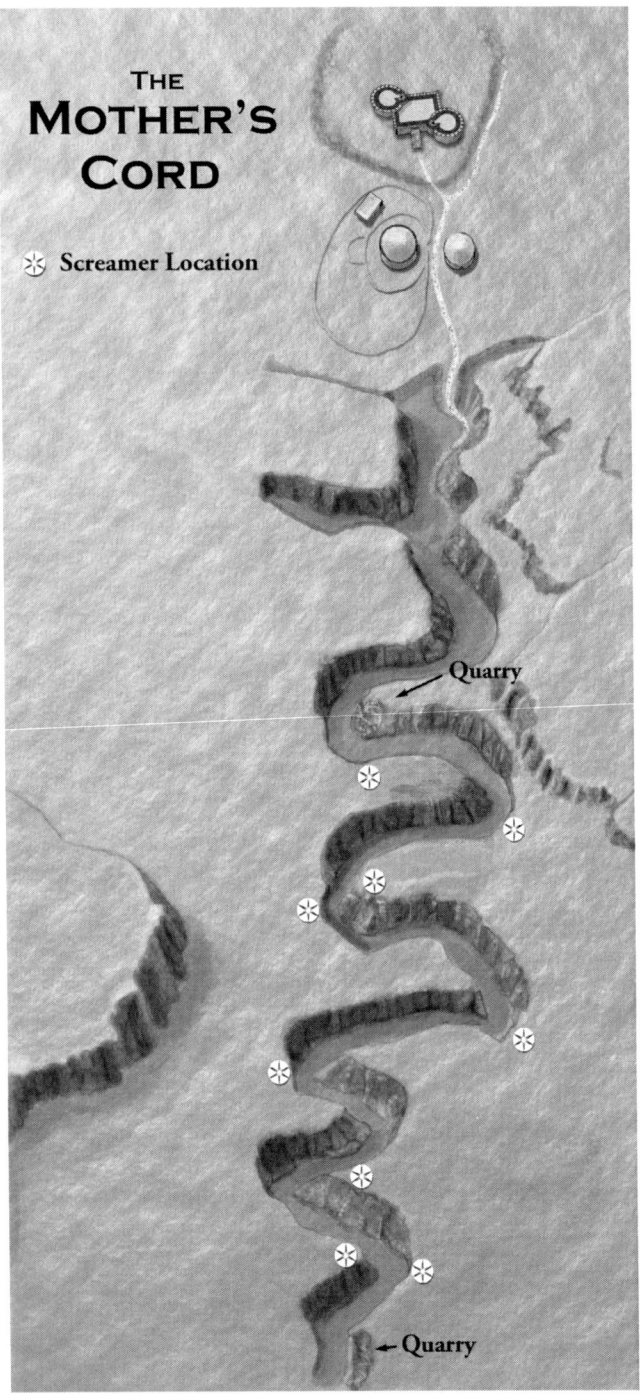

will probably attract the attention of some of these carrion eaters. They are unlikely to provide any greater threat than a distracting cawing - although they can be a danger to a small familiar or any crippled individual or creature. The greatest danger they pose is if the tower's garrison is alerted by their behaviour. There is the possibility that a bird will be tempted to fly off with an unattached but small object, which sparkles in the light.

THE SCREAMERS

A gruesome collection of nine experiments have been placed at intervals of around three hundred metres along the road that winds north up to Jedakiah's tower. Unfortunate individuals have been merged together using animal parts, foul sorcery and chaos matter. They are now a bewildering and nauseating fusion of thrashing limbs, exposed bones, staring eyes and screaming mouths that vanish and reappear in a quivering, obscene mass. They are totally insane and their shrieking and babbling is incomprehensible but echoes terrifyingly along the walls of the pass. Each monstrosity has been marked with a rune of Chaos and fused into the rocky slopes some ten metres or more from the trail's edge; their spinal columns and odd limbs being threaded through the ground and then melded together to hold the wretched thing fast. Their purpose is to scare away intruders, a living demonstration of the power and ruthlessness of Jedakiah, but they also function as a warning system for the tower's defenders. An especially loud commotion will alert the garrison and trigger the dispatching of 'Two Maws', a hunting and tracking beast, with a handler and a couple of guards to investigate.

The Screamers attack if a being or a weapon comes in reach of them, using a flailing mass of teeth and claws that stretch in an attempt to tear the life from the living. They have the ability to sense the mark of Chaos used by Jedakiah and his chosen followers. The fear this engenders quells the screams of rage and hatred into a quieter and pathetic wailing and gibbering.

THE GREY LURKER

Near the end of the gorge, a dark, dismal cleft, untouched by sunlight, extends deep into the mountainside. Here an early experiment of Jedakiah has made its lair. This creature resembles a colossal, pallid louse with two long tendrils located near its head, which it uses to sense and grasp prey. It is usually torpid as it continually undergoes a metamorphosis into a larger body, but on detecting living prey or on being summoned by the men of the tower it rouses itself and proceeds to secure a meal. It is wary of fire and if

intervals are a few depressions in the cleft's sides where stone has been quarried.

BIRDS OF ILL OMEN

A small flock of thirteen ravens roost near the tower and seem to have adapted to the changes Jedakiah's occupation has wrought. The birds all show various physical mutations, such as canine like mouths, or an odd number of eyes, or feet. They are able to find enough carrion to survive on, courtesy of the habitual cruelty of the sorcerer and his retinue. A party approaching the tower from the trail it is badly wounded without taking prey it might decide to retire to its lair. The mark of Chaos is formed on the upper side of its thorax, and it takes other victims in preference to those who bear a similar mark.

The Grey Lurker automatically senses the approach of beings within 100 metres. If a group of man-sized creatures nears the entrance to the lair the creature investigates if it makes an Easy Willpower roll, but requires a Hard Willpower roll if the party are carrying an enchanted Chaos rune medallion.

The Sorcerer's Lair

Bushes and trees within bowshot of the tower have been hacked down or burnt to reduce available cover for any attackers. When stocks of wood run low at the tower, a work party of 1d6+6 slaves and two Blessed One guards are sent to the woodlands further down the mountainside. They are equipped with a hand pulled cart, felling axes, hatchets and cord to accomplish their task.

The Outbuildings

(See the diagram on page 203)

These are primitive constructions that have utilized some of the stone from ruined subsidiary buildings of the stronghold. Roofs are made from a turf covering, supported by frameworks of branches.

Enclosures

Dry-stone walls are used as enclosures for livestock. Three dozen nervous and mangy sheep are kept to provide meat for the tower: fear of the creatures further down the trail keeps them from straying. An open-sided shelter gives some protection from the elements.

The Broch

This large structure has a sunken floor; its walls have iron brackets installed through which sets of chains and manacles can secure slaves. The low doorway is screened by a flap of hide. There is usually a handcart parked near the building.

A 'Blessed One' is usually on watch in the guard closet at night, sharing a watch with another two sleeping on the upper floor. No guards are generally placed outside the tower when darkness falls, as the Grey Lurker is believed to have once taken a watchman. When Jedakiah fears an assault he orders his men to incarcerate all the slaves in the main keep.

Beast Hut

Two Maws, a twin-headed cat-like monstrosity, is chained to a metal staple on the ground floor when it is not used for patrols and hunting forays. The upper level of the structure has a wooden floor some three metres from the ground, reached by a ladder. It is inhabited by the two handlers.

OLD STABLES

This dilapidated stone building has lost the original loft section and roof, although a new roof of turf has been added recently. Some bags of oats are hung up clear of the floor, which is carpeted with dry bracken.

THE SLAVER'S PARTY

On reaching the keep the slaves are inspected in the grounds outside the tower by Jedakiah, who then invites Lortt to the hall where he pays him the agreed sum and questions him on recent events in the outside world. The guards single-out a few slaves for various acts of abuse to intimidate the newcomers. The new slaves are kept bound overnight in the slave pen whilst the slavers are expected to bed down in the old stable block. Lortt or a slaver needs to make a Willpower Test to bother to ensure that a rota for setting a lone guard is maintained overnight. Slavers usually feel the need to drink alcohol to cheer themselves at their vigil, which adds an extra level of difficulty to their Perception tests. If any mules or horses are tethered nearby they are skittish and easily spooked.

The slavers' party leaves a few hours after dawn on the next day, whilst Jedakiah inspects the slaves closely later that morning so he can determine the purpose for each one. Hardy warriors will be considered for being moulded into Beast-Men, but those who earn his enmity are locked in the dungeons to be turned into Screamers when he finds the time. Especially powerful or important individuals may be kept to one side as hostages or potential sacrifices.

Occasionally Jedakiah terrorises newly arrived guests or batches of slaves by picking one out for sacrifice to the Grey Lurker. Victims are tied to a post near the tower and the creature is summoned by blowing rams' horns.

SLAVES

There are usually 2d6+6 slaves present at Distaff Peak, plus any that are brought by slavers or tribesmen. At night 1d6 of these slaves are kept in the tower while the rest are kept in the slave pen. Leaderless, they are too fearful to attempt an escape or revolt. Dynamic leadership from characters making Hard Oratory or Formidable Influence rolls will inspire the down-trodden wretches to attempt to overthrow their oppressors, especially when backed-up by initial successes in defeating their captors.

DARK CHILD'S TOWER

The rebuilt keep and towers present a dilapidated, listing appearance despite Jedakiah having used a greedy architect to help oversee its rebuilding. The dark-stoned masonry is cracked and irregular, its towers twisted out of true symmetry and a shortage of slates has resulted in turf being partially used.

The entrance is via a stone stairway reached by a drawbridge from the first floor of the tower. The underside of the bridge is clad with bronze sheeting and a latticework of bolted iron strips to protect it from assault. The doors beyond are similarly protected, and a large wooden beam is used to bar the gates from the inside. The arrow slits and windows are too small to permit entry, and those in the main building (and the turret rooms used as quarters), have simple wooden shutters that can be secured with a basic drop latch.

During the day, two barbarians guard the main doors of the first floor but the drawbridge is kept lowered: at night the bridge is raised. The garrison takes two-hour watches during the day and four-hour ones at night. A watchman is stationed on each turret and a guard placed at the stairhead outside Jedakiah's personal chamber. If the Lady Bria is a captive, a guard is assigned to protect the door leading to her room with instructions to prevent entry by anyone other than Jedakiah. Currently the garrison is depleted, as various warriors are away on missions gathering tribute. Routine and extra fatigue has sapped the stamina and alertness of the garrison. If no state of alert has been called Jedakiah's men will take an extra level of difficulty on all Perception tests.

The building itself is an unsettling sight. Skewed walls, doors, and uneven floors create a disorientating effect that is made worse by the influence of Chaos that has seeped into the very stones of the tower. Movement seems to occur out of the corner of an individual's vision; shadows flow and ebb, whilst doors and objects seem to have shifted slightly when they are unobserved. The Tower radiates the presence of Chaos to those sensitive to such forces. Strangers to the castle find that Perception rolls are subject to an extra level of difficulty when attempting to scan both its interior and exterior.

THE GROUND FLOOR

(See the diagram on page 206)

Ostensibly the tower's cellars, this level has a stone floor and a stone-vaulted roof containing a hatchway. The rear

THE BLESSED ONES

The warriors of Jedakiah's guard are all marked as favoured members of the Cult of the Chaos Mother with a distinctive rune. The 'Blessed Ones' bear individual physical mutations that have been gifted to them. They are also adorned with scars they have inflicted up themselves during frenzied religious rites. The hulking brute Skalgak is the Captain nominated by Jedakiah to give orders to them. All these barbaric warriors are fanatically loyal to both their Goddess and Jedakiah, and have sworn oaths to protect their lord at the cost of their own lives. If Jedakiah is killed they attempt to avenge him before commiting suicide. Moreover, they are frustrated by their inactivity and eagerly seize the opportunity to engage in hand-to-hand combat. All wear a cattle horn on a baldric round their shoulders when on duty: these can be used to try to summon the Grey Lurker if Jedakiah orders it. If a horn is sounded the monster leaves its lair if it makes a Standard Willpower test; each extra horn sounded makes the level of difficulty one grade easier.

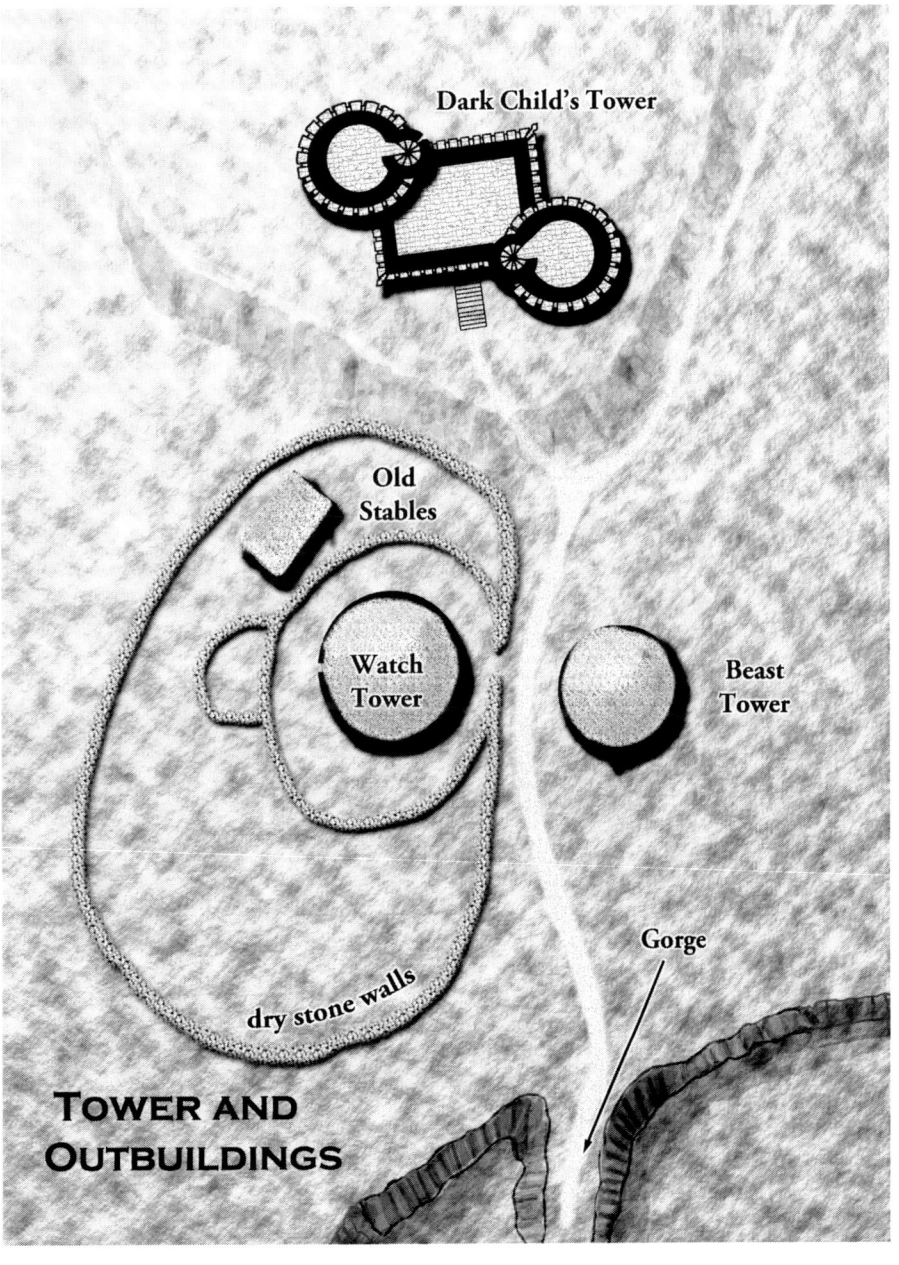

TOWER AND OUTBUILDINGS

turret's stairway leads down to the dungeon and the well chamber.

1A: Contains smoked meat, sacks of oats and root vegetables, jars of weak beer and cheap, imported wine.

1B: Contains small barrels of rusty nails, rotten rope coils and bundles of firewood.

1C: This door has a lock and slaves are often imprisoned in it overnight, or in times of crisis, huddling together for warmth.

1D: This chamber is bare, save for ancient moss covered traces of graffiti that were inspired by nightmare visions that drove one of the tower's original defenders into howling madness. A tinder box, lantern and torches are in an alcove. A set of trap doors are concealed by thin paving slabs cemented to their top sides. Some loose stones lift out to expose a couple of rope loops to pull them open. Underneath is a passage that snakes downwards some thirty metres until it reaches a stairway that spirals-down six metres into the Cavern of Changes.

THE FIRST FLOOR

GUARD ROOM

The main chamber is used as living quarters by Blessed Ones; their pallets and furs are sited against the walls along with bags and boxes of personal effects. The doors have a shuttered grill and spy hole set in them and are barred at night. A trap door is set in the floor; coils of rope, a pallet and a pulley suspended from the ceiling can be used to help load and unload the ground floor cellars.

KITCHEN

Iron, copper and wood utensils are used to prepare food. Bins and baskets are used to keep foodstuffs near to hand.

BRIA'S ROOM

This room is a guest room and has some imported furniture and a small brazier. An expensive collection of female attire and cosmetics (gathered by the sorcerer for The Pure Beauty) are stored in three chests. Thick furs and simple linens cover the bed.

OUTBUILDING PLANS

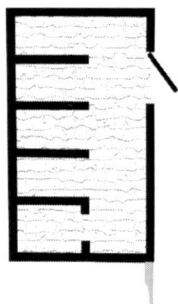

Old Stable Block

Watch Dun - Ground Floor

Watch Dun - Second Floor

Beast Tower - Ground Floor

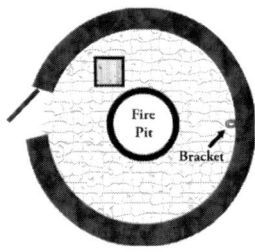

Beast Tower - First Floor

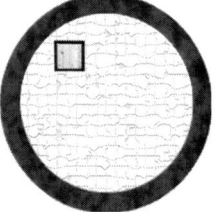

If Bria is present she is locked up here, Jedakiah and the Hooded One having the only keys. The recesses for the shutters in the wall are blocked-off by crudely-cemented stones. No sharp tools or implements can be found in this chamber, nor will any fuel or means of lighting the brazier be to hand. Bria is clad in warm, homespun cloth of Garthari manufacture to make her existence as comfortable as possible in the chill castle. Fisshazz, 'the Hooded One' feeds her an elixir in her meals which prevents her succumbing to illness from the cold.

THE SECOND FLOOR

MAIN HALL

This large stone-flagged hall was used on the rare occasions when Jedakiah needed to impress and entertain groups of chieftains. Benches and trestle tables are piled against the walls and two chests hold cloths, and tableware of pewter, wood and horn. Wooden panels partially divide the hall; all of them are daubed with crude Chaos symbols.

THE HOODED ONE'S CHAMBER

A brazier is kept constantly alight, fuelled by strange, slow burning bricks of alchemically treated peat. A bar can be used to secure the room from the inside. A small, locked box contains a dozen vials. Three copper vials contain a noxious black fluid that quickly turns to vapour when uncorked. If the fumes are inhaled, they confuse the user's perceptions for 3d6 seconds, but will subsequently modify the user's vision so that they perceive the infrared spectrum for 1d3 hours. The remaining nine vials are made of glass; three are empty but six contain a bitter purple fluid which, when ingested, acts as Ophidian venom; if resisted, the imbiber gains the power of Astral Projection (MYTHRAS, page 157) and can astrally travel up to POW x5 in kilometres for a period of minutes equal to his Magic Points.

JEDAKIAH'S STUDY

This room contains a table on which are an abacus and a brass orrery representing the heavenly spheres. Under these contraptions is a pile of astrological charts. Some sheets of vellum, covered with a scrawl of quotations, numbers and diagrams are placed on a lectern. The notes refer to the conditions and materials needed for the Dread Rite and mention that it will be performed in the Cavern of Changes. If a Very Easy Lore (Astrology) roll is made, the date and time required for Jedakiah's Dread Rite can be deduced.

The surrounding shelves hold a wide variety of books and scrolls, some stolen on Jedakiah's orders. These include a series of documents recording all that is known by the civilised world of the Chaos Mother's cult, and a collection of maps detailing The Realm and plans of its major cities. The original architect's drawings of the Gaze of Saylis, as the tower was once called, are amongst the clutter of paperwork. They mark the original chambers and rooms which correspond to those of the current tower, but do not show the Cavern of Changes. Some marginal notes refer to the probability that various tunnels are believed to exist besides the one that contains the water source to be used by the garrison.

The door to the study is kept locked and has a bolt on the inside.

THE THIRD FLOOR

THE CHAPEL

This was once sacred to the war god Sormund and had a small shrine to Sayalis. It has been deliberately profaned and converted to the worship of the Chaos Mother. A hide secured to one wall has been used for a crude painting of the Chaos Mother and her daughter. A large, crude, blood-encrusted table is used as an altar.

Here the influence of Chaos is especially powerful and any strangers attempting Skill rolls will find their chances of making a fumble doubled.

GUEST CHAMBER

This chamber is similar to the one on the first floor, but is unoccupied.

JEDAKIAH'S CHAMBERS

This chamber is usually locked, even when Jedakiah is present. Within are a desk, chairs, a bed and wardrobe.

On the desk is an especially prized possession, the skull of Nestor, Jedakiah's former tutor. Jedakiah can reduce the difficulty of *any* Lore roll he attempts whilst touching the skull if he spends a Magic Point. If anyone, other than Jedakiah, touches the skull their mind is filled with a scream of rage and pain, and images of Jedakiah laughing and gloating. The assailed individual must make a Willpower roll; if this is failed they gain the new Passion Fear (Jedakiah) at 80% - or will increase the passion, if they already have it, by 1d10. If the Willpower roll is made, they might be sufficiently moved and angered by the vestigial soul to *start* a Passion Hate (Jedakiah) or increase it by 1d10.

A large, locked chest holds 1,000 Founders and an assortment of jewellery that might fetch up to 25,000 Founders if sold in a city. Another locked box includes various maps and correspondence related to Jedakiah's schemes of conquest. One book includes a list of ciphers used by agents in the service of various cities (such as Xhago and Gul-Azar). Under a false bottom is Jedakiah's personal grimoire, The Entropic Revelations, a book bound with the skin flayed from his former tutor. It automatically gives a reader who studies it thoroughly the Lore (Chaos) skill or, a 2d6 increase if the skill is already known. However, the bizarre and blasphemous secrets and aspirations revealed unhinge a weak mind, and, if a Hard Willpower roll is failed the reader is driven insane. Those driven to madness by the text suffer disturbing dreams and nightmares and, during their waking hours, succumb to a debilitating paranoia.

A small alcove has been converted into a private shrine for communion with the Chaos Mother and includes an

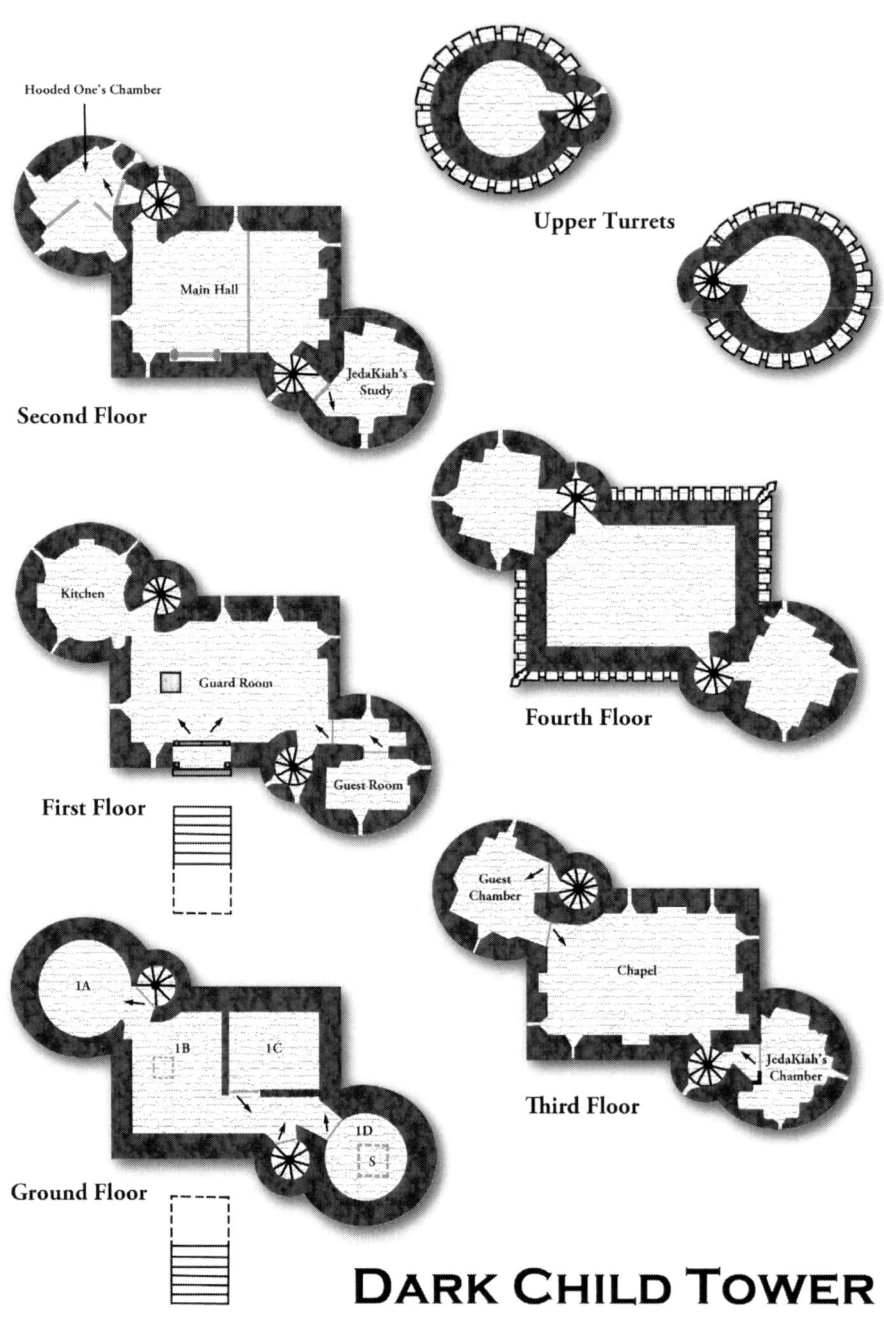

DARK CHILD TOWER

altar for burning incense or sacrificing small animals. It is made from a smoothed boulder of granite in which a depression has been carved.

THE FOURTH FLOOR

The top of the keep has machiolated battlements. A supply of rocks and stones is to hand for the defenders to drop through holes set in the overhang, on anyone attempting to breach or scale the walls. A barrel with a watertight lid contains bundles of fire arrows, and a flint and steel in case they are needed to mark targets, or to incinerate any siege equipment brought against the tower. A large chest holds four grapples and ropes for use against siege equipment and two strong forked sticks are available to use as levers against ladders. A huge, bronze gong and a long mallet are housed at the top of the tower for alerting the garrison. The stair turrets are capped with a small slate roof. Gargoyles at the corner incorporate drainage spouts.

TURRET ROOFS

The battlements are fortified in the same fashion as the roof of the keep. Improvised awnings made from branches and hides offer meagre protection from the elements.

THE DUNGEON

This subterranean level is reached by a stairwell from the rearmost turret. The room is sunk a metre below the entrance's doorway. The iron door set in the cell has a shuttered observation grill, and a small, bolted hatchway. A pair of manacles and chains is fixed to each wall and a stool, a bucket and a filthy, louse-infested mattress is the only furniture. Both of the doors are locked, the Captain of the Blessed Ones carries a set of keys and another is in Jedakiah's possession.

WELL CHAMBER

The stairwell from the dungeon above ends at a door that is usually unlocked. The room contains a few mildewed buckets, although one is in better condition and has a rope attached so it can be used for drawing water. A couple of coils of rope hang on a wall hook; one is knotted and is intended for use if anyone needs to inspect the well. A few tattered and grubby animal pelts are in one corner, as the guards sometimes take a slave down into this room so they can indulge their lust in some privacy. A wooden cover capped with bronze on the underside is used to protect the well. Two iron bolts are used to secure it with iron brackets, driven into the flooring. An iron ring in the centre of

---

THE ONE WHO HAS PURE BEAUTY

Bria is a stunningly beautiful young woman with brilliant blue eyes and hair of a pale, golden hue. Normally she has a kind and frank expression, though currently she is scared and haggard. Despite having passed through the hands of an assortment of Batrachians and barbarians she has managed to keep a firm hold on her sanity. She is helped in her resolve by a simple, but deep, faith in the Gods of her homeland. She is, however, deeply terrified of Jedakiah and senses that he has a horrible fate planned for her that involves more than making her a wife or a slave. She responds well to firm advice and leadership from characters who attempt to rescue her, and can offer a certain degree of help and insight into the sorcerer and his minions.

THE HOODED ONE

This cold hearted schemer is called Fisshazz, a centuries-old Ophidian scholar and devotee of the Chaos Mother. He is assigned to assist Jedakiah with his schemes but also to keep a close eye on his activities. The Ophidians believe that Jedakiah's plans will be of benefit to their own, revered, aspect of the Goddess of Chaos. They are convinced that their centuries long patience will finally witness mankind tear apart its civilisations and power when a new cycle of Chaos returns to the world, and the Ophidians will flourish again, using the survivors of mankind's wars as slaves and cattle.

Unless in secure privacy, Fisshazz always wears a voluminous, hooded robe which hides his tail, hands and head from observers. He tries to ensure that the hidden hand of his folk is not discovered. Jedakiah is an important tool but the Ophidian will prize his own life more highly. He is determined not to be captured alive and will try to flee into the cavern system to avoid this or, if cornered, he attempts to use his dagger on himself. He makes reports to some of the leaders of the subterranean city of his race by projecting his astral form. He has explored all the caverns under the tower in this form and is aware of the existence of the giant axolotl but has chosen to keep the existence of the creature to himself.

the cover's upper surface can be used to help lift it clear of the well opening.

The trap door has a resistance to being forced of 100%, although the verdigris-stained cladding of the trap door's underside can be cut using metal tools. If the bolts can be somehow slid free or cut, the Brawn roll of someone trying to open the trapdoor from below becomes Easy.

A chance to enter the well room occurs during the odd intervals of the day when the trap door is unbolted. A couple of slaves enter the room to draw water accompanied by a bored guard, who may elect to just stay at the head of the stairs.

The Cavern of Changes

This underground chamber is lit by torches and has various niches holding clay lamps. From the centre of the cavern floor grows a seven metre long, tangled and leprous root known as 'The Dream Root', from which lurid pustules of fruit and fungi sprout. A listless slave is wrapped in the coils of the plant, its vines and tendrils penetrating his eyes and orifices. A couple of slaves tend the quivering limb, tapping a vile milky fluid which is collected in bronze bowls. The viscous sap is poured into human-sized basins carved into the rocky floor, and are surrounded with etched runes covered with sigils of blood. Within all these vats, bar one, are blasphemous hybrids, curled into a foetal position as they gestate within the noxious, visceral fluid. These creations are currently helpless, though if the Games Master needs to pose a new threat to the characters, the hybrids can be at the point of maturity and emerge to do the bidding of their creator. The empty pool is deeper than the others and has a three metre-high wooden pillar sunk into the nearby ground. This is covered with crude carvings and painted with strange runes; it has a couple of iron rings for helping to secure a captive by the feet and upraised arms.

If the Chaos Mother's Chalice has been brought to Jedakiah's stronghold it will be placed in one of the rough-hewn niches in the cavern wall. A wooden crate, with its lid leaning against it, is on the floor near the niche. Inside, packed with straw, are half a dozen clay bottles. These contain cloying sap from the Root of Chaos intended for use in rituals to place the mark of Chaos on cultists. Other boxes scattered around the edges of the cavern contain tallow candles, and spare torches, rush wicks and flasks of oil.

Jedakiah

He wears his long, raven-black hair and beard in twisted locks. He is a long way along the ambitious path he has mapped out for himself and his dark and penetrating eyes normally gleam with the unsettling gaze of a maniac. He can choose to hide his insane demeanour, although this requires an opposed roll of his Deceit roll against another individual's Insight. He is capable of appearing calm and can speak persuasively with a cultured accent, but generally prefers to order his minions in a curt and intimidating manner. He habitually wears dark robes and an assortment of rings and talismans made from precious metals. He also carries a set of keys to various doors and chests in a leather purse that hangs from his belt.

Jedakiah has the idiosyncrasy of gloating to the skull of his old mentor, although the soul was torn from the shell of his tortured body and bartered to a foul being a decade or more ago.

Jedakiah's Tactics

If alerted to potential danger Jedakiah directs his forces to investigate and deal with any threats located, but he keeps at least two bodyguards close at hand. If he is warned that enemies are moving against him, and he is not facing immediate assault, he will he prepare to cast Consecrate on the tower.

Should a threat seem powerful enough to prevail against his forces, Jedakiah attempts to complete The Dread Rite as soon as possible, ordering Bria to be taken to the Cavern of Changes, and requiring the attendance of at least three guards and the Hooded One.

In the face of an especially dangerous threat from forces outside the tower, he orders the summoning of the Grey Lurker; he can also use his powers of mutating flesh and bone to release the Screamers. If he finds himself in harm's way from physical violence, he casts Damage Resistance on himself. Study the magic provided in Jedakiah's statistics on page 220. He has multiple ways of defending himself and attacking others, and is clever enough to always have both offensive and defensive magic prepared for immediate casting.

If all looks to be lost, Jedakiah attempts to escape using the Distaff Peak tunnels, but this is a last-resort: his is too near the creation of the Chaos Daughter to consider fleeing - and, if he is successful, he will become far too powerful for any mortal foe to vanquish.

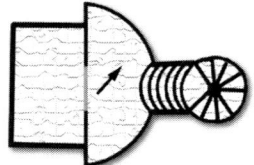
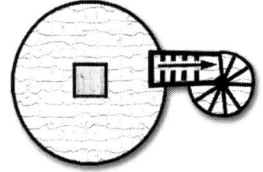

The Dungeon   **Well Chamber**

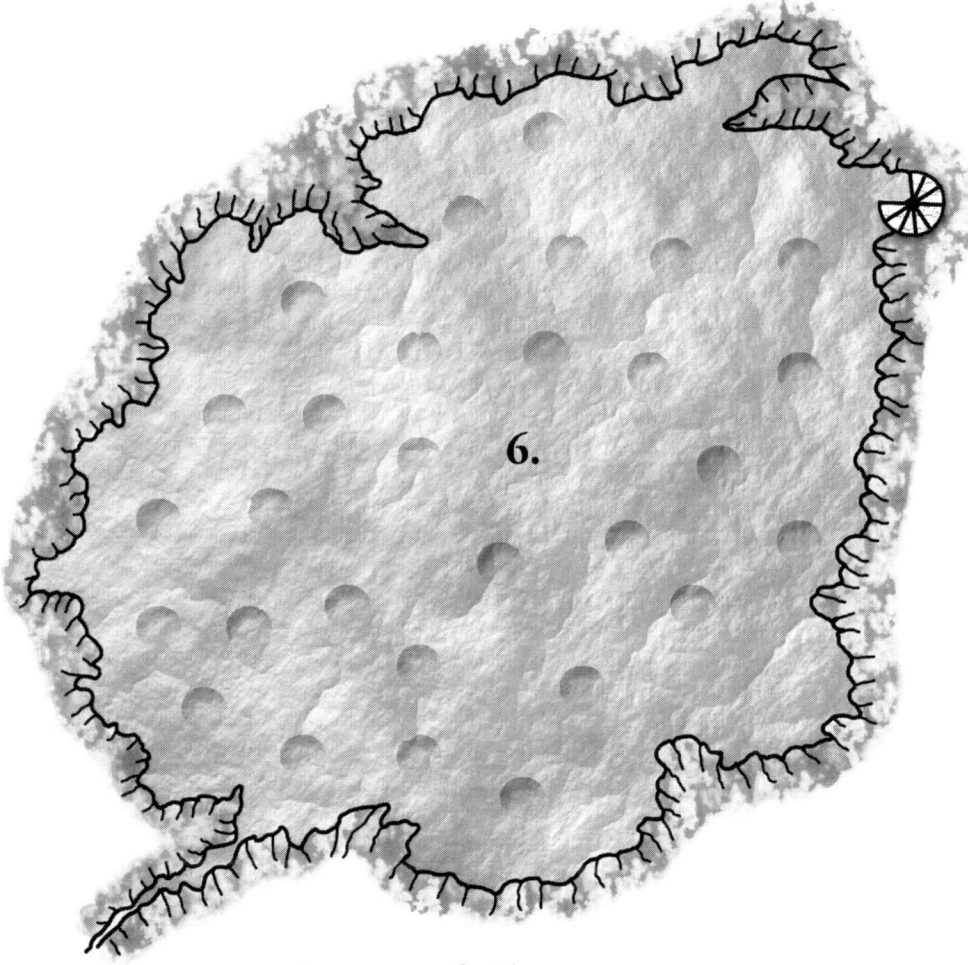

6.

Cavern of Changes

THE DREAD RITE

Although defeated centuries ago by the Founding Four, the power of the Chaos Mother still lingers, albeit in a vastly weakened form. Her perception and power in The Realm have been strengthened in recent decades, with the re-founding of a Chaos Cult based around the resurgent remnant of the Chaos Tree. Now, via her new disciple, Jedakiah, she senses an opportunity for rebirth.

Through the sacrifice of the One Who has Pure Beauty in a Dread Rite, the mortal's purity and innocence can be melded with the Chaos Mother's soul. The result will be the 'birth' of the Chaos Daughter, a new, powerful, god-like being. Jedakiah and the Chaos Daughter must be spiritually bound; the ritual, when complete, uplifting Jedakiah into the avatar of the new Chaos Father. He and his Daughter find that their power now transcends even that of the Chaos Mother when she was at the height of her influence.

The two deities vacate the world and a new reign of chaotic terror is brought upon The Realm.

To conduct the ceremony Jedakiah has Bria, or an acceptable substitute, taken to the Cavern of Changes, her hands bound behind her back. He is accompanied by three of the Blessed Ones and the slaves are sent to their quarters. Jedakiah has the sacrificial victim tied to the pillar in the chamber. He then starts his ritual by attempting to call forth the miracle Awaken (Chaos Avatar) which needs a Very Easy Exhort (Chaos Mother) roll. If his pleas are successful he then needs to have the victim anointed with the milk taken from the Chaos Chalice. The chalice will ideally be filled and carried by Fisshazz, though another individual can be delegated to this task. Whilst chanting a certain passage from the Entropic Revelations, Jedakiah slits his sacrifice's throat. After cutting her bons, he has her body thrown into the pool of chaos sap in front of the pillar. Jedakiah then needs to make a Very Easy roll of his Entropic Revelations skill; however the following circumstances each impose two levels of difficulty to the roll:

- Using a different innocent and fair maiden other than Bria.
- The sacrifice not being sufficiently 'pure'.
- Not using the milk taken from the Chaos Mother's Chalics
- Not using the Chalice (butt some other vessel).

If the roll is made, the body undergoes a transformation into a tall, powerful, female with multiple arms and breasts. This process takes 1d3+1 rounds, during which time characters may decide to flee, or else try to effect the slaying of Jedakiah. The Chaos Daughter, once created, will be immune from any power or attack a character can make. If irritated, assume she can make a physical counter-attack against an individual at 150% inflicting 1d6+1d12 damage.

Once the Chaos Daughter is fully-formed Jedakiah implores with her to grant him godhood which requires a Very Easy Devotion roll. If this is successful the Daughter of Chaos anoints him with the milk from her own breast: Then, Jedakiah must make a final Devotion roll. If this final Devotion roll is failed, Jedakiah is transformed into a raving creature identical to the Screamers he has himself created. The new goddess's screams drown out the cries of the monstrosity and she appears to grow larger before vanishing in triumph to start her new reign.

If Jedakiah's final Devotion roll is successful he starts to transform, transforming into a tall, cruel-featured being whose head sprouts long, twisting horns. He flashes a look of malice at those who tried to thwart him, and embraces his new bride. The pair take-on a colossal size, laughing wildly as they disappear, leaving behind the mortal world. With their vanishing, the Root of Chaos immediately wilts, dying as its energies are sapped. Rocked by the cosmic energies unleashed, Dark Child's Tower's foundations shake, rocks start to fall from the roofs of the caverns and the structure above totters as it starts to collapse.

The disturbance imposes a level of difficulty on any action, and doubles the chance of a fumble. After 3d6 minutes the whole tower collapses - as do the other structures in its vicinity. Those still trapped within the tower or its cellars take 6d6 damage to 1d3 locations, and those in the other buildings 4d6 to a single location. Individuals within 15 metres of the collapsing tower take 4d6 damage to a single location unless an Evade roll is made. The surviving Blessed Ones who have witnessed the apotheosis enter a state of Frenzy, slaughtering anyone not of their brotherhood. Other visitors and inhabitants are dazed or try to flee the site in panic. The Screamers find themselves freed and scuttle towards the ruins looking for men to slaughter; to make matters worse, the Grey Lurker will bestir itself looking for prey.

Conclusion

If either Jedakiah or the Chaos Daughter achieves a dark apotheosis into a being of divine power, then war and disasters rage across The Realm. The Games Master might choose to continue the campaign as all the Gods of The Realm are drawn into the cataclysmic conflict. Perhaps the characters are granted a chance to become avatars of The Four and are able to directly attack the new Gods of Chaos?

Should Jedakiah and his chief lieutenants be slain or captured the threat to The Realm is removed and the characters become renowned heroes. Perhaps one of them becomes romantically attached with Bria? Further activity might involve ferreting out traitors to The Realm who conspired with Jedakiah. The tribes of Gartharis fall back into their old pattern of raiding and squabbling with each other now that the guiding hand of an arch-manipulator is gone. If Jedakiah manages to escape at some point, it is up to the Games Master if he vanishes into obscurity or is able to successfully relocate and establish another base of power to further his insane schemes; which now include taking revenge against those who have thwarted him. Even being cornered and killed in his lair might not be the end of his cursed existence. The fickle Goddess he worships might yet have the power and inclination to see him resurrected in some fashion to plague The Realm once more.

Non-Player Characters

Gartharis Barbarian

A typical barbarian tribesman armed for battle. Their long hair and beards are braided and clothing is of dull coloured wool in striped or checked patterns, though successful raiders wear more colourful apparel. Piercings, tattoos and scarification are popular amongst warriors, some of whom also sport trophies such as scalps and ears from foes they have slain. If they are outclassed by superior tactics, or terrified by sorcery, they can be treated as Underlings with 5 Hit Points. Chieftains, however, use the Blessed One statistics given on page 214 but have no Chaos gifts.

Attributes	1d20	Location	AP/HP
Action Points: 2	1–3	Right Leg	1/6
Damage Modifier: +1d2	4–6	Left Leg	1/6
Magic Points: 11	7–9	Abdomen	2/7
Movement: 6 metres	10–12	Chest	2/8
Initiative Bonus: 10	13–15	Right Arm	1/5
Armour: Soft Leather Greaves and Sleeves, Padded Hauberk, Padded Leather Helm	16–18	Left Arm	1/5
Abilities: None	19–20	Head	2/6
Magic: None			

Skills: *Athletics 50%, Brawn 60%, Endurance 65%, Evade 50%, Locale 70%, Perception 55%, Stealth 50%, Survival 65%, Track 55%, Unarmed 50%, Willpower 35%*

Passions: *Fear (Jedakiah) 80%, Loyalty (Clan Chieftain) 70%., Loyalty (Jedakiah) 50%*

Combat Style: *Gartharis Warrior (Spear, Axe, Shield) 60%*

Weapon	Size/Force	Reach	Damage	AP/HP
Shortspear	M	L	1d8+1+1d2	4/5
Battle Axe	M	M	1d6+1+1d2	4/8
Target Shield	L	S	1d3+1+1d2	4/9

Gartharis Scout

These are typically adolescents with downy beards and are not allowed braids. They wear their hair in a pony tail. If used as Rabble they have 4 Hit Points.

Attributes	1d20	Location	AP/HP
Action Points: 3	1–3	Right Leg	-/5
Damage Modifier: +0	4–6	Left Leg	-/5
Magic Points: 9	7–9	Abdomen	-/6
Movement: 6 metres	10–12	Chest	-/7
Initiative Bonus: 13	13–15	Right Arm	-/4
Armour: None	16–18	Left Arm	-/4
Abilities: None	19–20	Head	-/5
Magic: None			

Skills: *Athletics 50%, Brawn 30%, Endurance 55%, Evade 60%, Locale 50%, Perception 60%, Stealth 60%, Survival 60%, Track 55%, Unarmed 40%, Willpower 25%*

Passions: *Fear (Jedakiah) 80%, Loyalty (Clan Chieftain) 60%*

Combat Style: *Gartharis Scout (Sling,) 70%, Gartharis Warrior (Spear, Axe, Shield) 40%*

Weapon	Size/Force	Reach	Damage	AP/HP
Dirk	S	S	1d3+2	6/6
Buckler	M	S	1d3	6/8
Sling	L	-	1d8	1/2
Shortspear	M	L	1d8+1	4/5
Battle Axe	M	M	1d6+1	4/8

RAVENS

The ravens of Gartharis are jet black, tenacious, and agile.

Attributes	1d20	Location	AP/HP
Action Points: 3	1–5	Right Wing	–/2
Damage Modifier: -1d8	6-10	Left Wing	–/2
Magic Points: 7	11-16	Body	–/4
Movement: 8m	17-20	Head	–/3
Initiative Bonus: 10			
Armour: None			
Abilities: Flying			
Magic: None			

Skills: *Athletics 75%, Endurance %, Evade 70%, Perception 75%, Survival 66%, Willpower 30%*

Passions: *Love Carrion 80%*

Combat Style: *Opportunistic Mobbing (Beak and Claw) 35%*

Weapon	Size/Force	Reach	Damage	AP/HP
Beak	S	T	1d3-1d8	As for Head
Claw	S	T	1d4-1d8	1/2

SCREAMERS

These wretched creations are immune to fatigue, disease and poisons. Their raging hatred makes them virtually mindless and any attempts to control their mind or influence their personality is at the Herculean difficulty grade.

If they are freed by any means they can drag and scuttle themselves along at speed of 1d3 metres a round.

Attributes	1d20	Location	AP/HP
Action Points: 1d3+1 per round	1–20	Body Mass	2/10
Damage Modifier: +1d4			
Magic Points: 1			
Movement: See Opposite			
Initiative Bonus: 10			
Armour: Bone, Rubbery Flesh			
Abilities: Chaos Tainted, Frenzy, Intimidate, Night Sight			
Magic: None			

Skills: *Athletics 25%, Brawn 31%, Endurance 32%, Evade 20%, Perception 45%, Survival 99%, Willpower 26%*

Passions: *Hate and Loathing of All Unmutated Things 120%*

Combat Style: *Insane gnashing and flailing 60%*

Weapon	Size/Force	Reach	Damage	AP/HP
Fangs	M	T	1d6+1d4	As for Body
Claw	M	L	1d6+1d4	As for Body

The Grey Lurker

The Grey Lurker possesses the Vampiric ability: After an opponent is bitten and wounded the creature automatically drains 1d8 points of CON per Combat Round. The creature can drain 80 points of CON before it is sated.

The Grey Lurker's tentacles are used to Grapple victims and draw them to the creature's maw.

Attributes	1d20	Location	AP/HP
Action Points: 2	1	Right Rear Leg	6/10
Damage Modifier: +2d6	2	Left Rear Leg	6/10
Magic Points: 8	3	Right Middle Leg	6/10
Movement: 6 metres	4	Left Middle Leg	6/10
Initiative Bonus: 9	5-11	Abdomen	6/20
Armour: Chitin exoskeleton, no Armour Penalty.	12-14	Thorax	6/12
Abilities: Chaos Features, Luminous, Night Sight, Wall Walking, Vampiric	15	Right Front Leg	6/10
	16	Left Front Leg	6/10
	17	Right Tentacle	6/9
	18	Left Tentacle	6/9
	19-20	Head	6/10

Skills: *Athletics 35%, Brawn 70%, Endurance 100%, Evade 18%, Perception 25%, WillPower 40%*

Passions: *Crave Vitality 95%*

Combat Style: *Grasp and Suck (Tentacles and Bite) 50%*

Weapon	Size/Force	Reach	Damage	AP/HP
Bite	S	T	1d3+2d6	As for Head
Tentacle	L	VL	1d4+2d6	As for Tentacle

Blessed One Guards

Chosen Garthari, granted Chaos Gifts through their loyalty to the Chaos Mother.

See the Blessed One Chaos Gifts box nearby for details on the gifts possessed by each guard.

Attributes	1d20	Location	AP/HP
Action Points: 2	1–3	Right Leg	2/7
Damage Modifier: +1d4	4–6	Left Leg	2/7
Magic Points: 11	7–9	Abdomen	6/8
Movement: 6 metres	10–12	Chest	6/9
Initiative Bonus: 6	13–15	Right Arm	6/6
Armour: Scalemail and Leather	16–18	Left Arm	6/6
Abilities: Chaos Tainted	19–20	Head	4/7

Magic: None

Skills: *Athletics 60%, Brawn 70%, Endurance 75%, Evade 50%, Locale 70%, Perception 55%, Stealth 35%, Survival 60%, Track 35%, Unarmed 65%, Willpower 50%*

Passions: *Loyalty (Jedakiah) 90%, Loyalty (Clan Chieftain) 60%*

Combat Style: *Gartharis Sworn Warrior (Spear, Sword, Shield) 80% Bow 45%*

Weapon	Size/Force	Reach	Damage	AP/HP
Falchion	M	M	1d6+2+1d4	6/10
Short Bow	L	-	1d6+1d4	4/4
Target Shield	L	S	1d3+1+1d4	4/9

Blessed One Chaos Gifts

- Warrior #1: Armoured. Has a tough, shark-like hide that gives +3 Armour Points.
- Warrior #2: Arms. Has an extra arm which can wield a bonus weapon. (Extra falchion)
- Warrior #3 (Captain Skalgak): Big, Siz 24; and increases Damage Bonus to +1d6 and Adds +2 Hit Points to each location.
- Warrior #4: Horned. A large horn projects from the warrior's forehead. It does 1d8 damage.
- Warrior #5: Nerveless. The warrior is covered with the scars of blades and burns. Cannot feel pain and does not suffer ill-effects of serious wounds.
- Warrior #6: Oversized Chest: The warrior's huge chest has 18 hit points.
- Warrior #7: Shaggy. A thick, hairy pelt provides + 2 Armour Points.
- Warrior #8: Strong. Is Strength 24 and increases Damage bonus to +1d6.
- Warrior #9: Toothed. Warrior has a dog like set of jaws that can bite for 1d8 damage.
- Warrior #10: Tough. Warrior is wiry and has 25 Con and adds +2 Hit Points to each location.
- Warrior #11: Ugly. The warrior has a misshapen and intimidating face (has the Intimidate Abilty, MYTHRAS, page 216).
- Warrior #12: Warped. The warrior has a crab-like claw instead of a shield arm. The limb has 8pts Armour Points and can use Sunder and all unarmed Combat Manoeuvres.

The warriors prefer hand-to-hand combat though they have been persuaded to take up the bow, normally a mere hunting weapon, as part of their arsenal. Defenders on duty generally carry either a shield or a bow and quiver, though if an alarm is sounded they ensure that they equip themselves with both these weapons.

Blessed One Handler Chaos Gifts

- Handler #1: Leaper. Handler has powerful but oddly joined legs that add two levels of ease to any Athletics tests attempted when jumping.
- Handler #2: Observant: Has large, avian like eyes that add two levels of ease to visual Perception tests.

Blessed One Handlers

The Blessed One Handlers are responsible for Two Maws, but, like the Blessed One Guards, also enjoy Chaos Gifts.

New Weapon – Whip

SIZ: Small
Reach: Very Long
Damage: 1d2
AP/HP: 1/3

Special Effects: Entangle, Grip, Stun Location and Take Weapon.

Grip and Take Weapon are usually Unarmed effects, but a skilled whip-user can wrap the cord around an item and then yank it clear.

Each 'cat whip' The handlers use contains a fine strip of hide that has been taken from Two Maws and plaited amongst the other thongs; and a rune is inscribed in the grip. Each whip adds two levels of ease to the wielder's Beast Handling skill when trying to control or intimidate Two Maws.

Attributes	1d20	Location	AP/HP
Action Points: 2	1–3	Right Leg	1/7
Damage Modifier: +1d4	4–6	Left Leg	1/7
Magic Points: 11	7–9	Abdomen	1/8
Movement: 6 metres	10–12	Chest	1/9
Initiative Bonus: 10	13–15	Right Arm	1/6
Armour: Leather and Padding	16–18	Left Arm	1/6
Abilities: Chaos Tainted	19–20	Head	2/7
Magic: None			

Skills: *Athletics 60%, Beast Handling 75%, Brawn 70%, Endurance 75%, Evade 75%, Locale 70%, Perception 55%, Stealth 60%, Survival 65%, Track 65%, Unarmed 60%, Willpower 50%*

Passions: *Loyalty (Jedakiah) 88%, Cruelty 85%*

Combat Style: *Beast Handler Weapons (Falchion, Torch, Whip) 70%*

The torch can be used by a handler in his off-hand without penalty

Weapon	Size/Force	Reach	Damage	AP/HP
Falchion	M	M	1d6+2+1d4	6/10
Torch	M	M	1d4 (Fire)	4/4
Whip	S	VL	1d2+1d4	1/3

Two Maws

This bizarre beast is similar to a large feline the size of a barbarian's pony. It has two heads that are strangely gaunt and somehow suggest a man's face - albeit with slanting, pale yellow eyes that lack pupils. A cruel ridge of spines runs along its back and down its lashing tails, the tips of which have a cluster of hard spikes. The beast has the mark of chaos on both its foreheads whilst an assortment of wheals, burns and brand marks mar its entire hide. The creature has a hatred for its handlers and would turn on them if they were ever helpless or careless enough let their guard down.

The creature attempts to knock an opponent to the ground and then use Choose Location to attack the victim's head and throat with one of its jaws. It uses its tail against foes who try to flank it, its twin heads giving it uncanny peripheral vision. Two Maws remains alive and conscious as long as a single head is conscious.

Attributes	1d20	Location	AP/HP
Action Points: 4	1	Right Hand Tail	4/8
Damage Modifier: +2d6	2	Left Hand Tail	4/8
Magic Points: 9	3-4	Right Hind Leg	3/11
Movement: 10 metres	5-6	Left Hind Leg	3/11
Initiative Bonus: 14	7-9	Hindquarters	4/12
Armour: Fur and Scales	10-12	Forequarters	4/13
Abilities: Multiheaded	13-14	Right Front Leg	3/11
Magic: None	15-16	Left Front Leg	3/11
	17-18	Right Head	3/11
	19-20	Left Head	3/11

Skills: *Athletics 70%, Brawn 68%, Endurance 60%, Evade 40%, Perception 60%, Survival 70%, Track 65%, Willpower 50%*

Passions: *Fear (Cat Whip) 75%, Fear (Fire and Whips) 55%, Fear (Jedakiah) 66%, Hate (Handlers) 75%*

Combat Style: *Red in Tooth and Claw (Jaws, Claws and Tail Bash) 65%*

Weapon	Size/Force	Reach	Damage	AP/HP
Jaws	M	T	1d8+2d6	As for Head
Claws	M	M	1d10+2d6	As for Leg
Tail	M	L	1d8+2d6	As for Tail

Giant Salamander

A hideous, sickly-white, salamander-like monstrosity with a voracious appetite.

Attributes	1d20	Location	AP/HP
Action Points: 3	1-3	Tail	3/11
Damage Modifier: +2d6	4-5	Right Hind Leg	3/11
Magic Points: 7	6-7	Left Hind Leg	3/11
Movement: 6 metres	8-10	Hindquarters	3/12
Initiative Bonus: 13	11-14	Forequarters	3/13
Armour: Thick Hide	15-16	Right Front Leg	3/11
Abilities: Cold Blooded, Regenerate	17-18	Left Front Leg	3/11
Magic: None	19-20	Head	3/12

Skills: *Athletics 47%, Brawn 99%, Endurance 78%, Evade 32%, Perception 49%, Swim 80%, Willpower 44%*

Passions: *Love Live Food 100%*

Combat Style: *Lurking Death (Jaws, Tail Sweep) 67%*

Weapon	Size/Force	Reach	Damage	AP/HP
Jaws	H	M	1d10+2d6	As for Head
Tail	H	L	1d8+2d6	As for Tail

SLAVERS AND SLAVES

The Slavers are used to fighting with the odds in their favour. The Games Master might decide that Lortt's lackeys count as Underlings with 5 Hit Points.

The Slaves can be used for the poor wretches encountered in the locality of the tower or as a captive of the slavers. Used as Rabble they have 4 Hit Points.

Slavers

Attributes	1d20	Location	AP/HP
Action Points: 3	1–3	Right Leg	1/6
Damage Modifier: +1d2	4–6	Left Leg	1/6
Magic Points: 12	7–9	Abdomen	1/7
Movement: 6 metres	10-12	Chest	2/8
Initiative Bonus: 11	13–15	Right Arm	1/5
Armour: Leathers	16–18	Left Arm	1/5
Abilities: None	19–20	Head	2/6

Magic: None

Skills: *Athletics 45%, Brawn 50%, Drive 40%, Endurance 55%, Evade 35%, First Aid 40%, Locale (Native land) 60%, Perception 55%, Ride 45%, Track 40%, Unarmed 55%, Willpower 36%*

Passions: *Greed 75%, Sadistic 70%*

Combat Style: *Slavers (Club, Net, Whip) 60%, Knife Fighting (Knives and Dirks) 55%*

Weapon	Size/Force	Reach	Damage	AP/HP
Club	M	L	1d6+1d2	4/4
Dirk	S	S	1d3+1d2	6/6
Whip	S	VL	1d2+1d4	1/3
Net	S	L	1d4+1d2	2/20

Slaves

Attributes	1d20	Location	AP/HP
Action Points: 2	1–3	Right Leg	-/4
Damage Modifier: -1d2	4–6	Left Leg	-/4
Magic Points: 9	7–9	Abdomen	-/5
Movement: 6 metres	10-12	Chest	-/6
Initiative Bonus: 10	13–15	Right Arm	-/3
Armour: None	16–18	Left Arm	-/3
Abilities: None	19–20	Head	-/4

Magic: None

Skills: *Athletics 28%, Brawn 25%, Endurance 28%, Evade 35%, Locale (Native homeland) 40%, Perception 38%, Survival 28%, Unarmed 25%, Willpower 25%*

Passions: *Hate Slavers 100%, Fear Jedakiah 110%*

Combat Style: *Desperate Improvisation (Club, Knife) 25%*

Weapon	Size/Force	Reach	Damage	AP/HP
Club	M	L	1d6-1d2	4/4
Knife	S	S	1d3-1d2	6/6

THE ROOT OF DREAMS

Although immobile, the Root can attack and defend itself. After an opponent is grappled and Entangled, the root automatically drains 1d8 points of POW in each succeeding round if it wins an opposed Willpower test.

Anyone witnessing the root must make a Willpower roll when they next sleep. If this is failed, dreams of disturbing - yet alluring - Chaos haunt the sleeping hours until they are somehow exorcised. Those who have been taken to 0 POW automatically fall into a delirious slumber of insanity which they cannot be woken from without powerful magic or the intervention of a divine being.

Attributes	1d20	Location	AP/HP
Action Points: 2	1–8	Stem	4/13
Damage Modifier: +1d10	9-11	Tendril #1	3/10
Magic Points: 28	12-14	Tendril #2	3/10
Movement: 0	15-17	Tendril #3	3/10
Initiative Bonus: 10	18-20	Tendril #4	3/10

Armour: Rubbery Flesh

Abilities: Chaos Tainted, Frenzy, Susceptibility (Fire), The Dark Kiss

Magic: None

Skills: *Athletics 35%, Brawn 80%, Endurance 65%, Evade 20%, Perception 25%, Willpower 74%*

Passions: *Lust for POW 100%*

Combat Style: *Grasp (Tendril) 55%*

Weapon	Size/Force	Reach	Damage	AP/HP
Tendril	M	L	1d6+1d10	As for Tendril

THE HOODED ONE – OPHIDIAN EMISSARY AND ACOLYTE OF THE SERPENT GODDESS

The Hooded One is a shadowy emissary from the Ophidians, an acolyte of the Chaos Mother cult and an adviser to Jedakiah, providing insights into the Ophidian's work and plans (where it suits them). The Hooded One is suspicious of the sorcerer - more from the point of view of what Jedakiah will become if he transcends into the Chaos Husband than anything else - but is still happy to advise him, carefully noting the outcomes to feed back to his own masters.

Characteristics	Attributes	1d20	Location	AP/HP
STR: 11	Action Points 3	1-3	Tail	1/6
CON: 13	Damage Modifier 0	4-5	Right Hind Leg	1/6
SIZ: 13	Magic Points 16	6-7	Left Hind Leg	1/6
DEX: 15	Movement 6m	8-10	Hindquarters	1/7
INT: 16	Initiative Bonus 16	11-14	Forequarters	1/8
POW: 16	Armour Scales	15-16	Right Front Leg	1/5
CHA: 8	Abilities	17-18	Left Front Leg	1/5
	Cold Blooded, Night Sight, Poison	19-20	Head	1/6

Skills: *Athletics 56%, Brawn 56%, Conceal 70%, Deceit 85%, Earth Sense 88%*, Endurance 66%, Evade 60%, Heart Slow 85%*, Immunity (Poison) 55%*, Influence 75%, Insight 75%, Language (Common Tongue) 80%, Lore (Alchemy) 65%, Lore (Ophidian History) 70%, Perception 75%, Squeeze 80%*, Stealth 90%, Swim 64%, Teach 50%, Unarmed 56%, Willpower 80%*
*Skill has similar effects as Mystic abilities

Passions: *Loyalty (Nest) 90%, Suspicious (Jedakiah) 60%*

Magic

Theism: *Exhort (Serpent Goddess) 65%, Devotion (Serpent Goddess) 85%*
Consecrate, Corruption, Fear, Rejuvenate (self)
Devotional Pool = 8

Combat Style: *Unseen Blade (Dagger) 45%*

Weapon	Size/Force	Reach	Damage	AP/HP
Bite	M	M	1d6	As for Head
Claw	M	T	1d4	As for Arm
Tail	M	L	1d4	As for Tail
Dagger	S	S	1d4+1	6/8

Bria, the Pure Beauty

Traded by the Batrachians (see *Beneath the Black Water*), Bria is Lord Drystan's daughter. She has precise idea what Jedakiah has planned for her, but his leering, sardonic smiles and occasional hints at 'Something great... something powerful' have the poor girl terrified. Despite her terror, Bria is no swooning damsel. Given the opportunity she is feisty and headstrong, capable of looking after herself and providing help as, and when, needed. She has been watching Jedakiah and his minions, noting what they do and how they act. She can offer advice and information to the characters if necessary.

If the Dread Rite is accomplished though, Bria ceases to exist, becoming the Chaos Daughter - a being of fierce and terrible power utterly loyal to her 'new' mother and sorcerous husband. She will, in fact, become more powerful than Jedakiah - although the sorcerer believes he, as the male, will always command the upper hand.

Characteristics	Attributes	1d20	Location	AP/HP
STR: 9	Action Points	3	1–3	Right Leg	0/5
CON: 12	Damage Modifier	-1d2	4–6	Left Leg	0/5
SIZ: 9	Magic Points	15	7–9	Abdomen	0/6
DEX: 15	Movement	6m	10-12	Chest	0/7
INT: 14	Initiative Bonus	15	13–15	Right Arm	0/4
POW: 15	Armour	None	16–18	Left Arm	0/4
CHA: 19	Abilities	None	19–20	Head	0/5
	Magic	None			

Skills: Athletics 34%, Brawn 18%, Courtesy 59%, Craft (Needlework) 50%, Dance 75%, Devotion (Aliya) 34%, Endurance 39%, Evade 40%, Influence 72%, Insight 55%, Locale ( ) 75%, Perception 42%, Sing 66%, Stealth 35%, Unarmed 24%, Willpower 58%

Passions: Fear (Jedakiah) 44%. Love (Family) 80%, Loyalty (Father) 70%

Combat Style: Defend Virtue (Dagger) 29%

Weapon	Size/Force	Reach	Damage	AP/HP
Dagger	S	S	1d4+1-1d2	6/8

Jedakiah

The archetypal mad and evil sorcerer, Jedakiah is a physically imposing man: strong, fit and fiendishly clever. He is tall with long, raven hair hair habitually tied back at the nape of his neck. He has a full beard, streaked with grey now, that is shaped into a double-pronged fork hanging at his chin. Sometimes he winds silver rings into the beard; sometimes knuckle bones, depending on his whim. His eyebrows are arched, heavy and thick. His eyes are piercing and he always has a fierce, wicked expression. He wears thick robes of black, silver and amber, covered in arcane symbols and runes. The Chaos, Mastery and Motion runes are prominent on his clothes.

His manner is always sardonic and condescending: his intellect is highly developed and he considers most to be his intellectual inferior. The one exception is his attitude towards the Ophidians, which he knows have highly developed intellectual capabilities - something he respects. It goes without saying that Jedakiah is cruel, amoral, and vengeful. He cares little for human life once he has extracted use from it. He is unfettered by notions of morality.

Magically Jedakiah has no equal in The Realm. As the creator of the grimoire of Entropic Revelations he has mastered spells of wrath and destruction. From his study of the runes and folklore he has command of a number of Folk Magic spells too. He is also a worshipper of the Chaos Mother and although she cannot ordinarily grant Miracles, Jedakiah has found a way to tap into her powers, granting him the Miracles listed, and creating a Devotional Pool from which to power them. He can be considered as the High Priest of the Cult of the Chaos Mother but is unlikely to exhort the Goddess for a Miracle when the time for his apotheosis nears, as he needs all his Devotional Pool to ensure he has his Goddess's favour and attention when he conducts The Dread Rite which involves the Awaken (Chaos Avatar) miracle.

Jedakiah also possesses the Staff of Mutation. This was taken from part of the God's Limb itself and looks to be composed of tightly wound tendrils of an indeterminate-coloured wood with an oily sheen. The head is an ovoid shaped cluster of vine-like strands that can unwind in a serpentine fashion. Jedakiah uses this symbol of office as a quarterstaff and he can control the tendrils of the staff to grasp at opponents or objects. In close combat he uses it to achieve an Entangle Special Effect. If an opponent is entangled by the staff, Jedakiah uses subsequent Combat Actions to cause an automatic Impale Special Effect to the location held; this ignores worn armour as the tendrils twist through the gaps in the protection. If Jedakiah casts Wrack against an opponent held by the staff (when it has entangled or impaled them, for example), he can choose to affect the location the weapon is attached to. If damaged, and unless it suffers the loss of all its Hit Points, the staff regenerate 1d3 Hit Points at the end of every Combat Round.

Characteristics	Attributes	1d20	Location	AP/HP
STR: 13	Action Points	3	1–3	Right Leg	0/6
CON: 17	Damage Modifier	+1d2	4–6	Left Leg	0/6
SIZ: 13	Magic Point	16	7–9	Abdomen	0/7
DEX: 15	Movement	6m	10–12	Chest	0/8
INT: 20	Initiative Bonus	18	13–15	Right Arm	0/5
POW: 16	Armour	None	16–18	Left Arm	0/5
CHA: 13	Abilities	Chaos Tainted	19–20	Head	0/6
	Magic	See Below			

Skills: Athletics 31%, Brawn 26%, Commerce 68%, Conceal 58%, Deceit 90%, Endurance 74%, Evade 60%, Influence 86%, Insight 85%, Locale 90%, Lore (Alchemy) 60%, Lore (Ancient History) 97%, Lore (Serpent Folk) 45%, Meditation 50%, Oratory 75%, Perception 81%, Sleight 48%, Stealth 70%, Survival 68%, Teach 64%, Unarmed 26%, Willpower 82%

Passions: Loyalty (Chaos) 90%, Hate (Family) 88%, Suspicious (Strangers) 75%, Arrogant 100%

Magic

Folk Magic 78%
Alarm, Avert, Beast Call (Chaotically Mutated), Befuddle, Bypass, Chill, Curse, Darkness, Demoralize, Fanaticism, Incognito, Lock, Phantasm, Protection, Shove, Spirit Shield, Voice, Witch Sight

Sorcery (The Entropic Revelations): Invoke 80%, Shaping 80%
Cast Back, Damage Resistance, Mark, Mystic (Sight), Neutralise Magic, Palsy, Protective Ward, Sculpt (Flesh and Bone), Wrack (Chaos)

Theism: Exhort (Chaos Mother) 80%, Devotion (Chaos Mother) 80%
Awaken (Chaos Avatar), Consecrate, Corruption , Fecundity
Devotional Pool = 16

Combat Style: Scholar Staff Fighting (Quarterstaff) 60%, Dastardly Knife Work (Dagger, Dirk) 66%

Weapon	Size/Force	Reach	Damage	AP/HP
Dagger	S	S	1d4+1+1d2	6/8
Quarterstaff	M	L	1d8+1d2	4/8

Index

A
Accursed Spring, the, 174
Adventurers, 17
Aganthus, 160-161, 164, 173, 181, 185
Aliana den Solis, 116-119, 125, 133, 145, 153
Aliya, 10-16, 28, 30, 59, 66, 88-89, 96-97, 103, 105-106, 123-124, 162
Alynoor, Princess, 55-56, 60, 66, 81
Apes, Winged, 173, 190
Ash-Dynad, 125, 129-130, 139
Astomvar, Duke, 15, 160-161, 164, 185
Athanax, Lord, 55
Axolotl, Giant, 216
Aylesford, 14, 20, 23, 25, 26-37, 168, 179

B
Bandits, 14, 22, 26, 90, 92-97, 110, 111, 166
Bath House, 125
Batrachians, 39-43, 50-52
Beast Men, 160-164, 168-169, 173, 174-176, 180-184, 186
Beneath the Black Water, 39-54
Benzaad ab Keffi, 139
Berec the Scowl, 133
Black Spires, the, 173
Black Vale, 8-10, 84, 87-88, 97, 99-101, 166
Blessed Ones, the, 201, 204-205, 209-210, 214
Boar-Kin, 9
Bria, 40-42, 51, 208, 219

C
Caravan, 19-38
Carnival of Baths and Exotica, the, 139
Cavern of Changes, the, 208
Chandanar, 12-14, 55-57, 77-78, 89
Chandanar, Power of, 59
Chaos Blessed, the, 114
Chaos Hybrid, 9, 19, 21, 28-29, 30, 32, 34, 37-38, 160-161, 178-179, 182-183, 185-186, 190
Chaos Mother, the, 6, 8-14, 16-17, 87, 192-196, 200, 205, 208-209
Chaos Mother's Chalice, the, 87-115
Chaos Root, the, 210
Climate, The Realm, 7
Complex, Ophidians', 179-182
Contessa, the, 116-119, 125, 133, 145, 153
Corrupted Temple, the, 103
Crystal Pool, the, 181, 185
Cultures, The Realm, 9
Curse of the Contessa, 116-159
Cylder, 14-15, 18, 46-47, 51, 55-56, 58, 60-65, 78, 87-89, 137, 166

D
Dagmar Shieldbiter, 56
Dalla, 24
Dark Child's Tower, 16, 192-193, 196, 202-211
Daughter of Chaos, the, 13, 17, 45, 178, 193, 209-210
Demon Horse Outlook, 161, 167, 171-173
Dread Rite, the, 45, 205, 209

Dream Root, the, 193
Drystan, Lord, 15, 18, 39-42, 45, 62, 87-89, 185-186, 192

E

Egg of Hylar, 40, 49, 51
Eglis, 173
Envoy, the, 161, 179, 185
Eyeglass of True Seeing, 137
Eyloi the Hare, 167, 188

F

Families, Westport, 124
Feather Eye, 116-117, 119-120, 124-125, 128-129, 131, 136, 142-143, 145-150, 156
Feyr, 9-13, 35
Founding Four, the, 6, 10-12, 14, 16, 57, 59, 63, 66, 89, 166, 193
Fredak, the Physician, 132
Frogfens, the, 40-42, 51
Fustilius Stump, 87, 97, 99

G

Gartharis, 7, 9, 12, 14, 17, 19, 22, 32, 58, 61, 65, 84, 86, 139, 192-194, 197, 212
General Mencios, 56, 58, 61, 65, 70-73, 77-78, 86, 81
Geris Lortt, 192, 196, 202
Governance, The Realm, 8
Great Cylder Market, the, 56, 65
Grey Lurker, the, 201, 214
Gul-Azar, 55-58, 61, 65-67, 71-75, 77, 82, 84-86

H

Hanno, 99, 113
Hareesh, 133
Healing, in Westport, 123
Hog's Trotters, the, 24, 25
Holding Cells, the, 180
Hooded One, the, 40-41, 45, 192, 205, 207, 210, 218

I

Ildray, 134-136
Inch, 116, 131, 138, 154
Investigations, 127

J

Jedakiah, 5, 15-16, 19, 33-34, 41, 45, 55-57, 78, 82, 84-85, 116-120, 138, 145, 147, 150-152, 160-161, 179, 185, 192-195, 200, 202, 204-210, 220-221
Jhonen, 20-24, 26-28, 35

K

Kalathus, 87-89
Kardash Weathervane, 55-56
Karl Pig-Axe, 87, 90, 92, 96, 110
Kerebas, 172
Kremathus, 165-166
Krytos, 116, 122, 124, 148, 153

L

Laimonis, 173
Law and Order, Westport, 122
Long Riding, 7, 9, 11, 13, 17, 21, 35, 40, 166
Lucius, Duke, 14, 88-89, 90, 93
Lump, 22
Lurien, 15, 20, 22, 28, 30, 34, 161, 168, 170

M

Mad Ester, 90, 94, 96, 110
Magic Points, 10
Magic, The Realm, 9
Mail-An, 130, 132, 134
Man'agan Herald, the, 123, 131, 138
Manuun, 19, 28, 30, 32, 34, 37, 179
Meatsheets, 47-48, 53, 180
Meggo, 124, 126, 130-131, 136, 141, 158
Mendrith-Ran's Guest House, 137
Menissa, 10-11, 124
Miguel ab Arranchez, 126
Miners, the, 100, 113
Minotaurs, 9
Mollonius, 87-88, 100, 103, 109, 113
Mother's Cord, the, 193, 199-200
Mutants, 88, 103, 105-106, 109, 113-115
Myur, King, 8, 13-14, 55-58, 73, 78, 82

N

Nests, the, 180
Non Humans, The Realm, 8
Norport, 15, 87-88, 97, 99, 162, 166, 187
Nyren, 15, 18, 35, 160-164, 166-167, 185

O

Old Stone Bridge, the, 32
Old Town Docks, 122
Ophidians, 9, 14, 19, 32, 37-38, 47, 53, 59, 161, 176, 178-182, 185, 193-194, 207, 218
Order of Truth, the, 6, 9, 13, 17, 51, 55, 59, 66, 88, 132, 136, 185
Otomars, 173
Outpost, the Forgotten, 45-48

P

Passions, 17
Perenge the Ink Stained, 126, 130, 134-136, 151, 155
Pyramid. Ophidians', 176

Q

Quicksand, 42

R

Raid on Yagelan's Bluff, 160-191
Ravens, 213
Realm, the, 7-18
Reckoning at Distaff Peak, 192-220
Religions, 10-14
Renamos, 9, 12, 172
Renegade Gods, the, 11-12
Root of Dreams, 194, 218
Rumours, Nyren, 166

S

Salamander, Giant, 199, 216
Sayalis, 10, 12-13, 15, 17, 59, 65, 121, 161, 164, 193, 205
Screamers, the, 200, 201, 209, 213
Senholm, 15
Shadows Behind the Throne, 55-86
Shaft, the, 179
Slavers, the, 202
Smokefoot, 90, 94, 111
Solisti Compound, 142 – 146
Son of Fury, the, 181-182, 185, 190
Sormund, 10, 11, 13, 124, 205
Spider, Giant, 42, 54
Stasis Tube, the, 179, 181-182
Steam Vents, the, 172, 175
Sweetwater Squid Inn, 56, 63, 67
Sweggen Nine Fingers, 117, 124, 126, 130-131, 136-138, 155

T

Terrain, The Realm, 7
The Moors, 9
The Vale, 9
Theatre of Shadows, the, 55, 65
Thorsen, 22-26, 170
Thuk, 87, 112
Travel Encounters, 168
Travel in The Realm, 14
Two Maws, 200, 201, 215, 216

U

Utuk, 20, 24, 25, 35

V

Viduva, 173
Viper, Marsh, 43, 53
Viper, Moor, 141

W

Westport, 15, 84, 87, 89, 94, 116, 118, 120-124, 166

X

Xalgith, 10, 11, 22, 30, 116, 124, 126, 134
Xhago, 116-120, 125, 128-130, 133-136, 138-152, 155

Y

Yagelan's Bluff, 160-161, 164, 167-168, 175-176, 178-182, 185, 191
Yoreth, 164

Z

Zakar, 87-88, 99, 101, 113, 114
Zoona, 23